Justice Connections

Justice Connections

Edited by

Patricia Easteal AM

CAMBRIDGE SCHOLARS
PUBLISHING

Justice Connections, Edited by Patricia Easteal AM
Copy edited by Skye Masters

This book first published 2013

Cambridge Scholars Publishing

12 Back Chapman Street, Newcastle upon Tyne, NE6 2XX, UK

British Library Cataloguing in Publication Data
A catalogue record for this book is available from the British Library

ISBN (10): 1-4438-4731-3, ISBN (13): 978-1-4438-4731-5

TABLE OF CONTENTS

CONTRIBUTORS

Amanda Alford is a legal officer at the Australian Law Reform Commission (ALRC). During her time at the ALRC she has worked on a number of significant inquiries, including in relation to family violence and mature age workforce participation. Prior to joining the ALRC, Amanda was a lawyer at the Australian Government Solicitor, practising largely in employment law. She has also spent time working on the Public Sector Workforce Development Program in Papua New Guinea and undertakes a range of pro bono work. Amanda has a particular interest in international, human rights, labour and employment law as well as anti-discrimination law.

Bruce Baer Arnold teaches law at the University of Canberra. His research interests centre on privacy, confidentiality, intellectual property and identity. He is general editor of the *Privacy Law Bulletin* and has written extensively in legal and other publications regarding biometrics, consumer protection, white collar crime, online child safety, life sciences patents and other matters. He blogs at barnoldlaw.blogspot.com.

Lorana Bartels (BA LLB LLM (UNSW) PhD (UTas) GDLP) is a Senior Lecturer in the School of Law and Justice at the University of Canberra. She is a member of the Australian Capital Territory Law Society Criminal Law Committee and the Australian and New Zealand Society of Criminology Committee of Management. Lorana has published over 40 research papers on a range of criminal justice issues, including sentencing law, and women and Indigenous people in the criminal justice system. Her first book, *Qualitative Criminology: Stories from the Field* (co-edited with Kelly Richards) was released in 2011.

Wendy Bonython is an Assistant Professor in law at the University of Canberra. She has a PhD in molecular medicine, and her research interests include medical law, mental health law, and torts.

Professor Rosalind Croucher BA(Hons) LLB PhD AMusA FRSA FACLM(Hon) FAAL TEP was appointed to the Australian Law Reform Commission in February 2007, and in December 2009 as President, after a distinguished period of 25 years in University teaching and management, including as Dean of Law at Macquarie University (November 1999–February 2007), where she still holds a Chair. She has lectured and published extensively, principally in the fields of equity, trusts, property, inheritance and legal history. At the ALRC Professor Croucher was the Commissioner in charge of six inquiries (2007–2013). She continues her academic writing where she can, around the exigencies and demands of ALRC inquiries.

Dr Dalma Demeter is an academic at the University of Canberra, teaching and researching international arbitration, international sales law and legal education. Dalma has a truly international background, encompassing both civil law and common law education and practice, being a member of several professional organisations, and arbitrating at the Willem C Vis International Commercial Arbitration Moot in both in Hong Kong and Vienna every year. Her academic work and contribution to legal education have been recognised by several awards and her research is strongly connected to her teaching.

Mirjana Drenovak-Ivanovic (Mag. iur., PhD) is an Assistant Professor in Environmental Law at the University of Belgrade Faculty of Law. She was an academic visitor at the University of Oxford Faculty of Law (Research topics: comparative and global environmental law; access to justice in environmental matters), visiting researcher at the *Institut für Rechts — und Sozialwissenschaften, Universität Hohenheim* in Stuttgart (Research topic: German environmental law), visiting researcher at the *Faculté de droit International et Européen de l'Université Nice-Sophia Antipolis* (Research topics: French environmental law; Court of Justice of the European Union and environmental protection).

Professor Patricia Easteal AM, PhD is a legal academic, author and advocate at the School of Law, University of Canberra.. She investigates justice and the law, specifically in the areas of criminal law, family law, discrimination law, employment law and immigration law. She has published 15 books and over 150 academic journal articles with a primary focus on access to justice for women. She was a finalist for the Human Rights Community Award in 2012, was 2010 Australian of the Year (ACT) and became a Member of the Order of Australia in 2010. Her achievements in learning and teaching have been recognised with national Australian Learning and Teaching Council awards.

Anthony Hopkins is an ACT Barrister and a Professional Associate at the University of Canberra, where he has taught since 2008. Anthony's teaching and research interests lie in criminal law, evidence law, advocacy and Indigenous Australians and the law, drawing upon his current practice and his past experience as a criminal defence lawyer at the Central Australian Aboriginal Legal Aid Service and the Northern Territory Legal Aid Commission.

Keziah Judd is a PhD candidate in the School of Law at the University of Canberra and a legal policy officer with the ACT Government. Her PhD is on feminism, sexual harassment law and the media. She is the co-author, with Professor Patricia Easteal, of 'He Said She Said: Credibility and Sexual Harassment Cases in Australia' (2008) 31(5) *Women's Studies International Forum* 336 and 'Sexual Harassment on Trial — the DJs Case' (2012) 36(4) *Alternative Law Journal*, with Professor Patricia Easteal, Skye Saunders and Bruce Arnold.

Jessica Kennedy is a lawyer at Farrar Gesini Dunn Family & Collaborative Law. She is in the final stages of her PhD, which looked at the impact and effectiveness of procedural changes aimed at protecting sexual assault victims throughout the criminal justice process. Jessica's Honours thesis looked at sentencing in sexual assault cases by relationship between victim and perpetrator. Jessica has authored/co-authored various articles and book chapters in this area.

The Hon Michael Kirby AC CMG was a Justice of the High Court of Australia (1996–2009). He earlier served as President of the New South Wales Court of Appeal (1984–95) and inaugural Chairman of the Australian Law Reform Commission (1975-84). In the ALRC he led the project on defamation law reform and privacy protection in Australian law. This resulted in his appointment to the OECD expert group on privacy (1978–80), which he chaired. He was the recipient of the Australian Human Rights Medal (1991) and the inaugural Australian Privacy Medal (2010). In 2011 he was named laureate of the Gruber Justice Prize.

Tony Krone PhD is Associate Dean Education Faculty of Business, Government and Law, University of Canberra. He does research in the area of transnational crime such as the on-line trade in precursor chemicals and cyber security, cyber crime particularly related to children, criminal law, and has looked at formal and informal justice mechanisms to promote lasting peace in Asia and the Pacific region.

Wendy Kukulies-Smith is a Teaching Fellow at the ANU College of Law. Wendy lectures in Criminal Law and Procedure. In addition, she specialises in sentencing law and works with the National Judicial College of Australia on the Commonwealth Sentencing Database. Her research interests include the re-examination of notorious criminal cases from colonial Australia, mercy in sentencing, and the development of practice and principles within the Criminal Justice system. She is undertaking a PhD at the ANU entitled *Punishing Parents: Mercy, Motherhood and Individual Justice in the Australian Sentencing Landscape*.

Christina Ashley Lewis completed a Bachelor of Commerce/Bachelor of Laws with Honours at the University of Canberra. Her Honours thesis was on Aboriginality and its impact, if any, on the sentencing process in the Australian Capital Territory. She also undertook a course on International Criminal Law at the University of Leiden, in the Netherlands in 2011. Since being admitted into the legal profession in December 2012 Ms Lewis has commenced practicing at Baker Deane & Nutt, Lawyers.

Skye Masters is a final year BA/LLB Honours student at the University of Canberra. She has authored/co-authored articles in the field of privacy law and is a member of the editorial board of the *Alternative Law Journal*, after having been a student editor of the *Canberra Law Review*.

Thilini Perera is a University of Canberra Law (Honours) Graduate. Her honours thesis topic was international investment arbitration. Thilini's specific area of interest is international commercial arbitration law. She represented the University of Canberra at the prestigious Willem C Vis (East) International Commercial Arbitration Moot in Hong Kong in 2012. Thilini currently works as the Company Secretary of a leading not-for-profit organisation in Australia while completing her Graduate Diploma in Legal Practice and hopes to be admitted as a solicitor in June this year.

Dr Susan Priest is an Assistant Professor in the Faculty of Business, Government and Law at the University of Canberra. She is also a legal practitioner in the ACT. Susan teaches the foundation law units in the undergraduate and postgraduate programs. Her particular research interests are in the areas of Australian legal history, colonial criminal law, and some human rights issues. Susan has given a number of seminars and conference presentations in these areas as well as published in several books and peer reviewed journal articles.

Skye Saunders is a lecturer in the Australian National University (ANU) College of Law. She teaches primarily in the Graduate Diploma of Legal Practice in units such as Legal Ethics, but also lectures in Foundations of Australian Law. Skye also teaches at the University of Canberra. Prior to joining the ANU, Skye practised as a solicitor, working on a diverse range of matters and developing a particular interest in the areas of discrimination and employment relations law. Skye is currently also pursuing doctoral research at the University of Canberra, the title of which is *Whispers from the Bush: The Sexual Harassment of Australian Rural Women at Work*.

Margaret Thornton is a Professor of Law at the Australian National University. She has degrees from Sydney, New South Wales and Yale. She is a Barrister of the High Court of Australia, a Fellow of the Academy of Social Sciences in Australia and a Foundation Fellow of the Australian Academy of Law. She has held visiting fellowships at various institutions, including Oxford, London, Columbia and York (Canada). Her research spans the areas of feminist legal theory, discrimination law, legal education, legal profession and the corporatisation of universities. Her most recent book is *Privatising the Public University: The Case of Law* (Routledge, 2012).

Lorraine Walker has degrees in Arts and Law from University of Sydney, started her Masters twice was (and remains) an officer in the RAAF, has been a Crown Prosecutor in the UK, a solicitor, a partner in a firm, a barrister and is now Chief Magistrate and Chief Coroner of the ACT. She has a particular interest in health law (especially mental health) and death law.

Helen Watchirs OAM was appointed as the ACT Human Rights & Discrimination Commissioner in 2004. She has supervised the handling of about 1000 discrimination cases, as well as conducting Human Rights Audits of detention facilities. Dr Watchirs has over 30 years' experience as a human rights lawyer working for Federal Government agencies, and several United Nations agencies, including UNAIDS, WHO, ILO, UNDP and the Office of the High Commissioner for Human Rights. Her PhD and Masters focus on HIV/AIDS human rights issues. She is a member of the Federal Ministerial Advisory Council on Blood Borne Viruses & STIs, and the Organ and Tissue Advisory Council.

FOREWORD

LORRAINE WALKER

As a lawyer, one is sometimes asked whether one considers that our legal system delivers "justice". This begs the question, what is justice? Over a number of years in the profession, I have come to answer this question along the lines that justice is a fortuitous but uncertain by-product of our legal system.

This superficially cynical response is in fact far from cynical. It is a reflection of my conclusion, based upon experience as a military lawyer, a prosecutor, a solicitor, a barrister and a judicial officer, that the complexities of legal processes are such that there is no replicable formula for "justice". In the end, law is truly an art, not a science. Attempts to reduce legal principles to mathematical or scientific formulae are, it seems to me, doomed to failure. That is because, unlike science, the variability in legal process is infinite. The rules may remain largely unchanged but the common denominator in all legal processes is people. Often people are not entirely honest, often not entirely reliable, often not entirely thorough and never entirely predictable, and that's just the lawyers. Throw in some litigants and judges and one can readily appreciate that each legal "experiment" will have a somewhat different outcome, despite a significant commonality of factors.

Furthermore, what is perceived as justice by one player in the legal theatre may well be perceived as injustice by another. Justice is unlikely to be an absolute. Here it is to be distinguished from fairness, which is more readily capable of external validation.

It is the essence of justice that it will be applied in accordance with all the strengths and weaknesses of those whose role it is to facilitate it. And because the "experiments" are not replicable, that may cause people to question its facilitation, as indeed they should.

Some of the mystery of the professions, including law, has been exposed in recent decades, with generally higher education and a proliferation of knowledge through the internet. Perhaps this has contributed to an increasing distrust of the legal process.

Certainly there is a trend towards legislative proscription of human relationships which runs the risk, despite the best intentions, of attempting to reduce justice to a formula. There has been significant comment about one such area of concern, that of overly prescriptive sentencing legislation. Largely reflecting an effort to placate public perceptions of undue lenience perceived by some community members as "injustice", a mandated formulaic approach adopted in some jurisdictions has significantly hampered judicial officers in the art of sentencing effectively. To an extent, sentencing has become an exercise in "ticking the boxes".

That is not to suggest that public opinion is a matter of no significance to creating and implementing law. Public opinion is the very essence of effective law-making and application. Unless the law is accepted by the majority, it cannot operate to regulate human relationships and a basic pillar of civilised society will fall. So "public opinion" cannot be arrogantly disregarded.

In assessing how justice is to best be achieved in any particular legal process, therefore, community standards and expectations are an essential consideration. But these cannot be achieved by the application of a proscriptive formula. Perfect justice may not be achievable at all. But public scrutiny of the process, so readily achievable now with the available options for communication, provides the potential for more informed assessment and critique of the application of legal process. Initiatives such as "You be the Judge" on the Victorian Sentencing Advisory Council website, leading to informed comment, are positive. Publically broadcast court proceedings are likely to also assist in greater public understanding of at least judicial application of the law. Such dissemination of cases may also produce more informed feedback and, possibly a reduced need for legislative intervention in the judicial system through increased confidence in the judicial system.

The Symposium that is reflected in this book brought together participants from academia and the legal and related professions. Each of the chapters is an insightful consideration of particular aspects of our justice system. Such communal reflection provides another avenue for the necessary ongoing review of our legal system, certainly one I very much appreciated. I trust that the reader is able to absorb, dissect, analyse and continue the "justice" conversation.

PART I

JUSTICE BEHIND THE SCENES

INTRODUCTION

ROSALIND F. CROUCHER

Common Threads

This part of the Justice Connections Symposium included three papers: one on a particular amending statute in the area of sexual and violent offences; and two on sentencing — the first concerning the relevance of Aboriginality in sentencing, the second on data collection. My challenge as "discussant" was to bring the intellectual threads of the three papers together.

I was delighted to undertake such a responsibility for the first *Justice Connections Symposium* held by the University of Canberra in 2011 and the set of papers I commented upon then was similarly grouped under the heading "Justice Behind the Scenes". On that occasion I was able to point to echoes in my own work. Curiosity about how legislation gets to where it is, revealed to me how accidental, or serendipitous, much law reform can be — especially when considered outside the arena of contributions by institutional law reform bodies, such as the Australian Law Reform Commission.[1] In drawing the threads together on that occasion I spoke of the power of people in law reform. A happy coincidence was the fact that the Symposium was held on Mabo Day, 3 June — the day on which the High Court delivered its judgment in *Mabo & Ors v Qld (No 2)*,[2] upholding the continuity of Koiki Mabo's title to his land on Murray Island and, with it, signalling the end of *terra nullius* in Australia. That litigation grew out of a meeting between a gardener and a couple of academics. The gardener was Koiki or "Eddie" as he was known. In 1974 Koiki had a conversation with James Cook University academics, Professor Noel Loos and Henry Reynolds, about his land on Mer (Murray Island) that started a ball rolling that ended up in the High Court, making legal history. It was a fortuitous — serendipitous — meeting, combining principle, passion and champions.

---

[1] Published in *Canberra Law Review*: Rosalind Croucher, 'Introduction: Justice Behind the Scenes' (2011) 10(2) *Canberra Law Review* 1.
[2] *Mabo & Ors v Qld (No 2)* (1992) 175 CLR 1.

Once law reform "happens", through the introduction of new laws — such as the *Sexual and Violent Offences Legislation Amendment Act 2008* (ACT)[3] — justice "behind the scenes" invites a different kind of consideration. It is now not about *how* the law happened, but rather, is it *working*? Is it *fair*?

Reflections on Justice as Fairness

To me, the linking theme in the chapters in this first part of *Justice Connections* is the idea of "fairness" in justice, interrogating it from both a subjective and objective perspective. The dominant approach is one of "reflection" — in both a practical and philosophical sense — that "justice" is improved, made fairer, by a process of reflecting; by capturing reflections as data; by critical analysis and commentary upon steps taken ostensibly to improve justice.

The chapter by Jess Kennedy and Professor Patricia Easteal, "View from the Inside: *The Sexual and Violent Offences Legislation Amendment 2008*" (Kennedy and Easteal), and that by Christina Lewis, Anthony Hopkins and Dr Lorana Bartels, "The Relevance of Aboriginality in Sentencing: The Potential of Pre-sentence Reports — Missed Opportunities in the Australian Capital Territory" (Lewis et al), focus principally upon the subjective aspect of justice and the lived experience of individuals within the justice system. For Kennedy and Easteal their reflective analysis is informed by surveys and interviews; for Lewis et al, it is through critical consideration of cases and by interviews. Each of these two chapters is concerned with justice as fairness at an individual level: to victims of sexual assault (Kennedy and Easteal); to Aboriginal accused and convicted offenders (Lewis et al).

The challenge in placing a critical lens on justice in the sense of "fairness" felt or perceived at an individual level, is to ensure that the systemic aspects of justice — the sense of a justice "system" in a wider society — also actively protect the right to a fair trial for an accused at the same time as extracting the best possible evidence from witnesses who may otherwise be at a disadvantage. The issue at a systemic level is, therefore, how to let the subjective in.

---

[3] The introduction of this legislation was the focus of the paper by Jessica Kennedy and Patricia Easteal in *Justice Connections I*, published subsequently in the *Canberra Law Review* as: Patricia Easteal and Jessica Kennedy, 'The Conception, Gestation and Birth of Legislation: The *Sexual and Violent Offences Legislation Amendment Act 2008* (ACT)' (2011) 10(2) *Canberra Law Review* 8.

The focus on the subjective aspect of justice as fairness is clearly evident in the title of the first of the chapters, by Kennedy and Easteal: "view from the inside". One of the key messages from their chapter is the importance of support for victims of sexual and violent offences.[4] As one of the participants in their study commented, "I felt I always had support with me and someone to talk to".[5] But there is also a reminder that overly protective responses, such as an almost automatic assumption that evidence will be given via CCTV, may override or fail to consider the autonomy of the victim in allowing choice as to the mode of presentation of evidence. Kennedy and Easteal refer to a victim witness who chose not to give evidence by CCTV "because she felt she had greater control and a greater presence in the courtroom". But, in such a case, a victim witness needs to be given a choice about other measures, such as the use of a screen, so that she or he does not have to see the accused. The interviews and survey, while working from a very small sample, provide some valuable suggestions as to aspects of the mode of supposedly 'protecting' witnesses that may be re-evaluated in practice.

The chapter by Lewis et al begins with the challenging question as to why Aboriginal and Torres Strait Islander offenders are overrepresented in the custodial population in Australia — 13 times higher than the general population on 30 June 2011.[6] Their work also demonstrates the power of a support person, this time in the form of a barrister or legal practitioner to

---

[4] This was also a message that came through very clearly in the work the Australian Law Reform Commission did in the area of family violence: Australian Law Reform Commission and New South Wales Law Reform Commission, *Family Violence — A National Legal Response,* ALRC Report No 114/NSWLRC Report No 128 (2010). See especially chapter 32 of the Report. A similar conclusion was identified in a different, but analogous context, in the review of the Women's Family Law Support Service, a joint initiative of the Family Court, Sydney registry, and the NSW Women's Refuge Movement: Lesley Laing, *Women's Family Law Support Service Evaluation — "They Should Have This in Every Court*" (University of Sydney, Faculty of Education and Social Work, 2011) <ses.library.usyd.edu.au/bitstream/2123/7917/1/WRM_WFLSS%20Evaluation%202011.pdf>. I had the privilege of launching this evaluation: *"They Should Have This in Every Court" — Women's Family Law Support Service Evaluation* (2011). See <www.alrc.gov.au/news-media/2011/%E2%80%98they-should-have-every-court%E2%80%99-womens-family-law-support-service-evaluation>.

[5] Jessica Kennedy and Patricia Easteal, 'View from the Inside: The *Sexual and Violent Offences Legislation Amendment Act 2008*', footnote 43.

[6] Citing: Australian Bureau of Statistics (ABS), *Prisoners in Australia, 2011*, Cat No 4517.0) (ABS, 2012).

put the case for the individual, bringing to the consideration of sentencing relevant issues of the individual's life and circumstances — including in this case the offender's Aboriginality. The signal role that pre-sentence reports may play in this context is identified. The challenge posed by this chapter is the appropriate way in which such matters can be considered. How do you recognise the "full complexity of post-colonial Indigenous experience" and its relevance "to achieving equal justice in sentencing"?[7] Lewis et al point to the Canadian model as an example of how "culturally relevant sentencing options" may be developed.[8] The sample in this chapter was also a very small one, but the questions are still key ones for future research. Particularly crucial in such research is achieving an appropriate balance between the subjective considerations of the individual offender's circumstances in the sentencing context, understanding what a recognition of the offender's Aboriginality means and its relevance in that context, and the objective considerations of a justice system working fairly and impartially across the entire Australian community.

The objective perspective of fairness is seen most strongly in the third of the chapters in this set, by Dr Lorana Bartels, "Sentencing in the Australian Capital Territory". In its consideration of sentencing data in the ACT, this chapter acts as a bridge between the idea of fairness or justice as subjective and the broader needs of justice in an objective or systemic sense. Bartels emphasises that the availability of public sentencing data and the role of sentencing councils play a vital part in developing evidence-based sentencing policy and improving public knowledge and understanding about sentencing.

Justice and Iconography

The systemic lens is one that reflects a more objective sense of justice, one that is embodied symbolically in the image of the statue of justice that dominated the program brochure for the Symposium and was projected on the screen throughout the day's proceedings. It is the image of the Roman goddess of justice, Justitia. She holds the scales of justice in her hand, evenly balanced, and in her other she bears a sword — the ultimate image of authority of the State. This particular statue stands in front of the City

[7] Christina Lewis, Anthony Hopkins and Lorana Bartels, 'The Relevance of Aboriginality in Sentencing in the Australian Capital Territory: Missed Opportunities and the Potential of Pre-Sentence Reports'.

[8] Ibid.

Hall in Frankfurt, Germany.[9] It forms part of the Gerechtigkeitsbrunnen (Fountain of Justice) and was built in 1543.[10]

Copper engraving, Caspar Merian (1627–1686) entitled: *Curia Francofurtensis ad Moenum. cum Foro Piscario. Römer. or Town Hall of Franckfurt am Mayn. Including the Square. called the Römerberg.*[11]

[9] The complex of buildings is referred to as the "Römer" which received its name in the 14th century from "Zum Römer" ("to the Roman"), denoting its long history as the site of the coronation of Holy Roman Emperors: *Römer Information and Pictures* (2012) Go There Guide <www.gothereguide.com/romer+frankfurt-place/>.

[10] *Römerberg* (2012) A View on Cities <www.aviewoncities.com/frankfurt/romerberg.htm>.

[11] *Curia Francofurtensis ad Moenum. cum Foro Piscario. Römer. or Town Hall of Franckfurt am Mayn. Including the Square. called the Römerberg* (2012) WikiMedia <http://commons.wikimedia.org/wiki/File:Frankfurt_Am_Main-Caspar_Merian-BUAAKUCEWUCA-111_112-Curia_Francofurtensis_ad_Moenum_cum_Foro_Piscario_Roemer_oder_Rathhauss_zu_Franckfurt_am_Mayn_Sampbt_dem_Platz_der_Roemerberg_genant.jpg>.

In reflecting upon the idea of justice as fairness as a theme expressed in the three chapters in this section of *Justice Connections,* and particularly the tensions between the subjective and objective senses of fairness, I found curious resonances in this particular statue and its representation of justice. There are two particular things I found intriguing. First, it is the fact that this statue is not blindfolded, where many images of justice are. The second is the way this particular statue is facing in its physical location.

The blindfolded image of justice is clearly one that signifies objectivity: that justice should be delivered fairly to all, regardless of the standing or wealth of those who come before her. It is the classical embodiment of impartiality. Interestingly, however, Roman depictions of Justitia showed her without a blindfold,[12] and it was only from about the same time as our particular statue of Justitia was born that she appeared with her eyes covered.[13] Many representations of Justitia continue with uncovered eyes: including the statue on top of the Old Bailey courthouse in London and the statute outside the Supreme Court of Queensland, Brisbane, Queensland. While the scales are evenly balanced in all the images — blindfolded or not — I was certainly struck by the particular significance of an open-eyed representation of justice in my musings upon the themes evident in the set of chapters under consideration.

The second intriguing thing about our statue in the context of a discussion of themes is that she faces *towards* the city hall. And without a blindfold she is staring into the place where justice is meted out — a symbolic expression of the tensions between subjective and objective conceptualisations and practice of fairness. I know it may be seen as drawing a considerably long bow, but as a discussant I am accorded such licence.

Accepting That Justice is Fair

Community understanding and acceptance of the justice system as one that is fair is played out on a daily basis in response to reports of sentencing decisions. The quote of an observation by the former Chief

---

[12] The helpful Wikipedia entry for "Lady Justice" cites: 'The Scales of Justice as Represented in Engravings, Emblems, Reliefs and Sculptures of Early Modern Europe', in G Lamoine (ed), *Images et Representations de la Justice du XVie au XIXe Siecle* (University of Toulose-Le Mirail, 1983) 8: *Lady Justice* (2012) Wikipedia <http://en.wikipedia.org/wiki/Lady_Justice>.

[13] Ibid, with link to the statue in the Fountain of Justice in Berne: *Berner Iustitia* (2012) Wikipedia <http://en.wikipedia.org/wiki/File:Berner_Iustitia.jpg>.

Justice of New South Wales, the Hon James Spigelman AC QC, included by Bartels in the opening section of her chapter, reflects that position acutely, namely that "sentencing engages the interest, and sometimes the passion, of the public more than anything else judges do. The public's attitude to the way judges impose sentences determines, to a substantial extent, the state of public confidence in the administration of justice".[14] That public confidence is well expressed in the imagery of the balanced scales of Justitia. Another way of expressing this is to ask whether the decision passes the *Daily Telegraph* test — does public confidence in the fairness of the justice system, as discussed over the breakfast table and in the morning tabloid press, remain strong, notwithstanding criticism of individual decisions.

The criminal justice system is tested all the time in terms of fairness. Writing in 1983, in his collection of essays, *Reform the Law*, the Hon Michael Kirby AC CMG remarked that "the sentencing of convicted criminals is a matter about which citizens have strong opinions".[15] Professor Arie Freiberg, quoted again by Bartels, amplified such a view in saying that sentencing is "played out not only in the courts but in the broader arena of public opinion" and that it is "as much about politics as it is about law or criminology".[16]

The three chapters weave between them the subjective and objective aspects of justice as fairness. Surveys and interviews capture very directly the subjective element - the lived experience of the law. Data collection of sentencing practices provides a connection to the objective of policy formation and law reform, as well as informing judicial decision makers on a daily basis. In reflecting on the value of such approaches, Kirby remarked that, while some are "dubious about the value of opinion surveys and detailed analysis of sentencing practices and statistics", "there is room for more science":

> Inconsistency and disuniformity in the name of individual judicial discretion may be no more than lazy self-indulgence on the part of a legal profession resistant to change. The defence of the right of the judge or magistrate to have his personal idiosyncratic views, at the cost of the citizen coming before him for judicial punishment, is no longer acceptable.[17]

---

[14] Lorana Bartels, 'Sentencing in the Australian Capital Territory', footnote 2.
[15] Michael Kirby, *Reform the Law* (Oxford University Press, 1983) 128.
[16] Bartels, above n 14, footnote 117
[17] Kirby, above n 15, 133.

Another metaphor to describe the common threads in the chapters is that of a mirror. The chapters reflect inwards, looking closely in the looking glass. But they also provide a challenge to turn the mirror outwards, to use the critical insights obtained to provide a basis for continuing reform of the law. Through a careful and, over time, a more extended consideration of the subjective, lived experiences of the justice system in the areas under review, those insights will increase in value and validity. Such a mirror needs to keep turning — from the inwards to the outwards view — so that the conversation continues.

With respect to sentencing and law reform, Michael Kirby reminds us that "the reform of the sentencing of convicted criminal offenders is a controversial task. The last word will never be spoken on sentencing and criminal punishment".[18]

Many words are required for improvement of the law: by academics — through critical analysis, building of data and by submissions to law reform and other bodies engaged in law reform projects; by sentencing councils and similar bodies, in continued analysis and the development of model guidance; and by law reform bodies — where appropriate Terms of Reference are given or independent research initiated. The suffragists of the late nineteeth and early twentieth centuries adopted and advocated the policy of "much speaking" in order to achieve their goals. It is a good rule of thumb in law reform and in interrogating "justice connections" — the theme and title of this book.

[18] Ibid, 152.

CHAPTER ONE

VIEW FROM THE INSIDE: *THE SEXUAL AND VIOLENT OFFENCES LEGISLATION AMENDMENT ACT 2008*

JESSICA KENNEDY
AND PATRICIA EASTEAL

Introduction

The experiences that sexual assault victims have in the criminal justice system can compound their trauma and victimisation, resulting in victims being discouraged from reporting and/or continuing with their case.[1] Indeed, research suggests that some women are so traumatised as a result of the preliminary hearing that they are either unwilling or unable to follow through with the complaint.[2] In addition there has been extensive research documenting the revictimisation of witnesses in sexual assault trials.[3]

The *Sexual and Violent Offences Legislation Amendment Act 2008* (ACT) was enacted in mid-2009 to address these issues with "the dual objectives of treating complainants in sexual and violent offence proceedings

---

[1] Office of the Director of Public Prosecutions (ACT) and Australian Federal Police, *Responding to Sexual Assault: The Challenge of Change* (2005) Director of Public Prosecutions
<http://www.dpp.act.gov.au/pdf/DPP%20SARP%20report%20(11Feb05).pdf>.

[2] See: Department for Women, *Heroines of Fortitude: The Experiences of Women in Court as Victims of Sexual Assault* (Office for Women: NSW Department of Premier and Cabinet, 1996); Patricia Easteal and Christine Feerick, 'Sexual Assault by Male Partners: Is the License Still Valid?' (2005) 8(2) *Flinders University Journal of Law Reform* 185.

[3] See: Office of the Director of Public Prosecutions and Australian Federal Police, above n 1.

and other vulnerable witnesses with respect and dignity during the prosecution process, and ensuring a fair trial for an accused" and were "designed to extract the 'best' evidence possible from witnesses who may otherwise suffer a disadvantage".[4] This Act amended the *Evidence (Miscellaneous Provisions) Act 1991* (ACT) and the *Magistrates Court Act 1930* (ACT) in relation to sexual and violent offences. The committal hearing process was modified by allowing a transcript or written statement of an audio or visual recording between police and a witness to be admissible as evidence for all sexual assault victims.[5] A "pre-trial hearing" for non-disabled, adult victims of sexual assault who are especially vulnerable[6] was to be held as soon after the committal as possible and before the actual trial[7] was introduced. And, other measures to protect the victim witness such as CCTV, screening and closing the court were introduced.

The Act, however, as drafted and enacted is permeated with indeterminacy.[8] For instance, who is eligible to participate in pre-trial hearings are deemed as those likely to suffer severe emotional trauma or most likely to be intimidated or distressed. The process itself is grey with the ordering of many of the provisions only decided by the judicial officer *if* the prosecution applies. There are no clear guidelines for the prosecutors to follow. Further, there is the use of the word "may" as opposed to "must" in a number of provisions as discussed later in this chapter.

Judicial and/or prosecutorial discretion in applying and interpreting indeterminate provisions may be influenced by prevailing notions of sexuality and sexual behaviour that come from a stereotypical definition of "real" or "legitimate" rape and stereotypical constructions of the "good" victim and "reasonable" responses.[9] Sexual assault myths continue to permeate society and judicial officers and legal practitioners, as members

---

[4] Revised Explanatory Statement, Sexual and Violent Offences Legislation Amendment Bill 2008 (ACT) 2.

[5] Magistrates Court Act 1930 (ACT) ss 33, 34.

[6] Evidence (Miscellaneous Provisions) Act 1991 (ACT) s 40P(1)(c).

[7] Revised Explanatory Statement, Sexual and Violent Offences Legislation Amendment Bill 2008 (ACT) 5.

[8] See: Jessica Kennedy and Patricia Easteal, 'Shades of Grey: Indeterminacy and Sexual Assault Law Reform (2011) 13(2) *Flinders Law Journal* 49.

[9] D Lievore, 'Intimate Partner Sexual Assault: The Impact of Competing Demands on Victims' Decisions to Seek Criminal Justice Solutions' (Paper presented at the Eighth Australian Institute of Family Studies Conference, Melbourne, 12–14 February 2003) 3.

of society, continue to be influenced by them.[10] In addition, balancing the rights of the accused and the victim may be somewhat problematic.[11] Therefore, our aim in this study was to identify how these indeterminate sections of the *Sexual and Violent Offences Legislation Amendment Act* are in fact being interpreted and thus assess if the Act is achieving its objectives.

Methodology

To answer our research questions, we used two targeted purposive samples to obtain the views and experiences of the implementation of the Act. The first consisted of nine legal practitioners including three of eight ACT Supreme Court judicial officers who oversee cases involving sexual assault, one ACT prosecutor and five legal barristers who had each represented a defendant in a sexual assault matter in the past five years. This represented a response rate of 31 per cent.

Three victim support workers and two victim witnesses either completed a second online survey or participated in a face-to-face interview.[12] The former were recruited using "respondent driven sampling".[13] As a result of an October 2010 story about the project in the *Canberra Times* newspaper, which included a participation invitation to victims of sexual assault who had experienced a trial, three victims of sexual assault contacted the researchers. One was not suitable since the defendant in that case plead guilty before the committal. The two victims who participated in the research gave evidence at the committal hearing (pre-reform) and at the trial (post-reform).

---

[10] See: Patricia Easteal, *Less Than Equal: Women and the Australian Legal System* (Butterworths, 2001); Hilaire Barnett, *Introduction to Feminist Jurisprudence* (Routledge, 1998); VicHealth, *National Survey on Community Attitudes to Violence against Women 2009: Changing Cultures, Changing Attitudes — Preventing Violence against Women* (2010); Jennifer Temkin and Barbara Krahe, *Sexual Assault and the Justice Gap: A Question of Attitude* (Hart Publishing, 2008).

[11] The right to a fair trial is discussed fully in: Jessica Kennedy, Patricia Easteal and Lorana Bartels, 'How Protected is She? "Fairness" and the Rape Victim Witness in Australia' (2012) 35 *Women's Studies International Forum* 334.

[12] The University of Canberra's Committee for Ethics in Human Research approved the project on 27 October 2010. Protecting the anonymity of participants and the well-being of the victim-witnesses were the main ethical consideration in this project.

[13] Douglas Heckathorn, 'Respondent-Driven Sampling: A New Approach to the Study of Hidden Populations' (1997) 44 *Social Problems* 174.

Each potential research participant was sent an email with a link to the particular survey on SurveyMonkey®. All instruments first asked some demographic and contact information questions. Questions for legal practitioners then asked how each of the indeterminate sections of the legislation were being interpreted in practice. The last section of the instrument sought the respondents' views on whether the changes were achieving their intended aims.

The victim support person survey was composed of questions asked of the practitioners and those asked of the victims. Participants were asked about the impact that a trial could have on sexual assault victim witnesses' wellbeing. Following this, a number of questions sought respondents' views on how the new provisions are being implemented and the effect (if any) that they have had on the experiences of victim witnesses.

Of the two victim participants, one completed an online survey using SurveyMonkey®, and the other chose to participate in a face-to-face interview using the same instrument. That interview was recorded and later transcribed. The victim witness research instrument first asked the participant to discuss her experiences of committal hearings, pre-trial hearings and trials, and how the processes had impacted on her wellbeing. Questions were then asked about the respondent's specific experiences in relation to the reforms, ie view of the accused, testifying in an open/closed court, and having a support person present.

Note that with both of these last two samples, participants were contacted by email again to clarify or expand on their answers. This method was ideal for eliminating errors and omissions in the original instrument.

Survey responses were examined qualitatively using an "open-coding" approach.[14] Due to the small number of respondents and the shortness of most answers, the process of thematic coding was informal and unstructured. The process of studying the interview transcript and each passage of every survey word-by-word and line-by-line led to the labelling of each passage with an adequate code. This process helped to identify the common themes that arose and to summarise and observe the patterns in the responses.

---

[14] Matthew Miles and Michael Huberman, *Qualitative Data Analysis: An Expanded Sourcebook* (2nd ed, 1994) 40–43.

Caveats

Due to the small sample sizes, we do not claim that the findings necessarily represent the views of all judges, lawyers, support workers and victims: it cannot be said that these few are representative of the whole. Further, due to the short research "window" the findings are preliminary. They can be used to demonstrate how the legislation is being or might be implemented and how it could affect victim witnesses' wellbeing.

View from the Inside: How are the Amendments being Applied?

New section 38C — Accused may be screened from witness in court

(1) This section applies to the complainant or a similar act witness (the "witness") giving evidence in—
 (a) a sexual offence proceeding …
(2) The court may order that the courtroom be arranged in a way that, while the witness is giving evidence, the witness cannot see—
 (a) the accused person; or
 (b) anyone else the court considers should be screened from the witness.

Research in other jurisdictions suggests that screens are rarely used in practice because of the preference for CCTV,[15] and that when screens are required, the discretionary practice is often not invoked.[16] The legal practitioners surveyed concur with none of the participants either making or observing an order made for the use of screens as all victims of sexual assault are eligible to give evidence via CCTV.[17]

---

[15] See: New South Wales Law Reform Commission, Questioning of Complainants by Unrepresented Accused in Sexual Offence Trials, No 101 (2003) [5.2.21]; New South Wales Attorney-General's Department, Report of the Children's Evidence Taskforce: Taking Evidence in Court (1994); Celia O'Grady, Child Witnesses and Jury Trials: An Evaluation of the Use of Closed Circuit Televisions and Removable Screens in Western Australia (Ministry of Justice of Western Australia, 1996) [10.3].

[16] Judith Oliver, 'The Legislation Changed, What About the Reality?' (2006) 6(1) *Queensland University of Technology Law & Justice Journal* 55.

[17] Participant no 6, legal practitioner (11 May 2011).

> I have never been asked to make orders under [section] 38C — the standard practice seems to be to rely on Divisions 4.2B and 4.3 and have the evidence given by audio-visual link from a remote witness room.[18]

> In practice all complainants give evidence remotely via video link and the accused is positioned so that the witness cannot see the accused… Because of the provisions almost mandating evidence by video link [section] 38C in my experience has never specifically arisen [19]

One judicial officer said that he "would rely particularly on any submissions from the accused or his/her counsel"[20] when deciding whether to make an order under this section.

> I interpret this section as giving the court a discretion to screen a witness from the accused in the relevant proceeding. I find it difficult to see who else should be out of sight of the witness. I would generally make an order when requested. It would really be up to the accused to justify why the measures should not be implemented.[21]

When asked to hypothesise when an order under this section would not be made, two judges responded:

> It is impossible to imagine the range of circumstances in which an order under [section] 38C would be sought, and accordingly impossible to identify any particular cases in which' such an order would be refused.[22]

> I find it difficult to imagine the circumstances. I suppose it is possible that there would be some circumstance, but I find it difficult to see it.[23]

However, others did hypothesise that "in the unusual situation where a witness is giving evidence in court rather than via CCTV",[24] an order for the use of screens would not be made if the "test [is] not satisfied"[25] or criteria not met.[26]

---

[18] Participant no 2, judicial officer (27 April 2011).
[19] Participant no 5, legal practitioner (4 June 2011).
[20] Participant no 3, judicial officer (7 April 2011).
[21] Ibid.
[22] Participant no 2, judicial officer (27 April 2011).
[23] Participant no 3, judicial officer (7 April 2011).
[24] Participant no 6, legal practitioner (11 May 2011).
[25] Participant no 1, judicial officer (1 June 2011).
[26] Participant no 9, legal practitioner (10 April 2011).

Although the victim support personnel surveyed had never seen the use of screens in court, they were asked about their potential burdens and benefits. One victim support worker reported that “people who want to sit in court usually do so because they want to see the defendant: most of the people I support are entitled to use CCTV so if they are in the courtroom it is because they have chosen to be and [chosen] to be able to see the accused”.[27]

Interestingly, the victim witness in our study who chose to give evidence in the courtroom was not offered screens for her protection. This victim stated that she “did not want to testify via CCTV because she felt that she had greater control and a greater presence in the courtroom”, however, she did want to be screened from the accused in the courtroom.[28] She had asked the prosecution about the use of screens, and was told that “they didn’t do that here — it wasn’t an option”.[29] It must be noted that this trial was held approximately three months after the introduction of the new legislation. Because screens were not used in this case, the victim felt “scared’ because she “had to walk right past him”, “anxious” while giving evidence, and she “had trouble breathing”.[30] She stated that the accused and his family were “unnerving and distracting” and that the accused was “glaring at her the whole time and trying to put her off”.[31] One victim support officer supported this finding, stating that if the victim is unable to see the accused, they are “able to speak with more confidence and certainty knowing they [cannot] see the accused but [knowing that the accused can] hear them tell their story”.[32]

New section 38E — Witness may have support person in court

(1) The court must, on application by a party who intends to call a witness, order that the witness have a person (a *support person*) in the court close to, and within the witness’s sight, while the witness gives evidence.

“An application for a support person to be present is commonly made in relation to people who are to give evidence by audio-visual link from a

---

[27] Participant no 10, victim support (7 June 2011).
[28] Interview with participant no 13, victim witness (28 October 2010).
[29] Ibid.
[30] Ibid.
[31] Ibid.
[32] Participant no 12, victim support (31 May 2011).

remote witness room".[33] Judicial officers surveyed indicated that the section "requires that where the prosecution … requests a support person to be with the witness, the court must comply with that request":[34]

> I have never had such an application opposed by the other party, and have never declined to make such an order when sought.[35]

This view was confirmed by the legal practitioners surveyed, one of whom stated that as the section is interpreted and applied "strictly, it is very seldomly opposed by defence".[36]

> In practice virtually all complainants give evidence remotely by video link and in the room with them is a sheriff's officer who hands exhibits etc and ensures that the support person — who is also in the room but not on camera — is not gesturing to the witness.[37]

> Usually a DPP staff member sits near the witness in the room from which the witness is testifying and is out of the sight of those watching the testimony in Court.[38]

> Routinely when evidence is given via CCTV, the court is advised that a support person is present in the remote room. Usually that person is the witness support officer from the DPP.[39]

Both victim witness participants in our study had support people from the ACT DPP and/or Canberra Rape Crisis Centre (CRCC) within their sight whilst giving evidence. The support people were described as "very helpful, friendly [and] approachable".[40] The victims felt that the support people improved their experience, and neither of them would have preferred to testify alone:

> [She] made me feel more comfortable. Improved the experience. Definitely no to testifying alone. Support is much better.[41]

---

33 Participant no 2, judicial officer (27 April 2011).
34 Participant no 3, judicial officer (7 April 2011).
35 Participant no 2, judicial officer (27 April 2011).
36 Participant no 4, legal practitioner (18 July 2011).
37 Participant no 5, legal practitioner (4 June 2011).
38 Participant no 7, legal practitioner (27 April 2011).
39 Participant no 8, legal practitioner (26 April 2011).
40 Participant no 14, victim witness (26 July 2011).
41 Ibid.

> I felt that I always had support with me and someone to talk to — even when I was walking to and from the court.[42]

The only problem reported to arise in relation to the application of this section is where "there is some issue as to the person who is the support person being an appropriate person".[43] One victim witness was faced with the question of who could be present whilst she gave evidence at the committal. At the hearing she had a witness support person from the DPP and a counsellor from the CRCC with her in the remote witness room. However, the counsellor was asked to leave before the witness gave her evidence because the defence counsel had objected to the fact that the counsellor was present when the victim gave her initial statement, and was worried that the counsellor was going to "coach her".[44]

Revised section 39 — Sexual and violent offence proceeding — evidence to be given in closed court

> (2) The court may order that the court be closed to the public while all or part of the witness's evidence (including evidence given under cross-examination) is given.
> (3) In deciding whether to order that the court be closed to the public, the court must consider whether—
> (a) the witness wants to give evidence in open court; and
> (b) it is in the interests of justice that the witness give evidence in open court.

Judges provided mixed responses as to how they interpreted the meaning of section 39(3)(b), with one stating that (s)he would allow the court to be closed "[i]f the vulnerability test is satisfied and it is otherwise fair to allow the evidence to be given".[45] Another judicial officer took a slightly different viewpoint on the meaning of "interests of justice":

> The interest is the need for complainants especially not being deterred from making complaints by the fear that some very personal details of their interaction with the accused will become public property because of the evidence that they give.[46]

[42] Interview with participant no 13, victim witness (28 October 2010).
[43] Participant no 6, legal practitioner (11 May 2011).
[44] Interview with participant no 13, victim witness (28 October 2010).
[45] Participant no 1, judicial officer (1 June 2011).
[46] Participant no 3, judicial officer (7 April 2011).

When asked what (s)he would do if there was a conflict between the victim's wishes and the interests of justice, this judge stated that (s)he "would mostly accept the wishes of the witness; … [(s)he could] see little justice in not doing so".[47] However, the other two judicial officers did not agree, with one saying that (s)he could not give either consideration more weight overall, that the "decision would depend on the details of each competing consideration".[48] This judge also stated that "I would need to consider why the witness was so keen to give evidence in open court, and the nature and degree of the impact of that on the interests of justice".[49]

The lawyer respondents reported that orders to close the court are "rarely sought and rarely made", "as it should be",[50] but that an order might be "requested if a complainant particularly wants the court to be closed during their evidence".[51] One practitioner stated that "so far there has been little occasion for recourse to this section".[52] Another reported that the "public interest points in the direction of evidence being given in open Court".[53]

Victim support workers stated that, in practice, "an order may be made for a court to be closed if it is going to enhance the person's evidence … application can be made up until the morning the person is supposed to give evidence".[54] However, despite the apparently equal weighting of the factors by judicial officers discussed above, one victim support worker believes that the "[p]ublic interest always trumps a victim's wishes or concerns. The victim is often treated as an afterthought or like an annoyance, despite the rhetoric that is heard in court".[55] This support person also confirmed the view that the power of the judicial officer to close the court to the public is rarely invoked: "victims have asked to have a closed court, but rarely is it granted or applied for".[56]

When asked about the victims' wishes, another victim support person stated that:

> Most people are fine for the court to be open as not many people sit in anyway. Some do not want the defendant's family in there, and some do

---

[47] Ibid.
[48] Participant no 2, judicial officer (27 April 2011).
[49] Ibid.
[50] Participant no 7, legal practitioner (27 April 2011).
[51] Participant no 6, legal practitioner (11 May 2011).
[52] Participant no 8, legal practitioner (26 April 2011).
[53] Participant no 7, legal practitioner (27 April 2011).
[54] Participant no 10, victim support (7 June 2011).
[55] Participant no 12, victim support (31 May 2011).
[56] Ibid.

> not want their own family in there, so in these cases a closed court application may be made.[57]

> They do not like that others can hear their evidence and are particularly concerned about the defendant's supporters being able to hear the evidence. They find the open court very intimidating.[58]

However, all victim support personnel reported that most victims would prefer the court to be closed to the public, and that a closed court improved their experience:

> … knowing that their personal life is not being portrayed to those who may not know them is definitely a confidence booster.[59]

> They are happy that there is not just anyone sitting in the courtroom listening to their evidence.[60]

The victim witnesses supported this view. Although both victims gave their evidence in an open court, each stated that she would have preferred the court to be closed to the public. In one of the victim participant's cases, the prosecutor said that it was not in the interests of justice for the court to be closed, so they did not even apply for an order. As a result, the victim reported feeling distracted and abused.[61] She felt that it was her story, not a story for the public — that she was talking about such personal things (including her own body) that she would rather not have talked about them in public.[62] She would also have preferred to only have specific people in the courtroom (no students) and would have liked it if people didn't keep coming and going.[63]

The other victim witness participant reported that she was concerned about the publicity of the trial, and would have preferred if this were avoided:

> I was nervous about it being printed in the paper as Canberra is small and my story was read by many people and confidentiality is difficult to maintain. People who know people, know people and two and two are put together very easily. Although trying to be positive, people read my story

[57] Participant no 10, victim support (7 June 2011).
[58] Participant no 12, victim support (31 May 2011).
[59] Participant no 11, victim support (31 May 2011).
[60] Participant no 10, victim support (7 June 2011).
[61] Interview with participant no 13, victim witness (28 October 2010).
[62] Ibid.
[63] Ibid.

> creating awareness, education and my story being heard and helping victims and criminals and the whole process. Having the choice and control over public access may have been nice.[64]

New section 40P — Meaning of witness — div 4.2B

> (1) For this division, a *witness* is a prosecution witness in a sexual offence proceeding who—
> (a) is a child; or
> (b) is intellectually impaired; or
> (c) is a complainant who the court considers must give evidence as soon as practicable because the complainant is likely to—
> (i) suffer severe emotional trauma; or
> (ii) be intimidated or distressed.

Once this definition of witness is satisfied, "a witness may give evidence at a pre-trial hearing [and] the evidence must be given by audiovisual link".[65] This recording then "must … be played at the hearing of the sexual offence proceeding".[66]

When asked how they would determine which witnesses fit within the definition of section 40P(C) judicial officer respondents stated that "it is not a comparative exercise"; that "it is an assessment of the particular witness":[67]

> There is no question of determining which witnesses are more likely to suffer trauma etc than others (it's not a choice or a competition). The determination is whether, for the reasons specified, a witness must give evidence as soon as practicable.[68]

Legal practitioners supported the view that "it's done on a case by case basis" and stated that "child witnesses are more vulnerable generally".[69] Although one practitioner remarked that "in practice ALL complainants in sexual matters are effectively 'deemed' to be likely to suffer intimidation or distress",[70] it does not seem that this view is translating into the application of the section in practice.

---

[64] Participant no 14, victim witness (26 July 2011).
[65] Evidence (Miscellaneous Provisions) Act 1991 (ACT) s 40Q.
[66] Ibid, s 40S.
[67] Participant no 1, judicial officer (1 June 2011).
[68] Participant no 2, judicial officer (27 April 2011).
[69] Participant no 4, legal practitioner (18 July 2011).
[70] Participant no 5, legal practitioner (4 June 2011).

> I have not yet seen [an application under this section made]. Presumably this would be done by affidavit, probably authored by a staff member from the DPP, annexing relevant reports. There may or may not be a need for cross examination.[71]

When asked how they would come to a decision under this section, judicial officers reported that it would "involve looking at what kind of evidence the prosecution raises", which might include an "expert report, from a medical practitioner or psychologist to support the claim",[72] and "whether the defence opposes a determination that the witness give evidence in a pre-trial hearing".[73]

Legal practitioners and victim support personnel confirmed this, albeit with the caveat that "these provisions have not been in operation for long in a small jurisdiction, [so] many of these questions cannot be answered conclusively yet":[74]

> I would expect that expert medical evidence would be required on this issue.[75]

One victim support worker stated that "often defence will agree and a date for a pre-trial hearing is set, [but at] other times we have had to get a letter from a psychologist outlining the issues".[76]

Legal practitioners and victim support personnel also illustrated the process prior to the decision by the judge:

> Through prior discussions with witnesses, the Prosecution usually is made aware when a person is likely to suffer trauma or be intimidated or distressed as a result of delay, and an application is made accordingly.[77]

> This [issue] is usually brought up by the witness who verbalises that they need to give evidence ASAP as they are not coping well. [The provision] has also been used where trials are being set a long time in advance. That causes people further distress.[78]

---

[71] Participant no 8, legal practitioner (26 April 2011).
[72] Participant no 3, judicial officer (7 April 2011).
[73] Participant no 2, judicial officer (27 April 2011).
[74] Participant no 7, legal practitioner (27 April 2011).
[75] Ibid.
[76] Participant no 10, victim support (7 June 2011).
[77] Participant no 6, legal practitioner (11 May 2011).
[78] Participant no 10, victim support (7 June 2011).

> [One victim] stated that they needed to give evidence as soon as possible so the prosecutor made an application in court.[79]

> [The need for this provision is usually determined] by the way in which the victim presents. The DPP will determine whether they are a suitable candidate …[80]

It therefore certainly does not appear that the prosecutors are routinely making these applications:

> It would usually only be once a person mentions that they are not coping or have some mental health conditions that we (the prosecutor or [victim support]) will bring up the possibility of a [pre-trial evidence] with them. Otherwise we would not inform them if they seem able to cope with the time.[81]

Two victim support workers stated that "both the AFP and the DPP explained the new legislation to each victim whose matter ends up proceeding".[82] However, one clarified that the victims are only actually made aware of those processes that are automatically available to them:

> All victims are advised about what is automatic for them, such as CCTV etc. For those provisions that are not automatic and need an application, they are only advised if the prosecutor (or [victim support worker]) thinks that they would be successful in the application and that it would assist them in giving evidence.[83]

One legal practitioner reported that (s)he had been involved in approximately 15 sexual assault trials involving adult complainants. Of these matters, two applications for pre-trial hearings were made, and both were made by consent, that is, the defence did not object to the victim's evidence being taken at a pre-trial hearing and so it was not necessary to argue in court why the pre-trial evidence should be given.[84] Another victim support worker estimated that the prosecution "don't apply for the pre-trial hearing … in about 80 per cent" of cases because "there is no severe emotional trauma or they are not particularly intimidated or distressed".[85] This finding suggests that the "filter" at the prosecutorial

---

[79] Ibid.
[80] Participant no 11, victim support (31 May 2011).
[81] Survey of participant no 10, victim support (7 June 2011).
[82] Participant no 11, victim support (31 May 2011).
[83] Survey of participant no 10, victim support (7 June 2011).
[84] Survey of participant no 6, legal practitioner (11 May 2011).
[85] Survey of participant no 10, victim support (7 June 2011).

stage, whereby the prosecutor or victim support worker assesses the eligibility of the victim, is acting as more of a barrier to the special provisions than objections by the defence or non-granting of the application by the judicial officer.

In this study, one victim was not made aware of the process at all and stated that she didn't "think it was available",[86] despite her trial being held almost four months after the introduction of the reforms. In the other case, the prosecutor offered to pre-record the victim's evidence, but the victim declined because she had her "mind set on giving evidence in court".[87] This was because the police officer that she had spoken to had told her that she would appear to be a strong witness if she gave evidence in the courtroom, and despite the fact that the victim support worker had told her that she should not give evidence in court. So although this victim was aware of the reforms and that her evidence could be pre-recorded, an application was not made.[88]

Interestingly, one judicial officer in the study also referred to the view that witnesses appear stronger in the courtroom:

> There is still a strong feeling that the evidence by CCTV is not as striking and effective as evidence in the courtroom. I have not seen research on this, but have a feeling that there may be some case to justify this.[89]

Victim support workers described the pre-trial hearing process as "stressful, [but] manageable"[90] and "streamlined and calmer".[91] It is reported to be very "organised" such that "both parties know what to expect", and provides victims and their supporters with "knowledge" and "empowerment" because they know "what is ahead" and can feel some control over the process: "victims finally feel they are not the ones on trial".[92] Having procedures in place for those more "vulnerable" was viewed as being "supportive" of victims.[93] One victim support worker reported that knowing that reforms have been put into place for them provides victims with "confidence in the criminal justice system".[94]

---

[86] Participant no 14, victim witness (26 July 2011).
[87] Interview with participant no 13, victim witness (28 October 2010).
[88] Ibid.
[89] Participant no 3, judicial officer (7 April 2011).
[90] Participant no 10, victim support (7 June 2011).
[91] Participant no 11, victim support (31 May 2011).
[92] Ibid.
[93] Ibid.
[94] Ibid.

Victims who had been involved in a pre-trial hearing were reported to have been "very happy" with the fact that they did not have to give evidence again at the actual trial: "They were glad that things were over and done with".[95] Victim support personnel also reported that victims were "more willing to become involved with the criminal justice system".[96] Furthermore, one victim support worker reported that (s)he had not seen any victims who gave evidence at a pre-trial hearing be recalled to give further evidence at the trial.[97]

New section 40T — Witness may be required to attend hearing

(1) This section applies if an audiovisual recording of a witness's evidence given at a pre-trial hearing is admitted in evidence at the hearing of a sexual offence proceeding.
(2) The accused person may apply to the court for an order that the witness attend the hearing of the sexual offence proceeding to give further evidence.
(3) The court must not make the order unless satisfied that—
  (a) if the witness had given evidence in person at the hearing of the sexual offence proceeding, the witness could be recalled; and
  (b) it is in the interests of justice to make the order.

Judicial officers and legal practitioners reported not having seen this section applied in practice, but were able to hypothesise about how it might be interpreted. One judicial officer outlined the importance of this section, as "there may be a chance that the trial would be decided one way or another because of the absence of that additional evidence".[98] When asked how (s)he would interpret the meaning of "interests of justice", one judicial officer stated that:

> [Section] 46 of the *Evidence Act 1995* (Cth) provides for the recall of witnesses, and there is a view that the rule in *Browne v Dunn* may permit recall of witnesses in some other cases as well. I have never been asked to make an order under this section, but I suspect that if recall of the witness was available under the *Evidence Act*/*Browne v Dunn* tests, then it would usually be in the interests of justice to do so.[99]

Legal practitioners provided slightly different interpretations:

---

[95] Participant no 10, victim support (7 June 2011).
[96] Participant no 11, victim support (31 May 2011).
[97] Participant no 10, victim support (7 June 2011).
[98] Participant no 3, judicial officer (7 April 2011).
[99] Participant no 2, judicial officer (27 April 2011).

> It would be seen as being in the interest of justice if it was necessary for the accused to obtain a fair trial.[100]

> [It would have to be] something of relevance that would justify recalling the witness and [which] could prejudice a fair trial not to have the matter followed up with the witness — as the legislation states.[101]

> At face value the provision is wide in the sense that the circumstances where someone may be recalled are broad, and the interests of justice are similarly broad. It would be expected however that the provision would be interpreted restrictively to limit the occasions where a person might be recalled.[102]

When asked to hypothesise about when the section might actually be invoked in practice, legal practitioners essentially shared the view that a victim would be recalled where new evidence became apparent after the witness had given evidence:

> [A witness would be recalled] in circumstances when new evidence comes to light after the witness gives his/her evidence — generally that is the only time.[103]

> It is likely they would be recalled only if a new issue not raised in their evidence was raised by another witness.[104]

New section 40V — Recording of witness's evidence at pre-trial hearing admissible in related hearing

(1) This section applies if an audiovisual recording of a witness's evidence given at a pre-trial hearing is admitted in evidence at the hearing of a sexual offence proceeding.

(2) The recording is admissible as the witness's evidence in a related proceeding unless the court in the related proceeding otherwise orders.

(3) However, the court in the related proceeding may—

  (a) refuse to admit all or any part of the audiovisual recording in evidence; and

[100] Participant no 4, legal practitioner (18 July 2011).
[101] Participant no 5, legal practitioner (4 June 2011).
[102] Participant no 8, legal practitioner (26 April 2011).
[103] Participant no 4, legal practitioner (18 July 2011).
[104] Participant no 6, legal practitioner (11 May 2011).

(b) if the court refuses to admit part of the recording in evidence—order that the part that is not admitted be deleted from the recording.

One judicial officer stated the admissibility, or non-acceptance, of evidence under this section would be subject to the same test as under section 40T (the *Evidence Act* and *Browne v Dunn* tests).[105] Other judicial officers and legal practitioners hypothesised that, in practice, the evidence could be rejected for a number of reasons:

> Where there is a clear indication that the witness had been asked blatant leading questions or a suggestion of prompting by the questioners.[106]
>
> In circumstances when it is necessary to ensure the accused gets a fair trial and is able to canvass all issues with the witness.[107]
>
> If there is something unfair to the accused in the questioning of the witness (ie cross examination of witness, suggesting answer in question) then that part of the interview can be excluded. The prosecution would then need to lead evidence on the excluded area in the usual way.[108]
>
> Presumably it would be in the interests of justice to refuse where the factual paradigms differ between the two cases despite the relatedness (eg occurrence the issue in one case, and consent in the second).[109]
>
> If it prejudices the case in some way.[110]

These findings demonstrate that if evidence is pre-recorded at a pre-trial hearing, there are still a number of opportunities for it to be challenged and reasons for it to be inadmissible in a related hearing, thereby reducing the intended effect of the section.

Revised section 43 — Giving evidence from place other than courtroom

(1) This section applies if the courtroom where a sexual or violent offence is heard and another place are linked by an audiovisual link.

---

[105] Participant no 2, judicial officer (27 April 2011).
[106] Participant no 3, judicial officer (7 April 2011).
[107] Participant no 4, legal practitioner (18 July 2011).
[108] Participant no 7, legal practitioner (27 April 2011).
[109] Participant no 8, legal practitioner (26 April 2011).
[110] Participant no 9, legal practitioner (10 April 2011).

(2) The evidence of the complainant and each similar act witness must be given by audiovisual link from the other place unless the court otherwise orders.
(3) The court may make an order under subsection (2) only if satisfied—
 (a) that—
  (i) for the complainant—the complainant prefers to give evidence in the courtroom; … or
 (b) if the order is not made—
  (i) the sexual or violent offence proceeding may be unreasonably delayed; or
  (ii) there is a substantial risk that the court will not be able to ensure that the sexual or violent offence proceeding is conducted fairly.

Participants did report that CCTV is routinely used, and most of them had not seen an order made under this section for the victim to appear in court. Judicial officers and legal practitioners indicated that the only time the use of CCTV might be challenged is "when there is some particular characteristic of the witness (such as size) which cannot be adequately assessed from the audiovisual transmission",[111] or where "it could be said the jury or judge could not assess the witness unless they see his/her body language etc".[112] Only one judicial officer reported that (s)he had made an order under this section, and it was for this exact reason:

> I have made an order under [section] 43 once, in a violent offence proceeding. The order was sought by the defence, who were planning to raise self-defence and wanted the jury to be able to see the respective sizes of the relatively slight accused and the rather bigger complainant. I was inclined to the view that this did raise an issue of fairness that might justify making the order, but in the event the complainant was willing to give evidence in person so the order was made, in effect, by consent. This meant that I didn't hear the accused's fairness arguments in favour of the order or any opposing arguments from the complainant, and didn't have to reach a conclusion on the fairness point.[113]

Victim support personnel reported that victims who gave evidence via CCTV were "able to speak with more confidence and certainty knowing they couldn't see the accused but [knowing] they could hear them tell their story".[114] The victim witness who used CCTV supported this view:

---

[111] Participant no 3, judicial officer (7 April 2011).
[112] Participant no 4, legal practitioner (18 July 2011).
[113] Participant no 2, judicial officer (27 April 2011).
[114] Participant no 11, victim support (31 May 2011).

> I chose not to see the accused and this was definitely the best option. Unfortunately when the trial finished we went out at the same time as the accused and I saw the accused and started crying at having to see him. Absolutely best avoided. Best avoided due to horrible feelings towards accused. Too confronting seeing accused.[115]

View from the Inside: Have the Aims of the Act been Achieved?

Aim: Reducing the trauma for sexual assault victim witnesses

The new subsection 90AA of the *Magistrates Court Act 1930* introduced the idea of a "paper committal" for sexual offence prosecutions, aiming to reduce the number of times victim witnesses have to give evidence. This section is one of the few mandatory sections introduced. It prohibits absolutely the attendance of victims of sexual assault at the committal hearing.

Victim support workers described the committal process (of the past) as often scary, repetitive, unnecessary, stressful, overwhelming, elongated, frustrating, traumatic, discouraging and unfair.[116] It was reported that these hearings "brought all of the negative thoughts up and was not good for their wellbeing".[117] Generally speaking, the process was detrimental to the victim witness's wellbeing.[118]

Therefore, by removing committals for all victims of sexual assault, victims are no longer exposed to retrauma at that preliminary stage. However, the main aim of the reforms was to alleviate the trauma of *all* sexual assault proceedings for all victims of sexual assault. Has this occurred?

The two victim witnesses described their experience as a witness in the trial as scary, overwhelming, intense,[119] hopeless, angering, long, enduring, complex and confusing.[120] One talked about the feelings of hopelessness while being cross-examined:

---

[115] Participant no 14, victim witness (26 July 2011).

[116] Participant no 10, victim support (7 June 2011); Participant no 11, victim support (31 May 2011); Participant no 12, victim support (31 May 2011).

[117] Participant no 10, victim support (7 June 2011).

[118] Participant no 11, victim support (31 May 2011). Participant no 12, victim support (31 May 2011). Participant no 10, victim support (7 June 2011).

[119] Participant no 14, victim witness (26 July 2011).

[120] Interview with participant no 13, victim witness (28 October 2010).

> The process was hopeless. I felt that it was a joke because it felt like it wasn't going anywhere and wasn't achieving what I had hoped it would achieve. They continued to go over the same questions and I felt that it didn't matter what they said, it wasn't going to change what happened — I knew the truth (and so did he). They were going to make what they wanted of it.[121]

The victims also identified some negative health impacts:

> [The trial] made everyday life more difficult and challenging. Harder to concentrate. Not able to talk to people openly. Difficult to go to work and get on with it at times. Impacted on my relationship with my boyfriend by adding stress to the relationship. At times I withdrew from people, so I could deal with my own feelings and cope without the added stress of their opinions.[122]

> [As a result of the trial I] was not sleeping, lost a lot of friends. I had nightmares, depression, lots of anger, and moodiness. [However] the process of talking to people about it and being heard was very validating because I got to tell my story and people — the police and DPP — understood and believed me.[123]

The victim support personnel surveyed confirmed that these may be the experiences of most victims both before and after the amendments. They described the process as scary, unnecessary, overwhelming,[124] frightening, stressful, long, confusing, painful,[125] traumatic, discouraging, debilitating and abusive.[126] One support person stated that "people are very fearful of giving evidence … they have to repeat themselves over and over … they have already given a statement and have to give evidence at trial as well … people often have sleepless nights … it is a very new experience for them".[127] Another highlighted other negative aspects of the process for victims: "[it is] confusing … with both sides arguing on points of law and requesting adjournments [and] painful … [the] bringing up of painful memories".[128]

---

[121] Ibid.
[122] Participant no 14, victim witness (26 July 2011).
[123] Interview with participant no 13, victim witness (28 October 2010).
[124] Participant no 10, victim support (7 June 2011).
[125] Participant no 11, victim support (31 May 2011).
[126] Participant no 12, victim support (31 May 2011).
[127] Participant no 10, victim support (7 June 2011).
[128] Participant no 11, victim support (31 May 2011).

However in their responses to the question of whether the aim of extracting better evidence had been achieved (see below), the support people inferred that the trials post-amendment have been less traumatic or at least less fear-provoking for victim witnesses.

There were mixed responses from legal practitioner participants as to whether this legislative aim has been fulfilled, although many noted that the changes have not been in place long enough to make full comment. Judicial officers were reluctant to give a definitive answer to this question:

> Not able to say — some witnesses appear more comfortable but that is a very subjective impression.[129]

> I had conducted two sexual assault trials before 1/6/09. In both cases the complainants gave evidence by audio-visual link from a remote witness room. I have not yet presided over a trial under the new provisions in which either pre-trial evidence or a police interview was admitted instead of evidence given during the trial, so I'm not in a position to assess trauma levels under new and old schemes, but in my limited experience every complainant reacts differently and it would require one to hear a lot of such cases before generalisations could be made, which would be in the nature of whether people seem more or less distressed at eg a police interview than they used to be at the time of the trial.[130]

The primary theme that arose from the question about the effect of the legislation was that the reforms have the potential to be effective:

> I think that witnesses often have a real fear of being in the same room as the accused. This has now improved. They appear to feel safer in giving the evidence from a distance.[131]

> … the change to paper committal proceedings removes the need for complainants to give evidence both at committal and trial, which is a significant improvement. The ability for sexual assault witnesses to give pre-recorded evidence also helps to alleviate the trauma associated with lengthy delays, although the need to establish trauma or distress as a criterion places a limitation on the utility of this provision.[132]

---

[129] Participant no 1, judicial officer (1 June 2011).
[130] Participant no 2, judicial officer (27 April 2011).
[131] Participant no 3, judicial officer (7 April 2011).
[132] Participant no 6, legal practitioner (11 May 2011).

> Many more people are entitled to CCTV and pre-trial hearings which make people much more comfortable about giving evidence. Some people have stated they would not have given evidence if they didn't have CCTV.[133]

> Victims are more willing to engage in the Criminal Justice System knowing that special provisions are now made for them.[134]

However, prosecutorial and judicial discretion may mean that special provisions are not used enough for adult, non-disabled victims:

> Pre-recording is a real positive, if only it could be utilised more often. The fact that victims do not have to give evidence at committals is a real positive. Pre-recorded children's evidence and cross is fantastic ... We seek supporting documentation from psychologists etc. This section had not been used more than twice when I was employed at ODPP.[135]

This means that although more victims might feel encouraged to engage with the system, and are no longer discouraged by their committal experiences, a substantial proportion of adult, non-disabled victims are not experiencing the significant benefits of some of the special provisions.

Whilst not prejudicing accused's right to a fair trial

It must be noted too that although the amending legislation aimed to reduce the trauma of a trial for victims of sexual assault, this was to be done without prejudicing the accused's "right" to a fair trial. The judicial officers surveyed were confident that this right had been maintained despite the changes, although, again, they were careful to explain that there have not been many trials to test it:

> An accused has a right to a fair trial. The changes have not derogated from that right.[136]

> I haven't observed any threat to this right, but as indicated have only conducted a handful of relevant trials.[137]

The legal practitioners were less confident. Interestingly, all defence practitioners surveyed indicated that the accused's right to a fair trial had been eroded to some extent:

---

[133] Participant no 10, victim support (7 June 2011).
[134] Participant no 11, victim support (31 May 2011).
[135] Participant no 12, victim support (31 May 2011).
[136] Participant no 1, judicial officer (1 June 2011).
[137] Participant no 2, judicial officer (27 April 2011).

> I think it has eroded some aspects of the fair trial. A jury should be able to see the witness completely and not via TV. Most cases are word on word and body language is so important to assess credibility.[138]

> It's early days, but I am concerned that the testing of a young complainant's testimony has been compromised when (as is in practice usually) there is a long delay between police interview and defence counsels opportunity to cross-examine.[139]

> There is a distinct disadvantage to the accused in the complainant giving evidence other than before the court. Cross-examination is less effective and, regardless of any warnings, the message is communicated clearly that the complainant is a genuine victim. This inherently undermines the presumption of innocence.[140]

> There is a significant danger that treating the evidence of the accuser in this way will be unfair as there is a danger of a perception arising that the accused is guilty — it flies in the face of the presumption of innocence.[141]

The opinion of the one legal practitioner who worked as a prosecutor was in line with those of the judicial officers surveyed: that the accused's rights were maintained despite the changes.

Aim: Extracting best evidence possible

Yet another aim of the legislation was to "extract the 'best' evidence possible from witnesses who may otherwise suffer a disadvantage".[142] The overall response from judicial officers and legal practitioners to the question of whether this aim had been fulfilled was negative:

> No — [it is the] same evidence — just taken differently.[143]

> It's too early to say. However I doubt it.[144]

---

[138] Participant no 4, legal practitioner (18 July 2011).
[139] Participant no 5, legal practitioner (4 June 2011).
[140] Participant no 8, legal practitioner (26 April 2011).
[141] Participant no 9, legal practitioner (10 April 2011).
[142] Revised Explanatory Statement, Sexual and Violent Offences Legislation Amendment Bill 2008 (ACT) 2.
[143] Participant no 4, legal practitioner (18 July 2011).
[144] Participant no 7, legal practitioner (27 April 2011).

> No. The changes allow less effective challenge to a complainant and thereby degrades the overall quality of the evidence before the court. Diminishing the testing of evidence diminishes its quality.[145]

> No — it is much harder to appear "real" on a TV.[146]

However, again, the legal practitioner responses differed between those who worked as defence counsel and those who worked for the DPP. The one participant from the DPP stated:

> The changes have not been in place long enough to make full comment in relation to this. Certainly, the ability for witnesses to give evidence early is likely to improve the quality of evidence as it is given closer in time to the offence than might otherwise be the case.[147]

The victim support personnel surveyed all agreed that the changes made to the legislation did improve the quality of the victims' evidence as victims are (potentially) able to give evidence sooner and are less fearful when they do have to give evidence:

> [The evidence is improved] in relation to people recalling their evidence so far after the event.[148]

> … giving evidence away from the courts means victims have the privacy of coming and going without being seen by the accused's family. This bolsters confidence when giving evidence as the fear of retribution is alleviated.[149]

> … the addition of the off-site room means victims are less fearful prior to giving evidence as they no longer have the fear of facing the offender or his supporters in the court precinct.[150]

One judge though believed that the view of a witness in the courtroom appearing stronger than a witness on a television screen continues to exist,

---

[145] Participant no 8, legal practitioner (26 April 2011).
[146] Participant no 9, legal practitioner (10 April 2011).
[147] Participant no 6, legal practitioner (11 May 2011).
[148] Participant no 10, victim support (7 June 2011).
[149] Participant no 11, victim support (31 May 2011).
[150] Participant no 12, victim support (31 May 2011).

despite research that suggests that the presence (or not) of the witness appears to have no effect on conviction rates.[151]

Conclusion

The *Evidence Amendment Act 2008* (Cth) came into force at around the same time as the *Sexual and Violent Offences Legislation Amendment Act*, and amended the Commonwealth *Evidence Act*. This Act also aimed to reduce the trauma of a trial for victim witnesses by amending the *Evidence Act 1995* (Cth), with section 41, which now makes it mandatory for judicial officers to intervene where they are of the opinion that a question put to the victim witness is "improper".[152] The amending Act also broadened the definition of improper questions, and now includes questions that are "misleading or confusing … unduly annoying, harassing, intimidating, offensive, humiliating or repetitive … belittling, insulting or otherwise inappropriate".[153]

All judicial officers surveyed stated that the changes to the wording of section 41 have not resulted in them disallowing more questions. One judicial officer provided an interesting explanation for the lack of change on his behalf: "I am always a little conscious that the Appeal Court is not necessarily composed of judges who understand the need to protect witnesses".[154] One legal practitioner stated: section "41 does provide a useful mechanism to challenge inappropriate questions, and I do rely upon it when necessary".[155] However, all legal practitioners surveyed confirmed the view that more questions are not being disallowed as a result of the changes.

It is therefore fair to assume that any reduction in trauma for victims of sexual assault in the ACT can be attributed to the changes made by the *Sexual and Violent Offences Legislation Amendment Act*.

Our findings show that although some of the provisions such as CCTV and support people are strictly applied and working well, a number of the provisions for adult victims of sexual assault who are not intellectually impaired are very indeterminate and are being interpreted differently by different judicial officers and prosecutorial personnel. Further, these

---

[151] Judy Cashmore and Lily Trimboli, *An Evaluation of the NSW Child Sexual Assault Specialist Jurisdiction Pilot* (NSW Bureau of Crime Statistics and Research, 2005).

[152] *Evidence Act 1995* (Cth) s 41(1).

[153] Ibid.

[154] Participant no 3, judicial officer (7 April 2011).

[155] Participant no 6, legal practitioner (11 May 2011).

victims are required to demonstrate vulnerability or distress in order to be eligible for some of the protections. The prosecutor must perceive the victim as vulnerable before informing them and making an application, and then introducing further hurdles such as obtaining expert reports for the trial in order to convince the judicial officer.

Although judicial officers said that they would make an equal assessment of victim and offender rights when determining whether to close the court, lawyers reported that these orders are rarely sought and rarely made, despite our findings that victim witnesses would nearly always prefer it. The provisions providing for the use of screens in court are also reportedly rarely used in practice, despite the reported benefit to victims, and in one case, screens were not available even though the victim asking specifically for them. It is unclear from our study why these provisions are not being used, but as a result, they are not having their intended effect of protecting victims from further trauma.

Our findings suggest that the pre-trial hearing process also provides many benefits for victims of sexual assault. However, there appear to be some issues with the process before this. These issues are resulting in the section not being utilised as often as it could be. Both victim witnesses in our research were not able to experience the benefits of a pre-trial hearing because they were either not informed that it was an option, or were convinced that giving evidence in court would be better for “their case”. Perhaps these issues are just “teething problems” and will be overcome with time. However, there is evidence in these findings that societal views about vulnerability and the manner in which evidence is given are affecting the implementation of this section. This means that victims who do not conform to the societal view of normal or “real” rape may not be perceived as especially vulnerable and therefore slip through the gaps and be left unprotected by the legislation.

CHAPTER TWO

THE RELEVANCE OF ABORIGINALITY IN SENTENCING: FINDINGS FROM INTERVIEWS IN THE ACT

CHRISTINA LEWIS, ANTHONY HOPKINS AND LORANA BARTELS

Introduction

Aboriginal and Torres Strait Islander (ATSI)[1] Australians come before courts to be sentenced in numbers far greater than would be statistically expected given the size of the relevant population. This overrepresentation is starkly reflected in our prisons. Though the ATSI population accounts for less than 3 per cent of the Australian population,[2] on 30 June 2011 ATSI prisoners made up 26 per cent of the custodial population.[3] The rate of imprisonment of ATSI Australians on 30 June 2011 was 14 times higher than the general population.[4] These statistics are tragic and depressingly familiar, all the more because they are trending steadily up rather than down.[5] In the Australian Capital Territory (ACT), the smallest jurisdiction in Australia,[6] the picture is little better. On 30 June 2011, the

---

[1] In this chapter, the terms Indigenous, Aboriginal and ATSI are used interchangeably, although it is acknowledged that there are differences between Aboriginal and Torres Strait Islander communities.
[2] Australian Bureau of Statistics (ABS), Population Distribution, Aboriginal and Torres Strait Islander Australians, 2006, Cat No 4705.0 (ABS, 2007).
[3] ABS, *Prisoners in Australia, 2011*, Cat No 4517.0 (ABS, 2012).
[4] Ibid.
[5] Ibid.
[6] For general information about the ACT, see: *About the ACT* (2012) ACT Government <http://www.act.gov.au/browse/about-the-act>.

rate of imprisonment of ATSI Australians in the ACT was 13 times higher than the general population.[7]

An appreciation of this overrepresentation necessitates the question: why? There is no simple answer. Indeed, the 1991 report of the Royal Commission into Aboriginal Deaths in Custody (RCIADIC) devotes a whole volume to exploring the underlying issues which explain these disproportionate rates of imprisonment.[8] In summary, the Commissioners found an answer in the history of colonial and post-colonial relations between Indigenous and non-Indigenous Australians and their institutions. They also found an answer in the legacy of discrimination, disadvantage and socio-economic inequality borne of this history.[9] Tasked to inquire into the deaths of 99 Indigenous Australians who died in custody, the Commissioners found:

> eighty-three were unemployed at the date of last detention; they were uneducated at least in the European sense — or under-educated — only two had completed secondary level; forty-three of them experienced childhood separation from their natural families through intervention by the State authorities, mission or other institutions; forty-three had been charged with an offence at or before aged fifteen and seventy-four at or before aged nineteen; forty-three had been taken into last custody directly for reasons related to alcohol and it can safely be said that overwhelmingly in the remaining cases the reasons for last custody was directly alcohol related … generally speaking the standard of health of the ninety-nine varied from poor to very bad (the average age of those who died from natural causes was a little over thirty years); their economic position was disastrous and their social position at the margin of society; they misused alcohol to a grave extent …[10]

What is dramatic here is that the Commissioners did not simply come to generalised conclusions about the reasons for custodial overrepresentation. They found these reasons reflected in the lives of the individuals who had died, and in their experience as Indigenous Australians:

> What did emerge was that to understand the last hours of life of each individual and to truly understand the circumstances of their deaths Commissioners had to know the whole life of the individuals and, equally important, had to understand the experience of the whole Aboriginal

---

[7] ABS, above n 2.

[8] Commonwealth Royal Commission into Aboriginal Deaths in Custody, *National Report* (1991) vol 2.

[9] Ibid.

[10] Ibid, vol 1 [1.2.17].

> community through their two hundred years of contact with non-Aboriginal society.[11]

But understanding the systemic and background factors that result in Indigenous Australians coming before sentencing courts in disproportionate numbers does not directly bear upon how these offenders' Aboriginality should or could be taken into account in sentencing. It is impermissible for a court to treat the reduction of general custodial overrepresentation as an objective in the sentencing of an individual.[12] The reason for this is that a court must sentence an individual, taking into account their personal circumstances and the circumstances of their offence. In turn, to be relevant to the sentencing process, these unique circumstances must bear upon the need for retribution, deterrence, protection of society and the potential for reform.[13]

How, then, does an understanding of the reasons for overrepresentation bear upon the sentencing of a particular Indigenous Australian? It does so only insofar as the systemic and background factors that result in this general overrepresentation are found to exist in the life of the individual offender being sentenced. These systemic and background factors may well be critical to understanding why the offender comes before the court and may, for example, illuminate an offender's moral culpability and potential for rehabilitation.

The fundamental premise of this chapter is precisely that which emerged from the Royal Commission: namely, that to understand the individual, we must understand the experience of the group to which they belong. And, that where facts relevant to sentencing emerge as a result of understanding an Indigenous offender within the context of their experience of Aboriginality, these should be taken into account in the interests of ensuring equal justice.

The case law supports this understanding of the relevance of Aboriginality in sentencing, though the issue has not received the same level of consideration in the ACT as it has elsewhere. However, the critical question is whether, in practice, Aboriginality and an offender's

---

[11] Ibid, vol 1 [1.2.15].

[12] *Western Australia v Richards* (2008) 185 A Crim R 413, 416 (Martin CJ).

[13] *Veen v R (No 2)* (1988) 164 CLR 465, 476 (Mason CJ, Dawson, Brennan and Toohey JJ); see also: *Crimes (Sentencing Procedure) Act 1999* (NSW) s 3A; *Penalties and Sentences Act 1992* (Qld) s 9(1); *Sentencing Act 1991* (Vic) s 5(1); *Sentencing Act 1995* (NT) s 5(1); *Criminal Law (Sentencing) Act 1988* (SA) s 10(1); *Crimes (Sentencing) Act 2005* (ACT) s 7; *Sentencing Act 1997* (Tas) s 3; *Crimes Act 1914* (Cth) s 16A.

experience of Aboriginality *are* being taken into account. This chapter seeks to answer this question through a consideration of sentencing in the ACT. It does so by drawing on published judicial decisions, but also by drawing upon the experience of Aboriginal Legal Service lawyers in the ACT who represent Indigenous offenders on a daily basis at the "coal face".

The conclusion reached is that, in general, the Aboriginality of offenders coming before 'mainstream'[14] sentencing courts receives limited attention. It is further concluded that one significant reason for this is that pre-sentence reports, which are extensively relied upon in sentencing, do not themselves explore the unique systemic and background factors impacting on the lives of Indigenous offenders. Accordingly, there is often limited, if any, material before the court from which the relevance of an offender's Aboriginality can be determined. Ultimately, it is contended that an opportunity is being missed and that the potential exists for pre-sentence report writers to do more to assist sentencing courts in their efforts to ensure the "even administration of criminal justice"[15].

Judicial Consideration of the Relevance of Aboriginality in Sentencing

The following section presents an overview of the case law on Aboriginality in sentencing.[16] The issue was first considered by the High Court in the case of *Neal*, where Brennan J explained:

> The same sentencing principles are to be applied, of course, in every case, irrespective of the identity of a particular offender or his membership of an ethnic or other group. But in imposing sentences courts are bound to take into account, in accordance with those principles, all material facts including those facts which exist only by reason of the offender's

[14] As compared to the Galambany Indigenous Sentencing Court, which will be discussed in brief later.

[15] *Neal v R* (1982) 149 CLR 305, 326 (Brennan J).

[16] For a fuller discussion, see Anthony Hopkins, 'The Relevance of Aboriginality in Sentencing: "Sentencing a Person For Who They Are"', *Australian Indigenous Law Review* (forthcoming). For a recent qualitative analysis of judicial views on Aboriginality and sentencing, see: Christine Bond, Samantha Jeffries and Heron Loban, 'Inequities, Alternatives and Future Directions: Inside Perspectives of Indigenous Sentencing in Queensland' (2012) *Psychiatry, Psychology and Law*.

> membership of an ethnic or other group. So much is essential to the even administration of criminal justice.[17]

This statement of general principle recognises that individual circumstances cannot be neatly separated from the circumstances of the group or community to which the individual belongs. Such recognition opens the door to a full consideration of offenders' circumstances, including their historical, cultural, socio-economic and psychological experience of Aboriginality. Arguably, the logical conclusion of *Neal* requires sentencers to engage with and understand the Indigenous experience in all its complexity.

Significantly, Justice Brennan did not circumscribe judicial consideration of Aboriginality in sentencing; his Honour left open what might be considered within the terms "all material facts" and how these facts might be material to the sentencing discretion. In addition, he made no attempt to restrict claims to group identity, for example, by suggesting that consideration of Aboriginality in sentencing is to be restricted to "tribal" or "traditional" Indigenous Australians. However, Aboriginality will only affect a person's sentence where that fact casts light on the individual's circumstances, which need to be explained in the context of their Aboriginality.

Hopkins recently described the decision in *Neal* as "an invitation to judges to throw off the yoke of their own experience and consider the particular circumstances of the Indigenous person before them through the lens of Aboriginal experience",[18] but subsequent interpretations have sought to limit its scope. This has created a "divisive and intolerable"[19] situation whereby some Indigenous offenders may be regarded as not "Aboriginal enough"[20] for the principle set out in *Neal* to apply.

Only some kinds of Aboriginality count

The leading NSW case is *R v Fernando*,[21] which involved an offender being sentenced for maliciously wounding his de facto partner with a knife while heavily intoxicated. The offence was committed in a rural NSW

---

[17] *Neal v R* (1982) 149 CLR 305, 326 (Brennan J). For comment, see Martin Flynn, 'Not "Aboriginal Enough" For Particular Consideration in Sentencing' (2005) 6(9) *Indigenous Law Bulletin* 15.

[18] Hopkins, above n 16, 5.

[19] Ibid, 7.

[20] Flynn, above n 17.

[21] *R v Fernando* (1992) 76 A Crim R 58.

town with a large Indigenous community. The offender was described as having a "deprived background" and a history of alcohol abuse. Wood J developed eight sentencing principles ("the *Fernando* principles") to be considered when sentencing an Indigenous offender. These can be summarised as follows:

- The same sentencing principles are to be applied in every case but a court should not ignore facts which exist only by reason of the offender's membership of an ethnic or other group;
- Aboriginality is relevant in terms of explaining the offence and circumstances of the offender;
- Alcohol abuse and violence within Aboriginal communities may not be solved through imprisonment;
- Indigenous communities should be protected from serious violence by drunken offenders in their communities (even in the absence of evidence proving the effectiveness of imprisonment);
- While drunkenness is not normally an excuse or mitigating factor, where the offender's abuse of alcohol reflects their socio-economic circumstances and background, that can and should be taken into account as a mitigating factor;
- Sentencing courts must avoid any hint of racism, paternalism or collective guilt when sentencing Indigenous offenders, but must recognise the offender's subjective circumstances;
- A sentence of imprisonment may be particularly harsh for an Indigenous person who is not familiar with non-Indigenous life or comes from a deprived background; and
- The need to ensure the punishment fits the crime is to be balanced against the need for rehabilitation.

A recent review of the impact of *Fernando* by the NSW Sentencing Council described the application of the principles in the appellate courts as "uneven".[22] The impact of *Fernando* and subsequent decisions[23] in NSW has been to restrict the application of *Neal* to cases involving

---

[22] Janet Manuell, *The Fernando Principles: The Sentencing of Indigenous Offenders in NSW* (Discussion paper prepared for the NSW Sentencing Council) (2009) 1.

[23] See *R v Ceissman* (2001) 119 A Crim R 535; *R v Pitt* [2001] NSWCCA 156 (14 May 2001); *R v Morgan* (2003) 57 NSWLR 533; *R v Newman and Simpson* (2004) 145 A Crim R 361; *R v Kelly* (2005) 155 A Crim R 499. See also: *Crawford v Laverty* [2008] ACTSC 107 (13 October 2008) (Penfold J), discussed below.

Indigenous offenders in specific rural or remote communities where alcohol abuse is endemic and who have committed violent offences while intoxicated. We would argue that such an approach fails to appreciate the full complexity of post-colonial Indigenous experience and the relevance of this to achieving equal justice in sentencing. Edney has described the decisions as "fundamentally misapprehending the nature of Indigenous identity in post-colonial society"[24] and "attempt[ing] to define the contemporary Indigenous experience and who may be entitled to rely upon Aboriginality for the purpose of sentencing".[25] Flynn has likewise argued that although

> some Indigenous defendants do not have a history of deprived socioeconomic circumstances and that many do not live on reserves, the same fact remains that every Indigenous person is a member of a visible racial minority in a community that is often not tolerant to racial minorities.[26]

A broader view of Aboriginality?

In her review of the *Fernando* principles, Manuell pondered "What does it mean to be an Indigenous person?" and whether any disadvantage experienced differs, "depending on whether the offender grew up in urban, regional or remote areas".[27] In contrast to the narrow approach taken in the cases above, some decisions have shown a more expansive approach to these issues. Significantly, in the 2007 decision of *Waters*, James J stated on behalf of the NSW Court of Criminal Appeal that "[c]ontrary to a submission made by the Crown, I would not regard the approach to sentencing Aboriginal offenders outlined in *Fernando* as being limited to Aborigines who live in isolated communities".[28] This statement was recently approved by Refshauge J of the ACT Supreme Court in *TM v Karapanos and Bakes*.[29]

The South Australian Court of Criminal Appeal has also demonstrated a clear willingness to consider the Aboriginality of offenders even where

---

[24] Richard Edney, 'The Retreat from *Fernando* and the Erasure of Indigenous Identity in Sentencing' (2006) 6(17) *Indigenous Law Bulletin* 8, 8.

[25] Ibid, 9.

[26] Flynn, above n 17, 15.

[27] Manuell, above n 22, 11.

[28] *Waters v R* [2007] NSWCCA 219 (2 August 2007) (James J, Giles JA and Hisop JA agreeing), [39]. Interestingly, Manuell, above n 22, did not refer to this decision in her review.

[29] *TM v Karapanos and Bakes* [2011] ACTSC 74 (12 May 2011) ('*TM*'), [112].

their circumstances are significantly removed from those present in *Fernando* or similar cases. In *R v Smith*,[30] the Court considered an appeal against the severity of a sentence of a 22 year old Aboriginal man, who had been raised in an urban setting and had no history of drug or alcohol abuse. However, according to an anthropological report before the court, his offending was closely entwined with his experience of Aboriginality. Specifically, he had been raised by his Aboriginal father, originally from a more remote Aboriginal community, who himself had a long criminal record and a history of drug abuse. His father was accorded respect within the Aboriginal community in Adelaide for his criminal history and his capacity to survive incarceration. And, through his own offending, the younger Smith sought to emulate his father in pursuit of the respect he believed he would be accorded by kin and community.

The offender was unsuccessful in his appeal. Nevertheless, two members of the Court made clear that consideration of Smith's Aboriginality and experience of Aboriginality was fundamental to the appropriate exercise of the sentencing discretion, regardless of his urban circumstances. Justice Gray stated that the offender's "urban Aboriginality raises important considerations",[31] adding that it "provides an explanation for his conduct. This factor is mitigatory".[32] In addition, Lander J observed:

> In my opinion no distinction is to be drawn between an Aboriginal person to whom European culture is foreign because of a lack of exposure to that culture (ie: a traditional Aboriginal), and an Aboriginal person to whom European culture is foreign, not because a lack of exposure to that culture, but simply as a result of that person's identity as an Aboriginal person …
>
> The heritage of Aboriginal people raised in urban settings is relevant in explaining matters personal to the offender. Insofar as that heritage throws light on such matters, and on the circumstances of the offending, there is no rigid distinction to be made between the approach to be taken to urban Aboriginal people and those Aboriginal people often described as "tribal".[33]

There have also been two notable Victorian decisions which have taken a broader approach to offenders' Aboriginality. The first of these was *R v Fuller-Cust*,[34] which involved consideration of the relevance of

[30] *R v Smith* (2003) 86 SASR 132.
[31] Ibid, [134] (Gray J).
[32] Ibid, [135] (Gray J).
[33] Ibid, [61]–[62] (Lander J).
[34] *R v Fuller-Cust* (2002) 6 VR 496.

Aboriginality in the sentencing of an offender who was removed from his natural parents as a young child. It was accepted that the offender's removal from his community and the aftermath of that removal resulted in an Aboriginal identity very different from that under consideration in *Fernando* or *Neal*, but an identity nonetheless Indigenous.

Fuller-Cust pleaded guilty to five counts of rape, two counts of indecent assault, one count of false imprisonment and one count of recklessly causing injury. He appealed against the sentence of 20 years' imprisonment, and succeeded on a ground unrelated to his Indigenous status, resulting in a three year reduction in his sentence.[35] In the decision, his background was set out in detail. He had been removed from his Aboriginal mother and non-Aboriginal father as a toddler and repeated requests for his return and access to him were denied by the Social Welfare Department. By the time the offender was two, he and his sister were living with non-Indigenous foster parents, who subsequently rejected him after instances of deprivation and physical discipline. He was also sexually abused by a foster uncle. He was reunited with his mother at the age of 15, but this was unsuccessful. A consulting forensic psychiatrist gave evidence to explain, amongst other things, the causal link between this dysfunctional and disadvantaged background and the offending for which he was to be sentenced.

Batt JA and O'Bryan AJA found that in the circumstances, community safety, and specific and general deterrence, as well as denunciation of the offender's conduct, were of far greater importance than any mitigation due to the offender's Aboriginality. The judges did, however, recognise the offender's background as a relevant mitigating factor, including the sexual abuse he had suffered, and the fact that he had been placed as an infant into unsatisfactory institutional and foster care.

Eames JA provided a powerful dissent, arguing that "to ignore factors personal to the applicant, and his history, in which his Aboriginality was a factor, and to ignore his perception of the impact on his life of his Aboriginality, would be to sentence him as someone other than himself".[36] With explicit reference to the principle in *Neal,*[37] Eames JA accepted the invitation, and indeed the responsibility, to consider the offender's

---

[35] Special leave to appeal to the High Court was sought and rejected on the basis that the appeal amounted to "a complaint about the individual sentencing of this applicant, rather than a point of general application or general principle": Transcript of Proceedings, *Fuller-Cust v The Queen* [2003] HCATrans 394 (3 October 2003) [3] (Hayne J).

[36] *R v Fuller-Cust* (2002) 6 VR 496, 520.

[37] Ibid.

circumstances through the lens of Aboriginal experience. To ask and answer the question of what material facts existed by reason of the offender's Aboriginality, Eames JA turned to insights drawn from the RCIADIC and the Stolen Generations "Bringing Them Home" report.[38] His Honour accepted as a partial explanation for the offender's circumstances and behaviour the common and documented experience of Indigenous Australians as a group. He identified facts material to the offender's life existing by virtue of his membership of the group of Indigenous Australians separated from their families, brought up without connection to kin and community.

The decision recognised that it is not just social and economic disadvantages which may lead an Indigenous person to commit an offence, but also acknowledged that the more complex issues of historical and cultural differences, such as being a member of the Stolen Generation, should be taken into account in order to ensure the individual is sentenced appropriately. Crucially, Eames JA was able to understand Fuller-Cust as a product of the particular historical and social impacts on Indigenous Australians and perceived him as "an Aboriginal person severed from and unable to embrace his Aboriginality".[39]

Eames JA's approach was approved by the Victorian Court of Appeal in *DPP v Terrick*,[40] where Maxwell P, Redlich JA and Robson AJA set out eight propositions relevant to the sentencing of Indigenous Australians, including that

- Circumstances of disadvantage, deprivation or (sexual) violence may be explanatory, if not causative, of the offending or (if relevant) of the offender's alcohol or drug addiction.
- The (relative) weight to be given to circumstances of disadvantage or deprivation is a matter for the sentencing judge, and will depend on: (a) the nature and extent of the disadvantage [and] (b) the nexus (if any) with the offending …
- Thus, Aboriginal offenders are not to be sentenced more leniently than non-Aboriginal persons on account of their race …
- When applying sentencing principles, which are common to all Victorians, a different outcome may result for an Aboriginal offender if it is shown that "mitigating factors in the background of the offender,

[38] Report of the National Inquiry into the Separation of Aboriginal and Torres Strait Islander Children from their Families, Bringing Them Home (Human Rights and Equal Opportunity Commission, 1997).

[39] Hopkins, above n 16, 17.

[40] *DPP v Terrick* (2009) 24 VR 457 ('*Terrick*').

> or [in the] circumstances of the offence, occurred or had an impact peculiarly so because of the Aboriginality of the offender".

Such considerations require a careful examination of the history of the offender. The relevance of Aboriginality to an offender's disadvantaged background must be established by appropriate evidence.[41]

These propositions were endorsed in the ACT by Refshauge J in *TM v Karapanos and Bakes*,[42] where his Honour described the propositions as "represent[ing] a comprehensive approach which will be helpful to sentencers who must deal with Aboriginal offenders whose deprived background lead them often and too often into the criminal justice system".[43]

The decision in *Terrick* clearly marked a return to the general principle propounded by Brennan J in *Neal* over 25 years earlier. Indeed, it expanded on it, as it was the first decision where a majority of an Australian appellate court agreed that historical and cultural disadvantages often found in Indigenous communities are powerful considerations when sentencing Indigenous offenders. There was no talk of restriction to cases involving alcohol abuse or to circumstances bound by offence type, location or other factors. Instead, the approach embraces the complexity of post-colonial Aboriginal identity, requiring a "careful examination of the history of the offender" and requires the court to take factors into account which exist by reason of the offender's Aboriginality.

However, as was made clear by the Victorian Court of Appeal in *Terrick*, facts that exist by reason of offender's Aboriginality and the relevance of these facts must be established by "appropriate evidence". In other words, there must be a basis in evidence to establish a link between the offender's Aboriginality and the circumstances of the offence or the circumstances of the offender. Hopkins recently drew attention to the failure of counsel to explicitly refer to the principles in *Fernando* or to make submissions and provide evidence which establishes a link between a defendant's experience as an Aboriginal person and their offending behaviour.[44] Hopkins further argues that this has caused a "recurrent theme in judgments disavowing the importance of Aboriginality in the

---

41 Ibid, 468–9 (Maxwell P, Redlich JA and Robson AJA). For discussion of the fact that Aboriginality appears to be regarded by the courts as synonymous with disadvantage, see Hopkins, above n 16.

42 *TM* [2011] ACTSC 74 (12 May 2011) ('*TM*').

43 Ibid, [114].

44 Hopkins, above n 16, 12, referring to the case of *R v Kelly* (2005) 155 A Crim R 499.

sentencing of particular Indigenous offenders".[45] We will return to the issue of the need for evidence to establish the offender's history and experience of Aboriginality — and the means of obtaining such evidence — in later sections of this chapter.

Aboriginality and Sentencing in the ACT

This chapter is concerned with the extent to which Aboriginality is taken into account by mainstream courts in the ACT. However, it should be recognised that an Indigenous sentencing court operates in the ACT and that this court is well placed to identify facts material to the sentencing discretion which exist by reason only of an offender's Aboriginality. These Indigenous courts do not apply Indigenous customary law, but rather provide a less formal means of sentencing and allow for the elders of the Indigenous community to play an active role in sentencing the offender.[46] The courts and their processes are designed to build trust between ATSI people, their communities and the criminal justice system, by allowing Indigenous communities to become involved in shaping the sentencing process.[47] The development of Indigenous courts in Australia has been driven, in large measure, by the recommendations in the RCIADIC report and in particular the over-representation of Indigenous people in prison.[48]

The ACT Galambany Circle Sentencing Court is one of over 50 Indigenous sentencing courts in operation in Australia.[49] This Court commenced on 5 May 2004, as a division of the ACT Magistrates Court and was previously known as the Ngambri Circle.[50] The name was changed to reflect diversity within the ACT ATSI population. "Galambany" means "we all, including you".[51] The Court's aims, objects and operations are set

---

[45] Ibid.

[46] Kathleen Daly and Elena Marchetti, 'Innovative Justice Processes: Restorative Justice, Indigenous Justice, and Therapeutic Jurisprudence', in Marinella Maro, Willem De Lint and Darren Palmer (eds), *Crime and Justice: A Guide to Criminology* (Thomson Reuters Australia, 4th ed, 2012).

[47] Ibid.

[48] Ibid, 462–463.

[49] Ibid, 463.

[50] His Honour Magistrate Shane Madden, 'The Circle Court in the ACT — An Overview and its Future' (Paper presented at the Indigenous Courts Conference, Mildura Settlers Hotel, 4–7 September 2007) <http://www.aija.org.au/Ind%20Courts%20Conf%2007/Papers/Madden.pdf>.

[51] *Galambany Circle Court* (20 July 2011) ACT Magistrates Court

out in practice directions issued by the ACT Magistrates Court.[52] In general the Court aims to involve the ATSI community in the process and provide a culturally relevant avenue for Indigenous people to be sentenced, in order to address the issue of Indigenous over-representation in the Australian criminal justice system and Indigenous offending behaviour.[53] The Court's processes are available, on application, to ATSI offenders who have pleaded guilty and whose offences can be finalised in the Magistrates Court and are not sexual offences. No similar court or process is available for those ATSI offenders who are sentenced by the Supreme Court.

There is now a presumption in favour of having the offender referred for assessment, designed to ensure that those offenders who wish to participate are given the opportunity to apply and be assessed.[54] The Magistrates Court does not publish statistics on the percentage of ATSI offenders who are sentenced in the Galambany Court as compared to the mainstream courts, but data for the June 2012 quarter indicated that there were 25 adults and nine young people referred to the Court in the 2011–2012 year and 24 adults and seven young people assessed and sentenced.[55]

As will be seen later, solicitors from the ALS support their clients' decision to attend the Galambany Court as, in some instances, they find it to be a more appropriate and beneficial sentencing method.

A broader view of the relevance of Aboriginality? Judicial consideration of the relevance of Aboriginality in sentencing in the ACT

Leaving to one side the Galambany Court, the relevance of Aboriginality in sentencing has received limited consideration in the ACT, at least insofar as published appellate decisions are concerned. The ACT Court of Appeal briefly considered the issue in an appeal against a sentence

---

<http://www.courts.act.gov.au/supreme/page/view/1363>.

[52] *Practice Direction No 1 of 2012 — Galambany Court* (2012) Magistrates Court of the Australian Capital Territory <http://cdn.justice.act.gov.au/resources/uploads/Magistrates/Practice_Direction_1_of_2012_Galambany_Court.pdf>.

[53] Ibid.

[54] Ibid.

[55] ACT Justice and Community Safety Directorate, *ACT Criminal Justice Statistical Profile — June 2012 Quarter* (ACT Government, 2012) <http://www.justice.act.gov.au/resources/attachments/ACT_CJSP_June_2012_-_FINAL_-_Att_C.pdf>.

imposed by a single judge of the Supreme Court in *Love v R*,[56] though no statement of general principle emerged. Critically, there are two conflicting decisions of single judges of the Supreme Court on appeal from the Magistrates Court in which the relevance of Aboriginality in sentencing is discussed, namely, *Crawford v Laverty*[57] and *TM v Karapanos and Bakes*.[58] These decisions will be discussed below. It will be argued that the former adopts a restrictive interpretation of the relevance of Aboriginality in sentencing, whilst the latter takes a broad, inclusive view consistent with the general principle established in *Neal.* While other published judgments of single judges of the Supreme Court consider the relevance of Aboriginality in sentencing,[59] they do not do so to the same extent, nor do they propound any alternative approach.

In general, what is common to the majority of these decisions is an apparent lack of evidence establishing the link between the Aboriginality of offenders and relevant sentencing considerations.[60] The result is that the relevance of Aboriginality is often either inferred or dismissed.

In *Crawford v Laverty*, Crawford appealed against eight sentences of imprisonment imposed in the Magistrates Court. The first ground of appeal was "that the learned Magistrate gave insufficient weight to the principles in *Fernando*".[61] Penfold J's decision with respect to this ground of appeal reflects the NSWCCA pre-*Waters*[62] approach to sentencing Aboriginal offenders. Specifically, her Honour stated: "It is apparent that the *Fernando* principles are of primary relevance to offences by Aboriginal offenders within Aboriginal communities, and in particular where the offences are associated with alcohol abuse and resulting

---

[56] *Love v R* [2012] ACTCA 8 (9 February 2012).

[57] *Crawford v Laverty* [2008] ACTSC 107 (13 October 2008) (Penfold J).

[58] *TM*, above n 43, [2011] ACTSC 74, [112].

[59] See, for example: *R v Monaghan (No 3)* [2012] ACTSC 45 (13 February 2012) (Refshauge J); *Khan v R* [2011] ACTSC 20 (8 February 2011) (Nield J); *R v Simonds* SCC 71 of 2011, [32] (Nield J) <http://www.courts.act.gov.au/supreme/sentence/view/1205/title/r-v-simonds>; *R v Weldon aka Williams* SCC 321 of 2009 (Refshauge J) <http://www.courts.act.gov.au/supreme/sentence/view/967/title/r-v-weldon-aka-williams>; *R v GD, DD, AK & BW* SCC 15 of 2012; SCC 19 of 2012; SCC 32 of 2012; SCC 40 of 2012; SCC 56 of 2012; SCC127 of 2012 (Penfold J) <http://www.courts.act.gov.au/supreme/sentence/view/1204/title/r-v-gd-dd-ak>.

[60] See, for example: *Khan v R* [2011] ACTSC 20 (8 February 2011), [26]–[27] (Nield J).

[61] *Crawford v Laverty* [2008] ACTSC 107 (13 October 2008) (Penfold J), [4].

[62] *Waters v R* [2007] NSWCCA 219 (2 August 2007).

violence within those communities".[63] This is further highlighted in her judgment at [23]:

> The appellant was not charged with an offence committed within an Aboriginal community, or offences attributable to the excessive use of alcohol. Rather, he is charged with a property offence (the refusal to submit DNA testing is consequential on the police investigation of his property offence) committed within and against the broader community … Those property offences were not committed as a result of alcohol abuse, but arose from the appellant's need to fund a heroin addiction.

It is not apparent whether there was any evidence before the Court linking the offender's Aboriginality to his offence or present circumstances, but the decision disclaims the relevance of Aboriginality except in circumstances analogous to those under consideration in *Fernando.* In so doing, the decision does not reflect the broader understanding of the relevance of Aboriginality in sentencing adopted most clearly by the Victorian Court of Appeal in *Terrick.* The limitations imposed by Penfold J have significant exclusionary consequences for judicial consideration of the relevance of Aboriginality in sentencing in the ACT, where many Indigenous people live in an integrated community, as part of urban Canberra. The decision denies the reality that complex historical and intergenerational factors uniquely experienced by Indigenous Australians bear upon them in myriad different ways, which too often lead to incarceration.

By contrast, in *TM v Karapanos and Bakes*,[64] Refshauge J endorsed a broader view of the relevance of Aboriginality in sentencing on an appeal from as sentence imposed by the ACT Children's Court, despite His Honour receiving limited submissions on the point.[65] The offender challenged the sentences imposed on her for three offences committed while in custody. The third ground of appeal was "that the principle for taking into account the Aboriginality of the appellant expressed in *R v Fernando* (1992) 76 A Crim R 58 should have been taken into account".[66]

By reference to the principles in *Fernando*, Refshauge J stated: "Those principles, though perhaps arising out of the difficult circumstances of sentencing Aboriginal offenders in remote communities, are not so limited".[67] Refshauge J went on to approve the principles established by

[63] *Crawford v Laverty* [2008] ACTSC 107 (13 October 2008) (Penfold J), [20].
[64] *TM* [2011] ACTSC 74 (12 May 2011), [112].
[65] Ibid.
[66] Ibid, [76].
[67] Ibid, [112], referring to *Waters v R* [2007] NSWCCA 219 (2 August 2007), [39].

the Victorian Court of Appeal in *Terrick,*[68] describing them as representing a "comprehensive approach",[69] which:

> … requires the sentencer to assess the extent to which the circumstances of the upbringing of the offender, here TM, including social, environmental and cultural factors, assumed significance in the application of sentencing principles, including identifying influences which have contributed to the commission of the offences relevant to the nature of the sentence to be imposed.[70]

The judgment does not explicitly disclose how these principles were taken into account in TM's case, or how the evidence explicitly linked the offender's Aboriginality to her offending. Notwithstanding this, the approach adopted by Refshauge J is inclusive, acknowledging the complexity of post-colonial Indigenous experience. Moreover, it is argued that the approach is entirely consistent with Brennan J's general statement of principle in *Neal*.[71] Refshauge J has continued to endorse the approach of the Victorian Court of Appeal in subsequent decisions.[72]

The ACT Court of Appeal had an opportunity to resolve the apparent conflict of authority in relation to the relevance of Aboriginality in sentencing in the case of *Love v R.*[73] Counsel for the appellant argued that there was a failure by the sentencing judge to take into consideration a rehabilitation opportunity available to the appellant by virtue of his Aboriginality, namely an Indigenous employment program at a mine site in remote South Australia. It was argued that this was a relevant sentencing fact existing by reason only of the offender's Aboriginality. Penfold, Burns and North JJ upheld the appeal on different grounds, and therefore found it unnecessary to address the issue in any detail.[74] However, in the course of their decision, they stated:

> We are not convinced that the connection between the appellant's Aboriginality and the availability of this rehabilitation program only to Indigenous offenders, as such, required any different treatment from the treatment that would be appropriate for evidence that any offender whose

---

68 *Terrick* (2009) 24 VR 457, 468–9.

69 *TM* [2011] ACTSC 74 (12 May 2011), [114].

70 Ibid, [116], referring to *Terrick* (2009) 24 VR 457.

71 *Neal v R* (1982) CLR 305, 326.

72 See, for example: *R v Monaghan (No 3)* [2012] ACTSC 45 (13 February 2012) [15]; *The Queen v King* SCC 164 of 2009 <http://www.courts.act.gov.au/supreme/sentence/view/1255/title/r-v-king>.

73 *Love v R* [2012] ACTCA 8 (9 February 2012).

74 Ibid, [8].

> early disadvantages had apparently contributed to his offending behaviour had a particular rehabilitation program open to him.[75]

It is apparent from this passage that the Court was not persuaded, on the evidence, that differential treatment was required on account of the appellant's Aboriginality. Notwithstanding this, the Court of Appeal had before it an Aboriginal offender who had been sentenced for 16 offences of burglary and theft committed in the general community of Canberra. He was not living and had not lived in a defined rural or remote Aboriginal community and whose offending was associated with a history of illicit drug use, in addition to his abuse of alcohol.[76] None of these factors was considered to render consideration of his Aboriginality irrelevant. What is apparent from the decision is that the Court of Appeal did not consider it necessary to indicate a position of support or otherwise for the approach adopted by the Victorian Court of Appeal in *Terrick*.

The legal position in relation to the relevance of Aboriginality in sentencing in the ACT remains to be clarified. What is apparent, from a review of decisions in the ACT, as elsewhere, is that for Aboriginality to be taken into account in sentencing, appropriate evidence supporting the link between that Aboriginality and relevant sentencing considerations must be before the court.

However, a review of published decisions is not sufficient to enable a conclusion to be drawn about the extent to which Aboriginality is being taken into account in sentencing in the ACT. In particular, it excludes from consideration the approach being adopted in the Magistrates Court, which does not publish sentencing decisions. It is therefore necessary, and desirable, to obtain an insider's view. The following section aims to do so by canvassing the views of those legal practitioners who are principally tasked to appear for Aboriginal offenders being sentenced by the Magistrates Court in the ACT, namely, lawyers at the ACT branch of the Aboriginal Legal Service (ALS).

The relevance of Aboriginality in sentencing in the ACT: Practitioners' view

In April 2012, face-to-face interviews were conducted with the three ACT defence lawyers in the ALS criminal law team, all of whom routinely represented Indigenous defendants in the ACT. Each of the participating

---

[75] Ibid.

[76] *R v Love* SCC 190 of 2010 (Nield J) <http://www.courts.act.gov.au/supreme/sentence/view/1037/title/r-v-love>.

solicitors was male and had one to two years' experience as criminal defence lawyers at the ALS in the ACT. However, collectively the group had over 35 years of experience as practicing solicitors.

The limitations of the research are acknowledged. Firstly, due to the research focus on the ACT, the sample size was limited to three. Secondly, the research is limited by the fact that the ALS solicitors do not represent all Indigenous offenders in the ACT; the participants' experience is necessarily limited to the Indigenous offenders that they have represented. The issue of self-disclosure also has the potential to limit the research findings. It could be expected that there would have been a degree of reluctance to provide negative answers to questions which refer to current practices and procedures. This may have occurred even though the identities of the solicitors were kept anonymous,[77] due to the small number of participants and the small size of the ACT. The participants were likely to have contemplated how their comments may reflect back on them.[78] In spite of these limitations, we suggest that the responses obtained provide an invaluable insight into how Aboriginality is taken into account in sentencing in the ACT.

The ALS solicitors were separately asked the following questions:

1. In your opinion does a person's Aboriginality affect the length or type of sentenced imposed on Indigenous offenders in the Australian Capital Territory? If so, in what way?
2. What is your opinion on how a person's Aboriginality is taken into account when sentencing Indigenous offenders?
3. What is your opinion of how section 33(1)(m) of the *Crimes (Sentencing) Act 2005* (ACT) is applied by judges and magistrates in relation to a person's Aboriginal cultural background?
4. Do judges and magistrates make distinctions between rural and urban offenders and what are the implications for your clients?
5. What recommendations, if any, do you feel are needed in this area of law in the Australian Capital Territory?
6. Do the pre-sentence report writers focus on a person's Aboriginality?

---

77 This project received ethics approval from the University of Canberra Human Research Ethics Committee. The Ngunnawal Centre at the University of Canberra also provided advice on the research.

78 Alan Goldstein and Irving Weiner, *Handbook of Psychology* (John Wiley and Sons Inc, 2003) vol 2, 164.

Aboriginality: Impact on length and type of sentence

The general consensus among the participants was that Aboriginality had limited, if any, effect on the length or type of sentence imposed on Indigenous offenders in mainstream courts. As highlighted by one participant, "I think it has very little bearing in the mainstream sentencing". Mainstream sentencing was the focus of the research, but it is interesting to note, by way of contrast, that all participants were of the view that Aboriginality was being taken into account by the Galambany Sentencing Court.

How is Aboriginality taken into account?

Participants were asked "What is your opinion on how a person's Aboriginality is taken into account when sentencing Indigenous offenders?" The common theme in the participants' answers was a person's upbringing. All participants acknowledged that, where an Indigenous offender's upbringing had a nexus with the offending behaviour which caused the person to offend, then that could be taken into account.

One solicitor answered that a person's Aboriginality does not on its own affect the sentence imposed on an offender; rather, Aboriginality would only be taken into account through its ability to cast light on common problems and issues facing the Indigenous community in the ACT, adding that if those issues or problems had a link to why the offences took place, then that could be taken into account. Another participant stated:

> Everyone is equal before the law, [but] if there are some circumstances which go towards the commission of an offence, which are unique to someone's upbringing, then that provides some mitigation in sentence.

Aboriginal cultural background and ACT sentencing legislation

The participants were asked about the impact for Indigenous defendants of the inclusion of "cultural background" as a relevant sentencing consideration contained in section 33(1)(m) of the *Crimes (Sentencing) Act 2005* (ACT). Responses were consistent with the overall view that Aboriginality has a limited impact on sentencing in mainstream courts in the ACT. With respect to the judicial application of the "cultural background" criterion, one participant stated:

> I'm not sure. I'm not sure you can really quantify how it is [taken into account?]. It's not often referred to by sentencing magistrates in their

> reasons for sentence. So, I'm not aware of any case law which gives a guidance to the Courts on how that's supposed to be taken into account.

Another participant said:

> Well that section refers also to: character, integrity, antecedents, and age, physical or mental condition of the offender. All of which carry a lot of weight. Ironically, cultural background carries very little weight and I don't think it has, it has little to no consideration, whereas the other factors, I mean character, antecedents, age, physical or mental condition play a substantial role.

Rural and urban Indigenous persons

The general consensus among the participants was that in the ACT, the distinction between urban and rural Aboriginal offenders is not referred too much at all. As one participant stated: "I don't see it referred to much, just in my experience … the [issue of] Aboriginality, full stop". Another participant stated: "Well, my experience has been submitting on these matters that it's not of so limited application, as to be applicable [only] to Aboriginal people in remote rural areas". This participant also commented on this change in approach by the ACT courts, stating:

> the tendered logic was that if people are so removed from the moral standards of the wider community then that could only really happen if they were living in remote areas and not part of the mainstream community. The reality is, there [are] significant pockets of isolation and disadvantage … right here in Canberra, the nation's capital city. Therefore, if you're going to limit it by limiting those principles to, as only applying to those people from remote areas, then you're ignoring, you're ignoring the obvious — that people from the same ethnic backgrounds live together, have relationships together, often don't move outside those ethnic backgrounds. Whether they live in remote geographical areas or whether they live in capital cities or urban areas.

Pre-Sentence Reports and Aboriginal Circumstances

Perhaps the most telling responses were received when participants were asked "Do the pre-sentence report writers focus on a person's Aboriginality?" Responses to this question appear, at first glance, to differ markedly. While all three mentioned that Aboriginality was referred to, to some extent, in the pre-sentence reports, two of the three solicitors took the view that Aboriginality was given insufficient attention. In particular, one participant was adamant that the pre-sentence reports which had been prepared for his clients were completely ineffective in taking a person's Aboriginality into account:

> Well yeah, they don't, they just don't … in those pre-sentence reports, they say, well, the offender is a 23 year old Aboriginal man and that's it, and that's supposed to cover the field.

As was noted by another participant, this results in a greater burden being placed on defence lawyers to provide evidence and make submissions on the importance of a defendant's Aboriginality in the sentencing process. Moreover, it is apparent from the responses that pre-sentence reports are not drawing explicit links between Aboriginality and offending. Nor, it would appear, judging from all the participants' responses, do pre-sentence reports address the potential for Indigenous- specific pathways for rehabilitation, reform or healing.

Two key recommendations were made by participants, each designed to ensure greater consideration of Aboriginality in sentencing. Firstly, in line with concerns about the absence of consideration of Aboriginality in pre-sentence reports, one participant advocated Indigenous involvement in the pre-sentence report writing process, and specifically, the recruitment of Indigenous pre-sentence report writers. A second participant advocated increasing access to the Galambany Court. In particular, he argued that this should be a right for Indigenous offenders for all offences. He expressed concern that his clients were not always successful in their application for Circle Sentencing, with the implication being that their Aboriginality was not then sufficiently taken into account in the Magistrates Court. We note that this response predated the most recent Galambany Court Practice Directions implemented in August 2012 which include a presumption that all and ATSI offenders be assessed for the program if they so choose and are not otherwise excluded.[79]

Conclusion

As has been argued, the principle of equality before the law requires sentencing courts to give close consideration to the relevance of an offender's Aboriginality in the determination of an appropriate sentence. Furthermore, "[c]onsultations with those who work at the sentencing 'coal face' … are an important site for understanding whether sentencing is an

[79] Magistrates Court of the Australian Capital Territory, above n 51.

equitable process — and not just simply an equal process — for Indigenous offenders".[80]

The fundamental question is whether facts material to the sentencing discretion exist by reason of an offender's Aboriginality. Whilst the issue has not been resolved in the ACT, there is growing acceptance of the need to consider the relevance of Aboriginality for all Indigenous Australians, regardless of how their Aboriginality is constituted. But, this requires sufficient evidence being placed before the sentencing court linking the Aboriginality of an offender, and their experience of Aboriginality, to their offending behaviour. It requires evidence of how uniquely Indigenous background and systemic factors have brought them to the point of sentence. Just this sort of evidence was found to exist in the lives of the 99 Indigenous Australians whose deaths in custody were investigated by the RCIADIC. However, it is apparent that this evidence is not being placed before the "mainstream" courts in the ACT, and may not routinely be placed before the "mainstream" courts elsewhere in Australia. Without this evidence, courts cannot be expected to meaningfully engage with the Aboriginality of offenders or the relevance of their Aboriginality in the sentencing process.

One concrete way to address this lack of evidence is to adopt a key recommendation of ALS criminal defence lawyers acting for Indigenous defendants in the ACT revealed in this chapter, namely, to increase the extent to which Aboriginality is a focus of attention within pre-sentence reports. To achieve this would require engagement with Indigenous expertise and the broader ACT ATSI community, a process that could draw upon existing relationships of trust built up through the operation of the Galambany Indigenous Sentencing Court. Indeed, such reports would usefully inform sentencing in the Galambany Court itself. Calls for Indigenous focused pre-sentence reports are not new.[81] A successful Canadian model exists, in the form of "Gladue Reports", implemented following the 1999 decision of *R v Gladue*.[82] These reports are produced by Indigenous caseworkers and set out the systemic and background issues affecting the lives of Aboriginal offenders, together with available culturally relevant sentencing options. The reports explain offending behaviour within the collective history of Aboriginal Canadians, highlighting the link between individual and collective experience.

---

[80] Bond, Jeffries and Loban, above n 16, 8.

[81] Eddie Ozols, 'Pre Sentence Reports on Aboriginal and Islander People: Overcoming the Myths and Providing Culturally Appropriate Information' (Paper delivered at Australian Institute of Criminology Conference: Aboriginal Justice Issues 2, Townsville, June 14-17, 1994).

[82] [1999] 1 SCR 688.

Furthermore, they explore options for healing and reform from the vantage point of this collective experience.[83] Drawing from this Canadian experience, it is argued that report writers, and ultimately the courts to whom these reports are addressed, must understand Aboriginality not simply as a yoke of collective disadvantage, but as offering the collective potential for positive change and uplift. However, on a cautionary note, this collective potential cannot be realised without the existence of Indigenous-developed programs of healing, rehabilitation and reform. Ultimately, whilst a sentence can be crafted with the aim of rehabilitating an offender and reducing the likelihood of reoffending, it is the pathways open to the offender from the time of sentence that can make this aim a reality.

---

[83] For a more detailed discussion of history, purpose and promise of Gladue Reports, see Hopkins, above n 16.

CHAPTER THREE

SENTENCING STATISTICS, SENTENCING COUNCILS AND THE QUEST FOR DATA IN THE AUSTRALIAN CAPITAL TERRITORY

LORANA BARTELS

Introduction

Sentencing legislation around Australia has undergone significant change in the past two decades, with all states and territories passing stand-alone legislation on this issue between 1988 and 2005.[1] Speaking extra-curially, the former Chief Justice of New South Wales (NSW), James Spigelman, observed that:

> [s]entencing engages the interest, and sometimes the passion, of the public more than anything else judges do. The public's attitude to the way judges impose sentences determines, to a substantial extent, the state of public confidence in the administration of justice.[2]

---

* The author acknowledges the helpful comments of Anthony Hopkins on an earlier version of this chapter.

[1] See Criminal Law (Sentencing) Act 1988 (SA); Sentencing Act 1991 (Vic); Penalties and Sentences Act 1992 (Qld); Sentencing Act 1995 (NT); Sentencing Act 1995 (WA); Sentencing Act 1997 (Tas); Crimes (Sentencing Procedure) Act 1999 (NSW); Crimes (Sentencing) Act 2005 (ACT). Sentencing for federal offences is governed by Part IB of the Crimes Act 1914 (Cth). In 2006, the Australian Law Reform Commission recommended the creation of a separate federal sentencing Act. See: Australian Law Reform Commission (ALRC), Same Crime, Same Time: Sentencing of Federal Offenders, Report No 103 (2006) Recommendation 2-1. To date, however, this recommendation has not been adopted.

[2] James Spigelman, 'Free, Strong Societies Arise From Participatory Legal Systems', *Sydney Morning Herald* (online), 16 May 2005

It is beyond the scope of this chapter to examine in detail the issues of public opinion in sentencing, including the role of penal populism and the media; the means of determining public opinion; and the extent to which it should be taken into account in individual cases.[3] However, the research generally indicates that increasing public information on sentencing is correlated with greater acceptance of and confidence in sentencing outcomes.[4] This chapter considers the issue of public information on sentencing by examining the collection and public dissemination of sentencing data in Australia, noting Freiberg and Krasnostein's recent observation that:

> In the criminal justice system generally, statistics are useful in many ways. They provide information about crime rates and criminals, about the operation of the courts and corrections and about dispositional outcomes. They make the law more accessible and transparent … For policy-makers and *for the community* they may promote informed debate as to whether sentences are inconsistent, whether sentencing levels are too high or too low and whether offences are prevalent (emphasis added).[5]

The role of sentencing councils in promoting public awareness and understanding of sentencing will also be considered.[6] In its 2006 review of

---

<http://www.smh.com.au/news/Opinion/Free-strong-societies-arise-from-participatory-legal-systems/2005/05/15/1116095851392.html>. See also: McHugh J in *Markarian v The Queen* (2005) 215 ALR 213, where his Honour observed at 236: "Public responses to sentencing, although not entitled to influence any particular case, have a legitimate impact on the democratic legislative process".

[3] For a recent discussion, see: Kate Warner et al, *Jury Sentencing Survey* (Report to the Criminology Research Council CRC 04/06-7, 2010) 8–24.

[4] Ibid. See also: Kate Warner et al, 'Public Judgement on Sentencing: Final Results From the Tasmanian Jury Sentencing Study' (Trends and Issues in Crime and Criminal Justice No 407, Australian Institute of Criminology, 2011).

[5] Arie Freiberg and Sarah Krasnostein, 'Statistics, Damn Statistics and Sentencing' (2011) 21(2) *Journal of Judicial Administration* 73, 82.

[6] For discussion of sentencing councils internationally, see: Karen Sampford, 'Sentencing Councils: An Overview of Models from Australia, New Zealand and the United Kingdom' (E-Research Brief No 2010/19, Queensland Parliamentary Library, 2010). See also: David Indermaur, 'Dealing the Public In: Challenges for A Transparent and Accountable Sentencing Policy', in Arie Freiberg and Karen Gelb (eds), *Penal Populism, Sentencing Councils and Sentencing Policy* (Hawkins Press, 2008); SuccessWorks, *Evaluation of Sentencing Advisory Council*, prepared on behalf of the Victorian Department of Justice (2008); Warren Young, 'Sentencing Reform in New Zealand: A Proposal to Establish a Sentencing Council', in Arie Freiberg and Karen Gelb (eds), *Penal Populism, Sentencing Councils and Sentencing Policy* (Hawkins Press, 2008).

federal sentencing, the Australian Law Reform Commission (ALRC) stated:

> State sentencing councils in Australia are to be commended. Better sentencing decisions and sound evidence-based policies can be promoted by disseminating sentencing statistics, analysing sentencing trends and conducting broad community consultation.[7]

The ALRC also suggested that sentencing councils "may promote better sentencing decisions".[8] In their book on sentencing councils, Freiberg and Gelb argued:

> the sentencing council can respond to, and influence, public opinion via its educative role ... the promulgation of accurate and up-to-date information on sentencing policy and practice would seem to be a key function of those bodies designed to promote and disseminate advice and information on sentencing ... education and information can play a major role in improving public perceptions of, and confidence in, the criminal justice system.[9]

Abadee, the foundation chair of the NSW Sentencing Council likewise saw such councils as "play[ing] a role in educating, informing and enhancing informed public opinion".[10] The need for informing the public and the potential role of sentencing councils was considered by Allen and Hough as follows:

> the public is woefully ill-informed — or indeed misinformed — about crime and justice. People think that crime is rising, and have thought so consistently over the whole decade it has been falling. People think that the courts are far too soft, and their views have not shifted significantly over a period in which we have almost doubled our use of imprisonment. Who can convincingly correct these deep-rooted misperceptions? The media have no interest in doing so. The government cannot command sufficient trust to deliver a credible message to the public. Opposition politicians certainly do not wish to support the government of the day in telling a good

---

[7] ALRC, above n 1, [19.33].

[8] Ibid [19.24].

[9] Arie Freiberg and Karen Gelb, 'Penal Populism, Sentencing Councils and Sentencing Policy', in Arie Freiberg and Karen Gelb (eds), *Penal Populism, Sentencing Councils and Sentencing Policy* (Hawkins Press, 2008) 14.

[10] Alan Abadee, 'The Role of Sentencing Advisory Councils' (Paper presented at the Sentencing: Principles, Perspectives and Possibilities Conference, Canberra, 10–12 February 2006) 6.

> story about law and order. Clearly there is a need for an authoritative, trusted institution that can perform this function.[11]

The chapter then presents a case study by exploring the position in the Australian Capital Territory (ACT) with respect to recent developments in relation to sentencing law and policy and the call for increased sentencing data. In this context, it is argued that public access to comprehensible sentencing data is required to promote community understanding of sentencing practices and that sentencing councils have a critical role to play as a bridge between the criminal justice system and the general public.

What are Other Jurisdictions Doing? Sentencing Data and Councils around Australia

National sentencing data

Since 1995, the Australian Bureau of Statistics (ABS) has published an annual report, *Criminal Courts, Australia*. The most recent iteration (at the time of writing), for the 2010–11 financial year, was released in February 2012, and includes sentencing data for the higher courts (Supreme and, as relevant, District/County Courts), as well as the Magistrates and Children's Courts.[12] The following national data are available:

- offence type (eg acts intended to cause injury) by sentence type (custody in a correctional institution; custody in the community; fully suspended sentence; community supervision/work orders; monetary orders; other non-custodial orders);[13]

[11] Rob Allen and Mike Hough, 'Does It Matter? Reflections on the Effectiveness of Institutionalised Public Participation in the Development of Sentencing Policy', in Arie Freiberg and Karen Gelb (eds), *Penal Populism, Sentencing Councils and Sentencing Policy* (Hawkins Press, 2008) 23.

[12] Australian Bureau of Statistics (ABS), *Criminal Courts Australia 2010–11*, Cat No 4513.0 (ABS, 2012). The 2011-12 iteration of these data was released in February 2013, but only presents the information in excel spreadsheets, rather than in a PDF format report, as in previous years.

[13] Ibid, Tables 2.7, 3.7, 4.7 for the Supreme, Magistrates and Children's Court respectively. See also Tables 2.1, 3.1, 4.1 for similar but less detailed data.

- annual trend data on the number of custodial orders and non-custodial orders (since 2005–6 for the Supreme and Magistrates Court and since 2006–7 for the Children's Court);[14]
- annual trend data on custodial and non-custodial orders by offence type;[15] and
- sentence type by age and gender of the offender.[16]

The following data are also available at the jurisdictional level:

- the number of custodial and non-custodial orders;[17] and
- annual trend data on sentence type.[18]

Data are also presented on the number of custodial and non-custodial orders for Indigenous and non-Indigenous offenders in some jurisdictions.[19] Additional data are available in excel spreadsheets on the ABS website (for example, the median and mean length of custodial sentence by offence type for each jurisdiction).[20]

It is arguably doubtful that many members of the public will access these data in their current form. Information of this nature is at times difficult to interpret even for those experienced in data analysis, let alone general members of the public who may not have the skills to interpret what they find. Accordingly, although there are data available, they are often too general to be of practical utility to members of the public (or, for that matter, sentencing officers[21]). In other words, what is required is a more digestible form of sentencing information.

---

[14] Ibid, Tables 2.2, 3.2, 4.2.
[15] Ibid, Tables 2.8, 3.8, 4.8.
[16] Ibid, Tables 2.9, 3.9, 4.9.
[17] Ibid, Tables 2.3, 3.3, 4.3.
[18] Ibid, Tables 2.11, 3.11, 4.11.
[19] Ibid, Tables 2.12, 3.12, 4.12.
[20] See: 4513.0: Higher Courts — Sentence Length by Type of Custodial Order, Selected States and Territories (ABS, 2012).
<http://www.abs.gov.au/AUSSTATS/abs@.nsf/DetailsPage/4513.02010%E2%80%9311?OpenDocument>.
[21] For recent discussion of the use and appropriateness of judicial officers relying on sentencing statistics in individual cases, see: Freiberg and Krasnostein, above n 5. See also: *R v Bloomfield* (1998) 44 NSWLR 734; Brian Preston, 'A Judge's Perspective on Using Sentencing Databases' (2010) 3 *Journal of Court Innovation* 248.

Commonwealth

Commonwealth sentencing data are available on the Commonwealth Sentencing Database,[22] which is produced by the National Judicial College of Australia, the Commonwealth Director of Public Prosecutions and the Judicial Commission of New South Wales. It is not available to the public, although members of the public may request a free password for access.

The establishment of a federal sentencing council was first proposed in 1980, as part of the ALRC's first major review of federal sentencing.[23] In its final report for that inquiry, the ALRC recommended that the council be part of the Australian Institute of Criminology (AIC) and that its functions include providing information on a systematic basis to the public through its own publications and through the mass media.[24] However, in its 2006 report, the ALRC recommended against the establishment of a federal sentencing council, on the basis that it would replicate work currently being undertaken by other agencies or that would be undertaken by proposed agencies.[25]

New South Wales

As Freiberg and Krasnostein have noted, NSW "has one of the oldest and most comprehensive sentencing databases, known as the Judicial Information Research System (JIRS)".[26] When the then Attorney-General, Bob Debus, commented on the establishment of the NSW Sentencing Council, he noted that "in New South Wales the government and public have access to the best sentencing statistical information in Australia, and arguably the world".[27] The JIRS sentencing data are very detailed, but are

---

[22] See: Welcome to the Commonwealth Sentencing Database (2012) Commonwealth Sentencing Database <http://njca.org.au/Projects/Cth%20Sen%20DB/CSD%20homepage.htm>.

[23] ALRC, Sentencing of Federal Offenders: Interim Report, Report No 15 (1980). For discussion, see: Michael Kirby, 'The Sentencing Council, Revisited', in Ivan Potas (ed), Sentencing in Australia: Issues, Policy and Reform: Proceedings of a Seminar, Sentencing: Problems and Prospects (Australian Institute of Criminology, 1987).

[24] ALRC, *Sentencing*, Report No 44 (1988). For discussion, see: ALRC, above n 1, [19.28].

[25] ALRC, above n 1, [19.34].

[26] Freiberg and Krasnostein, above n 5, 83.

[27] Bob Debus, 'The NSW Sentencing Council: Its Role and Functions' (2003) 15(6) *Judicial Officers' Bulletin* 45, 46. See also: Freiberg and Krasnostein, above n 5; Preston, above n 21, for discussion of JIRS.

not freely available to the public. Indeed, given that annual subscription fees for the NSW database range from $1600 to $3400,[28] it is highly doubtful that many, if any, members of the public would choose to inform themselves using this option.

Sentencing information is also available from the NSW Bureau of Crime Statistics and Research (BOCSAR), whose website (as at September 2012) lists 34 publications on sentencing published since 1990, including eight "sentencing snapshots" on common offences such as robbery and assault, published in 2011.[29] Detailed information on sentencing outcomes in the higher courts, Magistrates Court and Children's Court is also available in its annual criminal court report.[30] Finally, some data on individual cases are available on the NSW Public Defenders website. Sentencing tables "intended as a guide only" are provided for 13 key offences, including drugs offences, murder and sexual offences.[31]

Australia's first sentencing council was established in NSW in 2003, at which time its functions included:

> (c) to monitor and to report annually to the Minister on, sentencing trends and practices, including the operation of standard non-parole periods and guideline judgments; and
> (d) at the request of the Minister, to prepare research papers or reports on particular subjects in connection with sentencing.[32]

The Attorney-General at the time stated:

> It is hoped that the Sentencing Council's collective experience, expertise, independence and ability to consult with others will contribute to the

---

[28] See: *JIRS and SIS Subscriptions* (2012) Judicial Commission of New South Wales <http://www.judcom.nsw.gov.au/research-and-sentencing/sentencing-information-system-sis-subscription>.

[29] Publications and Statistics by Subject (Q to T) (2012) BOCSAR <http://www.lawlink.nsw.gov.au/lawlink/bocsar/ll_bocsar.nsf/pages/bocsar_pub_qtot#sentencing>.

[30] See, for example: BOCSAR, *New South Wales Criminal Court Statistics 2011* (2012). Annual reports since 1997 are available at: *Archived Annual NSW Criminal Court Statistics* (2012) NSW Bureau of Crime Statistics and Research <http://www.lawlink.nsw.gov.au/Lawlink/bocsar/ll_bocsar.nsf/pages/bocsar_court_stats_archived>.

[31] See: *Sentencing Tables* (2012) NSW Public Defenders Office <http://www.publicdefenders.lawlink.nsw.gov.au/pdo/public_defenders_sent_tables.html>.

[32] Crimes (Sentencing Procedure) Act 1999 (NSW) s 100J(1).

> strengthening of public acceptance and understanding of the sentencing process, and the maintenance of public confidence in that process.[33]

In 2006, the legislation was amended by the *Crimes and Courts Legislation Amendment Act 2006* (NSW) to include as one of the functions of the Council to "educate the public about sentencing matters",[34] thereby "foreshadowing a more proactive role in disseminating sentencing information to the general public".[35] The Council's website states that it is

> dedicated to strengthening public understanding and confidence in the sentencing process. To improve the public's confidence in the sentencing process, the Council provides an education program including public forums on sentencing and a plain language guide to sentencing in NSW.[36]

The inaugural Chair, Alan Abadee, argued that it was "of considerable importance that some body exists to not only gauge informed public opinion but also to participate in its creation".[37] As at March 2013, the Council's website listed 29 publications, including seven annual reports on sentencing trends and practices, although the most recent of these was released in 2009–10.

Victoria

In Victoria, sentencing data are primarily disseminated by the Victorian Sentencing Advisory Council (VSAC). The Judicial College of Victoria also publishes a sentencing manual,[38] which includes sentencing statistics, although most of these were being updated at the time of writing.

---

[33] Debus, above n 27, 46. See also: Alan Abadee, 'The New South Wales Sentencing Council', in Arie Freiberg and Karen Gelb (eds), *Penal Populism, Sentencing Councils and Sentencing Policy* (Hawkins Press, 2008); Kate Warner, 'Sentencing Review 2002-2003' (2003) 27 *Criminal Law Journal* 325.

[34] Crimes and Courts Legislation Amendment Act 2006 (NSW) sch 1.9 [7]. See now: Crimes (Sentencing Procedure) Act 1999 (NSW) s 100J(1)(e).

[35] Abadee, above n 33, 131.

[36] *NSW Sentencing Council* (2012) NSW Sentencing Council <http://www.sentencingcouncil.lawlink.nsw.gov.au/sentencing/sent_council_index .html>. The plain language guide, which is available on the Council's website, includes information on when an offender is sentenced; the sentence hearing; the purposes of sentencing; relevant factors determining a sentence; and sentencing options. See: NSW Sentencing Council, *Sentencing Information Package* (NSW Department of Attorney-General and Justice, 2011).

[37] Abadee, above n 10, 5.

[38] See: *Victorian Sentencing Manual* (2011) Judicial College of Victoria

The VSAC was established by the *Sentencing (Amendment) Act 2003* (Vic), with its functions from the outset including:

(b) to provide statistical information on sentencing, including information on current sentencing practices, to members of the judiciary and other *interested persons*;
(c) to conduct research, and disseminate information to members of the judiciary *and other interested persons*, on sentencing matters;
(d) to gauge public opinion on sentencing matters;
(e) to consult, on sentencing matters, with government departments and interested persons and bodies *as well as the general public* (emphases added).[39]

Perhaps unsurprisingly, the inaugural VSAC Chair, Professor Arie Freiberg, has described the Council in laudatory terms as "an innovative organisation performing the functions of a specialised law reform commission, bureau of statistics, sentencing guidelines panel and public education body combined".[40] These roles obviously overlap and are relevant in the context of ACT sentencing developments discussed below.

Freiberg noted that during debate on the legislation to introduce the VSAC, "the major concerns that were expressed related to the paucity of sentencing statistics in Victoria and the role of the Council in producing them".[41] In response to this, Freiberg went on to explain that "[e]arly in its life the Council agreed to a summary statement of its aim, as being 'to bridge the gap between the community, the courts and government by informing, educating and advising on sentencing issues'".[42] Crucially, the VSAC's role in terms of providing information "is not to produce statistical sentencing data but to provide sentencing information", which is intended to:

1. inform the public and others about what is happening in sentencing;
2. inform its own research into sentencing trends and issues;
3. provide greater transparency of the judicial and correctional processes; and

---

<http://www.justice.vic.gov.au/emanuals/VSM/default.htm>

[39] *Sentencing Act 1991* (Vic) s 108C(1)(b)–(e). For background, see: Arie Freiberg, 'The Victorian Sentencing Advisory Council: Incorporating Community Views Into the Sentencing Process', in Arie Freiberg and Karen Gelb (eds), *Penal Populism, Sentencing Councils and Sentencing Policy* (Hawkins Press, 2008).

[40] Freiberg, above n 39, 163.

[41] Ibid, 154.

[42] Ibid, 155. Reference omitted.

4. provide a basis for sociological critique or research into potential law reform.[43]

Clearly, such objectives go far beyond the mere provision of sentencing tables which, to the untrained eye, may yield little in terms of better understanding the sentencing process. Instead, the information on the VSAC's website "provides information about sentencing in Victoria in a simple, structured and accessible manner as well as providing its publications free of charge".[44]

The VSAC also created a virtual "You Be the Judge" exercise,[45] which seeks to improve "participants' understanding of the sentencing process and its complexities", and includes a "Socratic discussion … supported by written materials … examin[ing] the factors that a must consider when imposing a sentence and the difficulties in reconciling the various needs of the State, the defendant, and the victim",[46] which has been used repeatedly in community education contexts. Impressively, this function attracted over 7200 visitors in 2011–12 alone.[47] In addition, the VSAC delivered "You Be the Judge" sessions to 35 groups and gave presentations to more than 1100 participants in the 2011–12 year.[48]

In a 2008 evaluation, the Council was found to have undertaken 16 public education sessions involving over 1100 individuals and have distributed 780 teacher guides.[49] The evaluation also found that "[m]embers of the community are accessing SAC material in written and downloadable form"[50] and "[p]articipants in public education programs are thought to have improved their understanding of sentencing matters as a result of their participation".[51] In addition, it was found that "[m]edia commentators have made extensive use of their access to SAC statistical and other publications. The role of SAC in informing the media is valued by media representatives and other stakeholders".[52] It was concluded that the Council:

---

[43] Ibid, 156.
[44] Ibid, 159.
[45] See: *Virtual You Be the Judge* (2012) Sentencing Advisory Council <http://sentencingcouncil.vic.gov.au/page/education/virtual-you-be-judge>.
[46] Freiberg, above n 39, 159.
[47] VSAC, *Annual Report 2011-12* (VSAC, 2012).
[48] Ibid.
[49] SuccessWorks, above n 6.
[50] Ibid, 45.
[51] Ibid, 48.
[52] Ibid, 50.

> represents a best practice approach to sentencing law reform in relation to its consultation processes; quality of reports; accessibility; public education programs; lack of bias; diverse membership; high quality staff and chair; independence from government and judiciary; capacity to generate its own research and the provision of a voice for the community in the sentencing process.[53]

In October 2012, the VSAC released its annual report for the 2011–12 year, which strongly supports the ongoing and increasing relevance of the Council's work. In particular, there were 65000 visits to its website, a 32 percent increase on the previous year.[54] As at October 2012, the Council had disseminated over 120 publications, including guides for high school legal studies. The VSAC also recently released *SACStat*, an online tool providing sentencing data for 430 offences dealt with in the Magistrates Court. As evidence of the intended user-friendliness of the facility, it is "readily accessible on tablet devices and smart phones operating over 3G networks".[55] In a media release on 13 November 2012, Freiberg stated: "the public has the right to know what the courts are doing. Sentencing is not just for judges". He also stressed that "[p]roviding sentencing data is … a vital way to promote consistency and transparency in sentencing".[56]

Queensland

The Queensland Sentencing Information Services (QSIS), a database modelled upon the NSW sentencing system, JIRS, was established in Queensland in 2007. Unfortunately, it is only available to the court and to legal practitioners specialising in criminal law.[57] As discussed further below, the Queensland Sentencing Advisory Council (QSAC) was recently disbanded. Most of its publications are no longer accessible to the public, but a 2011 report called *Sentencing Profile: Queensland Court Outcomes 2006–10*[58] remains available on the Queensland Department of

---

[53] Ibid, 65.
[54] VSAC, above n 47.
[55] VSAC, 'SACStat Now Live' (Media Release, 2 October 2012).
[56] VSAC, 'Sentencing Is Not Just For Judges' (Media Release, 13 November 2012).
[57] See: *Welcome to Queensland Sentencing Information Service* (2012) Queensland Sentencing Information Service <http://www.sentencing.justice.qld.gov.au/>. For discussion, see: Freiberg and Krasnostein, above n 5.
[58] QSAC, *Sentencing Profile: Queensland Court Outcomes 2006–10* (QSAC, 2011) <http://www.justice.qld.gov.au/__data/assets/pdf_file/0008/155753/SPQldCourt.pdf>.

Justice website and includes a socio-demographic profile of sentenced defendants (gender, Indigenous status and age), as well as data on sentencing outcomes in the Magistrates, District and Supreme Court.

In February 2010, the former Queensland Government announced its intention to establish the QSAC.[59] The Council's mission was listed as "inform, engage, advise" and its functions included "publish[ing] information that improves the community's knowledge and understanding of sentencing in Queensland".[60] The introduction of the QSAC reportedly had the support of the then Opposition, which "sa[id] it should have been done a long time ago".[61] It was therefore surprising that the Liberal Government decided to abolish the QSAC shortly after coming to power in March 2012.[62] A spokesperson for the Attorney-General was quoted as saying that it "really duplicated the statutory functions that were being provided by the Queensland Law Reform Commission".[63] However, a brief examination of the 69 reports, 69 working papers and 42 miscellaneous papers published by that organisation between 1969 and 2011 indicated that none of them considered the issue of sentencing in detail.[64]

The decision to abolish the QSAC was criticised by the President of the Queensland Law Society, Dr John de Groot, who argued that "Queenslanders greatly benefit[ted] from the public education service provided, including newsletters and presentations". He described the Council as a "useful channel for Queenslanders to be informed on sentencing trends" and an

> important public organ that serves essential public functions, in particular, the provision of information to the community to enhance knowledge and understanding of matters relating to sentencing; the publication of

---

[59] Chris O'Brien, 'Community "Sentencing Council" to Advise on Legal Punishments', *ABC News* (online), 9 February 2010 <http://www.abc.net.au /news/2010-02-08/community-sentencing-council-to-advise-on-legal/324180>.

[60] *Publications* (2012) Queensland Sentencing Advisory Council <http://www.sentencingcouncil.qld.gov.au/publications>.

[61] Marissa Calligeros, 'Victims to Have a Say on Jail Time', *Brisbane Times* (online), 8 February 2010 <http://www.brisbanetimes.com.au/queensland/victims-to-have-a-say-on-jail-time-20100208-nlab.html>.

[62] Daniel Hurst, 'Workplace Rights Office, Justice Body Axed', *Brisbane Times* (online), 19 May 2012 <http://www.brisbanetimes.com.au/queensland/workplace-rights-office-justice-body-axed-20120518-1yvvw.html>.

[63] Ibid.

[64] See: *Publications* (2012) Queensland Law Reform Commission <http://www.qlrc.qld.gov.au/Publications.htm>.

information relating to sentencing; the research of matters relating to sentencing; and publication of the research results.[65]

South Australia

Some sentencing data are available on the website of the South Australian Office of Crime Statistics and Research (OCSAR). In 2011, OCSAR released *Crime and Justice in South Australia 2007, Adult Courts and Corrections*, which includes detailed information on sentencing outcomes in the Magistrates and higher courts, including the average length of sentence and non-parole period for custodial orders.[66] The data are sufficiently detailed to enable analysis, but somewhat out of date.

In February 2012, the South Australian Attorney-General "announced a new advisory group for criminal sentencing".[67] As at October 2012, however, the only mention of the proposed Council on the Attorney-General's website was an undated entry in the "2011 news archive". Headed "Call for expressions of interest for membership to the Sentencing Council of South Australia", the entry stated that the council would be an "advisory body of part-time members established to improve the quality and availability of information on sentencing in South Australia".[68] The proposed functions of the Council will reportedly include "publishing information relating to sentencing and conducting research on sentencing trends".[69] More recent information indicated that the Council would "assist in bridging a gap between the courts and the community … aim[ing] to strengthen public understanding of the sentencing process and by doing so enhanc[ing] confidence in the criminal justice system".[70]

---

[65] Queensland Law Society, 'Society Opposes Abolition of Sentencing Advisory Council' (Media Release, 22 May 2012).
[66] South Australian Office of Crime Statistics and Research (OCSAR), Crime and Justice in South Australia 2007, Adult Courts and Corrections (OCSAR, 2007).
[67] 'SA Gets Sentencing Advisory Council', *ABC News* (online), 7 February 2012 <http://www.abc.net.au/news/2012-02-06/rau-announces-sentencing-advisory-council/3814256>.
[68] 2011 News Archive: Call For Expressions of Interest for Membership to the Sentencing Council of South Australia (2012) South Australian Attorney-General's Department <http://www.agd.sa.gov.au/newsroom/news/news-archive/2011-news-archive>.
[69] Freiberg and Krasnostein, above n 5, 84.
[70] Draft Foreword from Council Chair, contained in personal communication from Amy Ward, 20 November 2012.

Western Australia

Sentencing data for the period 2006–2010 are available on the website of the Western Australian Department of Attorney-General.[71] As Freiberg and Krasnostein have noted, "[t]he statistics are framed broadly, giving information in relation to sentence types in the Magistrates, District and Supreme Courts as well as in relation to the Children's Court and Indigenous offenders".[72] In addition, the Crime Research Centre, based at the University of Western Australia, describes itself as "a major and innovative contributor to the collection and analysis of statistical data on crime in Western Australia".[73] Unfortunately, the information contained on the site appears to be rather dated, with the most recent sentencing data relating to 2006.[74]

Tasmania

The Tasmanian Sentencing Advisory Council was established in 2010. Its stated aims and functions include:

- improving the quality and availability of information on sentencing in Tasmania;
- undertaking research on sentencing;
- better informing the public on crime and sentencing issues; and
- gauging public opinion on sentencing matters.[75]

At the time of writing, the Council was "in the process of setting up a database of sentencing practices in Tasmania". The database will reportedly "improve the availability and usability of sentencing practices and will also be used to support judicial decision making, research and policy

---

[71] See: *Statistics* (2012) Government of Western Australia: Department of the Attorney-General <http://www.department.dotag.wa.gov.au/s/statistics.aspx>.
[72] Freiberg and Krasnostein, above n 5, 84.
[73] *Crime Research Centre* (2012) Western Australian Crime Research Centre <http://www.law.uwa.edu.au/research/crc>.
[74] See Nini Loh, Max Maller and Wendy Wrapson, *Adult Imprisonment, Western Australia 2006* (Annual Statistical Report Series No 3/2009) (Crime Research Centre, 2009); John Fernandez et al, *Adult Court Records, Western Australia 2006* (Annual Statistical Report Series No 5/2010) (Crime Research Centre, 2010).
[75] *Sentencing Advisory Council* (2012) Tasmanian Sentencing Advisory Council <http://www.sentencingcouncil.tas.gov.au/>.

making".[76] It is not yet clear, however, whether the database will be available to members of the public.

Northern Territory

There is some limited information on sentencing outcomes available on the Northern Territory Department of Justice website.[77] The data from the March 2011 quarter set out sentencing outcomes for specified drug and aggravated property offences,[78] but more recent data appear to focus on the number and rates of different offence types, rather than sentencing outcomes.

The establishment of a sentencing council in the Northern Territory was announced in August 2011.[79] It was suggested that the proposed Council would be "an advisory body, to better inform Government about sentencing trends".[80] The Council would be "charged with researching sentencing data, trends and community perceptions" and would "provide an important link between the courts, legislature and the community on areas of potential sentencing reform".[81] However, it is not clear to what extent it was intended that the role of the Council include informing the public (as opposed to informing the Government about the public's perceptions). There does not appear to be any further information about the (proposed) Council available and it is not clear whether the introduction of such a body accords with the policy of the recently elected Country Liberal Party.

---

[76] *Current Projects* (2012) Tasmanian Sentencing Advisory Council <http://www.sentencingcouncil.tas.gov.au/current_projects>.

[77] See: *Research and Statistics Unit* (2012) Northern Territory Department of Justice < http://www.nt.gov.au/justice/policycoord/researchstats/researchstats/NT_Quarterly_crime_statistics_Dec2012.pdf >.

[78] Northern Territory Department of Justice, *Northern Territory Quarterly Crime and Justice Statistics* (Issue No 35, 2011).

[79] Delia Lawrie, 'New Sentencing Council for the Territory' (Media Release, 26 August 2011). See also: Emma Masters, 'NT Worries About High Rate of Imprisonment', *ABC Alice Springs* (online), 29 August 2011 <http://www.abc.net.au/news/2011-08-29/20110829jail-sentence-inquiry/2860028/?site =alicesprings>.

[80] Lawrie, above n 79.

[81] Ibid.

Sentencing in the ACT: Where Have We Been and Where are We Going?

The ACT was the last Australian state or territory to introduce separate sentencing legislation, with the passage of the *Crimes (Sentencing) Act 2005* (ACT) ("the Act"), the majority of which came into effect on 2 June 2006. The Act "consolidate[d] existing sentencing laws … introduce[d] a number of new options for sentencing courts and modernise[d] the law".[82] Specific changes included the introduction of "combination sentences that allow for greater flexibility in sentencing", non-association and place restriction orders and extending the option of deferred sentences. In addition, the Act made changes to the process for making non-imprisonment orders, which "enables a consistent and simple procedure for dealing with breaches" and extended the scope of victim impact statements.[83]

The following presents a chronology of the key recent developments in sentencing law, policy and practice in the ACT. It should be noted that quarterly crime statistics dating back to 2006 are available on the ACT Justice and Community Safety website. The sentencing data have become more detailed over time and include restorative justice and circle sentencing data. Information on sentencing outcomes by principal offence is also presented for the Magistrates, Children's and Supreme Courts. Overall, the data are both up-to-date and detailed, but the discussion below indicates some concern about the accuracy and adequacy of the information. It should be noted that the ACT Government is currently reviewing these datasets, and is seeking information on the following issues:

1. How useful is the data set currently in the Profile?
2. Are there particular data sets that could be removed?
3. What new data could be incorporated into the Profile?
4. Could the data in the Profile be better presented? If so, how?
5. What analysis could enhance the presentation of the information contained in the Profile?[84]

---

[82] Explanatory Memorandum, Crimes (Sentencing) Bill 2005 (ACT) 2. For a recent discussion of the background to the review which informed the development of the Bill, see: Australian Capital Territory, *Parliamentary Debates*, Legislative Assembly, 21 September 2011, 4130 (Shane Rattenbury, Speaker).

[83] Crimes (Sentencing) Bill 2005 (ACT), Explanatory Memorandum, above n 82.

[84] ACT Government, Justice and Community Safety Directorate, 'Improvements to the Criminal Justice Statistical Profile – submissions invited' at http://www.justice.act.gov.au/page/view/387 viewed 8 March 2013.

Submissions to the Inquiry are due by 30 April 2013. The author has been invited to make a submission and will take the opportunity to consider possible improvements to the data.

In the lead-up to the 2008 ACT election, the Labor Government committed to spending $633 000 to create a sentencing council to gather evidence on sentencing in the ACT and make recommendations to the Government. In August 2009, the Standing Committee on Justice and Community Safety recommended that "the ACT Government consider the need to undertake a general review of sentencing in the ACT".[85]

In October 2009, the ACT Attorney-General established the ACT Law Reform Advisory Council (the LRAC). The Council's first reference was a review of the use of suspended sentences in the ACT. The author was engaged by the LRAC to conduct the reviewand the ensuing report[86] was endorsed by the Council and provided to the Attorney-General on 31 October 2010. The report noted:

> Our research raises concerns about the accuracy of the ACT data. We found significant coding errors in recording the sentencing data in the Supreme Court Registry. As well as this miscoding, our analysis of the ACT sentencing remarks indicates some inconsistency in how sentences are understood and, therefore, recorded. Further, it appears that essential aspects of the court's decision are not being recorded at all.[87]

The report made a number of recommendations in relation to data collection and dissemination, including that:

- the Supreme Court Registry be resourced to take urgent steps to establish sound administrative systems which ensure that sentencing data are recorded accurately and comprehensively.

---

[85] ACT Standing Committee on Justice and Community Safety, *Inquiry into the Crimes (Murder) Amendment Bill 2008*, Report No 2, ACT Legislative Assembly (2009) Recommendation 4.

[86] ACT Law Reform Advisory Council (LRAC), *A Report on Suspended Sentences in the ACT* (2010) <http://cdn.justice.act.gov.au/resources/uploads/JACS/PDF/LRAC_1_ Suspended_Sentences_31_Oct_final1.pdf>. See also: Lorana Bartels and Simon Rice, 'Reviewing Reforms to the Law of Suspended Sentences in the Australian Capital Territory' (2012) 14 *Flinders Law Journal* 254.

[87] LRAC, above n 86, 7.

- the Supreme Court Registry be resourced to establish an electronic database of remarks made on sentencing, to be made publicly available on the Court website and/or through AustLii.[88]
- the Attorney-General consider taking advantage of the opportunity created by systematic and reliable collection of sentencing data to make that data public on a regular basis.[89]

The Government tabled the report and its response to it in the ACT Legislative Assembly on 22 September 2011. In its response to the LRAC report,[90] the Government stated that it was "currently considering mechanisms to improve the sentencing data that is available and anticipates that further work will be undertaken in this area".[91] The Government noted the first of the recommendations above and agreed in principle to the latter two. In addition, it stated that work was "currently underway with the Judicial Commission of NSW to explore the feasibility of establishing a sentencing database for the ACT".[92]

In September 2011, shortly before the Government tabled its response to the LRAC report, the then Speaker of the Legislative Assembly, Shane Rattenbury MLA, introduced the Crimes (Sentencing) Bill 2011 (ACT).[93] The Bill sought to "require the Government to collect and publish information about how well sentences being imposed in the ACT are meeting the purposes of sentencing".[94] The Bill also called for a review of the Act, including consideration of "any options that exist to improve the general level of knowledge and understanding that exists in the community

---

[88] AustLII is the Australasian Legal Information Institute, which provides free public access to Australian legislation and case law. See: *Australian Legal Information Institute* (2012) AustLII <http://www.austlii.edu.au/>

[89] LRAC, above n 86, 8.

[90] Legislative Assembly for the Australian Capital Territory, *ACT Law Reform Advisory Council "A Report on Suspended Sentences in the ACT" – Government Response* (2011) <http://cdn.justice.act.gov.au/resources/uploads/JACS/PDF/Govt_Response_to _LRAC_Report1.pdf>.

[91] Ibid, 3.

[92] Ibid. For discussion, see 'Lack of Data Cruels Sentencing Report', *Canberra Times* (online), 25 September 2011 <http://www.canberratimes.com.au/act-news/lack-of-data-cruels-sentencing-report-20110925-1wrnv.html>.

[93] Crimes (Sentencing) Bill 2011 (ACT). For discussion, see: 'Greens Bid to Review Sentencing Laws', *Canberra Times* (online), 18 September 2011 <http://www.canberratimes.com.au/act-news/greens-bid-to-review-sentencing-laws-20110918-1wp7h.html>.

[94] Explanatory Memorandum, Crimes (Sentencing) Bill 2011 (ACT) 2.

about sentencing".[95] Rattenbury noted, when tabling the Bill, that the 2008 election promise to introduce a sentencing council "has not been actioned by government … due to concerns about value for money of a stand-alone ACT sentencing advisory council".[96] The Attorney-General, Simon Corbell, countered that "[t]he government is still considering its options on how best to meet this commitment".[97] As discussed below, however, this would no longer appear to be under consideration.

In October 2011, the ACT Government rejected the Crimes (Sentencing) Bill 2011, but gave "in-principle support for a sentencing review".[98] However, the Attorney-General noted that it

> would be difficult, if not impossible, without improvements to the collection of sentencing data to capture the historical sentencing information required for such a review. The currently limited data that is available will significantly fetter such a review at this time … a review would be better conducted after the establishment of a sentencing database and appropriately supported with the resources that are needed.[99]

In November 2011, the *Canberra Times* reported that "one ACT judge has called for the creation of 'sentencing ranges' which offer guidelines based on broader analysis of similar cases".[100] In the judgment itself, Justice Penfold noted that

> It is true that the ACT is a small jurisdiction, and that the number of sentences imposed in the Supreme Court each year is relatively small when compared with jurisdictions such as NSW. However, the Court imposes sentences for some hundreds of offences every year, and most sentences are for offences that fall into a fairly small group of common offences; there should be no insuperable obstacle to collecting enough sentencing information to identify ACT ranges for, say, the "top 5" offences in the categories of property offences, violence offences, sexual offences and pornography offences.[101]

---

[95] Australian Capital Territory, *Parliamentary Debates*, Legislative Assembly, 21 September 2011, 4131 (Shane Rattenbury, Speaker).
[96] Ibid, 4127–4128.
[97] Australian Capital Territory, *Parliamentary Debates*, Legislative Assembly, 19 October 2011, 4679 (Simon Corbell, Attorney-General).
[98] Ibid, 4678.
[99] Ibid, 4679.
[100] 'Judge in Appeal for Clarity on Sentencing', *Canberra Times* (online), 19 November 2011 <http://www.canberratimes.com.au/news/local/news/general/judge-in-appeal-for-clarity-on-sentencing/2363437.aspx?storypage=0>.
[101] *R v TW* [2011] ACTCA 25 (17 November 2011) [111] (Penfold J).

Although her Honour appears to have been concerned principally with sentencing consistency, the point remains apposite in the context of the present discussion about public education on sentencing.

Also in November 2011, the ACT Labor Government and Liberals passed the *Crimes (Penalties) Amendment Act 2011* (ACT), which increased the legislated maximum penalties for a range of offences, culpable driving of a motor vehicle[102] (increasing penalties from seven to 14 years, nine to 16 years, four to 10 years, and five to 12 years, depending on the circumstances). The amendments to the maximum penalty for culpable driving were prompted by the case of *R v Creighton*,[103] who was sentenced to two years and nine months' imprisonment after pleading guilty to culpable driving causing death. The amendment was opposed by Rattenbury, who argued that "harsher penalties did not reduce crime and called for research into community attitudes about sentencing".[104] Perhaps unusually, he had the support of the editor-at-large of the *Canberra Times*, Jack Waterford, who described Rattenbury as "sound on law and order matters". Waterford added that he "felt sorry for the relatives" of the man who had died at Creighton's hands, but was not convinced that their grief and anger "[would] or should be assuaged by a longer prison sentence".[105]

Writing in the *Canberra Law Review*,[106] Rattenbury contended that:

> There was no information or evidence provided by Government to support their rationale that the ACT community thought sentencing laws were deficient in this area. The argument at its highest pointed to laws interstate which imposed harsher punishments for similar crimes.[107]

---

[102] Crimes (Penalties) Amendment Act 2011 (ACT) ss 10–13.

[103] *R v Creighton* [2011] ACTCA 13. For discussion, see: 'Parties Unite Against Drivers Who Kill', *Canberra Times* (online), 16 November 2011 <http://www.canberratimes.com.au/act-news/parties-unite-against-drivers-who-kill-20111116-1v0vg.html>.

[104] 'Parties Unite Against Drivers Who Kill', above n 103.

[105] Jack Waterford, 'Justice Is Not There For "Closure" Or For Revenge', *Canberra Times* (online), 29 October 2011 <http://www.canberratimes.com.au/opinion/editorial/justice-is-not-there-for-closure-or-for-revenge-20111029-1v6pe.html>.

[106] Shane Rattenbury, 'Criminal Sentencing in the ACT — The Need for Evidence' (2011) 10 *Canberra Law Review* 170. See also: 'Greens Call for Data on ACT Sentencing', *Canberra Times* (online), 23 January 2012 <http://www.canberratimes.com.au/act-news/greens-call-for-data-on-act-sentencing-20120122-1te4b.html>.

[107] Rattenbury, above n 106, 176.

Indeed, it could be argued that the decision to increase the sentences in the absence of any information about actual sentencing patterns (rather than the outcome in one particular case) is akin to the edict of the Queen of Hearts in Alice in Wonderland: "Sentence first–verdict afterwards".[108]

Rattenbury suggested too that "[a] sentencing review in the ACT is the ideal way to update existing sentencing evidence and gather new emerging thinking and strategies",[109] adding that "[o]nly once we have conducted the review and gathered the data can we have a grasp of which areas we need to prioritise for attention and potential reform".[110]

This approach also has the support of the ACT Law Society, which at the time the *Crimes (Penalties) Amendment Act 2011* (ACT) was passed "urged the Government to begin an evidence-based review of sentencing". The President of the Law Society added that "The Society is concerned that available evidence does not support increasing penalties as an effective method of crime deterrent".[111] This view was confirmed in January 2012, when the *Canberra Times* noted that the Society had "previously expressed the view sentencing in the Territory should be studied before being reformed".[112]

In addition, the January 2012 media report noted that the ACT Government was continuing "to explore a partnership with the NSW Judicial Commission to improve the availability of sentencing information to the courts the legal profession, policymakers and the community".[113] In June 2012, the ACT Government announced its 2012–13 budget, which included an allocation of $2.2 million over four years for the creation of a new sentencing database, which would "provide clear data on sentencing laws and offence penalties".[114] When announcing the database, the Attorney-General added:

> The system will assist the judiciary, prosecution and defence in the sentencing process by allowing users to research sentencing information to answer specific or generalised queries as well as serve as a tool for judicial deliberation.

---

[108] Lewis Carroll, *Alice in Wonderland* (Bloomsbury, 2001) 166.
[109] Rattenbury, above n 106, 177.
[110] Ibid, 178.
[111] 'Parties Unite Against Drivers Who Kill', above n 103.
[112] 'Greens Call for Data on ACT Sentencing', above n 106.
[113] Ibid.
[114] Simon Corbell, 'Continued Investment in Community Safety' (Media Release, 5 June 2012).

> The availability of sentencing information promotes consistency, reduces the number of appeals and supports the evidence-based policy reform process.
>
> The ACT Labor Government went to the last election with a clear policy to improve sentencing practices in the Territory and this injection of funds fulfils that election commitment.[115]

This announcement raises two important questions: Does this mean the option of introducing a sentencing council has been abandoned? And will the sentencing database be available to the public?

In relation to the first question, it was recently reported that "the ACT Government says a sentencing council is not on the agenda". The Attorney-General added that "[t]he availability of reliable and comprehensive sentencing data is a necessary first step before further consideration is given to the possible establishment of a sentencing council".[116]

This approach is regrettable, as the discussion above suggests that sentencing councils can play a significant role in making reliable and comprehensive data available, as well as performing a wider role in engaging with and informing the public about sentencing practices. Furthermore, the initial proposed cost of the Council was less than a third that of the proposed database.

In relation to the second question, on 25 June 2012, Rattenbury asked the Attorney-General whether the data would "be made available, either in its entirety or in summarised form, to … interested members of the public".[117] The Attorney-General responded that "[e]xactly who will have access to the ACT's sentencing database will be determined following discussions with the NSW Judicial Commission and the work to develop the detail of the system".[118]

The proposed database is to be modelled on the NSW Judicial Commission's Sentencing Information System and developed in collaboration with the NSW Judicial Commission. The Attorney-General noted that, in NSW, the database is provided to a range of stakeholders, such as the

---

[115] Ibid.

[116] Michael Inman, 'Databank "Not Enough For Justice"', *Canberra Times* (online), 6 December 2012 <http://www.canberratimes.com.au/act-news/databank-not-enough-for-justice-20121205-2aw8m.html>.

[117] Legislative Assembly for the Australian Capital Territory, Select Committee on Estimates 2012–13, Answer to Question on Notice, E12-347, 6 July 2012. The question was informed by emails between the author and Rattenbury's then adviser, Richard Griggs, in June and July 2012.

[118] Ibid.

courts, prosecution services, legal aid agencies, and relevant government departments, as well as "some University libraries", adding that "if people outside of these categories wish to access the NSW [database] — such as defence barristers ... they can approach the New South Wales Judicial Commission and pay the annual subscription fee".[119] More recently, the Attorney-General indicated that "the database would be available to both criminal justice stakeholders and the community", but "no decision had been made on whether an annual subscription fee would be charged".[120] As noted above, subscription fees comparable to those currently charged in NSW would likely preclude widespread public uptake.

Although the proposed sentencing database is a welcome addition to the ACT sentencing landscape, and will doubtless answer many questions for judicial officers and policymakers about sentencing practices, it is arguably an incomplete response. Given the significant cost of the database, it would be highly desirable to provide free access to the public more broadly, as well as members of the media, in order to inform public discourse. Perhaps the current review of the ACT quarterly sentencing statistics is an attempt to ameliorate concerns about the limited utility of the present data publicly available, especially the questions 'How useful is the data set currently in the Profile?', 'Could the data in the Profile be better presented? If so, how?' and 'What analysis could enhance the presentation of the information contained in the Profile?'

However, as discussed above, the role of sentencing councils goes beyond the mere recitation of sentencing data. If the creation of a sentencing database is to be regarded as fulfilling the Government's policy of improving sentencing practices, then a more interactive model is desirable. In fact, the decision to spend over $2 million on a sentencing database appears to represent something of a missed opportunity in terms of giving the public bang for its sentencing buck. Ideally, the ACT public should have free access to sentencing data and a council which can disseminate and contextualise this information.

Conclusion

According to Freiberg, "[s]entencing is as much about politics as it is about law or criminology" and is "played out in the not only in the courts but in the broader arena of public opinion".[121] However, there is a critical

---

[119] Ibid.

[120] Inman, above n 116.

[121] Freiberg, above n 39, 148.

need for this opinion to be properly informed. Indeed, Indermaur has observed: "Without accurate information on crime and justice … how are people able to assess its performance?"[122] In an attempt to examine this issue, this chapter presented an overview of the extent of publicly accessible information on sentencing in Australia, the evolution of sentencing councils and their role in informing the public about sentencing, and recent developments in sentencing policy, law and data in the ACT.

The discussion indicated significant jurisdictional variation in the scope and currency of data made available to the public. In most jurisdictions, there appears to be a trade-off between the quality of the data and the extent to which information is readily available to the public. In particular, the sophisticated sentencing databases developed in NSW, Queensland and the Commonwealth are not available to the public and the ACT may soon follow suit in this regard (although the current moves to improve the publicly available quarterly data are of course noted). What is required, however, is information which is both comprehensive and disseminated in a timely fashion, but also in a format which is accessible and comprehensible to the public.

The majority of Australian jurisdictions have or are reportedly in the process of establishing sentencing councils, although the Queensland body has recently been disbanded. It would appear that the ACT Government has all but forgotten its 2008 election commitment to introduce such an organisation. This is lamentable, as such sentencing bodies "offer a more effective means of communication with the public about sentencing and penal policy than that which is available to the courts or to political representatives".[123] Indeed, Hutton added although sentencing councils may not "guarantee … a more rational approach to penal policy … [they] at least offer an opportunity for [its] development".[124]

Finally, the chapter presented a case study on the development of sentencing policy in Australia by considering recent developments in the ACT. This jurisdiction is doubtless not alone in responding in an ad hoc way to sentencing issues. It is argued that effective decision-making in this jurisdiction should include free public access to the proposed new sentencing database and a renewed consideration of the need to introduce a sentencing council. What is also required is an ongoing commitment to

---

[122] Indermaur, above n 6, 61.

[123] Neil Hutton, 'Institutional Mechanism for Incorporating the Public', in Arie Freiberg and Karen Gelb (eds), *Penal Populism, Sentencing Councils and Sentencing Policy* (Hawkins Press, 2008) 210.

[124] Ibid, 213.

developing evidence-based sentencing policy and improving public knowledge and understanding about sentencing.

PART II

DISCRIMINATION, WORKPLACES AND JUSTICE

INTRODUCTION

HELEN WATCHIRS

Sexual Harassment

Professor Patricia Easteal and Keziah Judd explore media reporting of sexual harassment, and demonstrate the negative use of language focusing on the credibility of the complainant, with sensationalist and melodramatic reports providing lurid details of unwelcome sexual encounters. The role of the media is very topical given the treatment of Australia's Prime Minister Julia Gillard, and the national as well as international discussions that this has provoked about misogyny. The media's presentation of a distorted or incomplete picture of the dynamics of sexual harassment in the workplace means that both men and women are less likely to understand their rights and obligations, or feel comfortable in asserting them in the workplace. A huge barrier women face in making complaints of sexual harassment is the realistic fear that their experience will be minimalised and trivialised, as well as that they will be blamed for inviting it.

The unfair allocation of responsibility on the victim is also a strong theme in Professor Patricia Easteal's and Skye Saunders' chapter on sexual harassment in the Australian bush. They found that many people expected women to "set the standard" of behaviour, assuming that women are responsible for men's behaviour, presumably as they are unable to control it themselves. The striking voices of women interviewed are similar to sexual harassment complaints we receive at the ACT Human Rights Commission: "The boss did tell me that I wasn't allowed to tell ya, but he pats me on the bum all the time. Which is a bit crap!" Women who do not put up with bad behaviours are perceived as being 'too precious', and aggressive rather than assertive. There is also an interesting finding that women in the youngest age bracket are far less likely to blame women for becoming targets of sexual harassment, which shows more recent cultural change possibly being achieved by improved education and community understanding.

Family Violence and Employment Law

Amanda Alford's chapter on Family Violence, Employment and Anti-Discrimination Law recognises that the workplace is a form of community, and one of the few common factors in family violence situations. Work provides long and short-term financial security, independence, confidence and safety for women. There have been recent developments in several large workplaces for example the NSW public service such as introducing paid access to leave on the ground of family violence in Enterprise Agreements and awards, as well as the Australian Public Service Commission broadening personal leave to include family violence. Australia is a world leader in providing this specific workplace support, which also makes economic sense by preventing the unnecessary loss of talented staff and associated recruitment costs.

The chapter highlights the important work in the Australian Law Reform Commission's 2011 Report and others, such as the Australian Council of Human Rights Agencies, the Human Rights Law Centre and Equality Rights Alliance around the inclusion of family violence as a protected attribute under Commonwealth anti-discrimination law.

Genetic Testing

Dr Wendy Bonython and Bruce Baer Arnold raise important legal and social issues of consumer protection, privacy, consent and discrimination in their chapter on Genetic Testing. The low level of genetic literacy among the general population, combined with an increased appetite for genetic information and direct availability of genetic tests to consumer is a dangerous prescription for new types of discrimination in the workplace and service delivery. The examples of the unintended potential future career consequences of testing conducted "for fun" remind us of the need to consider our approach to this area carefully. This work is overdue as the last major pieces of legal policy work were a decade ago, such as the Genetic Discrimination Project 2002–2005. The Australian Law Reform Commission 2003 Report recommended changes to the Commonwealth *Disability Discrimination Act 1992* to explicitly protect against genetic discrimination, although it appears to be generally covered in the protections against disability discrimination at the Federal and at State and Territory levels.

CHAPTER FOUR

MEDIA REPORTAGE OF SEXUAL HARASSMENT: THE (IN)CREDIBLE COMPLAINANT

KEZIAH JUDD
AND PATRICIA EASTEAL

Introduction: The Mass Media and the Court of Public Opinion

Studies of court and/or conciliation decisions about credible complainants and legitimate sexual harassment reveal that in determining what is reasonable and indeed in assessing whether behaviour was sexual and unwelcome and resulted in humiliation, it is often the complainant's identity, history and behaviour that are scrutinised and evaluated by conciliators and judicial officers.[1] Youth can enhance credibility if the alleged harasser is older. Also, credible victims fight back, report immediately, are consistent in their evidence, are able to particularise and testify either in a non- aggressive and not too "smart" manner or make an argumentative presentation coupled with confidence.[2] Judicial commentary about the complainant's relationships, dress and attitudes to sexuality is a chilling echo of Catharine MacKinnon's 1979 observation

---

[1] See Deb Tyler and Patricia Easteal, 'Sexual Harassment in the Tribunals: The Credibility Gap' (1998) 23(5) *Alternative Law Journal* 211; Patricia Easteal and Keziah Judd, '"She Said, He Said" Credibility and Outcome in Sexual Harassment' (2008) 31(5) *Women's Studies International Forum* 336; Patricia Easteal and Skye Saunders, 'The (Un)Successful Rural Workplace Sexual Harassment Complainant' (2011) 10(2) *Canberra Law Review* 84.

[2] Ibid.

that sexual harassment may be dismissed often as "trivial, isolated, and 'personal,' or as universal 'natural' or 'biological' behaviours …"[3]

These findings also confirm the feminist perspective that law must be looked at within the broader cultural context — in this instance in the broader context of beliefs about sexual harm. Those beliefs and the broader context are both reflected by and contributed to by the media. The media has been described as a shaper of attitudes through its use of narrative techniques:

> Stories create a causal chain: this happened because she did that, he responded by doing this. They identify notions of responsibility and blame; they make sense of the chaos of events "out there", and in doing so steer the audience's response towards one view of the world rather than another.[4]

In examining how female victims of sexual harassment are portrayed by the media, we must be aware that media reporting may be simplistic, misleading, and overly reliant on clichéd and "archetypal characters" as "ancient as they are inflammatory" — the seductress, the victimised man, and the man-hating woman.[5]

> The language of the media is limited: "Feminists" are always "ideologues". "Women in the workplace" invariably "threaten the place of men". "Complaints" of sexual harassment are constantly "on the rise". The tone ranges from flattened to melodramatic, often, without that much in between.[6]

Indeed it has been noted that feminism will always be working "against the grain" when engaging with the media:

> The forms of feminist theory and practice that most challenge the liberal status quo are the most likely to be misunderstood and/or mistreated by the media because of the media's own reliance on a liberal paradigm. This

---

[3] Catharine MacKinnon, Sexual Harassment of Working Women — A Case of Sex Discrimination (Yale University Press, 1979) 1.

[4] John Street, *Mass Media, Politics and Democracy* (Palgrave, 2001) 4.

[5] Jenna Mead (ed), 'Introduction — Tell it Like it Is', in *Bodyjamming — Sexual Harassment, Feminism and Public Life* (Allen and Unwin, 1997) 6.

[6] Ibid, 6. Mead's term "melodramatic" refers to classic tabloid journalism, with screaming simplistic headlines, highly emotive language, and a focus on scandal and gossip. While Mead herself does not define "flattened", we understand the term to refer to media commentary located beyond the front page, offering detailed but dry analysis to those readers who bother to dig for it.

> presents a significant challenge for those feminists who attempt to work with or within the commercial media.[7]

Much of the critical analysis of the media focuses on the idea of propaganda, with the media responsible for providing messages to subdue the populace, even in "enlightened" liberal democracies.

> The mass media serve as a system for communicating messages and symbols to the general populace. It is their function to amuse, entertain, and inform, and to inculcate individuals with the values, beliefs, and codes of behaviour that will integrate them into the institutional structures of the larger society.[8]

The media constructs a version of "reality" that favours those in power. Continuing in this vein, the media's use of clichéd characters can be seen as a shorthand method of reinforcing dominant social values about gender and the law. This use of media shorthand has been described as both political and problematic with television as "myopically focused on the foreground of ordinary experience"[9] favouring the simple (and indeed the simplistic) at the expense of the complex:

> It filters out: 1) more abstract and conceptual structures or relationships, including systems (which are relationships that interact over time to produce particular results or to maintain a particular balance); 2) causality, particularly remote causal histories and destinies, evolutionary change, and uncertain or incomplete processes of change; 3) context, which is likewise relational and causative; and 4) ambiguity, ie, uncertainty of meaning, and ambivalence, or uncertainty of value.[10]

This tendency for over-simplification, eschewing of context and reliance on broad-brush characterisation can be seen in media reporting of sexual harassment law, together with a love of drama and exaggeration. The latter would fall at the inflammatory, screaming headlines "tabloid"-style coverage of the spectrum in contrast with the more thoughtful,

---

[7] Donna E Young, 'Introduction', in Martha A Fineman, Martha T. McCluskey *Feminism, Media and the Law* (Oxford University Press, 1997) 7.
[8] Edward S Herman and Noam Chomsky, Manufacturing Consent — the Political Economy of the Mass Media (Vintage, 1994) 1.
[9] Jeffrey Scheuer, The Sound Bite Society — How Television Helps the Right and Hurts the Left (Routledge, 2001) 121.
[10] Ibid, 121–122.

detailed yet buried analysis associated with broadsheet articles beyond the front page.[11]

In "Ripples from the First Stone", Anya Poukchanski also identifies a blend of sensationalism and scepticism in the media when reporting sexual harassment cases. She comments, "A scandal-happy media armed with the lurid resources of the internet means privacy for victims is almost impossible, and reputation is easily, and enduringly, marred".[12] Poukchanski discusses the use of language to undermine the credibility of sexual harassment complainants, with particular attention to the term "alleged":

> Journalists refer to the "alleged victim", but it is the victim who is doing the alleging, against a person she claims to have committed a crime against her — the alleged assaulter. Referring to the "alleged" victim immediately casts the foundation of her claim into doubt; well she might be a victim, or she might be putting the whole thing on.[13]

Identifying the ties

In the following chapter we look at the style of writing in the reporting of a selection of Australian sexual harassment cases. We contrast broadsheets with tabloid, and the extent to which Mead's flattened/melodramatic dichotomy applies. We also particularly focus on how those who allege sexual harassment cases are characterised.

We analyse the reporting by a sample of Australian newspapers of five sexual harassment cases from mid-2010 through 2011. Using microfiche archives from the National Library of Australia and the online database Newsbank Newspapers Australia, we conducted an analysis of selected print media coverage of three New South Wales (NSW) based cases — Fraser-Kirk and David Jones, Bridgette Styles' complaint against Clayton Utz and Carole-Ann Britt's complaint against Patrick Stevedores and two Victorian matters — Susan Spiteri's complaint against IBM and Sallyanne Robinson's complaint against Rivers. For the NSW matters, articles appearing in three major Sydney newspapers — the broadsheet *The Sydney Morning Herald,* its weekend tabloid *The Sun Herald* and the populist tabloid *The Daily Telegraph* were identified. We used articles in

---

[11] Mead, above n 5.
[12] Anya Poukchanski (2011) 'Ripples from the First Stone' (2011) 39 *The Sydney Institute Quarterly* 10, 12 .
[13] Ibid.

the daily broadsheet *The Age*, and the tabloids *Herald Sun* and *Sunday Herald Sun* for the cases that took place in Victoria.

For each of the five, we looked at the "splash" period, focusing our attention on the first month of reporting of the case. This period was chosen because at this time the case was "fresh" in the minds of journalists and readers. In the IBM case, we looked at two distinct "splash" periods — when the case first hit the headlines in April 2011, and when the claim was filed in the Federal Court in October 2011.

Having developed a pro forma template, we recorded variables such as how the media portrayed the parties, the behaviour complained of, the relationship between the complainant and alleged harasser, whether the complainant's response to harassment was discussed and whether the age of the complainant was mentioned. We also noted and report below relevant "grabs" that are indicative of sensationalism and/or stereotyping and melodramatic versus flat reporting. After the textual analysis was complete, aside from looking at the aggregate findings, we compared the broadsheet to the tabloid coverage.

Caveat

The generalisability of our findings is limited both by the small sized sample and our focus on reportage in only several Australian newspapers. Any conclusions must be regarded as preliminary and not necessarily true for other print or visual media or for other types of cases.

"Facts" of the Five Cases

The facts of the David Jones case are well known to Australian readers. Junior publicist Kristy Fraser-Kirk made a complaint of sexual harassment against former CEO Mark McInnes. In her statement of claim, Ms Fraser-Kirk stated that Mr McInnes engaged in repeated unwelcome conduct of a sexual nature toward her, including telling her that a dessert was like a "fuck in the mouth", placing his hand under her clothing and touching her bra, trying to kiss her on the mouth and repeatedly asking her to accompany him to his home at Bondi.[14] Ms Fraser-Kirk also stated that when she reported these incidents to her supervisor at David Jones, she

---

[14] Fraser Kirk v David Jones & Ors, NSD 964/2010 Statement of Claim (2010) <http://resources.news.com.au/files/2010/08/02/1225900/118204-aus-bus-file-djs-statement-pdf.pdf> 3–7

was told to say "no, Mark" and her complaints were not addressed.[15] Some of the alleged harassment took place at work functions which were held away from the workplace or were text messages which were sent to the complainant whilst she was at home. (Therefore, if that matter had proceeded to a hearing, the test for vicarious liability may have failed.)

In the Clayton Utz case, Bridgette Styles complained of harassing behaviour by her colleagues, and described the law firm as a "hostile place to work", where managers failed to take action against a Facebook group called "Clayton Utz Workplace Relations (Sydney) Whorebags".[16] Ms Styles claimed that after her relationship with colleague Luis Izzo ended, she was harassed by other employees, who "posted a photo and montage of images of Mr Izzo with the caption 'I'm nice to look at' near her desk in the firm's workplace relations group".[17] Ms Styles also complained of sexual comments being made to her by colleagues during work functions, a failure by her employer to investigate her complaint of sexual harassment and victimisation in the workplace following the making of her complaint.[18]

In the IBM matter, the complainant Susan Spiteri alleged harassing behaviour by a former senior manager, which included telling her to "get those boobies out…to get sales".[19] Ms Spiteri's complaint also included allegations that this manager made sexual remarks in front of her during Christmas events, repeatedly placed his hand on her leg and up her dress at a work function, and engaged in bullying behaviour such as name-calling and phoning her late at night.[20] A *Herald Sun* article on the case noted that: "Despite complaining to four managers, no action was taken for 18 months, and only after the woman attempted suicide was the perpetrator forced to resign in mid-2009".[21] The article then quoted the complainant's legal representative Siobhan Keating: "IBM's inaction is impossible to understand".[22] In written judgment on an application for interlocutory relief, Jessup J commented:

---

[15] Ibid, 4.

[16] Louise Hall, 'Claims of Sexism as Young Lawyer Takes On Top Firm', *Sydney Morning Herald*, 8 June 2011, 3.

[17] Ibid.

[18] *Styles v Clayton Utz (No 3)* [2011] NSWSC 1452, [12]–[17], [21]–[22], [120] (MacCallum J).

[19] 'Woman Sues IBM for Bullying by Boss', *The Age*, 21 October 2011, 7.

[20] Marianne Betts, 'Woman Sues IBM for $1.1m — Sex Pest Legal Fight', *Herald Sun*, 15 April 2011, 9.

[21] Ibid.

[22] Ibid.

> I should emphasise that the applicant does not allege in her Statement of Claim that any of those respondents directly engaged in any conduct which would be unlawful under the *Sex Discrimination Act*. Rather, the case against them is that they failed to act to prevent the particular perpetrator from engaging in the conduct which was said to be unlawful on his part.[23]

In the Rivers case, former executive Sallyanne Robinson made a civil claim against the company for harassment by its owner and sole director,[24] Philip Goodman. Her statement of claim was reported as including complaints of unwanted sexual advances, unwanted touching of her breasts and bottom, being asked to model the company's underwear range, and being addressed as "honey bun" and "bunny".[25]

Dock worker Carole-Ann Britt in the Patrick Stevedores matter, complained of a hostile work environment, in which she was surrounded by "posters of naked women and piles of pornographic magazines and regularly asked about her sex life".[26] Alleged behaviours included the display of pornography on an overhead projector during a meeting.[27] Ms Britt said that she made a complaint to the maritime union after a male colleague drove her to a remote location on the port, touched her between the legs and encouraged her to have sex with him.[28]

Fanfare v Muted Coverage

While the David Jones (DJs) case appeared in the media with considerable fanfare, coverage of the other cases was considerably more muted. During August 2010, the DJs matter received front page coverage in *The Sydney Morning Herald* and *The Daily Telegraph* on five separate

---

[23] *Spiteri v IBM Australia Ltd* [2011] FCA 1318, [4] (Jessup J).
[24] Hamish Heard, 'Assault Payout', *Sunday Herald Sun*, 13 November 2011, 21.
[25] Cameron Houston, 'Rivers Tycoon on Sexual Assault Charge', *The Sunday Age*, 4 December 2011, 1.
[26] Tim Barlass, 'Sexist Port Workers in the Dock — Stevedore "Surrounded by Porn" — Blames Sexual Assault on Toxic Atmosphere', *The Sun Herald*, 11 December 2011, 3.
[27] Ibid.
[28] Ibid.

occasions.[29] For the other four cases in our sample, only two articles made the front page.[30]

The sheer volume of the coverage of the David Jones case was extraordinary. During its first month, the David Jones case was the subject of 26 articles in *The Sydney Morning Herald*, and 24 articles in *The Daily Telegraph*. However, the other cases in our sample have not attracted this level of coverage. The Clayton Utz case was the subject of two articles in *The Sydney Morning Herald*, and two articles in *The Daily Telegraph*. The IBM case appeared twice in *The Age*, and twice in the *Herald Sun*. The Rivers case was the subject of one article in *The Age*, one in the *Herald Sun* and one in the *Sunday Herald Sun*. The Patrick Stevedores case, which arguably made the most serious allegations in our sample, was reported in a single article in only one newspaper—*The Sun Herald*.

Melodramatic v Flat (Tabloid v Broadsheet)

We anticipated that there would be differences between the tabloid and broadsheet coverage. However, the cases in our sample showed that sometimes the line is not so clear. For example, much of *The Sydney Morning Herald* coverage of the David Jones case had a "scandal and gossip" element, with much of the reporting on the case done by the *Herald* gossip columnist Andrew Hornery for his "Private Sydney" column. In contrast, once the melodramatic "sex fight" headlines were stripped away, the *Herald Sun* provided some thoughtful commentary on the Rivers case.

We found that some of the coverage of the Fraser-Kirk case was nuanced but a flattened/melodramatic dichotomy was present in much of the media reporting, and ancient sexist stereotypes have continued to appear.

While the legal practitioners representing Fraser-Kirk, McInnes and David Jones competed for media attention and sympathetic coverage,

---

[29] Belinda Kontominas and Simon Mann, 'Are You Being Sued? Sordid Details of $37 Million DJs Sex Claim', *The Sydney Morning Herald*, 3 August 2010, 1, 6; Andrew Hornery, 'From Lawsuit to Swimsuit, DJs Dodges 'M' Word', *The Sydney Morning Herald*, 4 August 2010, 1–2; Janet Fife-Yeomans, 'Inside Australia's Biggest Harassment Case $37m SEX SUIT', *The Daily Telegraph*, 3 August 2010, 1–3; Nick Tabakoff, 'DJs to Set Up Bully Hotline', *The Daily Telegraph*, 7 August 2010, 1–2; and the front page teaser headline: 'New DJs Revelation: $37m Battle Turns Nasty, Page 3', *The Daily Telegraph*, 8 August 2010, 1.

[30] Houston, above n 25, 1; Shelly Hadfield, 'Millionaire Denies Woman's Harassment Claim - TYCOON SEX FIGHT', *Herald Sun*, 5 November 2011, 1, 4.

much of the reportage focused upon the size of the claim and the credibility of the complainant. In some of the more prominently placed articles, these newspapers provided a platform for the players to make their respective announcements, and argue their cases. Both the broadsheet and the tabloid newspapers highlighted the "scandalous gossip" aspects of the case, with the publication of provocative yet irrelevant sound bites from fashion designer Alannah Hill in the "Private Sydney" column, and speculation from *The Telegraph* about Sydney private investigator Frank Monte shadowing the complainant. In many articles, journalists provided their own critical analysis of the legal and social implications of the case, or its impact on the economic position of the David Jones brand. The most "flattened", yet detailed and legally accurate articles on David Jones were buried in the "Business Day" liftout section of the *Herald*, which is separate from the main newspaper. The bulk of *The Telegraph* coverage of the David Jones case fell predictably into the "melodramatic" camp, with a focus on the more colourful aspects of the case.

A critical difference between the melodramatic and flattened commentary in both newspapers was the treatment of the tortious component of the claim. In the melodramatic camp, commentators who chose to position Fraser-Kirk as the gold-digger generally did not concern themselves with the difference between compensatory and punitive damages. Miranda Devine's column for the *Herald* presents a typical example:

> Woman (sic) who are raped don't get that kind of money as victims compensation — they're lucky if they receive $100,000. A woman who was raped by a navy colleague at HMAS Cairns was awarded less than $500,000 in 2007 in a sexual harassment lawsuit. A David Jones employee who sustained a serious brain injury at work would get less than $300,000 in compensation under WorkCover. So why does McInnes's conduct qualify for such a grand cash grab?[31]

Although written with a fine rhetorical flourish, this statement fails to grasp the differences between an award of compensatory damages to return complainants to their original positions prior to the wrong suffered, compensation awarded under statutory no-fault schemes, and punitive damages to punish tortfeasors for their conduct. Such a basic error rendered the article very misleading in its analysis of legal issues.

A handful of commentators in the DJs articles did take pains to clarify the punitive nature of the claim. For example, in *The Sydney Morning Herald*, Kate Lahey commented:

---

[31] Miranda Devine, 'Nobody Died, So Why is She Demanding a King's Ransom?', *The Sydney Morning Herald*, 5 August 2010, 15.

> The figure is unusual for two reasons. Its sheer size is light years away from usual payouts in such cases and the nature of the damages sought is equally rare. It is designed as punishment, beyond general compensation damages for actions so egregious they warrant the extra penalty — unheard of in discrimination cases in Australia.[32]

However, such analysis was the exception rather than the rule. Only one of the *Telegraph* articles referred to the purpose of punitive damages: "If she wins, it would be the first time any Australian court has awarded punitive damages to punish an employer in a sexual harassment case".[33]

The flattened/melodramatic dichotomy was also seen in *The Daily Telegraph* reporting of the Clayton Utz case. At first, *The Daily Telegraph* appeared to have little interest in Styles' case, with its first report of the case being confined to a tiny "news in brief" column on page 13,[34] which was a classic example of "flattened" coverage. The brief article noted, "A former Clayton Utz lawyer who is suing the top-tier firm for sexual harassment and defamation said she never made a formal complaint because she feared for her job".[35] Melodramatic reportage began when the newspaper launched a blistering attack on the complainant, with a more sympathetic focus on her alleged harasser.[36] The melodrama escalated with an article on the victimised "man in the middle" of the case, and an unflattering portrait of the complainant as a scorned harridan: "Mr Izzo's brief fling with fellow lawyer Bridgette Styles triggered a volley of legal claims from his scorned lover".[37]

The Rivers case attracted the melodramatic headline "TYCOON SEX FIGHT" with its front page coverage in the *Herald Sun,*[38] but the article itself struck a good balance between the flattened and the melodramatic. While aspects of the complaint were spelled out in detail, the article appeared to take pains to describe both sides of the case without the use of further inflammatory language like "sex fight". The piece ended with the almost bland statement, "The matter is expected to be heard next year".[39]

---

[32] Kate Lahey, '"No" Gets No Firmer than a $37 Million Lawsuit', *BusinessDay*, *The Sydney Morning Herald*, 4 August 2010, 1.

[33] Fife-Yeomans, above 29, 2.

[34] 'Lawyer's Job Fears', *The Daily Telegraph*, 8 June 2011, 13.

[35] Ibid.

[36] Vanda Carson, 'Man in the Middle of $200K Claim — Law Firm's Sexual Harassment Case', *The Daily Telegraph*, 4 July 2011, 17.

[37] Ibid.

[38] Hadfield, above n 30.

[39] Ibid.

The *Herald Sun* took a similarly dramatic approach in its headlines for the IBM case, with the sensationalist titles: "Woman sues IBM for $1.1m — Sex pest legal fight" and "Woman sues IBM for $1.1m — Worker allegedly told to 'get boobies out'".[40] These headlines demonstrated the preoccupation with money and melodrama that we found in the David Jones coverage.

From headline to story: "Sex pest legal fight" opened with a focus on the most dramatic aspects of the case: the size of the claim, and the "salaciousness" of the harassment.

> A FORMER female executive is suing a major Melbourne company for $1.1 million after it allegedly failed to act on her repeated complaints of serious sexual harassment ... If she is awarded $1.1 million it could be the biggest sexual harassment payout in Australian history. Maurice Blackburn lawyer Siobhan Keating said the allegations included that a male colleague had rubbed himself against the woman and that he made comments such as, "if you get your breasts out, you will get more sales".[41]

In contrast, *The Age* reported on the case in its "Business" section, and adopted a more subdued tone, with less of a focus on describing the behaviour in gory detail, and a placing of the case in the context of recent legal history:

> A SEXUAL harassment claim for $1.1 million brought by a top IBM saleswoman shows the failure of companies to implement their own policies properly, the woman's lawyer says. The woman, whose lawyers will not name her because of her "delicate mental state",[42] is likely to lodge a Federal Court claim against IBM next week. She claims she endured almost two years of sexual harassment, discrimination and bullying at the hands of a male senior manager. Maurice Blackburn special counsel Siobhan Keating said the case, together with the lawsuit against against former David Jones chief executive Mark McInnes brought last year by

[40] Betts, above n 20; Ruth Lamperd, 'Woman Sues IBM for $1.1m — Worker Allegedly Told to "Get Boobies Out"', *Herald Sun*, 20 October 2011, 13.

[41] Betts, above n 20.

[42] No suppression orders of the complainant's name appear to be in place at this time. The complainant's full name has been used in judgments on the Federal Court website, and can be seen in the online court file of the case: *Susan Spiteri v IBM Australia & Ors* (2011) Federal Court of Australia, Victorian Registry VID1134/2011 <https://www.comcourts.gov.au/file/Federal/P/VID1134/2011/actions>.

publicist Kirsty Fraser-Kirk, showed "the gap in how far corporate Australia has come with sexual harassment".[43]

While the size of the claim was of interest and the article covered the same information as its *Herald Sun* counterpart, the selection of quotes from the complainant's solicitor demonstrated an interest in the legal rather than the "sexual" aspects of the case.

Credibility and Character

In their coverage of Fraser-Kirk, the *Herald* and *Telegraph* used similar criteria as the Courts (described in the Introduction above) in assessing her credibility. In both the "flattened" and "melodramatic" articles, her identity, history and behaviour were scrutinised and evaluated. At first glance, Fraser-Kirk appeared to fit the stereotype of the credible complainant in the Court discussed above. She was almost twenty years younger than her alleged harasser, and in a clearly subordinate position in the workplace hierarchy. She made a prompt, very vocal complaint of harassment. Her statement of claim documented the allegations of harassment with precision. This was certainly the picture of Fraser-Kirk that her public relations and legal team attempted to paint, when she addressed the media on 2 August 2010. Looking scared but brave, accompanied by her parents and boyfriend, she said, "I'm a young woman standing here today simply because I said it wasn't OK, because I said that this should never happen to anyone".[44]

Many of the articles did refer to Fraser-Kirk's relative youth. Thirteen *Herald* articles and eight *Telegraph* articles reported her age. In contrast, there appeared to be less interest in the age of McInnes, which was only reported in three *Herald* articles and one *Telegraph* article.

This interest in the age of the complainant was also apparent in the other cases in our sample. While Styles' age was not specifically mentioned in the media coverage, the two *Sydney Morning Herald* articles made a point of characterising her as a "young lawyer"[45] when reporting on her complaint against Clayton Utz.

As with Fraser-Kirk, there was a high level of scrutiny of her behaviour in some of the coverage. For instance, in *The Telegraph*:

---

[43] Ben Butler, 'IBM Saleswoman in $1.1m Sexual Harassment Claim', *The Age*, April 11 2011, 3.

[44] Kontominas and Mann, above n 29, 1.

[45] Louise Hall, above n 16, 3; Emma McDonald 'Life in the Firm Still No Picnic for Women', *The Sydney Morning Herald*, 9 June 2011, 15.

> When she told Mr Izzo how she felt about the photos at an after-work drinks session at Sydney's Ryan's Bar, Mr Izzo reported to the law firm management that he believed she was using the threat of a harassment claim as a bargaining chip with management. Just weeks after she joined the prestigious firm, Mr Izzo alleges Ms Styles accused him of "spading other girls", "looking for his next victim" and "being such a slut".[46]

In her choice of quotations, the journalist appears to make connections between Ms Styles' workplace rotations as a graduate solicitor and her complaint of sexual harassment, with some implications for her credibility as a complainant:

> They dated for three weeks before she joined the firm, but the couple agreed to end their relationship once Ms Styles began work. She said shortly after she began a rotation with the company's workplace relations department — which advises large companies and government on claims of unfair treatment by employees — she felt harassed.[47]

The last line of the article can be read as a parting shot at the complainant, her credibility and her work performance: "Ms Styles was sacked in December 2008. She is seeking at least $200,000 in damages".[48]

Indeed, analysis of reportage on these five cases shows that language may be used to paint a picture of incredibility. In a *Herald Sun* article on the IBM case, the reporter suggested that the complainant *may* be an archetypal incredible woman through repeated use of the word "allegedly". The complainant's legal representative is also mentioned as labelling her client's complaint as an allegation:

> Maurice Blackburn lawyer Siobhan Keating said the allegations included that a male colleague had rubbed himself against the woman and that he made comments such as, "if you get your breasts out, you will get more sales".[49]

The article went on, "He had also allegedly made sexual remarks in front of her during Christmas events, and had allegedly repeatedly placed his hand on her leg and up her dress several times at an evening function … He also allegedly bullied her …"[50]

---

[46] Carson, above n 36.
[47] Ibid.
[48] Ibid.
[49] Betts, above n 20.
[50] Ibid.

The Daily Telegraph gets the award for biggest turnaround in its Clayton Utz coverage. As we discussed earlier, its first article on the case was a miniscule "news in brief" item called "Lawyer's Job Fears". Then a few weeks later, it was a profile on the "man in the middle" of the allegations, and a blistering attack on the complainant's credibility.

Reportage on the Rivers matter showed that mental health issues could be a double-edged sword for complainant credibility, and presented competing pictures of an hysterical, incredible woman and an injured victim of "real" sexual harassment. Coverage of the Rivers case focused on the complainant, Robinson's mental health and the respondent Philip Goodman's wealth. An article in *The Age* included a description of the latter's lavish lifestyle:

> Goodman has made a fortune from a national chain of more than 150 Rivers stores. He owns two adjoining mansions in an exclusive Toorak court, where he keeps a fleet of prestige cars including a baby-blue Bentley and a red Ferrari California.[51]

Tabloid and broadsheet coverage alike devoted significant column space to the respondent, and defence attacks on the complainant's credibility. One *Herald Sun* article opened with a focus on Goodman and his wealth:

> A top retail tycoon has been accused of sexual harassment against a female worker, allegedly getting her to model underwear for him and spy on a business rival. Millionaire Philip Harry Goodman, 54, is the sole director of the Rivers Australia chain, which has 50 stores across Victoria.[52]

The remainder of the article devoted equal space to the complainant and respondent's respective cases, noting that the complainant, "claims in court documents that Mr Goodman:

- PATTED her on the bottom and grabbed her breast
- REQUIRED her to model underwear for him in private, during which time she claims he placed his hands over and under her bra.
- TOLD her to pretend to be his wife or girlfriend during product sample purchases and called her "honey bun".
- OFFERED her gifts and insisted she call in sick so they could go to lunch.

---

[51] Houston, above n 25.

[52] Hadfield, above n 30.

- REQUIRED her to wear glasses fitted with cameras to covertly photograph products and displays of a competitor".[53]

Then the defence's case was outlined:

> In a defence document responding to Ms Robinson's claims, Mr Goodman and Rivers allege she has a history of bipolar behaviour, and that she suffered a range of ailments and conditions during her time with Rivers, including alcohol abuse — a claim she denies. They said Ms Robinson at no time modelled underwear or was naked — but that she insisted on trying on underwear samples in front of Mr Goodman. They claim it was part of her duties as accessories product developer, charged with building the women's underwear range, that she try on samples. Mr Goodman denied touching Ms Robinson's breasts or bottom. Rivers claims in the course of her job, he and Ms Robinson went to shops to assess clothes, and he would have told her that if she was approached by sales staff, she should adopt the role of being a couple. Rivers and Mr Goodman admitted getting her to covertly photograph a competitor's goods but said that was not victimisation.[54]

These kinds of attacks on the complainant's credibility were also reported extensively by *The Age*:

> [The defence] claimed the Rivers employee did "nudie runs after having drunk too much alcohol" and "got so wasted on occasions at the end of a night out that she can't walk". Max Legal lawyer Terry McHugh slammed the personal attacks on his client.[55]

The complainant's mental health was also used by her own legal representatives in the media — albeit to present her sexual harassment claims as credible:

> Ms Robinson, now of Queensland, who claims she has suffered post-traumatic stress disorder, depression and panic attacks, declined to comment. Her lawyers say she is "attempting to re-establish her career".[56]

The limited reportage of the Patrick Stevedore complaint is markedly dissimilar to the other four with no aspersions or hints of victim incredibility. The portrayal of Britt, who described her workplace as a

---

[53] Ibid, 1, 4.
[54] Ibid, 4.
[55] Houston, above n 25.
[56] Hadfield, above n 30.

toxic environment, was quite sympathetic and focused on the details of the sexual harassment:

> Carole-Ann Britt claims that she, as a handful of female workers among 450 men at Patrick's Port Botany docks, she was surrounded by posters of naked women and piles of pornographic magazines and regularly asked about her sex life … The matter came to a head when she alleges she was driven at night to a secluded part of the port behind freight containers where a male employee placed his hand between her legs and encouraged her to have sex with him.[57]

The article quoted the complainant's legal representative's description of the matter as "the worst case of sexual harassment I have ever seen"[58] and a Patrick Stevedores spokesperson expressing disappointment over the failure of conciliation and the complainant's decision to speak to the media.[59]

Conclusion

A common feature of both media reporting and judgments is the focus upon the credibility of the complainant as opposed to the respondent. Discussion of the complainant's behaviour, response to harassment and mental health was a common feature of the newspaper coverage. While there was some discussion of the respondent's behaviour in the Rivers case, it was the complainant who held the most interest for journalists. Coverage of the IBM case and Rivers case placed considerable focus on the mental health of complainants.

In Court hearings, the credibility or character of the complainant appears to correlate with a finding in her favour.[60] In contrast, the media's presentation of the woman did not seem to affect the outcome. For example, coverage tended to be more sympathetic to the complainant in the other four cases than towards Fraser-Kirk. She was depicted in many of the stories as avaricious. Yet her matter settled for a reputedly higher amount than in the other four.

The melodramatic nature of the coverage did not necessarily equate to an exclusively credible or incredible picture of the complainant in a sexual harassment case. Generally, the melodramatic reporting focused on the

---

[57] Barlass, above n 26. As discussed above, this case only appeared in one newspaper story.

[58] Ibid.

[59] Ibid.

[60] Easteal and Judd, above n 1.

"sexual" aspects of the complaint in lurid detail, and the complainant's response to harassment. This could include either a sympathetic portrayal of the complainant, as in the Patrick Stevedores coverage, or an unsympathetic portrayal, as seen in the *Telegraph* coverage of the Clayton Utz case.

Although the more "flattened" commentary did not make the same judgments of complainant incredibility as the "melodramatic" coverage, its "buried" nature made it less accessible to all but the most interested readers. The more "flattened" commentary also did not necessarily equate to a more credible presentation of the complainant, or a discussion of the complainant at all. The *Telegraph* "news in brief" item on the Clayton Utz case amounted to a "burying" of the story, and gave no impression of Ms Styles as a complainant, either credible or incredible. The more "flattened" *Sydney Morning Herald* coverage in its "Business Day" liftout of the David Jones case did not make the same credibility judgments as the "Private Sydney" columns in the main paper, but its more nuanced coverage was not placed in a prominent position.

It is somewhat disturbing then to see how the mass media could be playing an important role in the shaping of community attitudes, by using stories to present its own "reality". It is this "reality" that gives the general community their information about sexual harassment and the law. The coverage was somewhat uneven in its focus, with some articles addressing relevant legal issues, and others showing a greater interest in using language to undermine the credibility of complainants. For instance, whilst it is important for the media to be careful in reporting of court cases and to show an understanding of key concepts like damages, and not to describe matters in dispute as established facts, the journalist's use of the word "allegedly" five times and "allegations" twice in the 300 word article about the IBM case does seem excessive.

Further, the melodramatic coverage presented patchy legal information for readers, and a continuing influence of sexist stereotyping. Many of the articles included irrelevant information, such as suggestions that the complainant in the Rivers case engaged in "nudie runs" when drunk, that presented a picture of an incredible complainant but did not have any bearing on her complaint of sexual harassment. Information of this kind can be challenged in a court of law before being admitted in evidence, but the complainant does not have this option if these statements are already in print.

Therefore, if the media indeed creates its own "reality", it could be presenting a problematic picture of sexual harassment law for potential complainants and respondents with a somewhat misleading impression of their respective rights and responsibilities. In the ways described here, it would seem that the Australian tabloid and broadsheet print media, like their overseas counterparts, do indeed frequently rely on broad-brush characterisation and evocative language, which may impact upon how sexual harassment complainants and perhaps sexual harassment itself, are regarded by the community.

CHAPTER FIVE

"I JUST THINK IT ALL COMES DOWN TO HOW THE GIRL BEHAVES AS TO HOW SHE IS TREATED": SEXUAL HARASSMENT "SURVIVAL" BEHAVIOURS AND WORKPLACE THINKING IN RURAL AUSTRALIA

SKYE SAUNDERS AND PATRICIA EASTEAL

The Bigger Picture: The Landscape

It is not uncommon for sexual assault victims and those who survive domestic violence to respond to the violence with feelings of shame/blame, minimisation and denial. It is also normative for some friends, family and others in the community to deny, minimise and blame the victim.[1] The last is a correlate of cultural beliefs that women who are victims of sexual or domestic violence have precipitated the violence with their behaviour. For instance, almost one half of the European Union respondents in one survey viewed the provocative behaviour of women as a cause of violence against women.[2] And, women who are victimised in the home are seen as in part responsible since they have remained there.[3] A similar "victim-blaming" ethos has been found in workplaces with sexual harassment:

---

[1] See, for example: Patricia Easteal, *Voices of the Survivors* (Spinifex Press, 1994); Patricia Easteal, *Less Than Equal* (Butterworths, 2001).

[2] Enrique Gracia 'Unreported Cases of Domestic Violence against Women: Towards an Epidemiology of Social Silence, Tolerance, and Inhibition' (2004) 58 *Journal of Epidemiology and Community Health* 536, 536.

[3] Patricia Easteal and Louise McOrmond-Plummer, *Real Rape, Real Pain* (Hybrid Publishers, 2006).

> Although many women officers experience sexual harassment, they have not united or taken coordinated action to press for change. Instead, women tend to reproach other women, asserting that those who get sexually harassed "ask for it" through their demeanor or behaviour. Such victim blaming makes the woman rather than her harasser the target of criticism.[4]

Minimising and/or trivialising abuse may be a psychological mechanism triggered by the dynamics of the violence.[5] Such feelings are also correlates of community attitudes that minimise some violence against women behaviours. For instance, in instances of partner rape, victims who disclose may experience responses that discount their harm such as being told that they are feeling sorry for themselves or that they are overreacting to something that is not really a "big deal" and since they stayed or returned that it couldn't have "hurt very badly".[6] In the context of sexual harassment, "Abuse, taunts, insults and other everyday micro-inequities of harassment that are sexed are trivialised and dismissed because they are deemed to be insufficiently *sexual*".[7]

These attitudes are conducive to both individual[8] and community denial.[9] For the victims or targets of violence, the "bizarre" and abusive actions may become normalised and unnamed. This is contributed to by their socialisation within a culture pervasive with mythology, which defines violence in narrow terms. In the context of sexual harassment, behaviours may become so "routine or habitual that they become functionally invisible".[10] The Australian Human Rights Commission accordingly found that "22 per cent of respondents who said they had not experienced 'sexual harassment' then went on to disclose about

---

[4] Susan Ehrlich Martin and Nancy C Jurik, Doing Justice, Doing Gender: Women in Legal and Criminal Justice Occupations (Women in the Criminal Justice System) (SAGE Publications, 2009) 73.

[5] Katreena Scott and Murray Straus, 'Denial, Minimization, Partner Blaming, and Intimate Aggression in Dating Partners' (2007) 22(7) *Journal of Interpersonal Violence* 851.

[6] Easteal and McOrmond-Plummer, above n 3, 180.

[7] Margaret Thornton, 'Sexual Harassment Losing Sight of Sex Discrimination' [2002] 26(2) *Melbourne University Law Review* 422.

[8] Karin V Rhodes and Wendy Levinson 'Interventions for Intimate Partner Violence Against Women Clinical Applications' (2003) 289(5) *The Journal of the American Medical Association* 601.

[9] Linda McKie, *Families, Violence and Social Change* (Open University Press, 2005) 152.

[10] Fiona Wilson and Paul Thompson, 'Sexual Harassment as an Exercise of Power' (2001) 8(1) *Gender, Work & Organization* 61.

behaviours that may in fact constitute sexual harassment under the *Sex Discrimination Act 1984*".[11]

A rural landscape drenched in masculinity

Australian rural mythology continues to revere "male dominance" as a norm, which is ingrained in daily rural life.[12] Masculinity is celebrated as being the essence of rural spirit and "is typically constituted in rural sites and spaces as visible marker of strength, courage and power, in familiar symbolic representations of the farmer, the frontier settler, the hunter, the stockman and the cowboy".[13] It is also known that through engagement in heavy manual labour (which is a feature of rural life and which "involves physical effort and often shared dangers"), a type of "group solidarity and a spirit of masculine camaraderie is created".[14]

> They believe that Jack is as good as his master, or even better; that mates must never bludge on one another; that a man's word is his bond; that women are inferior to men; and that the company of mates is preferable to the company of women. However, the opportunities for expressing such values and beliefs are severely limited.[15]

In combination with the ethos of male power in the bush, some academics and commentators have considered that the general "dangers of bush life' render the rural space as 'no place for a woman".[16]

---

[11] Australian Human Rights Commission *Sexual Harassment: Serious Business* (Australian Human Rights Commission, 2008). <http://www.hreoc.gov.au/sexualharassment/serious_business/index.html> 14.
[12] Elaine Barclay, Joseph Donnermeyer, John Scott and Russell Hogg, *Crime in Rural Australia* (Federation Press, 2007).
[13] Russell Hogg and Kerry Carrington, *Policing the Rural Crisis* (Federation Press, 2006) 164.
[14] Linda McDowell, *Identity and Place: Understanding Feminist Geographies* (Polity Press in association with Blackwell Publishers, 1999) 141.
[15] Kenneth Dempsey, 'Chapter 8: Mateship in Country Towns', in John Carroll (ed) *Intruders in the Bush: The Australian Quest for Identity* (Oxford University Press, 1982) 131.
[16] Kay Schaffer, *Women and the Bush* (Forces of Desire in the Australian Cultural Tradition) (Cambridge University Press, 1988) 52.

Our study

The view of "women as other"[17] in the bush has necessitated the implementation of survival mechanisms for rural women. It is within this context that we wanted to study the degree to which those in rural workplaces put the responsibility for sexual harassment on the targets and/or minimised or denied that the sexual harassment took place. We hypothesised that these types of attitudes would be consistent with the bush culture of "segregating and ridiculing of women, and the stereotyping of them as an inferior group", which "builds the bonds of mateship and strengthens the masculine identity of men".[18] To test the hypothesis, a sample of women employees and employers from different parts of remote and regional Australia were interviewed. For the purposes of this research project we have defined "rural" as an area at least 30 kms outside of outer boundaries of an "urban" centre, with relative dispersal of residence on relatively large parcels of land and with generally less than 50 000 people.

In this chapter we explore the way that harassing behaviour is perceived and reacted to in rural workplaces including: beliefs about the reactions/ responses of other women in the workplace to harassing behaviours ("She just keeps asking for it"); feelings of responsibility ("Saying 'no' makes me feel guilty"); minimising ("If you make a fuss you are just a big idiot"); and denial. We investigate whether there are differences in "survival" and cultural behaviours and thinking depending upon the occupation, degree of rurality, gender ratios, age, seniority and/or education of the respondents.

Methodology: Putting Out the "Coo-ee!"

In essence, the modern-day equivalent to the old "bush telegraph" (ie "word-of-mouth") was utilised for the recruitment of participants, through use of social networking tools such as Facebook and by email and word of mouth. The Facebook tool enabled Saunders to make contact with potential interviewees who were referred through the "private message" box function. Rurally located friends, families, colleagues and old school acquaintances all helped in "spreading the word" about this research.

Eighty-four women employees and 23 employers (two males) were interviewed. These took place between July and December 2011 following approval by the University of Canberra's Committee for Ethics in Human

---

[17] Ibid, 13–14.

[18] Dempsey, above n 15, 139.

Research. Protecting the anonymity of participants was the main ethical consideration in this project. Before responding to the survey, respondents were asked to read the participant information form and sign a consent form, both of which confirmed that all responses would be de-identified. Initially all respondents were interviewed face-to-face with Saunders travelling to rural and remote destinations in Western Australia, the Northern Territory, South Australia and New South Wales. Not wishing to lose the "voices" of the most remotely based participants though, it became apparent that telephone interviews would be a good complement. It was preferred too by some participants who required an evening interview time. Interviews were recorded and transcribed and took from 30 minutes to 90 minutes with an average of an hour, depending on the experiences of each participant. One researcher, Saunders, completed a recording form for each interviewee.

Data analysis

A single individual translated the recording forms into numerical variables; this ensured that there would be no inter-coder variation.[19] For analysis we merged certain occupations to allow for meaningful comparison: teachers and nurses are grouped as "professional"; agriculture and horticulture are one category and we have aggregated those working in retail, hospitality or fast food. We also designated our workplaces/locations by degree of rurality using the following population cut offs: high = 0–5000; average–high = 5001–15 000; average = 15 001–30 000; average–low = 30 001–50 000; and low = >50 000. In addition the responses to two questions ("How does sexual harassment make you feel?" and "Why do you think people sexually harass others in the workplace?") were aggregated into two categories to allow for some analysis, albeit limited by the low response rate. All serious effects ("angry", "hurt", "anxious", "hopeless", "humiliated and powerless", "degraded") were merged into one category and labelled as "serious". Other responses such as "can help you in your job", "depends on person", "didn't worry me", "you get used to it", were considered by us as "minimising". The answers given to why people sexually harass were grouped similarly. Examples of minimising responses included: "blokiness", "boys being pig-headed", "harmless", "joking, usually".

[19] Our thanks to Sally Bradford for her invaluable statistical assistance and guidance.

"Serious" included: "Exert power", "gain power", "power plays", "power thing", and "power trip".

Using PASW Statistics 19, the total data set (n=104) was cross-tabulated looking at variation in responses to relevant questions with sociodemographic variables such as age, seniority, education, rurality, occupation and ratio of men to women in workplace. In addition, employers (n=23) and employees' responses to some questions were compared. A Pearson's chi-square test of contingencies was used to evaluate statistical significance. Where appropriate, a series of unplanned 2x2 post hoc analyses were conducted to determine where statistical difference lay. The size of the cells in a number of cross-tabulations (eg more than one cell with less than five) precluded generation of statistically meaningful tests of variation.

Caveats

The number of rural workplaces with staff included in this study is not large enough to be representative of rural Australian workplaces. When disaggregated by occupation for instance, 11 per cent of respondents worked in the mines. It is unlikely that 11 per cent of females employed in rural areas are employed in the mining industry.

Further, people who participated in this research were self-selected as described above. It is possible that they were more likely to have experienced sexual harassment and were keen to discuss their experiences. Therefore the results reported next should be regarded as preliminary — providing indications but not necessarily absolutes.

Note too that whilst the definition of "rural" is a term that is intuitively ingrained into the psyche of most Australian people, most academics agree that the term "rural" is an elusive one[20] and that it is "constructed differently by different people".[21] Our sample is reflective of *our* definition and therefore our findings are limited by those boundaries. One issue with the categorisation of "rural" by number of people is that "some towns may be classified as rural based on population size, density or location, but still have ready access to many facilities owing to their proximity to major population centres".[22] In light of these obvious complexities in capturing the definition of rural, some academics prefer to define it as being

[20] Barclay et al, above n 12, 1.

[21] Sarah Wendt, *Domestic Violence in Rural Australia* (Federation Press, 1999) 15.

[22] Digby Race, Gary Luck and Rosemary Black, Demographic Change in Australia's Rural Landscapes: Implications for Society and the Environment (Springer, 2011) 4.

anything that does not fall within the definition of metropolitan.[23] Whilst this provides a relatively simple springboard from which to examine rural trends, we recognise that the danger is that if the term "rural" is used to classify most regions outside of the coastal metropolitan areas, "it may cease to have much in the way of descriptive veracity at all, despite its continuing cultural resonances".[24] While we had to impose population cut-offs for the degree of rurality, it is important, though, to also consider the predominant view of local residents in places such as Orange (which is a proud "rural community") and this involves the identification of "elements of rural place/landscape/society/existence which together provide an approximation of the overarching concept of rurality"[25].

Victim Blaming

> I feel — you know — we hear all about sexual harassment and things like that — but I also think that the female working in a male dominated business or area or whatever the situation may be — well, I think she has to set some standards herself and not just expect the men to come up to a standard. She has to set a standard for them to meet, if you understand what I am saying. So if she comes in all sort of "rah-di-rah" and you know, a fair bit of language, the men aren't going to have any boundaries. You have to set those boundaries by the way you are yourself. So that is just something that I feel is quite important … I just think that it all comes down to how the girl behaves. As to how she is treated. (Office administrator, aged 50, average level rurality)

That office administrator's view of victim responsibility was not a solo voice. Sixty per cent of 62 employee respondents and 83 per cent of 18 employer respondents believed that a woman contributes to her own victimisation. The following response encapsulated this type of thinking:

> Sometimes I have felt some of the things that I have talked about were my own fault. You know how it is when someone is talking in a really friendly way — and you are all getting on in a really friendly way and then the talk degenerates. Or maybe you have been part of a discussion that has been a little bit questionable in nature. Maybe you have been talking to another lady and someone comes along and assumes that it is open slather for them

---

[23] Robyn Mason, 'Building Women's Social Citizenship: A Five-point Framework to Conceptualise the Work of Women-specific Services in Rural Australia'(2007) 30 *Women's Studies International Forum* 299.

[24] Barclay et al above n 12, 4.

[25] Paul Cloke, Terry Marsden and Patrick Moody *The Handbook of Rural Studies* (SAGE Publications, 2006) 20–21.

> to be involved too. And if they are in a senior position to you and you are like me, you just try to pass it off and diffuse and finish it. The problem is, sometimes it works and sometimes it doesn't. (Teacher, aged 48, average level ruality)

Women were perceived as blameworthy because of their provocative behaviour:

> I honestly don't know, but I think it really comes down to how you react and how you conduct yourself, as to how people are going to react to you, a lot of it. You know, if you are going to walk around in mini skirts and you know, with half ya boobs hangin' out in front of you know, truck drivers and things like that — and if you don't expect to get comments from them in your dressing behaviour for example — then you're an absolute fool! (Grainary employee, aged 52, average level rurality)

This categorisation of a woman as a "fool" for conducting herself in such a way that might "invite" sexual harassment was referred to by other women in response to questions about barriers preventing women from reporting incidents of sexual harassment:

> … the community might be perceived as thinking that she is a trouble maker. So people will think she bloody well asked for it. (Environmental Scientist, aged 30, high level rurality)

More than one woman also spoke about the impact of her relationship status on the perception of her blameworthiness for acts of gendered harm in a rural community:

> And this is another aspect — in a rural community if you are a single mother, there is a perception that a single woman with a child is more likely to lose their moral code than just about anyone. When single mothers live in the bush they need to battle the quick assumption that "she invited it" or "watch that one". So in terms of the rural community supporting single mothers who are vulnerable to this sort of thing, I don't think this happens because they are seen as a threat to their own marriages. That makes life so hard and it makes you incredibly wary. (Teacher, aged 48, moderate–high level rurality)

Women working in more male dominated environments such as the grainary (less than 25 per cent of women) were significantly more likely to believe that women contribute to their own victimisation than participants in workplaces of 25–50 per cent women, ($\chi^2(1,N=52)=10.19$), and participants in workplaces of over 75 per cent women ($\chi^2(1,N=37)=11.16$). (See Table 5-1).

Table 5-1: Proportion of women in the workplace and responses to question of whether respondent believes that women contribute to their own victimisation

Proportion of women in the workplace		
	Yes	No
<25 (n=25)	92	8
25–50 (n=27)	52	48
50–75% (n=14)	57	43
>75% (n=12)	42	58

A female employer from a male dominated environment reflected on a situation, which required her to counsel a female employee about her choice of clothing — in the context of that employee having approached her with a complaint about offensive office conversation:

> I do remember one occasion where I had an employee who I did have to talk to about how she dressed for work. And she had come to me a little bit offended about some conversation in the office. (Senior Mining Consultant, aged 38, high level rurality)

Some women in occupations with token females conceded, however, that it was not *always* the victim's fault:

> Quite often you could not take responsibility for the way that a conversation turns out, though. I think that whole creep phenomenon is really important to consider. (Senior Manager in Mining, female, aged 42, high level rurality)

The belief that women contribute to acts of sexual harassment against them was also related to the participants' occupation (χ^2=(4,N=70)=15.13, p=0.004) as shown in Figure 5-1.

Figure 5-1: Occupation and belief that women contribute to their own victimisation

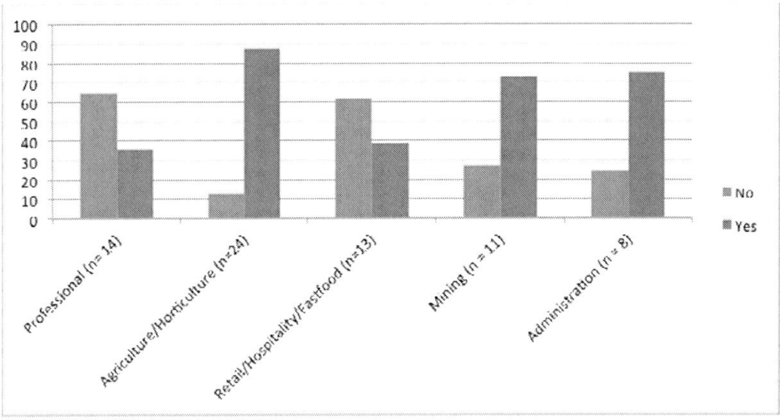

Those employed in agriculture/horticulture professions (21 of 24) were significantly more likely to believe that women contribute to their own victimisation than the five of 14 professionals ($\chi^2(1,N=38)=10.98$) and the five of 13 in retail/hospitality/fastfood occupations ($\chi^2=(1,N=70)=9.71$). For example, one agricultural employer would reframe harassment complaints, putting the focus on the targets' responses:

> I would say to them that they need to learn to cope with it. You just need to be cut out for it and some girls are obviously not … Yeah, people often ask me what it is about me that makes me able to handle men. You need to be assertive but not aggressive. If you are aggressive you just hear 'em say "Geez, she is a cranky bitch". If you are just assertive they will take your shit and make friends with you. You just need to show 'em you are not a weak little girl who needs looking after. (Senior Manager, Grainary, high level rurality)

There was also a tendency for some women to blame themselves for finding pornography offensive. One participant was asked about how she felt about the presence of the "dick mags" that she had identified as being prevalent on the cattle station:

> Oh I was usually pretty disgusted I guess. I was a pretty uptight sort of a person … Like I shouldn't judge myself for my reaction, but I wasn't particularly open to all that. (Jillaroo, aged 28, high level rurality)

A female senior winemaker from South Australia made a number of references to her belief that women, including herself, contribute to acts of sexual harassment. Asked about her response to receiving sexually explicit emails from a colleague, she said:

> Yes, it was revolting. I suppose in the most obvious way. I would get emails all the time to my home account. I felt very inadequate because as I said, we have had all this training and I still felt that I had done something wrong in the first place. I never took it any further because I didn't want to upset anyone in the community. This guy was married. It would have been terrible if the community had known — a married man with kids. (Aged 48, moderate–high level rurality)

This participant further defended the propensity for sexual harassment by male employees by highlighting that sometimes women are the inflictors of the behaviour:

> Yes, people have complained to me about innuendo or direct sleazy jokes. In the vineyards there were some women who would talk about sex all the time, though. And even young guys were scared of these women, too.

The only other significant variable was age (χ^2=(4,N=80)=12.18, p=0.016): Table 5-2 shows that only one of the eight respondents under the age of 20 believed that women contribute to their own victimisation.

Table 5-2: Do respondents of different ages believe that women contribute to their own victimisation

Age of employee	Do they believe that women contribute to their own victimisation?	
	Yes	No
<20 (n=8)	13	87
21–25 (n=16)	75	25
26–35 (n=29)	69	31
36–45 (n=11)	82	18
>46 (n=14)	57	43

A 19 year old female sandwich maker from Western Australia spoke vehemently about the need to put a stop to sexually harassing text messages:

> I told them to back off and all it took was the one firm message and there was no problem at all. I was clear that the feelings were just not reciprocated. (Low–moderate level rurality)

Another 19 year old woman who worked in a hardware store spoke about how her male colleagues were "misguided" in their behaviour:

> Um, looking back at it now I think it was one of those things where they really misguidedly thought that people were going to be impressed by their behaviour. (Hardware store assistant, low–moderate level rurality)

Minimising/Normalising

The interview instrument included a question about how sexual harassment made the respondent feel. There was a low response rate to this query: 45 of the 75 who did reply expressed a "serious" response. The remaining 30 minimised. For instance, one woman explained why "it didn't bother" her:

> It's everywhere. You know, screensavers, magazines lying around in crib rooms or on the floors. I know where all the hidey places are! At the end of the day, though, I would rather them look at magazines than me, so it doesn't bother me. (Electrical engineer, aged 30, high level rurality).

In response to a question about why people harass, two thirds (of 54) minimised. The 18 respondents who appeared to appreciate the seriousness tended to mention "power" in their reasoning. Professionals were more likely to see sexual harassment as a serious concern (5:6), as compared to 2:20 agriculturalists, 2:5 retail assistants, half of those in mining and none of the three working in administrative positions. Accordingly, a Livestock Agency Officer (female, aged 30, average level rurality) stated: "I just don't think people take it seriously out here", while a public servant (female, aged 26, moderate level rurality) said "It's probably an unconscious sort of thing, but yeah, I probably treat things as a joke generally. That's probably my personality as well. I don't want to make a fuss of something".

As illustrated in Table 5-3, employers were more likely to minimise the reasons for sexual harassment than employees (χ^2=(1,N=54)=4.34, p=0.037); however the effect size was small, (Φ=-0.28).

Table 5-3: Do employers and employees minimise or understand the seriousness of why people sexually harass

Do people minimise or understand the seriousness of why people sexually harass?				
	Minimise		Recognise seriousness	
	N	%	N	%
Employees	25	59.5	17	40.5
Employers	11	92	1	8

The following comment from a grainary manager is illustrative of a management perspective that minimises and normalises the behaviours as part of the culture:

> Yes, I have had complaints from the girls at the grain stand. Like they might say "that truck driver has just sworn at me" and I might have to remind 'em that they were made aware of it when they took on the role. But it is just not easy for me to change the workplace behaviour itself. That is a whole other thing and you can't just change the behaviour like that … (Aged 26, high level rurality)

Figure 5-2 indicates that participants who believed that women contribute to their own victimisation were also likely to minimise the reasons why people sexually harass (χ^2=(1,N=46)=5.72, p=0.017 with a moderate effect size, Φ=-0.35).

Figure 5-2: Beliefs about why people sexually harass by a belief that women contribute to their own victimisation

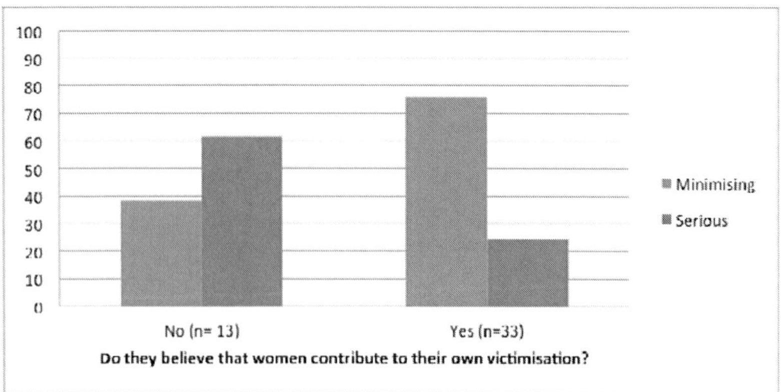

The words of a female manager in the trucking industry reflect this combination of victim-blaming and minimising:

> But if you work in rural Australia in a male dominated environment people like the drivers and farmers just think that it is normal and OK to make a dirty joke. Like, especially about your appearance … Like, if you are butch for example, you would hear lots of comments about what you get up to and what you look like. You either learn to handle it and fire it back at 'em like me or, you don't. I know that the guys don't mean it as being distasteful. (Aged 28, high level rurality)

Another Manager interviewee blamed her own dress style for unwanted staring or leering:

> … but that is probably my fault. You can see how I am dressed this morning. I never do my top buttons up … it is probably not being particularly careful either. But I have never dressed any different so … yeah. (Rangeland Manager, 50 years, high level rurality)

"It's all a bloody big boy's club out here"

A part of the minimising or normalising ethos seems to be an attitude about sexual harassment that it is just "boys being boys". Of the 70 who responded to the question "Do you regard sexual harassment as just 'boys being boys'?" 50 (71 per cent) answered affirmatively. There were no significant differences based on age, employer/employee, seniority, education, marital status or degree of rurality. The type of workplace, as shown in Figure 5-3, had a moderate effect (χ^2=(4,N=60)=16.10, p<0.001).

Participants working in agriculture/horticulture (χ^2=(1,N=38)=13.21) and those working in mining (χ^2=(1,N=21)=8.24) were significantly more likely to believe that sexual harassment is just "boys being boys" than participants within professional occupations. For example, one female who was employed as a geotechnical engineer for a mining company described having experienced unwanted physical touching, rude jokes, sexual banter and exposure to various types of pornography in the workplace. She maintained that it was preferable not to report these behaviours:

> I know it sounds bad, but you do get used to it. It's again — "boys being boys" or "men being men". Because it is a male dominated environment that is just how they are. It feels like, I suppose, you have to accept it. The way I see it, it is their workplace — oh that sounds very wrong! But it does just seem like it is their workplace. (Aged 26, high level rurality)

Figure 5-3: Occupation by belief that sexual harassment is about "boys being boys"

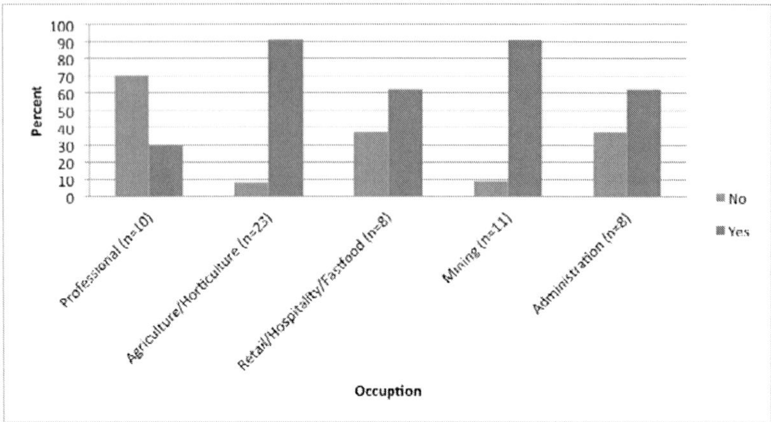

A horticulturalist, who identified as a lesbian, spoke of the reality of the "boys' club" in her outdoor workplace:

> I think it is just like a footy club. You get sweaty men together doing manual work and feeling good about being blokey. That drives it. It is quite usual when the boys are sitting down having smoko and they will be talking about their experiences of sex on the weekend. (Horticulturalist, 43 years, lesbian, average level rurality)

Similarly, a remote-area jillaroo reflected on her experience of the "boys club":

> Yeah, there was a bit of that (rude comments in general). I put it down to boys being boys. It sounds horrible but that was what it was … you are living with these people too. You can't just go home from work and that is it. 'Cause it was just like you would see them in the staff common room for dinner … And you would see these people at lunch time and on coffee breaks and in the laundry. (Aged 22, high level rurality)

The belief that sexual harassment is just "boys being boys" was also related to the proportion of women in the workplace of the participant (χ^2=(3,N=67)=14.23, p=0.003, with a moderate effect size, Φ=.46) (see Figure 5-4).

Those working in workplaces predominantly staffed by men were significantly more likely to hold this belief than participants in workplaces of over 75 per cent women (χ^2=(1,N=35)=10.64). Accordingly, a senior female manager in a mostly male staffed mining industry expressed the view that the small town "boy's culture" contributed to the gradual acceptance of pornography in the workplace:

> But professionals also develop a sense of tolerance for the other lifestyle — so the topless becomes OK. And then you suddenly realise — or I did — that it is not OK that you have developed such a tolerance for being served by a woman without a shirt or bra on. And with that you realise that you have to get out before you forget that it is not normal. (Aged 28, high level rurality)

Figure 5-4: "Boys being boys" by proportion of women in the workplace

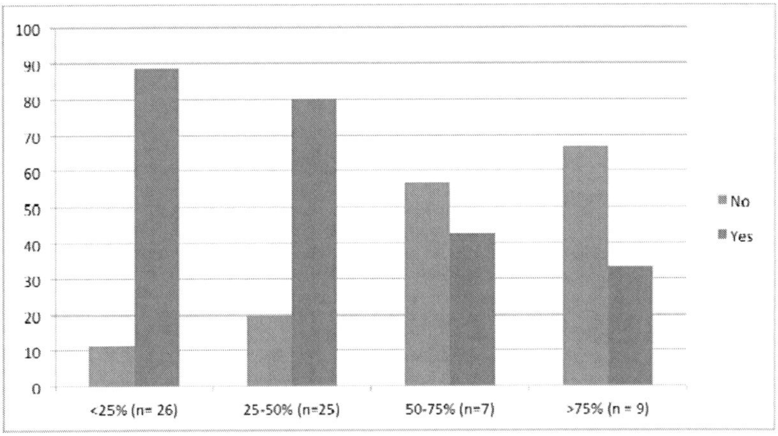

Denial

Forty-one per cent of employees and more than two thirds (68 per cent) of employers appeared to deny sexual harassment (χ^2=(1,N=102)=5.02, p=0.025), although the effect was small, (Φ=.22). One female manager of a large sheep station spoke of the harassment by her male co-workers in a relatively dismissive manner:

> I think some thought that I was probably going to be an easy lay — there is no proper way of saying it. It was just because I was there and they thought I was that way inclined — and I wasn't. And this was a rude shock for some of them. (Aged 40, high level rurality)

Is banter harassment?

An aspect of denial is not recognising certain behaviours as sexual harassment. A third of the sample did not answer the question about whether banter is harassment; tests of significance were therefore limited. Overall the majority (37:69) responded negatively. One participant, employed as a geotechnical engineer in a mining community, commented on the disparity between perceptions of banter in the workplace:

> People are just — the guys just look at it as fun. Fun and banter. Whereas girls may not see it that way. So they would say "it's just fun" and then a girl complains, procedures are followed and so forth — then it may look bad on her part because she took it to a wrong level or it wasn't meant in that way. But that is the same for anyone really. (Female, aged 26, high level rurality)

Significantly fewer employers believed that banter is sexual harassment (24 per cent) as compared to employees (56 per cent) ($\chi^2(1,N=69)=6.18$, $p=0.013$, with a small effect size, $\Phi=0.229$). One woman, for instance, who managed a cattle station in the northern part of Australia with her husband, spoke of the tendency for jackaroos to engage in banter on the job:

> Yeah, I mean they are suggestive and rude. But you can hear a joke like that and find it funny as against plain old outright "filthy". That's the difference between something that is funny and something that is plain and outright "crap". And I don't think the boys here would tell me something like that that had no funniness to it. (Station manager, female, aged 30, high level rurality)

Is pornography harassment?

Almost two thirds did not answer the question about whether pornography constituted sexual harassment; this made the data highly unreliable and statistical testing problematic. Twenty of the 28 employees who did respond believed porn to be sexual harassment while only six of the 14 employer participants had that view. For example, a female employer based in Kalgoorlie running an environmental consultancy for the mines seemed to feel that topless pin-up girl posters were benignly ubiquitous stating that, "It doesn't bother me at all". She also asserted that she would not interfere with people clustering at desks to look at pictures unless it was taking up a lot of their time and distracting them from doing their work.

All the professionals who responded to this question (n=6) replied "yes". And, 86 per cent of those employed in mining (n=7) saw pornography as harassment in contrast to half of the agriculture/horticulture (n=16) and retail/hospitality/fast food (n=2) and 60 per cent of the five administration workers who answered.

Turning a blind eye

Either reflecting denial or contributing to it were the 85 per cent (n=72 respondents) of employees and 77 per cent of employers (n=22) who believed that it is best to ignore the behaviour.

> I have experienced a man physically exposing himself to me. And not just to me — to anyone else who was around. Repeatedly. Countless times … This was an underground person who was in middle management. So when I would be underground he would often be too. There seems to be an old-school group of men who believe that women don't belong underground. And I've even heard it said that women are bad luck underground. And there is a group of men who think that it is funny to try to shock you underground. Or make you feel uncomfortable … I would ignore it! I certainly never did anything about it! … To me, if someone wants to show themselves it is more a reflection of them than a reflection of me. (Environmental Advisor in Mining, aged 36, high level rurality)

In response to a question about whether she felt confident that she would be free from workplace sexual harassment in the future, one woman's answer demonstrated that — on balance — she thought it best to ignore physical touching in the workplace and to contextualise the experience as "humorous":

> Here — yes, I am confident that I won't be harassed. Although the boss did tell me that I wasn't allowed to tell ya, but he pats me on the bum all the time. Which is a bit crap! (laughs). He said "Now don't you tell that girl anything!" (Laughs again). But that's the kind of fun that we have without being — you know — that's what I mean by "humour". Something like that is funny but it does have some overtones at times, I suppose … (fades thoughtfully). (Agricultural office administrator, aged 50, average–high level rurality)

Is sexual harassment an issue in rural Australia?

This was another question that tested or screened for attitudes that correlate with denial. Evidently, if looking at sexual harassment in the abstract and not in one's own workplace, far more people see it as an issue and do not deny that sexual harassment is an issue. Three quarters of the respondents (n=89) answered affirmatively.

One respondent spoke about the perils of being employed in a position, which required working in isolated bush areas. In her response she referred to broader issues of "sexual stuff" affecting women and which she ultimately regarded as "part of life, to be honest" (Rangeland manager, aged 50, very rural).

Those working in low degree of rurality places were significantly more likely to believe that sexual harassment is a big issue in rural Australia (24:26) than those participants living in more remote areas (17:33) (Fisher's=(4,N=89)=17.63, p=0.001, with a medium effect size, Φ=0.45).

> No, I don't. Don't get me wrong, I think there is prejudice against women, but you do have to — I don't know — you just have to put more into your job to prove your worth, maybe? (Geotechnical engineer, aged 26, high level rurality)

Conclusion: "It Sounds Bad — But You Just Get Used to it. It's Just 'Boys Being Boys' …"

Our research confirms that the tendency to make sexual harassment invisible, or if not invisible a mere shadow of the targets' reality, appears fairly widespread in rural workplaces. We have seen how apportioning (some of) the responsibility onto the victims or targets and constructing abusive behaviours in a trivial way contribute to denial.

A disturbing proportion of respondents — two thirds — believed that the women's behaviour, including how they respond to these types of incidents, contributes at least in part to their victimisation. Not surprisingly such attitudes were more common in workplaces that were more masculinised — those with a low ratio of women. Participants from these workplaces were also more likely to believe that sexual harassment is about "boys being boys", with those employed as horticulturalist/agriculturalists or in mining and staff from workplaces with few women most likely to ascribe to this viewpoint. This is unsurprising because we know that in male-dominated workplaces, the affirmation of men as "mates" occurs "through bonding and rituals within homosocial (white, heterosexual) groups"[26]) In occupations (such as those from which

---

[26] Michael Flood, Judith Gardiner, Bob Pease and Keith Pringle (eds), *International Encyclopaedia of Men and Masculinities* (Routledge Press, 2007) 400.

our participants were likely to accept sexual harassment as "boys being boys") this masculine bonding may involve the elements of "physical effort" and "shared dangers"[27] referred to above, as well as the enforcement of male power "in talk and workplace jokes".[28] Regardless of the manifestation of the male bonding, it is widely acknowledged that "one of the obvious exclusionary characteristics of the concept is that women tend not to be included in most understandings of mateship and what it means to be a mate".[29] For this reason, women in male dominated occupations were likely to accept sexual harassment as part of the workplace norm.

Although 60 per cent of respondents identified that sexual harassment had "serious" effects, two thirds had minimising responses to the question about why people sexually harass. Professionals were most likely to see power at the core and were also the occupation most apt to identify pornography as a type of sexual harassment. It is possible that through ongoing education, professionals may have developed a higher order, moral understanding of pornography as an assertion of male power in the workplace, rather than viewing it as a mere form of "naughty entertainment". The professional values associated with elite positions may also create a heightened awareness of potentially destructive workplace problems such as the blatant (or even subtle) display of pornographic material at work. It has been suggested that professionalism means "being productive and maintaining social distance with colleagues at work".[30]

The majority of respondents, however, did not appear to understand the dynamics of sexual harassment and its aetiology. Not surprisingly there was a correlation between these people and those who possessed victim-blaming beliefs.

Perhaps our most disturbing finding concerned the attitudes of employers/managers. A troubling proportion — more than four fifths of employers — believed that the women's behaviour, including how they respond to these types of incidents, contributes at least in part to their victimisation. Of some alarm too, employers appear significantly less knowledgeable about the dynamics/causes of sexual harassment. Employers

---

[27] Linda McDowell, *Gender, Identity and Place: Understanding Feminist Geographies* (Polity Press in association with Blackwell Publishers, 1999) 141.
[28] Ibid, 136.
[29] James S Page, 'Is Mateship a Virtue?' (2002) 37(2) *Australian Journal of Social Issues* 193, 195.
[30] Abigail C Saguy, *What Is Sexual Harassment: From Capitol Hill to the Sorbonne* (University of California Press, 2003) 119.

were also more likely than their staff to deny that sexual harassment takes place with less than one quarter considering banter to be harassment. In this context, Joan Acker discusses the phenomenon that "the willingness to tolerate sexual harassment is often a condition of the job, both as a consequence and a cause of gender hierarchy".[31]

Given that the rural workplace is deeply entrenched in tradition, it is unsurprising that workplace norms — such as the establishment of sexually harassing culture — are fixed and are not easily transformed. For this reason, rural employers and employees alike become accustomed to the saturation of sexual harassment in the workplace. "Unchallenged behaviour" was the way a female public servant from rural Western Australia described it. In support of the weight attributed to entrenched tradition, sexual harassment remains unchallenged regardless of the employer's gender. This is further exemplified by the prevalence of the "*fit in or f#$% off!* policy" that was cited by both employers and employees as a male catch-cry. This informal "policy", which serves to reinforce the entrenched tradition, is literally and shamelessly utilised in the rural workplace for maintaining gendered hierarchy in a traditional male space.

One potentially optimistic finding — an indication that these attitudes could in fact be changing — came from the seven of eight employees under the age of 20 who did not apportion any responsibility onto the targets. However, we must note that three quarters of those in their early- to mid-20s did express victim-blaming beliefs and so the other data may be an anomaly and not a significant harbinger of change.

The other finding that could bode well for tomorrow's targets: the three quarters of respondents who identified sexual harassment as an issue for rural Australia. The recognition of the issue as a general proposition is indeed very good at least in theory, but problematically, the *same* participants were often reluctant to identify "sexual harassment" with their *own* negative workplace experiences. It may be that the combination of the intensely "male" tradition in the rural workplace with women's gradual acquisition of "a kind of gut knowledge that they are outsiders"[32] leads to personal disempowerment which makes it easier for women to identify sexual harassment as a real threat in the *general* rural community. This may be compounded by the participants' awareness of the difficulties associated with "making a fuss" about harassment issues in their own workplace. That is, women understand that the backlash for identifying

---

[31] Joan Acker 'Hierarchies, Jobs, Bodies: A Theory of Gendered Organizations' (1990) 4(2) *Gender and Society* 139, 152.

[32] Miriam Dixson, The Real Matilda — Women and Identity in Australia 1788 to the Present (UNSW Press, 1999) 21.

sexual harassment in their workplace may include being deemed to be "making a fuss about nothing", being deemed to have "invited" any sexual harassment that is identified, the possibility of a complaint not being believed at all or the potential incitement of community gossip.[33] In view of these real possibilities, it may be that *not* identifying sexual harassment as an immediate problem in their *personal* workplaces is a self-defence mechanism in itself: the recognition of an issue as affecting *other* women is acceptable, but the recognition of an issue as being one of concern for herself adds to the woman's sense of vulnerability, and so she denies its impact. It has been suggested that this type of defence strategy is relatively common for victims of harassment:

> Coping strategies that manage the cognitions and emotions associated with the event are generally more common; such strategies include simply tolerating the harassment, denying that it is happening or that it has any effect, reinterpreting the behaviour as benign, trying to forget about it and (less commonly) blaming oneself.[34]

It is evident then that people in the rural workplace need to learn more about what constitutes sexual harassment and its effects and remedies. This was shown by the huge majority of respondents who expressed the view that it is best to ignore sexual harassment behaviours. It was also evident in the way that some respondents expressed "confused" understanding about the experience of sexual harassment and who is at fault.

The National Guidelines[35] explain that there is "no uniform standard expected of employers in taking all reasonable steps" to prevent sexual harassment, although at "*minimum*" employers should "have an appropriate sexual harassment policy which is effectively implemented, monitored and communicated to all workplace participants". The design and implantation of appropriate workplace policy in rural Australia first requires that employers understand prescribed legislative requirements. It is clear from our discussions with rural employers that these laws are not always fully understood or enforced at the senior level. For this reason, we recommend that "sexual harassment consultants" travel a strategic rural

---

[33] Skye Saunders and Patricia Easteal, '"Fit in or F$%# Off!" The (non)Reporting of Sexual Harassment in the Rural Workplace' (Paper presented at the National Rural, Regional Law and Justice Conference (UNE), Coffs Harbour, May 2012).

[34] Louise Fitzgerald, Suzanne Swan & Karla Fischer, 'Why Didn't She Just Report Him? The Psychological and Legal Implications of Women's Responses to Sexual Harassment' (1995) 51 *Journal of Social Issues* 117.

[35] Australian Human Rights Commission, above n 11.

Australian circuit, offering training seminars, workshops and consultations specifically to rural employers and senior managers, with a view to educating at a senior level.

This might then have a flow-on effect permeating the workplace culture. Employers would become equipped to communicate comprehensive policies to their employees, either with the ongoing assistance of a "sexual harassment consultant" or independently. "Sexual harassment consultants" would also offer tailored services to rural employees. These might include seminars, workshops and consultations focused on: identifying sexual harassment in the workplace; reporting that harassment with confidence; examining the legislative rights of the employee through that process; and emphasising the importance of supporting other employees who have experienced sexual harassment.

In the context of "supporting other employees", our findings show that there is a tendency in the male-dominated rural workplace for women to exhibit what they refer to as "narky" or "bitchy" behaviours — that is resenting the "attitudes" of their female colleagues or the way that they dress or present themselves to men in the workplace. It is perhaps ironic that in the anxious quest for "mateship", "men hunger for the kinds of friendships they believe women have with each other",[36] yet in the context of the sexual harassment experience "women can resent other women and perceive women as deceitful and untrustworthy".[37] Educating women in rural workplaces about supporting female colleagues may be particularly important in view of the finding that women tend to engage in behaviour which "blames" other women for their experience of sexual harassment. This type of revitalised understanding of other women is a critical component in shattering the myths that underpin the sexual harassment experience for rural women and stripping away the layers of denial, thereby making this type of gendered harm far more visible.

---

[36] Terry Colling, *Beyond Mateship* (Simon & Schuster Australia, 1992) 126.

[37] Gloria Cowan, 'Women's Hostility Toward Women and Rape and Sexual Harassment Myths' (2000) 6 *Violence Against Women* 238.

CHAPTER SIX

FAMILY VIOLENCE, EMPLOYMENT AND ANTI-DISCRIMINATION LAW: THE CHALLENGE FOR LAW REFORM

AMANDA ALFORD

Introduction

The search for law reform solutions to a significant and multifaceted issue like family violence is a challenging one. While family violence "knows no geographical, socio-economic, age, ability, cultural or religious boundaries",[1] there is one common characteristic that many people who experience family violence in Australia share — their participation in paid employment. Indeed, two-thirds of Australian women who report violence by a current partner are in paid employment.[2] Accordingly, and in the face of significant shifts in the nature and regulation of employment in Australia and the evolution of workplaces into our 'new communities', there is increasingly a role for employment and anti-discrimination law in responding to family violence.

---

* This chapter draws upon the author's work as part of the Australian Law Reform Commission's Inquiry team which produced Australian Law Reform Commission, *Family Violence and Commonwealth Laws—Improving Legal Frameworks,* ALRC Report No 117 (2011). To the extent that comments or conclusions in this chapter go beyond those expressed in the Final Report, they are the author's. The author acknowledges the assistance of Professor Rosalind F Croucher in offering comments on drafts of this chapter. The law in this chapter is current as at 21 March 2013.

[1] National Council to Reduce Violence against Women and their Children, Background Paper to Time for Action: *The National Council's Plan to Reduce Violence against Women and their Children 2009–2021* (2009) 16.

[2] Australian Bureau of Statistics, *Personal Safety Survey*, Cat No 4906.0 (ABS, 2005) 11, 34.

The intersection between family violence and the workplace is most compellingly highlighted by the circumstances of those people in paid employment who experience family violence. For example, the story of Jenny:

> Jenny is a very experienced accountant whose employment with a large commercial firm was initially undermined when her abusive partner, Paul, began phoning her workplace to speak to her work colleagues about his failing relationship with Jenny. When Jenny was badly assaulted by Paul in front of her two children, she and the children moved into her mother's small unit. Police charged Paul with assault, and over the following months, Jenny was required on numerous occasions to take time off work to attend both the local court for the assault charges and related Apprehended Violence Order and the Family Court for parenting orders. Jenny also needed to take time off work to have maxillary surgery as a result of the injuries she sustained in the assault. During the court process, Jenny described herself as desperate to attend counselling with her children, but was afraid to ask for any more time off work. When Jenny did request a day's leave to organise alternative accommodation, she was called to a formal meeting at her workplace and was accused by colleagues of "not pulling her weight". Jenny resigned and now has casual employment as a bookkeeper, and as a result has not been able to afford to move out of her mother's small unit.[3]

Stories like Jenny's informed the Australian Law Reform Commission's (ALRC) search for law reform solutions in this area in its Family Violence and Commonwealth Laws Inquiry. This chapter draws upon work done by the ALRC in that Inquiry. Beginningwith the premise that workplaces are the new communities, this chapter examines the capacity of the Australian employment and anti-discrimination law systems to identify and respond to family violence. It discusses the challenges of identifying law reform solutions in this area and identifies and responds to three key questions: First, why is family violence a workplace issue? Secondly, should the employment and anti-discrimination law systems identify and respond to family violence? Finally, what is the best approach to reform?

Background to the ALRC's Inquiry

Increasingly, attention has shifted to the connection between family violence and the workplace and subsequently the potential role for

[3] Redfern Legal Centre, Submission No 15 to Australian Law Reform Commission, *Family Violence and Commonwealth Laws Inquiry*, 5 April 2011.

employment law in this area. The foundational work of academics,[4] bodies such as the Australian Domestic and Family Violence Clearinghouse (ADFVC) and unions,[5] as well as the ALRC has been of particular importance in identifying family violence as an issue in relation to which the employment and anti-discrimination law systems can and should respond.

In July 2010, the then Attorney-General of Australia asked the ALRC to inquire into and report on the treatment of family violence in a number of Commonwealth laws, including employment law. The ALRC was asked to identify what, if any, improvements could be made to relevant legal frameworks to protect the safety of those experiencing family violence. The ALRC was required to consider legislative arrangements across the Commonwealth that affect those experiencing family violence and whether they impose barriers to providing effective support to those adversely affected by this type of violence.[6]

The Inquiry culminated in the release of *Family Violence and Commonwealth Laws—Improving Legal Frameworks*, ALRC Report 117

---

[4] See, for example: A Moe and M Bell, 'Abject Economics: The Effects of Batterings and Violence on Women's Work and Employability' (2004) 10(1) *Violence Against Women* 29; J Swanberg, T Logan and C Macke, 'Intimate Partner Violence, Employment and the Workplace: Consequences and Future Directions' (2005) 6 *Trauma, Violence and Abuse* 286; M Costello, D Chung and E Carson, 'Exploring Pathways Out of Poverty: Making Connections Between Domestic Violence and Employment Practices' (2005) 40 *Australian Journal of Social Issues* 235; L McFerran and R Braaf, 'Domestic Violence is a Workplace Issue' (Paper presented at Balance Brings Everything to Life Conference, Sydney, 11 September 2007); C Reeves and A O'Leary-Kelly, 'The Effects and Cost of Intimate Partner Violence for Work Organisations' (2007) 22 *Journal of Interpersonal Violence* 327; S Franzway, C Zufferey and D Chung, 'Domestic Violence and Women's Employment' (Paper presented at Our Work, Out Lives National Conference on Women and Industrial Relations, Adelaide, 21 September 2007); S Murray and A Powell, *Working it Out: Domestic Violence Issues in the Workplace* (2008).

[5] In 2009, following work by the Australian Domestic and Family Violence Clearinghouse (ADFVC), the Community and Public Sector Union and NSW Public Service Association and ADFVC resolved to develop a model domestic violence clause to log in the 2010 round of enterprise bargaining in the NSW university sector. In July 2010, the Centre for Gender Related Violence Studies at the University of New South Wales, of which the ADFVC is a project, received a Commonwealth Department of Education, Employment and Workplace Relations grant to promote the domestic violence clauses nationally.

[6] Attorney-General of Australia, Terms of Reference for the Australian Law Reform Commission: Impact of Commonwealth Laws on those Experiencing Family Violence (9 July 2010).

(2011). It followed an Inquiry concluded by the ALRC in conjunction with the New South Wales Law Reform Commission (NSWLRC) in October 2010.[7] Both inquiries emanated from the work of the National Council to Reduce Violence against Women and their Children,[8] which was tasked with the development of the *National Plan to Reduce Violence against Women and their Children 2010–2022* (National Plan). Importantly, several of the strategies under the National Plan, aimed at ensuring that communities are safe and free from violence, are relevant in the employment context. They involve, among other things: promoting community ownership and engagement, including by workplaces; promoting "positive and equitable workplace cultures"; and developing "workplace measures to support women experiencing and escaping" from family violence.[9]

Defining family violence

In the Australian legislative context, definitions of family violence have come to vary significantly between the *Family Law Act 1975* (Cth), criminal law and other Commonwealth, State and Territory legislation. However, the *Family Law Legislation Amendment (Family Violence and Other Measures) Act 2011* (Cth) amended the *Family Law Act* to introduce a new and broader definition of family violence,[10] substantially implementing a recommendation made by the ALRC and the NSWLRC in their joint 2010 report, *Family Violence—A National Legal Response*.[11]

---

[7] Australian Law Reform Commission and New South Wales Law Reform Commission, *Family Violence—A National Legal Response,* ALRC Report No 114/NSWLRC Report No 128 (2010).

[8] National Council to Reduce Violence against Women and their Children, Time for Action: The National Council's Plan for Australia to Reduce Violence against Women and their Children 2009–2021 (2009).

[9] Ibid, Outcome One, Strategies 1.1–1.3, 3.1, 4.3.

[10] *Family Law Legislation Amendment (Family Violence and Other Measures) Act 2011* (Cth) s 4AB(2).

[11] Australian Law Reform Commission and New South Wales Law Reform Commission, above n 7. The Act was introduced as a response to a number of reports, but substantially implements the ALRC's recommendation. See, for example: R Chisholm, *Family Courts Violence Review* (2009); Family Law Council, *Improving Responses to Family Violence in the Family Law System: An Advice on the Intersection of Family Violence and Family Law* Issues (2009); Australian Institute of Family Studies, *Evaluation of the 2006 Family Law Reforms* (2009).

The two-part definition of family violence contained in the *Family Law Act* is relied upon for the purposes of this chapter. It provides that family violence means "violent, threatening or other behaviour by a person that coerces or controls a member of the person's family (the family member), or causes the family member to be fearful". It also sets out a non-exhaustive list of behaviour that may constitute family violence, including:

(a) an assault; or
(b) a sexual assault or other sexually abusive behaviour; or
(c) stalking; or
(d) repeated derogatory taunts; or
(e) intentionally damaging or destroying property; or
(f) intentionally causing death or injury to an animal; or
(g) unreasonably denying the family member the financial autonomy that he or she would otherwise have had; or
(h) unreasonably withholding financial support needed to meet the reasonable living expenses of the family member, or his or her child, at a time when the family member is entirely or predominantly dependent on the person for financial support; or
(i) preventing the family member from making or keeping connections with his or her family, friends or culture; or
(j) unlawfully depriving the family member, or any member of the family member's family, of his or her liberty.[12]

Family Violence — A Workplace Issue?

The connection between family violence and work is increasingly clear. This is in part a result of recognition of family violence as a systemic issue arising from broad social, economic and cultural factors, rather than one relegated to the 'private' sphere. It is also a result of the prevalence of family violence in the lives of those who participate in paid employment.[13] However, the connection is also increasingly clear in light of the benefits of employment for people experiencing family violence on the one hand and, on the other, the effect of family violence on employees, co-workers and workplaces andworkplace productivity and safety. The recognised role of business under the National Plan also emphasises that the government has "rejected the notion that businesses are somehow separate from the society in which they operate and instead [considers

---

[12] Family Law Act 1975 (Cth) s 4AB(2).

[13] See, for example, Australian Bureau of Statistics, above n 2, 11, 34. See also: Australian Domestic and Family Violence Clearinghouse, *ADFVC National Domestic Violence and the Workplace Survey* (2011).

them] integrated institutions vested with benefits that concomitantly impose responsibilities".[14]

In the course of the Inquiry, the ALRC consistently heard that employment is vital in providing people experiencing family violence with financial security, independence, confidence, and an environment in which they are safe and treated respectfully. The importance of financial security and independence through employment has been emphasised by Elizabeth Broderick, the Sex Discrimination Commissioner:

> The primary way the majority of us lay the foundations of our economic security is through participation in paid work. We must develop better workplace responses to domestic and family violence to ensure that women can stay attached to the workforce. Doing this will mean three things. Firstly, we will protect women's financial security in the immediate term — women will be less likely to lose their job in a period of crisis. Secondly, if we can keep women attached to the labour market, we will better protect their economic security in the longer term — they will be less likely to live in poverty in their twilight years. But thirdly, and most importantly from an employer's perspective, individual businesses will be better able to prevent the unnecessary loss of talented staff.[15]

Conversely, the effect of family violence on the potential economic contribution of employees is significant. For example, women like Jenny who have experienced family violence generally have a more disrupted work history, receive lower incomes, and are often in casual and part-time employment.[16]

Family violence also directly and indirectly manifests in the workplace. The results of the National Domestic Violence and the Workplace Survey conducted in 2011 on behalf of the ADFVC indicated that, of those who reported experiencing family violence, nearly half the respondents stated that the violence affected their capacity to get to work—the major reason being physical injury or restraint. In the previous 12 months, 19 per cent of respondents reported that family violence continued in the workplace. Specifically, 12 per cent indicated it occurred in the form of abusive phone calls and emails, 11 per cent stated that it occurred by way of the violent

---

[14] B Smith and T Orchiston, 'Domestic Violence Victims At Work: A Role for Anti-Discrimination Law?' (2012) 25 *Australian Journal of Labour Law* 209.

[15] E Broderick, 'Launch of Domestic Violence Clause' (Paper presented at Launch of UNSW Domestic Violence Clause, Sydney, 15 April 2010).

[16] M Costello, D Chung and E Carson, 'Exploring Pathways Out of Poverty: Making Connections Between Domestic Violence and Employment Practices' (2005) 40 *Australian Journal of Social Issues* 235, 256; S Franzway, C Zufferey and D Chung, above n 4.

person attending the workplace, and 16 per cent reported a negative effect on work performance arising from being distracted, tired or unwell.[17] The effect on co-workers can also be significant where it results in increased workloads due to absenteeism or dealing with disruptions, such as harassing phone calls in the workplace.[18] In the most extreme cases family violence may result in family violence-related homicide in the workplace.[19]

Finally, the substantial social and economic cost of family violence and its broader implications for employers and the economy cannot be underestimated. Family violence is projected to cost the Australian economy an estimated $15.6 billion in 2021–22.[20] In 2004, it reportedly cost the corporate and business sectors over $1.5 billion through direct costs, including absenteeism, decreased productivity, and staff turnover resulting in recruitment and training costs and the loss of corporate knowledge.[21]

---

[17] Australian Domestic and Family Violence Clearinghouse, above n 13. The survey sample was 3611 respondents of which 81 per cent were women and 90 per cent were either a member of the National Tertiary Education Union or the NSW Nurses Association.

[18] See, for example: International Labour Organisation, (Bureau for Gender Equality), 'Gender-Based Violence in the World of Work: Overview and Selected Annotated Bibliography' (Working Paper No 3, 2011) 13.

[19] See, eg, L McFerran and R Braaf, 'Domestic Violence is a Workplace Issue' (Paper presented at Balance Brings Everything to Life Conference, Sydney, 11 September 2007); C Reeves and A O'Leary-Kelly, 'The Effects and Cost of Intimate Partner Violence for Work Organisations' (2007) 22 *Journal of Interpersonal Violence* 327.

[20] National Council to Reduce Violence against Women and their Children, above n 8 (2009), 43; KPMG, *The Cost of Violence against Women and their Children* (2009), prepared for the National Council to Reduce Violence Against Women and their Children.

[21] See, for example: Victorian Community Council Against Violence, *Family Violence is a Workplace Issue: Workplace Models to Prevent Family Violence* (2004); Australian Domestic and Family Violence Clearinghouse, *Why Domestic Violence Entitlements Makes Economic Sense: The Economic Costs of Domestic Violence on the Workplace*, referring to: Australian Human Resources Institute, 'Love 'Em don't Lose 'Em: Identifying Retention Strategies that Work' (2008) 2(1) *HR Pulse* 1; International Labour Organisation, above n 18, 13, 14.

The Role of the Employment Law System

The objectives of the employment law system in Australia include the provision of a balanced framework that promotes labour market engagement and economic productivity, as well as providing flexibility and a minimum safety net of terms and conditions.[22] In light of the benefits of employment for people experiencing family violence, its prevalence and enormous social and economic costs, ensuring the employment law system appropriately identifies, responds to and addresses family violence, is central to achieving these objectives.

The employment law framework

The employment law landscape is one in which significant changes have occurred in recent years. The *Fair Work Act 2009* (Cth) is Australia's key piece of industrial legislation.[23] The *Fair Work Act* provides for terms and conditions of employment and sets out the rights and responsibilities of employees, employers and employee organisations in relation to that employment. It regulates 'national system' employers and employees.[24] From 1 January 2010, all states other than Western Australia referred their industrial relations powers to the Commonwealth, essentially creating a new national industrial relations system. Employment that is not covered under the national industrial relations system remains regulated by the relevant State industrial relations systems. However, some entitlements under the *Fair Work Act* extend to non-national system employees.[25]

The *Fair Work Act* covers approximately 96 per cent of private sector employees.[26] The *Fair Work Act* also creates a compliance and enforcement regime and establishes several bodies to administer the Act,

---

[22] Fair Work Act 2009 (Cth) s 3.

[23] It replaced the *Workplace Relations Act 1996* (Cth) and most provisions of the Act took effect on 1 July 2009.

[24] The definition of 'national system employee' and 'national system employer' are contained in ss 13 and 14 of the *Fair Work Act 2009* (Cth) and are extended by ss 30C, 30D, 30M and 30N to cover employers in referring states: *Fair Work Act 2009* (Cth) ss 13, 14, 30C, 30D, 30M and 30N.

[25] For example, non-national system employees are entitled to unpaid parental leave, notice of termination, payment in lieu or notice and protection from unlawful termination of employment: *Fair Work Act 2009* (Cth) pts 6-3, 6-4.

[26] Fair Work Act Review Panel, Towards More Productive and Equitable Workplaces: An Evaluation of the Fair Work Legislation (2012), 49.

including the Fair Work Commission (FWC), formerly Fair Work Australia, and the Fair Work Ombudsman (FWO).

In December 2011, the Australian Government announced a review of the *Fair Work Act* (the Fair Work Act Review),[27] to examine and report on the extent to which the legislation is operating as intended and areas where the operation of the legislation could be improved consistent with the objects of the Act. The Fair Work Act Review was the subject of much controversy and attracted submissions from a wide range of stakeholders.[28] In August 2012, the Australian Government released the Fair Work Act Review Panel's Final Report. Although the Fair Work Act Review found that the effects of the *Fair Work Act* "have been broadly consistent with the objects" of the Act and that it is "operating broadly as intended", there were 53 recommendations for reform.[29]

On 1 January 2013, provisions of the *Fair Work Amendment Act 2012* (Cth) took effect, implementing some of the Fair Work Act Review recommendations.[30] In March 2013, the Fair Work Amendment Bill 2013 (Cth) was introduced into Parliament. Significantly, the Bill extends the right to request flexible working arrangements on the basis recommended by the ALRC, an issue discussed later in this chapter.

Within this framework, in the search for an appropriate role for the employment law system in responding to family violence, the ALRC was faced with a number of difficult overarching issues. In addition to those concerning terminology, these included: barriers to disclosure of family violence; privacy and confidentiality concerns; issues associated with the verification of family violence, where necessary; and the limits of law.

Disclosure in the workplace

People experiencing family violence may consider disclosing family violence to individuals and representatives within the employment law system

---

[27] The Hon Bill Shorten (Minister for Employment and Workplace Relations), 'Fair Work Act Review Announced' (Media Release, 20 December 2011). The Australian Government had committed to reviewing the operation of the Act two years after its commencement: Explanatory Memorandum, Fair Work Bill 2008 (Cth).

[28] The Review Panel received more than 250 submissions: Department of Education, Employment and Workplace Relations, *Fair Work Act Review* <www.deewr.gov.au/fair-work-act-review>.

[29] Fair Work Act Review Panel, Towards More Productive and Equitable Workplaces: An Evaluation of the Fair Work Legislation (2012).

[30] *Fair Work Amendment Act 2012* (Cth).

required? In the Final Report, the ALRC expressed the view that there is a need to ensure that employees accessing family violence leave are subject to the same requirements to demonstrate their entitlement to the leave as other forms of leave.[38] However, in light of the difficulties associated with disclosure of family violence, it is vital that people experiencing family violence are provided with choice as to the documentary verification provided to support a claim of family violence. Such documents may include those issued by a police officer, court, health professional, lawyer, family violence service or refuge worker, or the employee, in the form of a signed statutory declaration. For example, in Jenny's situation, had she been entitled to access leave or other entitlements, she would have been in a position to provide verification in the form of police reports, court documents and medical certificates.

The limits of law

In examining the potential role for the employment law system in identifying and responding to family violence, the ALRC made a number of complementary recommendations in relation to the development of a whole-of-government national education campaign, guidance material, research and monitoring initiatives.[39] The key overarching recommendation was for the development of a campaign focusing on the nature, features and dynamics of family violence, and its potential impact on employees and the workplace. It was intended that such a campaign would complement work being undertaken within the framework established by the National Plan.[40] Other recommendations emphasised the need for ongoing education, training and awareness-raising about family violence as a possible workplace issue and the development of guidance material suitable for a range of organisations and industries. In order to inform future policy development, the ALRC also emphasised the need for further research, data collection and monitoring of initiatives.

The September 2012 government announcement of the establishment of a National Centre of Excellence to Reduce Violence Against Women, tasked with leading a 'national research agenda' is a positive development

---

[38] Australian Law Reform Commission, above n 31, 428–429.

[39] See, for example: Ibid, recs 15–1, 15–2, 15–4, 15–5, 16–2, 16–3, 16–5.

[40] Australian Government, The National Plan to Reduce Violence against Women: Immediate Government Actions (2009) 12.

in this area and is discussed later in this chapter.[41] In addition, a number of stakeholders have made significant contributions to these parallel approaches to reform, both prior to and following the ALRC's Inquiry. For example, the Domestic Violence Workplace Rights and Entitlements Project coordinated by the ADFVC has been central in promoting and progressing the adoption of family violence clauses in enterprise agreements and other workplace instruments and the development of a range of guidance material to assist employees and employers.[42] The work of organisations like White Ribbon, which is conducting a pilot workplace accreditation project, and CEO Challenge, has also been central to efforts to raise awareness about the connection between family violence and the employment sphere and in transforming workplace culture.[43]

Approaches to Reform

In considering the most appropriate approach to reform in this area, there are three key areas of possible legislative reform: the *Fair Work Act*, anti-discrimination legislation and work health and safety legislation. The ALRC considered each of these in its Final Report.[44] The focus of this chapter is on possible amendments to the *Fair Work Act*; however it also briefly considers relevant developments in anti-discrimination law. In addition, in considering the most appropriate strategy for implementation of reform, this chapter outlines the ALRC's suggested phased approach to reform and highlights potential approaches in light of developments since the ALRC's Inquiry.

There are a number of aspects of the *Fair Work Act* that present opportunities to assist people experiencing family violence, like Jenny, including: leave and flexible working arrangements and statutory protection

---

[41] The Hon Julia Gillard, Prime Minister, 'Speech for Equal Futures Partnership Launch' (Speech delivered at Launch of Equal Futures Partnership, New York, 24 September 2012).

[42] Australian Domestic and Family Violence Clearinghouse, *Keeping You and Your Job Safe: Information for Workers Experiencing Family Violence* (2012); Australian Domestic and Family Violence Clearinghouse, Domestic Violence Workplace Rights and Entitlements Project, *How To Guides* (2011) <www.dvandwork.unsw.edu.au/how-guides-model-policies-procedures-and-safety-plans>.

[43] See, for example: White Ribbon, *White Ribbon National Workplace Program* <www.whiteribbon.org.au/programs/workplaces>; Australia's CEO Challenge <ceochallengeaustralia.org/>.

[44] Australian Law Reform Commission, above n 31, ch 15–18.

from discrimination. However, as discussed above, it is also necessary to recognise the limits of the law and the crucial role education, increased awareness and cultural change must play at broader societal and individual workplace levels.

Leave and flexible working arrangements

One of the key aims of the *Fair Work Act* is to assist employees to "balance their work and family responsibilities by providing for flexible working arrangements".[45] Leave and flexible working arrangements are key mechanisms in assisting people experiencing family violence to enter, re-enter or remain in paid employment. This is particularly important in light of the benefits of employment for people experiencing family violence, but the difficulties often faced by them in entering the paid workforce or retaining paid employment. In many instances, employees experiencing family violence are able to utilise existing leave and workplace policies and procedures which provide for flexible working arrangements. However, as Jenny's case illustrates, people experiencing family violence often exhaust their leave entitlements. Whereemployers are not willing to provide access to flexible working arrangements, examining legislative and regulatory mechanisms for ensuring access to such arrangements is necessary. As a result, this chapter examines leave and flexible working arrangements under the National Employment Standards (NES), enterprise agreements and modern awards.

The NES and family violence leave

The NES enshrine 10 statutory minimum requirements that apply to all 'national system'employees. The NES replaced the Australian Fair Pay and Conditions Standards,[46] and provide a minimum safety net of terms and conditions of employment encompassing areas such as working hours and arrangements, leave, and termination and redundancy pay. The NES cannot be excluded by an enterprise agreement or modern award. Under the NES, employees are entitled to access a number of categories of paid and unpaid leave, including: parental leave; annual leave; personal/carer's

---

[45] Fair Work Act 2009 (Cth) s 3.

[46] Introduced by the Workplace Relations Amendment (Work Choices) Act 2005 (Cth) which amended the Workplace Relations Act 1996 (Cth).

leave; compassionate leave; community service leave; and long service leave.[47]

An employee who is experiencing family violence may use a combination of leave entitlements to take time off work for purposes related to family violence. However, there are limitations on the use of particular types of leave under the NES;[48] and where family violence occurs over a prolonged period, people experiencing family violence may quickly exhaust their leave entitlements. As a result, existing leave provisions set out in the NES may not adequately provide for the needs of these employees.

In the course of the Inquiry, the ALRC was faced with divergent stakeholder views on the issue of paid family violence leave. Almost all stakeholders agreed that people experiencing family violence should be appropriately supported in the workplace. However, industry representatives and employer groups emphasised that the introduction of additional leave must be accompanied by a 'strong case' for its introduction and highlighted potential cost implications.[49] Other stakeholders emphasised the importance of minimum statutory entitlements to leave.

The provision of family violence leave under the NES is important in providing a universal and enforceable entitlement. In addition, the symbolic effect of such leave cannot be underestimated — it would build upon national developments around recognising and responding to family violence and recognise the relationship between family violence and workplaces outlined earlier in this chapter. As a result, the ALRC ultimately formed the view that the provision of a minimum statutory entitlement to paid family violence leave is necessary and appropriate. However, the ALRC tempered its recommendation by reference to a

---

[47] *Fair Work Act 2009* (Cth) ch 2, pt 2-2, div 5-9. Contravention of the leave-related NES (other than unpaid parental leave) is prohibited under s 44 of the *Fair Work Act*, which is a civil remedy provision. If an employer breaches the NES, an employee, employee organisation or an inspector may make an application for orders in relation to that contravention and the employer may be liable to pay a civil penalty of a maximum of 60 penalty units for each contravention: *Fair Work Act 2009* (Cth) pt 4-1, div 2. Notice and evidence requirements relating to leave under the NES are provided for under s 107 of the *Fair Work Act 2009* (Cth).

[48] For example, under the NES paid personal/carer's leave can only be used in circumstances of personal illness or injury or caring responsibilities: *Fair Work Act 2009* (Cth) s 97.

[49] Australian Chamber of Commerce and Industry, Submission No 19 to Australian Law Reform Commission, *Family Violence and Commonwealth Laws Inquiry*, April 2011.

phased approach to implementation and additional suggestions with respect to data collection and economic modelling.[50]

The ALRC's recommendation was cast broadly, but the Final Report explored a number of options for reform of the NES to provide access to leave for family violence-related circumstances.[51] First, the ALRC suggested amendment of s 97 of the *Fair Work Act*, under which personal/carer's leave can be taken, to include circumstances arising from family violence. Secondly, the ALRC considered the introduction of either a new statutory minimum entitlement to family violence leave under the NES, or additional leave for family violence purposes as a subset of personal/carer's leave under the NES. Rather than expressing a view on the preferable option, the ALRC concluded that the introduction of family violence leave should be accompanied by a number of basic requirements. These requirements includedthat the leave is paid, flexible and easily accessible where necessary, whilst containing sufficient safeguards to maintain the integrity of the leave system.[52]

Family violence clauses in enterprise agreements and modern awards

In 2010, the first Australian family violence clauses were included in the enterprise agreements for the Surf Coast Shire and University of New South Wales professional staff.[53] At the conclusion of the ALRC's Inquiry in November 2011, approximately six enterprise agreements across Australia and a number of awards in NSW included such clauses. By November 2012, approximately one million public and private employees had access to family violence-related leave under numerous enterprise agreements, modern awards and a range of policies and directives.[54]

---

[50] Australian Law Reform Commission, above n 31, rec 17–2.

[51] Ibid, 422–429.

[52] See: Ibid, 424–425.

[53] Both agreements were subsequently approved by the FWC. An enterprise agreement only comes into operation after approval by the FWC: *Fair Work Act 2009* (Cth) s 54. In addition to ensuring several pre-approval steps have been undertaken by the employer, the FWC must be satisfied as to a number of things, including that certain content requirements are met, there are no unlawful terms and that the agreement passes the 'better off overall' test: *Fair Work Act 2009* (Cth) ss 186–188, 193, 196–200.

[54] See, for example: Australian Council of Trade Unions, 'One Million Workers Now Have Access to Family Violence Leave' (Media Release, 23 November 2012); Australian Domestic and Family Violence Clearinghouse, Submission to Senate Standing Committee on Legal and Constitutional Affairs, *Exposure Draft of Human Rights and Anti-Discrimination Bill 2012*, December 2012.

The strong preference expressed by employers, employees, and their representatives was that clauses should contain clear and enforceable entitlements, but be tailored to suit the particular circumstances of the workplace and workforce. As a result, the ALRC ultimately recommended that the Australian Government support the inclusion of family violence clauses in enterprise agreements. At a minimum, the ALRC recommended such clauses should contain several basic requirements and provisions in relation to: when verification of family violence is required and the type of verification; confidentiality; reporting, roles and responsibilities; flexible work arrangements; and access to paid leave.[55]

The clauses have subsequently been incorporated into enterprise agreements across industries including aged care, banking, education and training, electrical contracting, railways, water and local government.[56]

---

[55] Australian Law Reform Commission, above n 31, rec 16–4.

[56] For example, family violence clauses have been included in: University of New South Wales (Professional Staff) Enterprise Agreement 2010; Surf Coast Shire Enterprise Agreement 2010–2013; Brimbank City Council Enterprise Agreement No 6 (2010); Moyne Shire Council Enterprise Bargaining Agreement No 6 2010; TransGrid Employees Agreement 2010 (NSW); Women's Health West Incorporated Enterprise Agreement 2010; ACOSS Collective Agreement 2011; Catholic Healthcare Residential Aged Care Enterprise Agreement (New South Wales) 2011–2013; Presbyterian Aged Care, NSWNA and HSU East Enterprise Agreement 2011–2014; Eastern Ranges GP Association Inc, ANF Enterprise Agreement 2011; Amnesty International Australia Employment Agreement 2011; Melaleuca Refugee Centre Enterprise Bargaining Agreement 2011; Banyule City Council Enterprise Agreement No 5, 2011; Barwon Region Water Corporation Enterprise Agreement 2011; Baw Baw Shire Council Enterprise Agreement 2011; Central Goldfields Shire Council Enterprise Agreement No 5, 2011; City of Greater Geelong Enterprise Agreement No 7, 2011; Loddon Shire Council Enterprise Agreement No 6, 2011; Mornington Peninsula Shire Council, Enterprise Agreement No 7, 2011; Manningham City Council Enterprise Agreement 5, 2011; Mitchell Shire Council Enterprise Agreement No 5 2011–2014; PACCAR Trucks Melbourne, Enterprise Agreement 2011; People's Choice Credit Union SA 2011; Swan Hill Rural City Council Enterprise Agreement No 5, 2011; Thoroughbred Racing SA Ltd Barrier Staff/AWU Enterprise Agreement 2011; West Gippsland Regional Library Corporation Enterprise Agreement 5, 2011; Whitehorse Manningham Regional Library Corporation Enterprise Agreement 2011; Whittlesea City Council Enterprise Agreement, No 6, 2011; Wyndham City Council Enterprise Agreement No 6, 2011; Rail Tram Bus Union and Hodge Rail 2012–2015; Rail Tram Bus Union and Nash Rail Enterprise Agreement 2012–2015; Rail Tram Bus Union and Vital Rail Trackwork 2012–2015; Geraldton Port Authority Enterprise Agreement (2012); State Water Corporation Enterprise Agreement 2012.

In May 2012, the ACTU Congress endorsed a Work, Life, Family Policy which states that "in workplace bargaining, the ACTU strongly encourages unions to include provisions designed to protect and support employees who are employees experiencing family or domestic violence". It outlines a number of principles for bargaining, including the provision of additional leave, access to flexible working arrangements, confidentiality, referral to services, workplace safety strategies and education and training.[57]

While enterprise agreements covering the majority of Commonwealth agencies do not currently include specific family violence clauses, the Government has expressed support for the inclusion of such clauses,[58] and there is some provision for leave for family violence-related purposes. For example the Department of Families, Housing, Community Services and Indigenous Affairs (FaHCSIA) *Enterprise Agreement 2012–14* provides that the Secretary may approve paid leave under a miscellaneous leave provision "in short term special/emergency situations or other exceptional personal or family circumstances not covered by the personal/carer's leave provisions of this Agreement, including domestic violence".[59]

In November 2012, the Australian Public Service Commission issued Circular 2012/3: *Supporting Employees Affected by Domestic or Family Violence*.[60] The Circular provides background information about family violence and its impact in the workplace, encourages consideration of the issue, and outlines support and leave arrangements for employees experiencing family violence. In particular, it provides that in accordance with agencies' enterprise agreements, access to personal leave entitlements should be allowed for reasons including attending medical appointments, moving into emergency housing, attending court or police, obtaining legal advice or organising children's care arrangements. Similarly, in 2012 at a state level, governments in Tasmania and Queensland have issued directives and developed policies in order to provide State public sector

---

[57] Australian Council of Trade Unions, *Work, Life, Family Policy* (ACTU Congress, 2012).
[58] G Marcus, 'Interview with Hon Kate Ellis, Federal Minister for Status of Women' (2011) 44 *Australian Domestic and Family Violence Clearinghouse Newsletter* 12.
[59] See: FaHCSIA Enterprise Agreement 2012–2014 [2012] FWAA 3549, cl 7.65.
[60] Australian Public Service Commission, Circular 2012/3: Supporting Employees Affected by Domestic or Family Violence (2012).

employees experiencing family violence with access to personal or special leave for purposes relating to family violence.[61]

While these are important steps, the inclusion of family violence clauses in Commonwealth, State and Territory government agency enterprise agreements, including the basic requirements suggested by the ALRC, would be preferable and is consistent with role of governments as a model employer. At a Commonwealth level it is also consistent with a June 2012 motion proposed by Amanda Rishworth MP which received bipartisan Parliamentary support. The motion recognised the connection between family violence and employment, the "positive impact of the inclusion of domestic violence clauses in contracts of employment" and urged "all private companies and public sectors to include domestic violence clauses in their enterprise agreements to provide victims with important protections such as access to leave in addition to existing entitlements".[62]

In addition to enterprise agreements, there is also scope for the inclusion of family violence clauses in awards. The key Australian precedent for the recognition of family violence in awards is the *Crown Employees (Public Service Conditions of Employment) Award 2009* (NSW). The award was amended in 2011 and entitles NSW public servants to five days special leave and use of other forms of leave for the purposes of responding to family violence, as well as flexible working arrangements. A range of other NSW awards have now been varied to include family violence provisions. In November 2012 the Tasmanian Government announced the variation of awards covering all State public service employees to enable access to personal leave for purposes relating to family violence.[63]

At a Commonwealth level, it is likely that existing provisions of the *Fair Work Act* are sufficiently broad to allow the inclusion of family violence-related terms in modern awards.[64] However, to date no Commonwealth modern awards include such clauses. The inclusion of family violence-related terms appears to be consistent with the modern

---

[61] Queensland Government, Minister for Education and Industrial Relations, Directive 2/12: Special Leave, 2012; Tasmanian Government, Ministerial Direction No 28: Family Violence — Workplace Arrangements and Requirements, 2012.

[62] Commonwealth, *Parliamentary Debates*, House of Representatives, 25 June 2012, 7856–69.

[63] L Giddings (Premier, Tasmania), 'Launch of the Family Violence Workplace Policy for Tasmanian Public Servants' (Media Release, 20 November 2012).

[64] *Fair Work Act 2009* (Cth) s 139(1).

awards objective of promoting social inclusion through increased workforce participation.[65] Such inclusion would ensureemployees experiencing family violence are able to access leave and flexible working arrangements to deal with circumstances arising from family violence, which increases the likelihood of their retaining employment. As a result, the ALRC recommended that in the course of the 2012 and 2014 reviews of modern awards by the FWC, the inclusion of a model family violence term should be considered.[66]

At the time of writing, the FWC is undertaking a review of all modern awards, based on applications to vary modern awards, as part of a range of reviews required under the *Fair Work Act* and associated legislation.[67] The scope of the current review is limited to considering whether modern awards achieve the modern awards objectives and are operating effectively, without anomalies or technical problems arising from the award modernisation process. The 2012 modern award review is unlikely to revisit issues already determined during the award modernisation process unless there are cogent reasons, such as where there has been a significant change in circumstances[68] and is therefore unlikely to consider the issue of family violence. However, the FWC has indicated that the 2014 review, also the focus of the ALRC's recommendation, will be broader in scope than the 2012 review.[69] This later review presents an opportunity to consider the inclusion of a model family violence term.

The right to request flexible working arrangements

Under the NES, an employee who is a parent or otherwise has responsibility for a child who is under school age, or who is under 18 and has a disability, may request a change in working arrangements to assist with the care of that child.[70] To be eligible to request flexible working

---

[65] Ibid, s 134(1).

[66] Australian Law Reform Commission, above n 31, recs 16–6, 16–7.

[67] See *Fair Work (Transitional Provisions and Consequential Amendments) Act 2009* (Cth) sch 5, s 6. The *Fair Work Act* provides for review of each modern award every four years: *Fair Work Act 2009* (Cth) s 156. There is also a process for varying modern awards outside the four yearly review: *Fair Work Act 2009* (Cth) s 157.

[68] *Modern Award Review 2012* [2012] FWAFB 5600, [89], [99]. For an outline and timetable see: *Modern Award Review 2012—Timetable* [2012] FWA 5721.

[69] *Modern Award Review 2012* [2012] FWAFB 5600 at [99].

[70] *Fair Work Act 2009* (Cth) s 65(1), 65(2). The note to s 65(1) states that examples of changes in working arrangements include changes in hours of work, patterns of work and location of work.

arrangements the employee must satisfy certain service requirements.[71] Such a request may only be refused on "reasonable business grounds".[72] The Australian provision was based on the UK right to request provision which has been incrementally extended to apply to parents and carers of children up to the age of 16 and those with caring responsibilities for a wide range of adults requiring care, including: relatives, spouses, civil partners and other household members.[73]

In its Final Report, the ALRC recommended that the Australian Government should consider amending the right to request provision to provide that an employee who is experiencing family violence, or who is providing care or support to another person who is experiencing family violence, may request the employer for a change in working arrangements to assist the employee to deal with circumstances arising from the family violence.[74]

In order to ensure recognition of the diversity of families and household structures, it is vital that any extension of the right to request on this basis is broadly formulated to include children or other dependants who may have been affected by family violence, as well as a range of similarly important relationships, recognising the role of extended kinship networks for Indigenous peoples as well as of neighbours and close friends "who may well be more likely to be called upon to care or support a victim of family or domestic violence than a member of the family or household".[75]

Significantly, the Fair Work Act Review Panel noted the work of the ALRC and recommended that, in order to increase workplace equity and

---

[71] In order to be eligible to request flexible work arrangements, the employee must have 12 months of continuous service, or for a casual employee, be a long-term casual employee with a reasonable expectation of continuing employment on a regular and systemic basis: *Fair Work Act 2009* (Cth) s 65.

[72] *Fair Work Act 2009* (Cth) s 65(5). Note, the Fair Work Amendment Bill 2013 (Cth) includes a non-exhaustive list of what might constitute reasonable business grounds.

[73] Employment Rights Act 1996 (UK) ss 80F, 80G; Flexible Working (Eligibility, Complaints and Remedies) Regulations 2002 (UK) (SI 2002 No 3236); Flexible Working (Procedural Requirements) Regulations 2002 (UK) (SI 2002 No 3207). For discussion of the evolution of the provisions see: Centre for Employment and Labour Relations Law, Submission to Fair Work Act Review Panel, Fair Work Act Review, 17 February 2012, 5.

[74] Australian Law Reform Commission, above n 31, rec 17–1.

[75] Australian Council of Trade Unions, Submission No 100 to Australian Law Reform Commission, *Family Violence and Commonwealth Laws Inquiry*, 30 September 2011.

remove current inequities, section 65 should be amended to "extend the right to request flexible working arrangements to a wider range of caring and *other circumstances*" (author's emphasis).[76]

The nature of the ALRC's Terms of Reference precluded from examining the possible extension of the right to request on grounds other than family violence. In the author's view however, there are clearly a number of potential grounds upon which the provisions could be extended. Since the ALRC's Inquiry, a number of other bodies and reports have recommended the extension of the right to request. For example the House of Representatives Standing Committee on Family, Community, Housing and Youth recommended in 2009 that the right to request be extended to all employees "who have recognised care responsibilities, including to those who are caring for adults with disabilities, mental illness, chronic illness or who are frail aged".[77] The Advisory Panel on the Economic Potential of Senior Australians recommended that the right be extended to persons aged 55 and over.[78] In February 2012, Adam Bandt MP introduced the Fair Work Amendment (Better Work/Life Balance) Bill 2012, which would, among other things, amend the *Fair Work Act* by extending the right to request to all employees and remove the flexible working arrangements provisions from the NES and create a new part of the Act.[79]

Significantly, as mentioned earlier in the chapter, in March 2013 the *Fair Work Amendment Bill 2013* (Cth) was introduced. It extends the right to request flexible working arrangements to a number of classes of employees, including those experiencing family violence and those providing care or support for people experiencing family violence.[80] If enacted, this would implement one of the ALRC's key recommendations.[81]

---

[76] Fair Work Act Review Panel, Towards More Productive and Equitable Workplaces: An Evaluation of the Fair Work Legislation (2012), 96, rec 5.

[77] House of Representatives Standing Committee on Family, Community, Housing and Youth, Parliament of Australia, *Who Cares ...? Report on the Inquiry into Better Support for Carers* (2009) rec 40.

[78] Advisory Panel on the Economic Potential of Senior Australians, *Realising the Economic Potential of Senior Australians —Turning Grey into Gold* (2011) rec 15.

[79] The Bill was referred to the House of Representatives Standing Committee on Education and Employment which reported in June 2012: House of Representatives Standing Committee on Education and Employment, *Advisory Report on the Fair Work Amendment (Better Work/Life Balance) Bill 2012* (May 2012). The Bill was read a second time in September 2012 and at the time of writing was before the House of Representatives.

[80] *Fair Work Amendment Bill 2013* (Cth) cl 17.

[81] Australian Law Reform Commission, above n 31, rec 17–1.

It is necessary, however, to recognise the significant limitations with the provision in its current form. Broadly, concerns centre on its procedural rather than substantive nature, the limited availability of enforcement mechanisms and the grounds for refusal. The ALRC emphasised two particular aspects of the provision that are likely to be particularly restrictive for people experiencing family violence — eligibility and the employer response period.[82] The ALRC did not make any systemic recommendations in relation to the provision, aside from its extension. However, in the author's view, these limitations detract from the usefulness of the provision and amendment should be considered, at least with respect to enforceability and rights of appeal to ensure consistency with other standards under the NES.[83]

Since the ALRC's Inquiry, a range of evidence assessing the existing right to request provisions has emerged. Lack of awareness of the provisions has emerged as a significant issue. In November 2012, the FWC released a report on the operation of the NES provisions relating to the right to request and extension of unpaid parental leave.[84] The Report indicated that the estimated rate of awareness of the right to request provision was 66% among employers and 48% among employees.[85] In addition, the Australian Work and Life Index (AWALI) 2012 indicated that 20.6 per cent of employees had made a request for a change to working arrangements in the past 12 months.It is unclear the proportion that relied upon the formal right to request provision in making such a request.[86] Significantly, the survey indicated that a majority of employees are unaware of the existence of the right to request provisions.[87]

As a result, while the ALRC recommended an extension of the right to request, its additional exposition of the limitations of the provision in its

---

[82] Ibid, 417–419.

[83] There are limited enforcement or appeal mechanisms under the *Fair Work Act 2009* (Cth) where an employee considers a request has been unreasonably refused. For example, s 44 specifically states that an order cannot be made under the civil remedy provisions in relation to a contravention of s 65(5). See also: *Fair Work Act 2009* (Cth) s 739.

[84] The General Manager of the FWC is required to produce such research reports: *Fair Work Act 2009* (Cth) s 653.

[85] Fair Work Australia, *General Managers Report into the Operation of the Provisions of the National Employment Standards Relating to Requests for Flexible Working Arrangements and and Extensions of Unpaid Parental Leave 2009–2012* (2012) [4.2.1], [4.2.2].

[86] N Skinner, C Hutchinson and B Pocock, Australian Work and Life Index 2012: The Big Squeeze: Work, Home and Care in 2012 (2012) 62.

[87] Ibid, 61.

current form and suggestions and recommendations with respect to supporting education, training and awareness raising are vital in ensuring the effectiveness of the provision.

Statutory protection from discrimination

Legislation in a number of overseas jurisdictions prohibits employers from terminating an employee's employment or otherwise discriminating against them where the employee is, or is perceived to be, a victim of family violence, or where they take time off work, for example, to testify in a criminal proceeding, seek a protection order or medical attention related to experiences of family violence.[88]

There is currently no such protection under Australian anti-discrimination legislation. In an Australian context, by way of brief chronology, in August 2010 the Queensland Working Women's Service first raised the potential for the inclusion of family violence as a protected attribute under Australia's anti-discrimination legislation.[89] The ALRC considered the possibility in the course of its Inquiry, raising the issue in its Issues Paper in February 2011 as well as in its later Discussion Paper, and in November 2011 the ALRC submitted its Final Report, *Family Violence and Commonwealth Laws — Improving Legal Frameworks,* to the Attorney-General.

In September 2011, the Australian Government released a discussion paper seeking submissions in relation to the consolidation of Commonwealth anti-discrimination law. It noted that submissions to the consolidation had recommended that victims of family violence be protected from unlawful discrimination.[90]

---

[88] California Labor Code (US) §§ 230, 230.1; Victims Economic Security and Safety Act 820 Illinois Compiled Statutes 180 (US) § 30; New York State Executive Law (US) §§ 296-1(a); New York City Administrative Code (US) § 8-107.1; Revised Code of Washington 49 § 4976 (US) § 49.76; Unlawful Action Against Employees Seeking Protection 2007 Fla Stat § 741-313 (US) § 741.313; Colorado Revised Statutes (US) § 24-34-402.7; Anti-Violence Against Women and Their Children Act 2004 (Philippines) s 43.

[89] A Heffernan and L Matahaere, 'Domestic Violence Discrimination in the Workplace: Is Statutory Protection Necessary?'(Paper presented at Our Work, Our Lives Conference, 2010).

[90] Australian Government Attorney-General's Department, *Consolidation of Commonwealth Anti-Discrimination Laws: Discussion Paper* (September 2011), 85.

In late 2011 the ALP National Conference resolved to "ensure that the Fair Work and anti-discrimination legislation frameworks provide appropriate protection to victims of domestic violence in the workplace".[91] At this stage a number of academics contributed to the development of thinking around the scope for inclusion under anti-discrimination law.[92]

In early 2012, the Australian Government tabled the ALRC's Report containing a recommendation that the Australian Human Rights Commission (AHRC), in the context of the consolidation, should examine the possible basis upon which status as an actual or perceived victim of family violence could be included as a protected attribute under Commonwealth anti-discrimination law.[93] The AHRC implemented the ALRC's recommendation and made a submission to this effect to the Attorney-General's Department as part of the consolidation process.[94] A range of other organisations made similar submissions.[95]

In May 2012, the ACTU Congress' Work, Family and Life Policy expressed support for the inclusion of a new ground of discrimination under Commonwealth and State and Territory anti-discrimination legislation as well as the *Fair Work Act* to "better protect employees who are experiencing, have experienced, or are perceived to be experiencing family or domestic violence, against adverse action".[96]

---

[91] See: *Motions from National Conference 2011, Amendment 448A* (2012) Our ALP <http://ouralp.net/2011/12/04/all-the-motions-from-national-conference-2011/#448>.

[92] See, for example: B Smith and T Orchiston, *Domestic Violence Victims at Work: The Role of Anti-Discrimination Law* (Working Paper, Sydney Law School, University of Sydney, 12 December 2011).

[93] Australian Law Reform Commission, above n 31, 16–8.

[94] Australian Human Rights Commission, Supplementary Submission to Australian Government Attorney-General's Department, *Consolidation of Commonwealth Anti-Discrimination Laws*, 23 January 2012.

[95] See for example: Australian Domestic and Family Violence Clearinghouse, Submission to Australian Government Attorney-General's Department, *Consolidation of Commonwealth Anti-Discrimination Laws*, 23 January 2012; Equality Rights Alliance, Submission to Australian Government Attorney-General's Department, *Consolidation of Commonwealth Anti-Discrimination Laws*, 19 December 2011.

[96] Australian Council of Trade Unions, *Work, Life, Family Policy,* above n 57.

There have also been several successful motions in Parliament in relation to this issue.[97]

On 20 November 2012, the Australian Government released a draft consolidated bill, the Human Rights and Anti-Discrimination Bill 2012 (Cth). Unfortunately, however, family violence was not included as a protected attribute in the Bill. The accompanying Regulatory Impact Statement (RIS) notes that

> human rights organisations and legal practitioners strongly supported the inclusion of other attributes, such as domestic violence and criminal record. Business groups opposed these on the basis they were uncertain and imposed significant new regulatory burden.[98]

The RIS notes that the Government does not propose to implement the introduction of other new attributes, including domestic violence, as part of the consolidation project "given its largely deregulatory focus".[99]

In March 2013, the Australian Government indicated that aside from amendments to the *Sex Discrimination Act 1984* (Cth) in relation to sexual orientation, gender identity and intersex status, the consolidation process involved a number of issues requiring "deeper consideration" and that the Attorney-General's Department will "continue working on this project".[100]

The failure to include family violence appears to be a missed opportunity to consider this issue. This is particularly so given there is a clear roadmap for the inclusion of family violence as a protected attribute under Commonwealth anti-discrimination legislation in light of the contribution made in submissions to the consolidation process including

---

[97] For example, on 27 June 2012, Senator Lee Rhiannon successfully moved a motion that the Senate note the prevalence, impact and cost of family violence and called on the Government to: "consider introducing domestic and family violence as a separate ground of discrimination; consider making discrimination related to domestic and family violence unlawful in the workplace; and urge all private companies and public sectors to include domestic violence clauses in their enterprise agreements": Commonwealth, *Parliamentary Debates*, Senate, 27 June 2012, 4692–3. On 14 August 2012, Senator Rhiannon successfully moved a motion that the Senate take note of the Attorney-General's response to the original Senate resolution: Commonwealth, *Parliamentary Debates,* Senate, 14 August 2012, 5188.

[98] Australian Government, Consolidation of Commonwealth Anti-Discrimination Laws: Regulatory Impact Statement (2012) 85.

[99] Ibid, 87.

[100] The Hon Mark Dreyfus (Attorney-General) and Hon Penny Wong (Minister for Finance and Deregulation), 'New Anti-Discrimination Laws to Cover Sexual Orientation, Gender Identity and Intersex Status' (Media Release, 20 March 2013).

by the AHRC,[101] and more broadly by academics such as Smith and Orchiston.[102] It is currently unclear whether the Human Rights and Anti-Discrimination Bill 2012 (Cth) will be introduced into Parliament prior to the Federal Election announced for September 2013.

If the Bill is not introduced, or if family violence is not included in the final text of the Bill, the author suggests there are a number of possible strategies for pursuing its ultimate inclusion in anti-discrimination legislation. These include for example, considering its inclusion in State and Territory anti-discrimination legislation, and encouraging an expansion of the proposed three-year review of the exceptions under the Bill to include matters such as the inclusion of additional protected attributes.[103]

Recent developments

Beyond a requirement that the government table the ALRC's reports in Parliament, implementation is a matter for government. However, in its Final Report the ALRC suggested it might be appropriate to implement its recommended reforms by way of a whole-of-government five-phased approach to reform.[104]

There has been a number of developments following the ALRC's Inquiry, some of which have extended upon the initial work done by the ADFVC and implemented several of the ALRC's recommendations in this area. For example, as noted earlier, the Australian Government announced the establishment of a National Centre of Excellence to Reduce Violence

---

[101] See, for example: Australian Domestic and Family Violence Clearinghouse, Submission to Senate Standing Committee on Legal and Constitutional Affairs, *Exposure Draft of Human Rights and Anti-Discrimination Bill 2012*, December 2012; Australian Domestic and Family Violence Clearinghouse, Submission to Australian Government Attorney-General's Department, *Consolidation of Commonwealth Anti-Discrimination Laws*, 23 January 2012.

[102] See, for example: B Smith and T Orchiston, 'Domestic Violence Victims At Work: A Role for Anti-Discrimination Law?' (2012) 25 *Australian Journal of Labour Law* 209.

[103] Clause 47 of the Human Rights and Anti-Discrimination Bill 2012 (Cth) provides that the "Minister must arrange for a review of the exception in this Division to be conducted, and for a written report on that review" within three years of commencement and that the report must be tabled in Parliament.

[104] For further detail on the suggested approach to reform see Australian Law Reform Commission, above n 31, ch 15.

against Women in January 2013.[105] The Centre will be based in Sydney but is a collaborative project between the Commonwealth, States and Territories. The Centre will receive funding of $3 million a year to "develop a national research agenda to improve policy and service delivery in the prevention of violence against women across Australia".[106]

In addition, the ADFVC received additional funding to expand its Workplace Rights and Entitlements Project; and DEEWR implemented a number of research and data collection recommendations.[107] Significantly, as recommended, issues relating to family violence were considered in the course of the Fair Work Act Review as well as by the AHRC and subsequently raised in the process surrounding the consolidation of anti-discrimination legislation.[108]

Further, legislation amending the *Fair Work Act* and implementing some of the ALRC's key recommendations is currently before Parliament.[109]

There have also been interesting developments in the broader employment and anti-discrimination law and international landscape. A number of existing international conventions are relevant to the legal framework in relation to violence in the family, and acknowledge that violence against women and children is a violation of human rights.[110] In

[105] The Hon Julia Gillard, above n 41; J Collins (Minister for the Status of Women) and P Goward (NSW Minister for Women), 'New National Centre to Reduce Violence Against Women' (Media Release, 28 November 2012).
[106] J Collins (Minister for the Status of Women) and P Goward (NSW Minister for Women), 'New National Centre to Reduce Violence Against Women' (Media Release, 28 November 2012).
[107] Australian Law Reform Commission, above n 31, recs 15–1, 15–4, 15–5.
[108] Ibid, recs 16–1, 16–8
[109] Australian Law Reform Commission, above n 31, rec 17–1.
[110] *Universal Declaration of Human Rights,* 10 December 1948 (entered into force on 10 December 1948); *International Covenant on Civil and Political Rights,* 16 December 1966, [1980] ATS 23 (entered into force on 23 March 1976); *Convention on the Elimination of All Forms of Discrimination against Women,* 18 December 1979, [1983] (entered into force on 3 September 1981); *Convention on the Rights of the Child,* 20 November 1989, [1991] ATS 4 (entered into force on 2 September 1990); *Convention on the Rights of Persons with Disabilities,* 30 March 2007, [2008] ATS 12 (entered into force on 3 May 2008); *Declaration on the Rights of Indigenous Peoples,* 13 September 2007, GA Res 61/295, UN Doc A/RES/47/1.

addition however, there are important moves at an international level with respect to employment and family violence.[111]

The Future Path to Reform

The search for law reform solutions reveals that if workplaces are the new communities, given the prevalence and impact of family violence, then a wide range of actors in the employment law system have a role to play in responding to and addressing family violence. The ALRC's Final Report, in combination with the National Plan and other initiatives in this area, provides an important blueprint for reform. Ultimately, the measure of our law reform success must be whether the experiences of Jenny and others like her would be different under an employment law system reformed to encompass the measures outlined in this chapter. To date the answer is mixed and depends on whether Jenny has access to family violence-related leave and entitlements under an enterprise agreement or modern award and whether Jenny's workplace has adopted the necessary policies, procedures and safety plans. In time, the employment and anti-discrimination law systems must be able to appropriately identify and respond to family violence in order to make a difference in the lives of all Australians experiencing family violence, including people like Jenny.

---

[111] For example, in July 2011 and October 2012 a representative from the ADFVC was involved in discussions with the Bureau for Gender Equality at the International Labour Organisation to discuss the development of international standards as well as the European Trade Union Confederation on implementing their domestic violence and work action plan: Australian Domestic and Family Violence Clearinghouse, *What's New?* (2012) <www.austdvclearinghouse.unsw.edu.au/whats_new.htm>.

CHAPTER SEVEN

REGULATION, DISCLOSURE, AND VOLUNTARY GENETIC PROFILING

WENDY BONYTHON AND BRUCE BAER ARNOLD

Direct-to-consumer (DTC) availability of genetic testing is a relatively new phenomenon, which has, until recently, largely escaped the attention of regulators. Made possible by the results of large-scale research projects such as the Human Genome Project, DTC genetic testing offers consumers the ability to access their personal genetic information for a range of uses, from the relatively benign to the potentially catastrophic, including information about predisposition to life-threatening illness. Although genetic tests relied on by clinicians in the context of diagnosis must comply with strict accreditation and quality control procedures, and demonstrate their clinical validity and utility before they are approved on a nation by nation basis, DTC genetic tests are available across borders and until recently have avoided enforcement by regulators of compliance with regulatory frameworks.

This chapter examines DTC genetic testing, focusing specifically on regulatory, privacy and consumer-protection issues. The cross-border marketing of low-cost multinational DTC genetic testing poses questions for Australian and international regulators, health service practitioners and consumers regarding consistency with privacy, data protection and consumer protection laws, the development of coherent international regulatory mechanisms and issues of genetic discrimination (the "GATTACA Problem"). The authors discuss current industry practice, and critique efforts to bring DTC genetic testing within the scope of regulatory bodies, including: the Food and Drug Administration (FDA) and the Therapeutic Goods Administration (TGA) in the US and Australia, respectively; proposed Australian National Health & Medical Research Council (NHMRC) Guidelines aimed at supporting doctors when confronted with DTC test results by patients; and legislative reforms against genetic discrimination, such as the *Genetic Information Non-discrimination Act* (GINA) in the US. Drawing on previous experiences with Australian privacy law and its application to genetics, the authors argue that some efforts in Australia potentially further weaken the Australian privacy regime, and leave doctors exposed to liability. The authors suggest that the development of an international consumer protection framework regarding DTC genetic testing is both desirable and possible, although not, apparently, on the current international agenda.

This is the Meaning of Life?
Genes, Genomes, and DTC Genetic Testing

Genetic testing

In 2000, the heads of two research consortia (one publicly funded, the other private) fronted a press conference at the White House as the then-President of the United States of America, Bill Clinton, announced that the first draft of the entire human genome was complete. It was to be another three years before the "finished" draft of the genome would be released by the Human Genome Project, the international publicly funded consortium who had been chipping away at the project since October 1990.[1]

For biologists, this milestone was viewed as the equivalent to man landing on the moon, heralding a new era of genomic medicine, whereby analysing the genomic sequence of specific individuals would reveal susceptibility to medical conditions, permit tailoring of treatments for disease based on the individual's genetic make-up, provide myriad other

[1] Victor McElheny, *Drawing the Map of Life: Inside the Human Genome Project* (Basic Books, 2010); Kevin Davies, *Cracking the Genome: Inside the Race to Unlock Human DNA* (Simon & Schuster, 2001). See also: Timothy Murphy and Marc Lapp (eds), *Justice & the Human Genome Project* (University of California Press, 1994).

diagnostic and therapeutic benefits or simply address a market for "designer babies".[2]

Amid talk of a "genomics gold rush",[3] ready access to venture capital and the absence of systematic regulation over the past decade resulted in the emergence of a range of start-up DTC testing enterprises located in the US, Iceland and other jurisdictions.[4] They have been marketing their services worldwide, synergising with celebrity events, corporate websites, invitations in social network services and co-marketing through partnerships with bodies that range from the US National Geographic Association to Australian private health insurer NIB. Marketing strategies have very much focused on forming partnerships with credible entities, to detract attention from the lack of scientific data underpinning the tests themselves.[5]

Despite these high hopes, and the expansion of commercial research in the area, sequencing of the human genome is yet to yield some of the expected breakthroughs. Experience since 1990 has shown that human genetics is far more complex than was initially thought, and that DNA

---

[2] Elizabeth Finkel, *The Genome Generation* (Melbourne University Press, 2012); Jon Turney, *Frankenstein's Footsteps: Science, Genetics and Popular Culture* (Yale University Press, 1998); Dorothy Nelkin and Susan Lindee, *The DNA Mystique: The Gene as a Cultural Icon* (Freeman, 1995). See also: Margaret Sleeboom-Faulkner (ed), *Frameworks of Choice: Predictive and Genetic Testing in Asia* (Amsterdam University Press, 2010); Glenn McGee, *The Perfect Baby: Parenthood in the New World of Cloning and Genetics* (Rowman & Littlefield, 2000); and Gregory Stock and John Campbell, *Engineering the Human Germline: An Exploration of the Science and Ethics of Altering the Genes We Pass to Our Children* (Oxford University Press, 2000).

[3] Eric Topol, Sarah Murray and Kelly Frazer, 'The Genomics Gold Rush' (2007) 298(2) *Journal of the American Medical Association* 218–221. See also: James Evans, Eric Meslin, Theresa Marteau and Timothy Caulfield, 'Deflating the Genomic Bubble' (2011) 331(6069) *Science* 861–862.

[4] See, for example: Roxanne Mykitiuk, 'Caveat Emptor: Direct-to-Consumer Supply and Advertising of Genetic Testing' (2004) 27(1) *Clinical & Investigative Medicine* 23–32; Janneke Gerards et al, *Genetic Discrimination and Genetic Privacy in a Comparative Perspective* (Intersentia, 2005).

[5] See, for example: European Academies Science Advisory Council and the Federation of European Academies of Medicine, *Direct-to-consumer Genetic Testing for Health-related Purposes in the European Union: The View from EASAC and FEAM* (August 2012); Gregory Kutz, 'Direct-to-consumer Genetic Tests: Misleading Test Results Are Further Complicated by Deceptive Marketing and Other Questionable Practices', Testimony Before the Subcommittee on Oversight and Investigations, Committee on Energy and Commerce, House of Representatives (US Government Accountability Office, 22 July 2010).

sequence alone provides limited clinically useful information.[6] And while DTC genetic testing companies are ideally positioned to contribute to our understanding of genetics and disease, it is premature to assign clinical validity to the tests they use. In essence, although we can see the letters in "the book of life", we cannot yet understand the meaning of much of the text in that book, and act on the basis of that understanding. Misunderstanding of those letters by consumers and misrepresentation by testing providers pose challenges for regulators, consumers and medical practitioners alike. To understand those challenges we first need to look at what the genome is, and its significance.

The human genome and disease

The human genome consists of three billion bases — pairs of chemical molecules — arranged in sequence to form genes. These sequences are then further packaged as chromosomes, of which humans have 22 pairs, and the two sex chromosomes, XX for women, and XY for men. Each chromosome carries a copy of each of the genes located on that chromosome, again with the exception of the sex chromosomes — women have two copies, one on each of the X chromosomes, while men only have a single copy, only having one X chromosome. Genes frequently act as a template or pattern for proteins — other molecules — that perform specific functions within the cell. Errors within the sequence can either lead to the protein produced being incorrect, or may affect the production or distribution of that protein.

According to the simplest models of disease caused by genetics, a single defect within a gene — potentially as minor as one error affecting a single base in the sequence of three billion bases — directly causes a change in how the cells of the body function, ultimately causing disease. This is most obvious in sex-linked disorders, such as haemophilia, where males, having only a single copy of the affected X-chromosome located gene, are affected much more severely and frequently than their female relatives; however for other genes, if a person has mutations within the both copies of an autosomal gene they can develop a wide range of disorders.

A large number of diseases do not follow this simple model. Increasingly, genome wide association studies (GWAS) are being used to

[6] Elizabeth Finkel, The Genome Generation (Melbourne University Press, 2012) 211. See also: Jeffrey Augen, Bioinformatics in the Post-genomic Era: Genome, Transcriptome, Proteome, and Information-based Medicine (Addison-Wesley, 2005).

identify candidate regions within the genome that appear to be associated with certain diseases. However, in many cases it is not entirely clear whether the region identified is a cause of the disease, or merely correlates with it, and these tests fails to detect the interactions between products of multiple genes, or account for environmental factors contributing to disease development.[7] Consequently, GWAS data, rather than providing a simple yes/no answer to the question of whether an individual will develop a disease, tends to rely on complex statistical analysis to determine whether a particular individual is at increased risk of developing a condition based on a combination of factors, both genetic and environmental. While useful in revealing genetic targets suitable for further research, they are not definitive diagnostic tools.

Many of the companies operating in this market utilise GWAS-derived testing platforms, such as microarrays or other high through-put technology, and market them directly to consumers, either directly, or by implication. In doing so, DTC providers are implicitly overstating the clinical validity and utility of these platforms. Companies frequently use commercially available testing platforms, such as Affymetrix and Illumina microarray and single nucleotide polymorphism chips, as the basis of their testing. It is worth noting, however, that the commercial market for which these platforms are designed was traditionally the life-sciences research market, rather than the clinical diagnostic market. The very fact that the platforms are commercially available does not, as some consumers assume, mean that the testing platforms themselves have been approved for diagnostic use — they have not — or that the test results are readily interpretable.

Although tests for some multifactorial conditions have been validated by scientific evidence and are now used as legitimate clinical diagnostic tools, in many cases the associations between gene variants and altered risk of developing diseases, in isolation from other risk factors, are currently too weak to be of clinical significance, and are, at best, indicative only, rather than predictive. While this makes them exciting research targets, these tests should not be used for diagnostic purposes.

The ability to generate a complete *and reliable* predictive profile of a person's health, intelligence, physical appearance, and other attributes simply from the sequence of their DNA remains, therefore, a scientific impossibility at the present time, due to the substantial gaps in knowledge,

---

[7] Cecilia Bellcross, Patricia Page , and Dana Meaney-Delman, 'Direct-to-consumer Personal Genome Testing and Cancer Risk Prediction' (2012) 18 *Cancer Journal*, 293–302.

including about models of complex multi-gene and environmental factor interactions.

The traditional business model for DTC testing consisted of a potential client registering interest with a company, often via a website, which would then send a collection kit to the address of the client. The kit contained a collection vessel, and sometimes a swab. The client then either self-administered a buccal swab — brushing the inside of the cheek to collect epithelial cells — or simply spat into the collection vessel, which was then mailed back to the testing facility of the company. In exchange for fees, the company performed genetic sequencing tests against the genetic markers of the client's choice, and the company then produced a report summarising the findings. The client was frequently required to access their results via a login website, and pay an ongoing subscription fee in order to maintain their access to their results. Although some sites provided access to genetic counsellors, often via telephone or email, this was by no means always the case.

Regulation: Who has the power?

Most Western jurisdictions — notably Australia, the US, Canada, Japan, and the EU — have regulatory bodies who are authorised by law to regulate pharmaceuticals and medical products. Their powers include granting or withholding regulatory approval for marketing. In the event that approval is not forthcoming, generally the product cannot lawfully be marketed in that country, noting that there are some exceptional circumstances which are recognised.

DTC genetic tests meet the criteria for in vitro diagnostic devices which fall within the purview of these regulatory agencies. Wording of the laws varies from jurisdiction to jurisdiction, but as a sample, the definition from the Australian *Therapeutic Goods (Medical Devices) Regulations 2002* (Cth) is provided below:

> IVD medical device, or in vitro diagnostic medical device, means a medical device that is:
> (a) a reagent, calibrator, control material, kit, specimen receptacle, software, instrument, apparatus, equipment or system, whether used alone or in combination with another diagnostic product for in vitro use; and
> (b) intended by the manufacturer to be used in vitro for the examination of a specimen derived from the human body, solely or principally for:
> (i) giving information about a physiological or pathological state or a congenital abnormality; or
> (ii) determining safety and compatibility with a potential recipient; or

(iii) monitoring therapeutic measures; and

(c) not a product that is:

(i) intended for general laboratory use; and

(ii) not manufactured, sold or presented for use as an IVD medical device.[8]

Clearly, therefore, a DTC collection kit from a company running tests which can provide information about a client's likely risk of developing a particular condition will appear to meet these criteria and, logically, should fall under the notice of the relevant regulator.

Once it has been established that a test is an in vitro diagnostic medical device, the regulator considers whether it should receive approval, permitting it to be marketed in that jurisdiction. Such approval for devices, including genetic tests, will only be granted if the applicants can demonstrate that the test is both safe and effective for patient use: safe, meaning that it will not cause the patient harm — and effective — meaning that it does what it claims to do, based on scientific data.

The majority of tests being marketed by DTC genetic testing companies are generally "safe": the consumer is not exposed to any test reagent, and swabbing the inside of the mouth to obtain buccal cells, and mailing the swab to the company in a sealed container poses little physical risk to the consumer. However, many of the tests are inadequately supported by scientific evidence to justify claims that they are effective. It is on this ground that many of the DTC genetic tests available are likely to fail to obtain regulatory approval. They thus pose questions under Australian and overseas consumer protection law.[9]

Tests for diseases following the simpler model, based on mutations in a single gene, discussed above, generally have a high predictive power. Based on the genetic sequence of an individual, conclusions can be drawn about whether they will or will not develop that disease. Such tests are both clinically valid — they accurately predict disease — and clinically useful — they provide information that, in many cases, is relevant for treatment.

As the model becomes more complex, and more factors are involved in development of disease, the predictive power of genetic testing decreases markedly, and results are instead expressed in terms of risk. Rather than providing a determinative yes or no type answer, they consider the increased or decreased risk associated with a genetic sequence, either with

[8] Therapeutic Goods (Medical Devices) Regulation 2002 (Cth).

[9] See, for example: the *Competition and Consumer Act 2010* (Cth) sch 2, ss 18, 29, replacing the *Trade Practices Act 1974* (Cth) ss 52, 53.

or without consideration of confounding factors such as the role of other genes and environmental factors involved in development of the disease. Analysis of risk associated with confounding factors is complicated by the incomplete identification of all contributing factors in many instances. For many diseases, it is clear that although there is a genetic component associated with risk of developing disease, other as-yet unidentified risk factors, including other genes, also have a role to play. The majority of tests marketed DTC are of the latter type.

Yet despite legitimate concerns frequently expressed about the validity and utility of these tests by the scientific community,[10] and the fact that, prima facie, they appear to fall squarely within the scope of regulation, until recently, providers of DTC genetic testing generally escaped the detailed attention of the regulators. That inattention reflected the newness of the technologies, resourcing and other problems within bodies such as the FDA and TGA, the absence of an incident that gained bureaucratic/media attention and thus affected institutional priorities, and the strategic location of some genetic testing services within jurisdictions (such as Iceland) with weak privacy and clinical regulatory frameworks.

Gertz, for example, notes

> legislation passed by the Icelandic government not for the benefit of scientists in general, but for one specific commercial company and enabling deCODE Genetics, a firm registered in the USA and based in Iceland, to set up a database consisting of the medical and genealogical records of the entire Icelandic population, living and dead, as well as tissue samples of every living Icelander.[11]

This lack of regulatory attention abruptly ground to a halt in mid-2010, when the business model of DTC providers evolved in a way that made it impractical for regulators in the US to ignore it any longer. Pathways Genomics announced that it was further advancing its business model by selling collection kits directly on shelves at Walgreen's drugstores throughout the US, finally prompted the US government, and the FDA in particular, to investigate DTC genetic testing.

---

[10] Above n 5.

[11] Renate Gertz, 'An Analysis of the Icelandic Supreme Court Judgment on the Health Sector Database Act' (2004) 1(2) *SCRIPTed: A Journal of Law, Technology and Society* 241, 242.

Consumer Protection, Genetic Discrimination, and Privacy — The Issues

Genetic literacy — Not understanding what you don't know?

In spite of the slow process of developing legitimate clinical diagnostic tools for multifactorial diseases, public interest in DNA technology, and the information it can reveal, has never been stronger. It is reflected in dramas such as *CSI*, where genetic information serves as a criminological silver bullet, and in journalism that embodies more enthusiasm than expertise.[12] This interest has not, unfortunately, been accompanied by an increase in the genetic literacy of the population.[13]

A consequence of the increased publicity genetic research has received in recent years is heightened enthusiasm about genetics, which has not been accompanied by a popular understanding of the limitations of the current state of scientific knowledge, or its implications.[14] Daily reporting in mainstream media headlined with "Scientists discover link between gene and (insert medical condition here)",[15] frequently based on the results of GWAS reported in scientific literature directed at an informed

---

[12] See, for example: Simon Cole and Rachel Dioso-Villa, '*CSI* and its Effects: Media, Juries, and the Burden of Proof' (2007) 41(3) *New England Law Review* 435; Tom Tyler, 'Viewing CSI and the Threshold of Guilt: Managing Truth and Justice in Reality and Fiction' (2006) 115 *Yale Law Journal* 1050.

[13] See, for example: D H Lea et al, 'Communicating Genetic and Genomic Information: Health Literacy and Numeracy Considerations' (2011) 14(4–5) *Public Health Genomics* 279; K D Christensen et al 'Understandings of Basic Genetics in the United States: Results from a National Survey of Black and White Men and Women' (2010) 13(7–8) *Public Health Genomics.* 467.

[14] See, for example: Caron Molster, Taryn Charles, Amanda Samanek and Peter O'Leary, 'Australian Evidence of a Literacy Gap in Lay Knowledge of Genetic Science and Related Concepts' (Paper presented at the Human Genetics Society of Australasia 32nd Annual Scientific Meeting, 2–6 August 2008); Caron Molster, Taryn Charles, Amanda Samanek and Peter O'Leary, 'Australian Study on Public Knowledge of Human Genetics and Health' (2009) 12(2) *Public Health Genomics* 84; Sandra Taylor 'A Population-Based Survey in Australia of Men's and Women's Perceptions of Genetic Risk and Predictive Genetic Testing and Implications for Primary Care' (2011) 14(6) *Public Health Genomics* 325.

[15] A Factiva database search of the terms "gene" and "link" identified 78 published articles (duplications omitted) in the past two years, claiming to identify new genetic links to diseases including Alzheimer's' disease, Motor neurone disease, cannabis addiction, alcoholism, migraine, risk of miscarriage, risk of cot death, diabetes, obesity, ADHD, and a range of other conditions.

researcher audience, rather than the layperson, creates a misperception amongst the public that: a) a comprehensive and very accurate diagnostic test may now be available; that b) treatment will be available, either immediately or in the near future; and that c) the results of testing are readily interpretable. This perception conflicts with the reality that such testing is generally only extremely preliminary in nature, and that the association between the gene and the condition may never be substantiated sufficiently to form the basis of an approved diagnostic test, for a range of reasons.

Misperceptions such as these create the perfect environment for the exploitation of genetically interested but naïve individuals, who are parted from their money in exchange for statistically complex, but clinically weak, genetic tests purporting to identify whether a person is at risk of developing a particular condition. The low level of genetic literacy among most consumers means that those people are potentially vulnerable in purchasing and acting on tests that are marketed as having a diagnostic rather than entertainment function.[16]

Even so-called "recreational genetics" service providers may be a cause for concern, as many of the consumer protection and privacy issues remain the same.[17] Those services target their marketing towards people interested in ancestry — see which genes you share with Martin Luther King, Kylie Minogue or Barack Obama — or physiological markers (or simply acquisition of a fashion statement, alongside companies that offer to turn a map of your DNA into "unique artwork"),[18] rather than in clinical predictors.

It is against this background that we have witnessed the rise of global DTC models of marketing genetic testing. Consumers appear to be

[16] Donna Messner, 'Informed Choice in Direct-to-consumer Genetic Testing for Alzheimer and Other Diseases: Lessons from Two Cases' (2011) 30(1) *New Genetics and Society* 59.

[17] See, for example: *My Ancestry* (2012) 23andME <www.23andme.com/ancestry/>.

[18] DNA Art, for example, indicates that "We create the ultimate in personalised art – ready-to-hang wall art based on your own genetic code. The image on your DNA Art™ is achieved by creating a unique DNA profile. A fragment of your DNA is tagged with fluorescent dyes and photographed in a professional genetic lab. The result is a series of bands and highlights that creates the image that we print and mount".

engaging with the services because provision of samples is fashionable,[19] because individuals are concerned to gain information that supposedly allows early diagnosis and even treatment of disorders, because provision benefits all humanity by contributing to a better understanding of the "book of life" or because DTC genetic testing resonates with the values of autonomy and self-actualisation that are apparent in contemporary popular culture.[20]

The multinational nature of some DTC genetic testing companies raises concerns on several fronts. Some companies have adopted strategies of distributing the activities of their business amongst jurisdictions that provide more permissive data storage, laboratory accreditation, privacy, and consumer protection regimes. Concerns about distribution of roles and responsibilities across jurisdictions are not restricted to the genetic testing sector — they are increasingly being voiced in relation to the data storage and processing in the global "cloud" and in much e-tailing activity. It is important to recognise, however, that the global collection of genetic data by an enterprise located in Iceland, Alaska or the Caymans is potentially more problematical than the purchase by an Australian consumer of a woolly jumper or DVD from Amazon.com. A framework for cross-border e-tailing is provided by UNCITRAL. There is no such accepted framework for DTC genetic test or for cross-border pharmaceutical retailing.[21]

Buyer beware? Consumer protection and DTC

Consumer protection is one of the most obvious issues in relation to this model. Although costs are rapidly falling, DTC testing is not cheap. Depending on the test, consumers can typically expect to pay several hundred to several thousand dollars.[22] Samples are returned from

---

[19] Allen Salkin, 'When in Doubt, Spit It Out: Spit Parties for Folks Who Want to Break Their Own DNA Code', *New York Times*, 12 September 2008. See also: Lone Frank, *My Beautiful Genome: Exposing Our Genetic Future One Quirk at a Time* (Oneworld, 2011).

[20] See, for example: Micki McGee, Self-Help Inc: Makeover Culture in American Life (Oxford University Press, 2005); Barbara Ehrenreich, Smile or Die: How the Relentless Promotion of Positive Thinking has Undermined America (Granta, 2009); Brian Pronger, Body Fascism: Salvation in the Technology of Physical Fitness (University of Toronto Press, 2002).

[21] Amir Attaran et al, 'How to Achieve International Action on Falsified and Substandard Medicines' (2012) 345 *British Medical Journal e7381.*

[22] Malorye Allison, 'Direct-to-consumer Genomics Reinvents Itself' (2012) 30(11) *Nature Biotechnology* 1027, 1028.

consumers to the company by mail, and results are typically returned by email or website. Access to that website might be for a limited period.

There have been several reported instances of consumers simply not getting what they pay for: either the test is from someone else's sample (eg male clients returning female-specific test results), or experiencing substitutions in the tests performed.[23] Additional consumer issues have arisen when consumers have purportedly had identical tests performed by two separate providers, and received contradictory results, something that raises questions about the proficiency of the testers and about the way that the data is expressed.[24]

A joint report released by the European Academies Science Advisory Council and the Federation of European Academies of Medicine in 2012 was scathing in its assessment of the industry, stating

> On the whole, DTC GT (Direct-to-consumer genetic testing) has little clinical value at present and, on occasion, has potential to be harmful. We would not wish to encourage European Union citizens to use DTC GT at present. We suggest special caution about DTC GT in several specific respects, for example relating to testing for high penetrance, serious disorders, prenatal screening, and nutrigenomic and pharmacogenetic testing. In developing general principles for the management of consumer genetic services, we emphasise that regulation must be on the basis that claims about the link between genetic markers and disease are scientifically valid. Other key issues to address include quality assurance, transparent supply of accurate information, consideration of the implications for established health services and clarification of consent procedures, including any use of data for research purposes.[25]

The US Government Accounting Office in 2010 condemned the DTC testing sector for deceptive advertising, nonsensical claims, "test results that are misleading and of little or no practical use", "contradictory results" and "DNA-based disease predictions that conflicted with … actual

---

[23] Gregory Kutz, 'Direct-to-consumer Genetic Tests: Misleading Test Results Are Further Complicated by Deceptive Marketing and Other Questionable Practices', Testimony Before the Subcommittee on Oversight and Investigations, Committee on Energy and Commerce, House of Representatives (US Government Accountability Office, 22 July 2010).

[24] Ibid.

[25] European Academies Science Advisory Council and the Federation of European Academies of Medicine, above n 5.

medical conditions".[26] It is notable that those criticisms are consistent with authoritative medical and scientific literature on DTC, some of which is noted in citations throughout this chapter, but are independent of the specialist regulators. In Australia for example the NHMRC has identified concerns as late as 2012.

Just as importantly, there are questions about consumer interpretation of the information provided by the services. The DTC model is, in essence, one of convenience rather than authority and meaningful interpretation by specialist medical practitioners.

DTC genetic testing is problematical because the services operate across national borders and outside conventional regulatory frameworks that centre on diagnosis by medical practitioners or the promotion and delivery of pharmaceuticals. Those services are also problematical because there are persistent questions about the quality of testing (different services provide substantially different reports regarding samples from the same people) and about the advice consumers receive on the basis of those tests.

In many instances, the multinational structure of providers and the use of opaque online boilerplate makes it unclear to consumers what their rights are.[27] As indicated above, they may mistakenly believe that the consumer protection laws in Australia apply to these services, when in actual fact the services may be performed in the US, Asia, or Europe, under a vastly different (or indeed non-existent) consumer protection regime.

Consent and privacy protection: Yours, mine, or ours?

Consumer protection is not the only issue raised by the multi-national operation of DTC providers. From a privacy perspective three additional concerns are apparent.

The first is that of consent. It is unclear whether consumers are aware of what use currently is or might in future be made by the service providers and third parties with information gathered through sample

---

[26] Gregory Kutz, 'Direct-to-consumer Genetic Tests: Misleading Test Results Are Further Complicated by Deceptive Marketing and Other Questionable Practices', Testimony Before the Subcommittee on Oversight and Investigations, Committee on Energy and Commerce, House of Representatives (US Government Accountability Office, 22 July 2010).

[27] Margaret Radin, Boilerplate: The Fine Print, Vanishing Rights, and the Rule of Law (Princeton University Press, 2012).

collection. What rights do consumers have under national and international law?[28]

In orthodox clinical medicine, it no longer acceptable for a clinician to leave a patient floundering in the dark with respect to understanding their choices. As the Australian High Court decision in *Rogers v Whitaker*[29] makes crystal clear, a patient's consent must be based on an understanding of the risk factors which are important to them — not the factors a "body of medical men",[30] or anyone else, would consider to be important, but the factors that could reasonably be expected to be of importance to the patient.

Although the Court rejected the use of the terminology "informed consent",[31] as placing too much emphasis on the provider of the consent, and not enough on the provider of the information the consent was based on, the concept has still crept into Australian law. What is clear, based on the decision, is that valid exercise of consent can only occur when patients or consumers have a complete understanding of all the relevant information.

The reliance some clients of DTC services are likely to place on the results they receive is of concern, given that some consumers will perceive "DNA as destiny", based on their own lack of genetic literacy, and lack of access to the support of professional counsellors. Some may make fundamental life choices (eg commit suicide, not have children, not invest for old age on the basis of expectations about an early death) or experience severe depression attributable to what they incorrectly construe from a DTC report as their genetic fate.

In the event that Australian regulators do not address the shortcomings of DTC both adequately and publicly, there is the potential for consumers who do undertake testing to be driven underground, and feel too embarrassed to discuss the results of their test with their own doctors, in case their doctor feels that they lack trust in them, or because they feel stupid for having the tests done, or even because they feel stupid for not fully understanding them. In the event that regulatory intervention drives

---

[28] Jasper Bovenberg, Tineke Meulenkamp, Ellen Smets and Sjef Gevers, 'Your Biobank, Your Doctor? The Right to Full Disclosure of Population Biobank Findings' (2008) 5(1) *Genomics, Society and Policy* 55.

[29] *Rogers v Whitaker* (1992) 175 CLR 479, [16] (Mason CJ, Brennan, Dawson, Toohey and McHugh JJ).

[30] Bolam v Friern Hospital Management Committee (1957) 1 WLR 582.

[31] *Rogers v Whitaker* (1992) 175 CLR 479, [16] (Mason CJ, Brennan, Dawson, Toohey and McHugh JJ).

the DTC market underground, there is a significant risk that patients will make decisions by giving undue weight to the results of DTC.

Although data from recreational providers is less likely to be considered in clinical patient decision-making, it still raises similar additional issues to clinical DTC that are inadequately considered by many consumers, particularly pertaining to privacy and disclosure concerns. Many of these providers are storing leftover samples for the purposes of creating DNA biobanks suitable for sale to third parties for further exploitation, often without the knowledge or consent of the consumer.[32] Consumers do not own the results of the tests and typically the buccal swabs or other samples become the property of the service provider.[33] There are no global protocols for rights in those samples or associated data if the service provider is acquired or goes into receivership, at which time its most significant asset might be data collected about people across the globe.[34]

The second concern is that consumers may not realise that by providing samples of their own DNA for analysis, they are by implication revealing genetic information about their relatives, potentially allowing the service provider and associates to build a genetic profile of those relatives. When you provide a spit sample or swab from your cheek you are implicitly providing genetic data about your siblings, a gift of data that may be received, processed and disseminated in a legal regime that has significantly lower privacy protection than Australia. Those relatives of course have not consented to the provision of information, and indeed may be unaware that individual/familial profiling is taking place in a jurisdiction that lacks the regulatory protections that are axiomatic in their place of residence.

Recent amendments to the Australian *Privacy Act* now provide scope for doctors whose patients have genetic conditions to contact the relatives of those patients, *without the patient's consent*, and advise those relatives that they may potentially have the same genetic predisposition.

To be permitted to disclose genetic information, such as is obtained from DTC genetic testing, to another person, such as a genetic relative, without the authorisation of the patient, the doctor must *reasonably believe*

---

[32] James Evans, 'Recreational Genomics: What's in it for You?' (2008) 10(10) *Genetic Medicine* 709. See also: Gert van Ommen and Martina Cornel, 'Recreational genomics? Dreams and Fears on Genetic Susceptibility Screening' (2008) 16(4) *European Journal of Human Genetics* 403.

[33] Shubha Ghosh, Identity, Invention, and the Culture of Personalized Medicine Patenting (Cambridge University Press, 2012).

[34] *FAQs* (2012) Navigenics <www.navigenics.com>.

that disclosure is necessary to prevent a serious threat to the life health or safety of a genetic relative of the patient.

The NHMRC, in its recently released for comment draft guidelines for practitioners on DTC testing, advises that doctors may, under the amended *Privacy Act*, be able to advise relatives of a patient of the results of that patient's DTC testing, again *without the consent of the patient*. In a submission to the public consultation process, these authors raised concerns about that advice, primarily that disclosure without consent, under the amended *Privacy Act*, requires that there be a reasonable belief that disclosure is necessary to lessen or prevent a serious threat to the life health or safety of their genetic relatives.[35]

As discussed above, the evidentiary base underpinning DTC genetic testing is weak; while many of the tests may be of utility in research, in the vast majority of cases there is either insufficient evidence of a statistically significant association between the test and manifestation of the disease; inadequate understanding of the role of other genetic factors in contributing to manifestation of a multi-factorial disease; or the association is simply too weak to be of any clinical use.

Having regard to these well-documented limitations of DTC genetic testing, therefore, it is inconceivable that a doctor could form a reasonable belief that disclosing the results of such tests would lessen or prevent a serious threat to anyone — including the patient they directly relate to — much less a genetic relative. Advising the genetic relatives of a patient that the patient has tested positive for a weak genetic marker which may or may not be clinically relevant in diagnosis of a specific medical disease, according to a mail-order laboratory which may or may not meet the accreditation requirements for criteria including sample handling and quality control, without at the very least seeking confirmation through clinically validated and regulatory approved tests, is not going to advance the health interests of the patients relative in any meaningful way, and the disclosure is, therefore, unreasonable. This lack of reasonableness will therefore render the doctor's disclosure unlawful.

Furthermore, even referring to the provisions permitting disclosure without patient consent in the draft guidelines induces a belief that there may be grounds under which disclosure under the amendment might be permitted, which, if a practitioner were to rely on, could conceivably see them facing litigation for breach of privacy and confidentiality.

The authors have opposed the inclusion of the textbox in the guidelines on the basis that the scientific literature comprehensively opposes the use

---

[35] *Privacy Act 1988* (Cth) s 95AA.

of DTC genetic testing as a diagnostic tool, based on its lack of clinical utility and validity, and as such it could *never* be reasonable for a doctor to contact a patient's relatives and advise them of the results of the patient's DTC genetic testing, because the link between the disease and the gene is, at this stage, far too tenuous to justify breach of the patient's confidence on those grounds alone. Clearly, legislative interpretations such as these from a body entrusted with drafting guidelines on implementation of the *Privacy Act* in the medical context calls the independence and objectivity of the NHMRC, as advisors to the regulators entrusted with protecting the privacy rights of Australians, into question.

This recent development demonstrates that even in a country like Australia, which claims to have a high degree of regard for individual autonomy, our privacy protections are vulnerable, especially in the context of genetic privacy.

In considering those concerns we might look to two framework documents: the 2011 Opinion on Consent produced by the Article 29 Working Party and the 2012 *Privacy and Progress in Whole Genome Sequencing* report from the US Presidential Commission for the Study of Bioethical Issues.

The Article 29 Working Party is an independent European body concerned with data protection and privacy. It was established under Article 29 of *Directive 95/46/EC* (ie the overarching European Data Protection Directive that shapes national privacy law in the EU member states).[36] Its 38 page Opinion (15/2011)[37] reflects the European Commission's commitment to "clarifying and strengthening the rules on consent", given a recognition that although the current EU rules provide that the individual's consent for processing personal data should be a "freely given specific and informed indication" of wishes, those conditions are currently interpreted differently in the EU member states.

The Opinion confirms that consent should be freely given, specific and informed, giving individuals enough detail to make a decision about how

[36] The Working Party's tasks are described in article 30 of *Directive 95/46/EC* and article 15 of *Directive 2002/58/EC*. See: Yves Poullet and Serge Gutwirth, 'The Contribution of the Article 29 Working Party to the Construction of a Harmonised European Data Protection System: An Illustration of "Reflexive Governance"?', in Verónica Perez Asinari and Pablo Palazzi (eds), *Challenges of Privacy and Data Protection Law — Challenges of Privacy and Data Protection Law* (Bruylant, 2008) 570–610.

[37] The Opinion is accessible at: *Opinion 15/2011 on the Definition of Consent* (2011) Article 29 Data Protection Working Party <http://ec.europa.eu/justice/policies/privacy/docs/wpdocs/2011/wp187_en.pdf>.

their personal data will be used. Where explicit consent is required to process sensitive personal data (such as health records) the Opinion indicates that an individual must expressly agree — whether orally or in writing — to the processing of the personal data. Consent on the basis of an individual's inaction is not sufficient. Individuals should also be able to withdraw their consent, preventing any further processing of their personal data.

The Working Party states that —

> Consent is one of several legal grounds to process personal data. It has an important role, but this does not exclude the possibility, depending on the context, of other legal grounds perhaps being more appropriate from both the controller's and from the data subject's perspective. If it is correctly used, consent is a tool giving the data subject control over the processing of his data. If incorrectly used, the data subject's control becomes illusory and consent constitutes an inappropriate basis for processing.

The Opinion further notes that

> The relevance of consent as an enabler of the individual's autonomy and self-determination relies on its use in the right context and with the necessary elements. Individuals who have consented should be able to withdraw their consent, preventing further processing of their data.

Is that withdrawal of consent meaningful when consumers are dealing with a DTC testing provider that is located in another jurisdiction and that may have been dealing with genetic information in a way that has not come to the individual's attention and that may not be readily verifiable?

The Opinion, in identifying specific elements of the EU legal framework related to consent, comments that

> For consent to be valid, it must be freely given. This means that there must be no risk of deception, intimidation or significant negative consequences for the data subject if he/she does not consent … Consent must be specific. Blanket consent without determination of the exact purposes does not meet the threshold.
>
> Consent must be informed … the information provided must be sufficient to guarantee that individuals can make well informed decisions about the processing of their personal data. The need for consent to be "informed" translates into two additional requirements. First, the way in which the information is given must ensure the use of appropriate language so that data subjects understand what they are consenting to and for what purposes. This is contextual. The use of overly complicated legal or technical jargon would not meet the requirements of the law. Second, the information provided to users should be clear and sufficiently conspicuous

> so that users cannot overlook it. The information must be provided directly to individuals. It is not enough for it to be merely available somewhere.

Those statements in the Opinion are not part of Australian law. However, they highlight questions about whether Australian and overseas consumers are truly informed and validly consenting when using DTC testing services that are located in another jurisdiction and that rely on vague (or difficult to identify) indications of how genetic information will be used, shared and deleted.

The *Privacy and Progress in Whole Genome Sequencing* report, by the US Presidential Commission for the Study of Bioethical Issues,[38] also has no force under Australian law and may be disregarded by US legislators. It does however complement the Article 29 Working Party Opinion by highlighting concerns about genetic data.

The Commission concluded that:

> to realize the enormous promise that whole genome sequencing holds for advancing clinical care and the greater public good, individual interests in privacy must be respected and secured. As the scientific community works to bring the cost of whole genome sequencing down from millions per test to less than the cost of many standard diagnostic tests today, the Commission recognizes that whole genome sequencing and its increased use in research and the clinic could yield major advances in health care. However it could also raise ethical dilemmas.

The report accordingly considers:

> the most feasible ways of reconciling the enormous medical potential of whole genome sequencing with the pressing privacy and data access issues raised by the rapid emergence of low-cost whole genome sequencing. The life-saving potential of genome sequencing depends on gathering genetic information from many thousands (perhaps millions) of individuals, most of whom will not directly benefit from the research. Those who are willing to share some of the most intimate information about themselves for the sake of medical progress should be assured appropriate confidentiality … Without such assurance in place, individuals are less likely to voluntarily

---

[38] Presidential Commission for the Study of Bioethical Issues, *Privacy and Progress in Whole Genome Sequencing* (2012).

supply the data that have the potential to benefit us all with life-saving treatments for genetic diseases.[39]

Unsurprisingly the report emphasises

> the principle of respect for persons, which requires strong baseline protections for privacy and security of data, while public beneficence requires facilitating ample opportunities for data sharing and access to data by clinicians, researchers, and other authorized users. Respect for persons further requires that any collection and sharing of individual data be based on a robust process of informed consent. Responsible stewardship calls for oversight and management of whole genome sequence information by funders, managers, professional organizations, and others … Respect for persons implies not only respecting individual privacy, but also respecting research participants as autonomous persons who might choose to share their own data. Public beneficence is advanced by giving researchers access to plentiful data from which they can work to advance health care. Regulatory parsimony recommends only as much oversight as is truly necessary and effective in ensuring an adequate degree of privacy, justice and fairness, and security and safety while pursuing the public benefits of whole genome sequencing. Therefore, existing privacy protections and those being contemplated should be parsimonious and not impose high barriers to data sharing. While the Commission supports the intellectual freedom this access will encourage, clinicians and researchers must also act responsibly to earn public trust for the research enterprise.

A girl called GINA? Or something else …

Other privacy-related issues raised by DTC genetic testing include mandatory disclosure of results under some circumstances, which may be unfavourable in the case of analysis of behavioural traits, for example, and the potential for discrimination on the basis of genetics. Referred to as the "GATTACA" problem, based on the 1997 film of the same title, it relates

---

[39] The Report also notes, at 2, that "the potential for unauthorized access to and misuse of information … eg by a spouse as evidence of unfitness to parent in a custody case (or) in a social networking space, which could adversely affect that individual's chance of finding a spouse, achieving standing in a community, or pursuing a desired career path".

to the geneticisation of opportunities afforded to individuals on the basis of their DNA profile.[40]

In Australia, it is unlawful for providers of health insurance to refuse to provide, or adjust premiums on, the basis of genetic predisposition to certain conditions. This is not, however, the case with respect to life insurance or travel insurance, or other classes of risk-based personalised insurance. Under Part IV of the *Insurance Contracts Act 1984* (Cth), any information which is relevant to the policy issuer must be disclosed, otherwise any payments made under the policy can be challenged on the basis of non-disclosure. Relevant information requiring disclosure would include the results of genetic testing, including DTC genetic testing.[41]

While it is unlikely that many insurers would significantly alter their practices on the basis of DTC test results at this stage, in the future, once a greater number of GWAS are scientifically verified as being of clinical utility and validity, this situation may change. Unfortunately, however, the patient's genome will not. The results of that "fun" test they took as a teenager to determine how much they have in common with Justin Bieber may come back to haunt them as a 50 year old when they are refused life insurance on the basis that they are at an increased risk of having a heart attack based on updated knowledge about those gene associations.

Other areas where the potential for genetic discrimination is ripe include employment and migration. Similar to the experiences of some employees who participated in "team-building" personality profiling activities, only to discover that their "profile" made them "unsuitable" for their job, the clear potential exists for employers to utilise DTC genetic in a similar way. Want to make someone redundant, but can't decide who? What better way than to take a look at their DTC genetic testing profile,

---

[40] David Kirby, 'Extrapolating Race in *GATTACA*: Genetic Passing, Identity, and the Science of Race' (2004) 23(1) *Literature and Medicine* 184-200. See also: Henk ten Have, 'Genetics and Culture: The Geneticization Thesis' (2001) 4(3) *Medicine, Health Care & Philosophy*, 295–304; Abby Lippman, 'Prenatal Genetic Testing and Screening: Constructing Needs and Reinforcing Inequalities' (1991) 17(1/2) *American Journal Of Law and Medicine*, 15–50.

[41] Kristine Barlow-Stewart et al, 'Verification of Consumers' Experiences and Perceptions of Genetic Discrimination and its Impact on Utilization of Genetic Testing' (2009) 11(3) *Genetics in Medicine* 193; and Margaret Otlowski et al, 'Investigating Genetic Discrimination In The Australian Life Insurance Sector: Use Of Genetic Test Results In Underwriting 1999–2003' (2007) 14(3) *Journal of Law and Medicine* 367. More broadly see: Mark Rothstein (ed) *Genetics and Life Insurance: Medical Underwriting and Social Policy* (MIT Press, 2004) and Janneke Gerards et al, *Genetic Discrimination and Genetic Privacy in a Comparative Perspective* (Intersentia, 2005).

and hazard a guess which employee will use more sick leave in the next few years, and get rid of them? Likewise, it is conceivable that in the absence of legislation and international legal frameworks specifically prohibiting the use of genetic data in this context, countries considering citizenship applications may be influenced by the information in their decision-making processes, to avoid absorbing the long-term costs of providing healthcare resources to chronically ill people.

Although recent research in Australia shows that the incidence of genetic discrimination is relatively infrequent,[42] it is still there — which is frightening in itself, considering how much DTC genetic testing has taken off since the research was completed. Although our federal *Disability Discrimination Act*[43] includes "genetic discrimination" as a type of prohibited discrimination, it is by no means comprehensive, and there will continue to be situations where DTC test results, in the wrong hands, can be used to exploit people, either intentionally, or through lack of understanding of what those results actually mean. The US has recently released new legislation dealing specifically with the issue of genetic discrimination. Called the GINA — *Genetic Information Non-discrimination Act*[44] — it specifically prohibits discrimination against people in employment and access to health insurance on the basis of their genetic makeup. Only time will tell how effective this legislation proves to be for clients of DTC genetic testing services discriminated against by US entities; problematically, though, it will provide no protection to them offshore.

Regulation — The Solutions, or Adding to the Problem?

Should DTC genetic testing be regulated?

One response might be that DTC consumers are adults who can be reasonably expected to take responsibility for their actions and who, in a liberal democratic State, are free to act autonomously without interference by the State except where that action places themselves or other actors at serious risk. Adults may accordingly choose to waive protections that are potentially available under national or provincial privacy law. However this position does not adequately address the issue of children and other

[42] See: Barlow-Stewart et al, ibid; Otlowski et al, ibid.

[43] The *Disability Discrimination Ac 1992* (Cth) in its definition of "disability", includes disability "which may exist in future (including because of a genetic predisposition to that disability)".

[44] Genetic Information Non-discrimination Act (2008) 122 Stat. 881.

vulnerable people who may be tempted to participate in DTC genetic testing. The literature on DTC genetic testing does not feature accounts of minors providing genetic samples, and it is likely that such provision is minimised by the commercial basis of the services; minors are assumed not to have access to the credit card that is typically required by the testers.[45] However, it is notable that at least one prominent site displayed photos of teenage children, and referred to discussing your results with "your friends", and utilisation of social networking devices for sharing of information.[46] Other client profiles include families who have had their minor children tested. It is difficult to imagine any compelling reason for undertaking DTC genetic testing that could not sensibly be delayed until the child was of a sufficient age to consent to testing for themselves, especially in light of the mandatory disclosure issues arising under insurance law.[47]

After ignoring the issue of DTC genetic testing for years, the period since mid-2010 has seen a flurry of activity by regulators and policymakers, indicating that in their view, the answer to the question of regulation is a resounding "yes". By proposing to distribute collection kits through a chain of pharmacies in the US, the sector forced the regulators to take a stand. The results of that action will have, and have already had, profound impacts on the market.

Shortly after Pathway Genomics and Walgreens' Drugstores announced their partnership, the FDA started sending letters to DTC genetic testing providers, both US and foreign-registered, stating that they had not approved DTC genetic tests as in vitro devices, and demanding they demonstrate why they didn't think their product met the requirements for in vitro devices requiring pre-market FDA approval.[48] This was accompanied by a round of congressional hearings on DTC genetic testing.[49]

---

[45] The authors argue that this assumption is baseless, as we know that some teenagers have access to credit cards to pay for testing of themselves, their friends, or even the family pet.

[46] See: Sandra Lee and LaVera Crawley, 'Research 2.0: Social Networking and Direct-to-consumer (DTC) Genomics' (2009) 9 *The American Journal of Bioethics* 35.

[47] Heidi Howard, 'Are the Kids Really All Right? Direct-to-consumer Genetic Testing in Children: Are Company Policies Clashing with Professional Norms?' (2011) 19 *European Journal of Human Genetics* 1122.

[48] See: Letter from FDA to DeCODE, 10 June 2010 <http://www.fda.gov/downloads/MedicalDevices/ResourcesforYou/Industry/UCM215241.pdf>.

[49] United States House of Representatives Committee on Energy and Commerce.

While all of this was conducted with a great deal of fanfare and publicity, at least in the initial stages, there has been very little in the way of public engagement occurring recently. Behind the scenes there may have been quite a lot of negotiation between a resource-strapped regulator and the more credible providers of DTC genetic tests — certainly the recent crackdown has led to changes in the business models being employed in this market.[50] The Genetics and Public Policy Centre, of Johns Hopkins University, released an updated version of its list of DTC genetic testing providers in 2011, after the FDA commenced its enquiry into the industry. In the 2011 list, 20 companies providing tests directly to consumers were identified,[51] down from the 39 identified in the earlier 2008 version.[52] While neither list is exhaustive, it does indicate that, in the face of the current uncertainty facing the industry, some companies have either suspended doing business, gone out of business altogether, or changed their practices away from DTC marketing.

Psynomics is an example of the former.[53] Located in San Diego in the US, it marketed tests directly to consumers, targeting those with specific concerns around bipolar and their responsiveness to Selective Serotonin Reuptake Inhibitors (SSRIs), a class of commonly-prescribed antidepressants. The tests provided, Psynome and Psynome 2, claimed to test for mutations in the region associated with G protein receptor kinase 3, and mutations in the promoter of the L-allele of the serotonin transporter gene, respectively. Unfortunately, the data these tests are presumably based on is extremely preliminary. While it identifies these areas as candidate regions, neither the material released on the Psynomics website nor within the peer reviewed medical literature indicates that the association has been established to a clinically valid standard.[54] As this company is specifically targeting customers who may have, or at the very least are concerned that they may have, a significant mental illness, this

---

[50] Malorye Allison, 'Direct-to-consumer Genomics Reinvents Itself' (2012) 30 *Nature Biotechnology* 1027.

[51] List of DTC Genetic testing Companies, Updated 8/11/2011 (2012) Genetics and Public Policy Center <http://www.dnapolicy.org/resources/DTCTableAug2011Alphabydisease.pdf>.

[52] List of DTC Genetic testing Companies, Updated 5/27/2009 (2012) Genetics and Public Policy Center <http://www.dnapolicy.org/resources/DTCcompanieslist.pdf>.

[53] Welcome to Psynomics (2012) Psynomics <http://www.psynomics.com/index.php>.

[54] For example: T B Barrett et al, 'Evidence that a Single Nucleotide Polymorphism in the Promoter of the G Protein Receptor Kinase 3 Gene is Associated with Bipolar Disorder' (2003) 8(5) *Molecular Psychiatry* 546.

raises a number of ethical and clinical concerns. One of the gravest is the potential for consumers who have been prescribed SSRIs to stop taking them without medical supervision, in reliance on the results of as-yet unsubstantiated genetic tests. According to the Psynomics website, the company is not accepting orders for testing at the present time.

The company whose actions triggered the FDA enquiry by its decision to sell collection kits directly to consumers through pharmacies, Pathway Genomics, is one that has significantly changed its business model since mid-2010. Whereas it was previously engaged in a bold strategy to broaden its consumer marketing, it now provides testing only via a physician intermediary. A doctor must register a client for a test, and the results of the client's tests are sent to the doctor, not the patient.[55] This is a far cry from the ambitious earlier model where any bored consumer could walk in off the street and order a test, with no guarantee they would be able to understand the results.

Navigenics, which triggered Australia's brief flurry of mainstream publicity on DTC genetic testing with its plan to offer policyholders of health insurer NIB discounted rates on their Compass testing program, has recently been acquired by Life Technologies, and is no longer accepting test orders.[56] Since its acquisition, it is unclear what business model the new owners intend to implement; however it seems unlikely that it will embrace DTC marketing in the same way the original company did.

Two of the remaining high-profile broad-based screening providers, DeCODE and 23andMe, appear to be retaining their DTC models of marketing in the face of the FDA's interest. DeCODE is located in Reykjavik, Iceland; presumably it expects to avoid some of the consequences of regulation on the basis that it is outside the US, but markets primarily to clients in the US, thereby minimising the impact of both US and EU regulation on the basis of regulatory arbitrage. DeCODE has had a somewhat chequered past. It filed for bankruptcy in the US in November 2009, but after a restructure and partial sale in early 2010,[57] remains a provider of DTC genetic testing services. It is continuing to market broad based tests claiming to screen for 47 conditions, as well as more specific tests focused on particular diseases. The DeCODE Scan retails for US$1100; the terms and conditions page focuses specifically on applicable laws in US states.[58] Notably, when the FDA first sent out letters

---

55 *Home* (2012) Pathway Genomics <http://www.pathway.com/>.

56 *Home* (2012) Navigenics <www.navigenics.com>.

57 *Science Insider* (2012) Science AAAS <http://news.sciencemag.org/scienceinsider/2010/01/decode-genetics-1.html>.

58 *Home* (2012) deCODE Genetics <www.decode.com>.

to DTC providers demanding that they demonstrate why their products did not require FDA approval, DeCODE was included in the first raft, indicating that the FDA does not think they are outside the FDA's regulatory jurisdiction.[59]

23andMe is located in California. One of its founders, Anne Wojcicki, is the wife of Google founder, Sergey Brin, who has financed some of the company's projects. Historically, it has tended to capitalise on its high profile, engaging extensively with the media to promote itself through activities such as "spit parties" at New York's fashion week. Like DeCODE, 23andMe offers broad-based tests examining some 244 disease risk factors and characteristics, at US$299. Unlike DeCODE, 23andMe appears to be planning to conform with the FDA's proposed regulatory framework, albeit somewhat reluctantly, recently announcing that it had applied for FDA approval for seven of its tests, and planned to lodge applications for approval of more in future.[60] This in itself is somewhat curious — nowhere have the authors been able to find any public documentation of a "grace" period being offered to 23andMe to give them time to become compliant with the regulatory requirements, and yet they are continuing to market their tests, in spite of the fact that none currently have regulatory approval. Normally, one would expect a regulatory authority such as the FDA to force them to suspend their business, at the very least, or face some form of sanction, however there appears to be no sign of this occurring.

In Australia, regulators are grappling with a somewhat different problem to that facing the FDA. While the FDA can pursue providers of tests within its jurisdiction supported by the weight of market size, the Australian market isn't really large enough to provide any threatened sanctions with much bite. That most DTC providers specifically target the US market is evident from their privacy statements and pricing policies; Australian legal provisions don't even rate a mention. Therefore, the US regulators can, presumably, threaten to bar providers from the US target market if they refuse to comply, a threat that would be far emptier coming from Australian regulators.

Deprived of this perceived "stick", Australian regulators have apparently instead opted for prohibition. Under the framework established by the TGA in 2011 in response to the Global Harmonisation Task Force,

---

[59] Letter from FDA to DeCODE, 10 June 2010 <http://www.fda.gov/downloads/MedicalDevices/ResourcesforYou/Industry/UCM215241.pdf>.

[60] *Press Releases* (2012) 23andMe <http://www.23andme.com/about/press/fda_application/>.

the TGA claims that in vitro diagnostic devices for self-testing or in-home use, without the supervision of a healthcare provider, will be among those it regulates as a result of its broadened scope of regulation. It specifically notes that "tests to determine genetic traits; (and) IVDs used to test for serious disorders, for example cancer or myocardial infarction" will be among those prohibited from supply.[61] DTC genetic tests are done at home, without the supervision of a healthcare provider; presumably it is exactly this type of test that the TGA intended to prohibit under its new framework.

While this prohibition may appear to make the problem simply go away, it will actually have minimal effect on the access of Australian consumers to DTC in the absence of other provisions. DTC is marketed primarily over the internet, via international sites. As these are outside the regulatory scope of the TGA, there is nothing they can do to prevent them being used by Australian consumers, or to regulate the claims and information being provided to consumers on these sites.

Conclusion

The preceding paragraphs have highlighted that the regulation of aspects of DTC genetic testing is fragmented and jurisdiction-specific: different rules (and varying levels of enforcement) in particular countries.[62] Regulators in each nation are concerned with the protection of consumers within that nation through rules that cover the operation of test providers and/or other parties such as medical practitioners that are located within the specific jurisdiction, but limited in terms of regulating the activities of off-shore providers of those tests who market their services via the internet. There is an indifference to and even non-recognition of marketing across borders to consumers within other jurisdictions. That indifference about regulation of the "export market" is reflected in the scholarly literature. Both regulators and academic commentators continue to conceptualise DTC genetic testing as a national problem with a national solution, ignoring the emergence of a global market that is addressed by service providers with global ambitions and global marketing opportunities, ie through use of the internet.

---

[61] Overview of the Regulatory Framework for In-vitro Diagnostic Medical Devices (2012) Therapeutic Goods Administration <http://www.tga.gov.au/industry/ivd-framework-overview.htm> (under the heading *Access to IVDs for Self-testing (Home Use)*).

[62] Sirpa Soini, 'Genetic Testing Legislation in Western Europe — A Fluctuating Regulatory Target' (2012) 3(2) *Journal of Community Genetics* 143.

Inconsistencies and incapacity in national policy-making and enforcement regarding DTC genetic testing encourage regulatory arbitrage. At this time it is unclear whether such arbitrage will be a substantive problem. We can hypothesise that testing costs will continue to decline, that the FDA is likely to authorise some DTC testing, that bodies such as the US National Geographic Society and insurers will continue to be attracted to promotion of DTC testing, and that enterprises in light-touch (or no-touch) jurisdictions such as India, South Korea and Iceland will emphasise marketing across borders. Policymakers in India and South Korea, for example, may well encourage an export-oriented DTC sector as a way of strengthening their life-sciences industries and building human capital.[63]

There is thus a need for co-operation between consumer protection agencies and health regulators in the advanced economies regarding development of a coherent global framework regarding DTC genetic testing. A model for that framework is provided by the *2008 Protocol (CETS No 203) to the 1997 Council of Europe Convention on Human Rights and Biomedicine (ETS No 164)*.

In the absence of an effective global framework, what might be done to restrict the operation in Australia of DTC genetic testing services that are based offshore?

One response might simply be that there is no need for restriction, with the national government (supported by medical practitioner organisations) instead concentrating on measures that increase the genetic literacy of consumers. Such a public education program would respect individual autonomy. It would result in benefits such as the reduction of stigma associated with particular genetic attributes and the reduction of unnecessary testing (and thence lower overall health costs) highlighted by economists such as Baumol.[64]

There is no express reference to genetics or health testing in the Australian Constitution; that statute indeed is silent regarding both health and consumer protection. It does, however, provide scope for the regulation of DTC genetic testing by enterprises that are located within Australia or that market from outside the national border. At a basic level sections 51(i) and 86 deal with international trade and commerce and with customs respectively. Section 51(v) encompasses the internet under the posts, telegraph and like services head of power. Section 51(xx) encompasses the regulation of corporations.

---

[63] Joseph Wong, Betting on Biotech: Innovation and the Limits of Asia's Developmental State (Cornell University Press, 2011).

[64] William Baumol, The Cost Disease: Why Computers Get Cheaper and Health Care Doesn't (Yale University Press, 2012) 166.

In principle an activist national government could therefore shape the Australian DTC genetic testing market through an outright prohibition on DTC test provision by Australian enterprises that is independent of medical practitioners, through interdiction of test kits and samples passing into/from Australia, and through directions to payment processors (banks and credit card services) not to handle transactions relating to offshore test service providers. There might even be attempts to restrict online advertising of offshore test services. In practice, the Australian Customs Service is much more likely to focus its capabilities on the interdiction of illicit drug shipments and, with less vigour, on unauthorised imports of pharmaceuticals and herbal medicines.

A far more comprehensive solution would be establishment of an international regulatory agreement, whereby each participating nation agreed to regulate the activities of DTC genetic testing providers within its borders at the supply end, rather than the demand end. This would see regulators cracking down on the online presence and marketing outreach of service providers within their jurisdiction, in exchange for similar activity being undertaken by regulators in other jurisdictions hosting DTC service providers marketing into their jurisdiction. As mentioned before, a difficulty in achieving such a framework is the potential for commercial exploitation offered by development of this market in some light-touch regulatory jurisdictions. Nonetheless, as many of the light-touch jurisdictions are dependent on regulatory approvals for marketing and exporting pharmaceuticals and other biological products into jurisdictions with an interest in regulating DTC genetic testing, and they are also interested in the results of further scientific and clinical research performed in these countries, there are options for negotiation that should be explored in the interests of establishing an international framework.

Sequencing the human genome was a monumental achievement in the timeline of human endeavour, made possible only by international collaboration and co-operation. It would be fitting if a global framework for the regulation of some of the derivative activities of this landmark could be established in the same spirit.

Authors note: It was announced on 10 December 2012 that life sciences company Amgen had purchased deCODE for $415 million. On 12 December 2012, Amgen confirmed that it would not be offering DTC genetic testing services after acquiring the company. Concerns about control of all the Icelandic DNA samples held by the company the time of sale passing to an American company have been raised, however no formal resolution on the issue has been reached as of December 2012.

PART III

JUDICIAL PRINCIPLES, PRAGMATISM AND PROPORTIONALITY

INTRODUCTION

THE HON. MICHAEL KIRBY

Principle and Pragmatism

In these remarks, I will confine myself to observations upon the two chapters in this section of the book.

The first, a collaborative effort by Bruce Baer Arnold, Wendy Bonython and Skye Masters, addresses "Law, Cultural Exceptionalism and the Body". It deals with a number of diverse topics loosely linked by an aspect of spirituality and religion as those forces impact on the human body and human life as it is lived. Bruce Baer Arnold begins the chapter by examining cultural exceptionalism. He is intrigued by the way in which Australia has evolved to be a kind of post-secular society. To establish this proposition, he refers to the well-known fact that the fastest growing category of religious adherence is not (as some might think) Islam. Instead, it is the category of "No Religion", the reply to the non-compulsory census question of about 20 per cent of the Australian population, and growing. Ironically, an irreverent identification with the religion of Jedi is also growing strongly.

So, one might ask, why do the traditional churches still have such a big say in Australian legislation and public life? Why, for example, in a supposedly secular country, have the churches been so successful in securing funding for private and religious schools? A recent report showed that, in terms of government subventions for religious schools, Australia is the third in rank in the OECD, just behind Belgium and Chile. Most Australians would think of their country as secular. In the nineteeth century, Roman Catholics established their own educational system. For a very long time it was entirely self-funded by persons of that religious denomination. However, in the 1950s, the Menzies government made an exception by providing a special grant to Catholic schools for science laboratories. This soon expanded into ever-growing federal grants. In the aftermath of the Great Split in the Australian Labor Party in the 1950s, both sides of Australian politics offered increasing funding for Catholic schools, in order to win the denominational vote. The challenge to this practice in the *Defence of Government Schools Case* in the High Court of Australia failed, with Justice Murphy dissenting.

Then in the 1990s, also in pursuit of political advantage, the Howard Government not only increased the federal grants to private and religious schools. It did so in what was, respectfully, a specially objectionable way. It funded the National Chaplaincy Program. Not only did this help to underwrite religious activities in private schools, but it also introduced school chaplains into public schools. From the 1880s, they had observed a principle of secularism so that all children, religious or non-religious, would feel comfortable in the school space. In pursuit of votes, the Rudd and Gillard governments have continued the chaplaincy scheme. Nearly $500 million has so far been expended on it. This is so, despite the serious neglect of infrastructure and financial support for public schools in Australia. The proposals of the recent Gonski committee enquiry are designed, in part, to redress the disadvantage public schools have suffered in governmental funding.

That is not an end to it, as Bruce Baer Arnold points out. Although repeated opinion polls in Australia have shown that majorities of citizens are comfortable with the idea of marriage equality for gay, lesbian, bisexual, transgender persons in Australia, the Howard government introduced into the *Marriage Act 1961* (Cth) a provision limiting marriage in Australia to the union of one man and a woman. Copying the successful strategy of Karl Rove in the United States, this measure was designed to pander to the demands of religious organisations and to ignore the civil rights of sexual minorities and their families and friends.

The role of organised religion to browbeat politicians, to threaten and bully them will one day be told. The story is not a pleasant one. It is the more surprising because of the secular traditions of Australia, and before that the secular bequest of British constitutionalism reflected in the Australian Constitution of 1901, and specifically in section 116. Although the present Prime Minister, Julia Gillard, openly confesses to having no religious belief, and lives in the official residence with her partner, to whom she is not married, her ardent embrace of the demands of religious minorities is puzzling to many Australians on both sides of politics.

Although the conference of the Australian Labor Party altered its national platform to include a commitment to marriage equality, a vote on the issue in the Australian Federal Parliament resulted in the overwhelming defeat of a Bill to amend the *Marriage Act*. This coincided neatly with moves to amend the law on marriage in the United Kingdom, New Zealand and France. Already, many developed countries have embraced marriage equality, including the Netherlands, Belgium, Spain,

Portugal, Canada, South Africa, Argentina and more than 10 states of the United States of America.

Once, Australia would have regarded itself as a secular State. Its population may still do so. But religious organisations want to keep their control over the human body and to impose, by law, discriminatory restrictions that forbid sexual minorities to enjoy the legal status of marriage, with its obligations and privileges. To many Australians, gay and straight, this is a shocking state of affairs. Given the powerful evidence of the physical, emotional and spiritual benefits that stable human relations can bring to those who enjoy them and given the now incontestable evidence that people do not choose their sexual orientation and cannot change it, these acts of discrimination are very wrong. But they persist in contemporary Australia. And the prospects of their changing, with a change of government, look bleak. So the democratic course has run its race. Absent a national Bill of Rights or charter, there is nowhere for the citizens most personally affected to go. The law offers them no remedy or redress against the injustice that they feel.

Skye Masters examines another aspect of spirituality in Australia. This concerns the spiritual feelings of Australia's Aboriginal people. Specifically, it relates to the conduct of autopsies on the bodies of Indigenous persons, said to be in breach of the spiritual beliefs of the family. Early in the life of the Australian Law Reform Commission, which I led between 1975–1984, we received a reference from Attorney-General Robert Ellicott to enquire into, and report on, the recognition of at least some aspects of Aboriginal Customary Laws. The report was duly delivered and substantially written by Professor James Crawford, then of the University of Adelaide, later the University of Sydney and now Cambridge University in the United Kingdom. His investigation showed some of the difficulties of accepting without qualification Aboriginal customary laws. Some of them, at least, appear inconsistent with current legal norms, affecting other Australian citizens. Some appear inconsistent with universal human rights, and especially as those rights that protect women. Yet other aspects of customary law could quite safely be taken into account, including a recognition of punishment already inflicted according to custom, so as to avoid the risk of double jeopardy.

An autopsy is a procedure often required by a coroner (the most ancient public officer in the English legal system) where there is some concern about the manner and cause of the death of the deceased. Sometimes the autopsy is ordered where foul play is suspected, so as to enhance the possibility of criminal process. Sometimes the autopsy is ordered for reasons of public health or community safety. Accordingly, a demand that an autopsy should be forgone because of its offence to traditional customs and beliefs runs headlong into the competing demands of society expressed in its criminal, health and other laws. Once the feelings of an Indigenous family would have been waved aside as incapable of overriding community interests. However, by analysis of recent cases in the Northern Territory of Australia, Skye Masters has shown how the Australian judicial system has become more sensitive and more nuanced in its respect for Aboriginal customs.

Wendy Bonython extends this analysis to another attribute relevant to Australia's multicultural society, namely blood transfusion in the case of an adherent to the Christian denomination of Jehovah's Witnesses. She does so by reference to Australian experience, specifically by illustration from a case before the Irish High Court relating to an African woman from Congo who was a Jehovah's Witness and who preferred not to receive a blood transfusion because it was contrary to the religious instructions of her faith.

Cases where transfusion of a child is presented for judicial decision are somewhat easier to resolve. The Crown or the State is regarded in law as the *parens patriae* of the child, or its ultimate guardian. The child can be made a ward of State for the relevant proceedings. A judge can then, if convinced and paying due respect to the views of parents and the consequences on the child, authorise blood transfusion in the name of the whole community.

But what of the case where the person requiring transfusion is an adult of full capacity? In such a case, what is the duty of medical practitioners? What is the authority of courts of law to force a person, if necessary with restraint, to receive blood against their sincere religious beliefs?

The decisions in the cases of autopsies and blood transfusions are not absolute. They involve pragmatic evaluations by the courts of the multiple considerations that are in play. Those considerations will include the instruction of particular religious beliefs. But they will also include perceptions of the best interests of the patient concerned. The point that each of the chapters in this section of the book demonstrates is that pragmatic examination of problems by an independent decision maker, guided by law and precedent, but weighing the various considerations presented, is the best mechanism that societies have yet devised to reach conclusions in such sensitive cases that are at once principled and pragmatic. The law generally gives respect to the private religious beliefs of its citizens, particularly in houses of worship. However, normally, in a country like Australia, those religious beliefs cannot have the final word. This is because there are other considerations at stake. They involve public concerns. In the case of gay marriage, they involve the public concern to eliminate the last vestiges of mediaeval, prescientific discrimination addressed to sexual minorities. And they include ensuring that gay people enjoy the same rights as other people in their capacity as human beings and citizens. The mere fact that other, religious people are upset at the very idea of marriage equality is no reason to deny it to those most intimately involved. Otherwise, the threshold of legal protection is put too low.

Similarly, in the case of autopsies, the mere fact that a parent (Aboriginal or non-Aboriginal) is upset by the idea of an autopsy on a family member is not enough, of itself, to warrant a court forbidding an autopsy. If a crime is suspected or if interests of public health are raised, a court will give those considerations its attention. Likewise, in instances of blood transfusion for those whose religion regards it as biblically impermissible, the law will give due respect to religious views. Sometimes they will prevail. But not invariably.

Proportionality

The second chapter in this part of the book is the gripping description by Wendy Kukulies-Smith and Susan Priest of the shocking case of a gang rape in Sydney on 11 September 1886. Sadly, the case bears some comparison to an event that took place in New Delhi in India on 16 December 2012. In the intervening period of more than a century, there have been many cases of gang rape that have come before the courts with their accusations, trials, verdicts and punishment.

The case in 1886, like that in 2012, started with a public transport driver. In Sydney it was a cab driver and in Delhi a bus driver. The victim in Sydney was a 16 year old girl, Mary Jane Hicks. She was driven by the cab driver to scrubland in Moore Park and was then brutally raped by nine young men, all between the ages of 17 and 22 years. At the time, under the criminal law of New South Wales, the punishment for the offence of rape was death by hanging. The accused were all apprehended, as later were the five accused and bus driver in Delhi. The Sydney accused were tried in the Central Criminal Court at Darlinghurst. The trial was conducted jointly before a jury, presided over by Justice Windeyer. The nine Sydney accused were all found guilty by the jury. They were convicted by the judge. Despite a rider to the jury's verdicts involving a recommendation for mercy, the judge refused their pleas. He sentenced all nine to death. The cab driver was also found guilty for his part in the crime. He was sentenced to 14 years imprisonment with hard labour and two floggings.

The trial was closely followed in the colonial media in Australia. In a settlement still of relatively small numbers, and before Federation, the prospect of the hanging of so many young men attracted huge attention and hotly contested views.

Pleas for mercy were advanced to the Governor of New South Wales, who was very distressed by the fact that his somewhat graceful life was interrupted by such an unpleasant decision. He spared five of the nine men from hanging. Those who were spared all served more than 10 years' imprisonment. Four of the young men were hanged. Mary Hicks reportedly left the Colony for New Zealand.

The trial of the young men in New Delhi likewise captured a great deal of media attention. In that case, the young woman who was sexually assaulted was thrown from the moving bus, together with her male companion who had boarded the bus with her. She was already grievously injured. Police were immediately called to the scene by a mobile phone. The accused were described. The young woman was treated in a Delhi Hospital and later flown to Singapore for emergency care. However, she died of her injuries. Demands were made in the Indian Parliament for the introduction of the death penalty for rape. An enquiry was established under the former Chief Justice of India, JS Verma. It recommended an increase in penalties and other reforms. However, it held back from recommending the reintroduction of the penalty of death that formerly existed for rape in the Indian Penal Code.

The media presentation of the legal players in the two dramas was not always flattering, either in 1886 or 2012. Justice Windeyer was described in the contemporary newspapers as ferocious and bent on securing the conviction of the accused. Cartoons display him with fierce eyes, a jutting jaw and brutal mien. In Delhi, legal practitioners refused to accept the brief to appear for the six accused persons (including the bus driver). This shameful act was a reminder of the shocking conduct of the advocates in Pakistan after the Governor of Pakistani Punjab was gunned down by one of his own bodyguards after he had urged repeal and reform of the law on blasphemy. Reportedly, when the accused was brought to court for the first time, advocates refused to appear for the prosecution and instead sprinkled the accused with rose petals, ostensibly to express their support for his action in defence of Islam. In India, the Chief Justice of the Supreme Court appealed to senior advocates to take up representation of the accused, to ensure that they would have a fair trial. This was duly done.

In cases of this kind, courts and the judicial process are tested for their fidelity to due process and natural justice. It is in horrific cases that the presumption of innocence, the necessities of scrupulously fair hearings and precise scrutiny of the law and evidence become of the greatest importance. In the Indian trial, according to reports, the most significant evidence against the accused will allegedly be DNA evidence gathered from a scientific examination of the bus in which the fatal attack was alleged to have occurred. Of course, back in 1886 there was no such DNA evidence. The accusations against the accused relied substantially on the testimony of Miss Hicks and confessional and circumstantial evidence called by the Crown.

The horror of the ordeal suffered by the two young women, in events separated in time and space, is obviously such as to demand condign punishment of those proved guilty of such conduct. But was the fourfold penalty of death ultimately imposed on the prisoners who did not receive the Governor's clemency in 1886 a just disposition? Of course, this question would be answered differently today than would have been the case back then. But even then, as the contemporary newspaper reports described in this brilliant chapter demonstrate, some observers thought it was disproportionate. In effect, if nine people could be sentenced to death and four actually executed in a case where the victim's life had been spared, what inducement would exist to an offender to hold back from destroying the life of the person best able, in the circumstances of that time, to describe the offenders, to give evidence against them and to bring them to justice?

Proportionality in punishment is always a contested virtue. In India, the mother of the deceased young woman, in despair, called for the penalty of death for the killers of her daughter. In the Australian case, the imposition of that penalty upon four young accused appears disproportionate. But what is proportion? According to what criterion can it be assessed? Here, there was no live question of proportion in the punishment imposed by the judge as between the several accused. Each of them was punished equally. Each was sentenced to death. Only the intervention of the Governor introduced a differential. One can imagine the pain of the prisoners whose sentences were confirmed, sitting in their cells in the Darlinghurst Gaol as, nearby, those who had been reprieved were crying with relief and the joy of life restored. The challenge for judges and others involved in criminal punishment is to reflect wisely, proportionately and in accordance with law on all of the relevant considerations necessary to a proper sentence. Often those considerations will be highly contested. Quite often, courts will divide in applying them. This happened in the High Court of Australia during my service.

In *Ryan v The Queen* (2001) 206 CLR 267, the High Court had to decide an appeal concerned with the sentencing of a Roman Catholic priest who had been convicted of sexual offences against 12 young boys over a period of 20 years. Testimonials were received from former parishioners, priests and others concerning the accused's good character, reputation and valuable good works as a parish priest. However, the sentencing judge, whilst acknowledging the pleas, said he could see no good in the accused. He held that his "unblemished character and reputation" before the crimes did not entitle him to "any leniency whatsoever".

The Court of Criminal Appeal of New South Wales rejected an appeal against the sentence of 14 years' minimum term imprisonment imposed at trial. In the High Court of Australia, Justices McHugh, Callinan and I upheld the appeal, with Justices Gummow and Hayne dissenting. The majority concluded, in effect, that when a person stands before a court for punishment, he or she is entitled to have taken into account both the considerations that aggravate the seriousness of the offence and those that mitigate the circumstances and represent positive features in the accused's life that stand to that person's credit at the moment of sentencing. Behind this notion lies an objective of securing proportionality in punishment and avoiding excess. We tend to be more sensitive today, at least in Australia, to the extremity involved in terminating a human life. Back in 1886, both in Australia and India, capital punishment was much more common. But even at that time, the disproportion of the punishment, and the number upon whom it was imposed, captured a great deal of discussion and debate. In matters of criminal punishment, such discussion and debate are inescapable. Amongst reasonable people, views will constantly differ. Scalograms, analysing judicial punishments (and many other judicial decisions) tend to show, in a semi-scientific way, what is discussed in bar common rooms: some judges tend to be hard in sentencing; some tend to be more lenient. It is impossible (and maybe undesirable) to completely eliminate these human variables from the judicial system. But appeal courts exist (ultimately, in Australia, the High Court) to scrutinise the resulting judicial orders and to make sure that they are not inconsistent with the enacted law or unacceptably out of kilter with due proportionality.

The similarities and differences between the offences of gang rape occurring in Sydney in 1886 and New Delhi in 2012 show the enduring features of the legal system and sadly the enduring features of human cruelty and criminal conduct. By examining contemporaneous records, and the debates that swirled around the trial of the nine in Sydney in 1886, Wendy Kukulies-Smith and Susan Priest have presented us with a fascinating and gripping story, full of interesting and still relevant legal and criminological questions. They have also demonstrated, once again, the importance of legal history to a proper understanding of the law. It is hard to imagine how young lawyers today can be readied for a life in the law without a thorough appreciation of the history of our discipline and the constant need for reform that that history demonstrates. But alas it does happen. This chapter is a welcome corrective.

CHAPTER EIGHT

LAW, CULTURAL EXCEPTIONALISM AND THE BODY

BRUCE BAER ARNOLD, WENDY BONYTHON AND SKYE MASTERS

> *M Jourdain:* Good Heavens! Then I have been speaking prose for more than forty years without knowing it. I couldn't be more grateful to you for teaching me that …
>
> *Philosophy Master:* But you must embroider it a bit.
>
> *M Jourdain:* No, I tell you. I want nothing else in the note but just those words, but arranged in a smart and up-to-date way. Let me hear the various ways in which they can be put, so that I can choose which I like best.[1]

This chapter is about blood, pain and power: three preoccupations of contemporary and past law. It is not about *Gladiator* and *Apocalypto*, the Butlerian abject body[2] or a Foucauldian deconstruction of the "monstrous"[3] and consensual sado-masochism in the *Spanner* case.[4] Instead it looks at notions of cultural exceptionalism and the body in Australian law through two lenses: autopsies and blood transfusions. We draw on legal pragmatism in interrogating recent case law. We highlight questions about

---

[1] Molière, 'The Would-be Gentleman', in Ian Maclean and George Gravely (eds) *Don Juan and Other Plays* (Oxford University Press, 1998 [first performed as 'Le Bourgeois Gentilhomme', 1670) 281.

[2] Judith Butler, Bodies That Matter: On the Discursive Limits of "Sex" (Routledge, 1993) 190.

[3] Andrew Sharp, Foucault's Monsters and the Challenge of Law (Routledge, 2010).

[4] *R v Brown* [1993] 2 All ER 75; Chris White, 'The Spanner Trials and the Changing Law on Sadomasochism in the UK' (2006) 50(2/3) *Journal of Homosexuality* 167.

medico-legal authority and tensions in human rights, concluding that Australian courts and legislatures reconcile conflicting values using a framework that is practical and that accommodates but does not necessarily privilege "ethno-religious particularism". That law embodies instance by instance accommodation of difference rather than a shift towards legal pluralism in which specific communities enjoy discrete legal systems within the same jurisdictions.

The aim in this chapter, which reflects ongoing research by the three authors,[5] is not to provide a detailed exegesis of specific judgments or to offer a comprehensive critique of how Australian law recognises (and selectively respects) conflicting cultural values. Instead the chapter examines areas of dispute — choices at the borders of law — in order to ask questions about authority, rights and difference.

The chapter has four parts. The first part provides an introduction to the concept of cultural exceptionalism and the philosophy used by the authors in considering legal snapshots. The second part looks at some recent Australian case law about autopsies, highlighting conflicting rationales and pointing to overseas legal frameworks as points of reference. The third part examines the relationship between principle and practice by looking at law regarding blood transfusions, in particular the refusal by members of the Jehovah's Witnesses to receive transfusions. The final part offers conclusions, arguing that the snapshots indicate that lawmaking by Australian courts and legislatures is essentially pragmatic — a matter of workable compromises rather than a doctrinaire insistence on principle that denies deeply held beliefs and values.

Making Sense of Exceptions

Contemporary Australian jurisprudence tacitly enshrines "one nation under the Constitution" rather than "under God". That Constitution does not provide a comprehensive freedom of religion or other faith; instead it is a *fin de siècle* artifact that sought to address cultural and religious anxieties by forbidding an established church. Baptists, Methodists, Roman Catholics, Presbyterians, Episcopalians, Theosophists, Sikhs, Buddhists and adherents of Judaism alike would be able to flourish

[5] The chapter for example reflects submissions, articles and doctoral research by the authors regarding organ donation, circumcision, capacity, consent and cultural identity.

without the complications posed by a national faith and national religious institution.[6]

That compromise — arguably a key aspect of the "Australian Settlement" espoused by figures such as Alfred Deakin[7] — has fostered the emergence of a heterogeneous post secular[8] society in which the "artificial" religion of Scientology enjoys some official recognition,[9] a large number of Australians irreverently identify their religion as Jedi,[10] and the common law offence of blasphemy has passed into desuetude.[11]

Legislatures and courts are however continuing to grapple with challenges posed by religious claims to exclusive authority in vilification of other faiths or street preaching,[12] religious speech in public places,[13] State funding of private schools,[14] the duties of people where there is a

---

[6] Luke Beck, 'The Constitutional Prohibition on Religious Tests' (2011) 35(2) *Melbourne University Law Review* 322; Carolyn Evans, *Legal Protection of Religious Freedom* in Australia (Federation Press, 2012).

[7] Paul Kelly, *End of Certainty: The Story of the 1980s* (Allen & Unwin, 1994) 1. See however: Geoffrey Stokes, 'The "Australian Settlement" and Australian Political Thought' (2007) 39(1) *Australian Journal of Political Science* 5.

[8] Juergen Habermas, 'Notes on Post-Secular Society' (2008) 25(4) *New Perspectives Quarterly* 17. Note however: Veit Bader, 'Post-Secularism or Liberal-Democratic Constitutionalism?' (2012) 5(1) *Erasmus Law Review* 5.

[9] Church of the New Faith v Commissioner of Pay-Roll Tax (Vic) [1983] HCA 40; (1983) 154 CLR 120.

[10] Gary Bouma, *Australian Soul: Religion and Spirituality in the 21st Century* (Cambridge University Press, 2006) 82. See also: Todd Nachowitz, 'New Zealand as a Multireligious Society: Recent Census Figures and Some Relevant Implications' (2007) 2(2) *Aotearoa Ethnic Network Journal* 1.

[11] Bede Harris, '*Pell v Council of Trustees of the National Gallery of Victoria*: Should Blasphemy Be a Crime? The "Piss Christ" Case and Freedom of Expression' (1998) 22 *Melbourne University Law* Review 217. See also: Helen Pringle, 'Regulating Offence to the Godly: Blasphemy and the Future of Religious Vilification Laws' (2011) 34(1) *University of New South Wales Law Journal* 316.

[12] *Catch the Fire Ministries Inc & Ors v Islamic Council of Victoria Inc* [2006] VSCA 284. See also: Nicholas Aroney, 'The Constitutional (In)validity of Religious Vilification Laws: Implications for their Interpretation' (2006) 34(2) *Federal Law Review* 287.

[13] The Corporation of the City of Adelaide v Corneloup & Ors [2011] SASCFC 84 and Attorney-General for the State of South Australia v Corporation of the City of Adelaide & Ors [2013] HCA 3.

[14] Leilani Ujvari, 'Non-Discrimination Laws and Religious Schools in Australia' (2009) 30(1) *Adelaide Law Review* 31–56; *Williams v Commonwealth of Australia* [2012] HCA 23; *Attorney-General (Vic); Ex Rel Black v Commonwealth* [1981] HCA 2; (1981) 146 CLR 559.

conflict between secular law and religious authority,[15] for example Shari'a and Indigenous customary law.[16] Those challenges are complicated because faith potentially melds with national origin or ethnic identity, reflected for example in the wording of section 9 of the *Racial Discrimination Act 1975* (Cth), which refers to "race, colour, descent or national or ethnic origin".[17]

Markus Davidsen, in discussing "Jediism" referred to "salad bar spirituality": identity as entertainment.[18] Despite growing secularism, faith, or a broader ethno-religious identity, still matter. It matters because particular communities are perceived to be powerful or susceptible to vote-seeking by individual politicians and political parties.[19] It matters because particular communities may be identifiable as the potential targets of discrimination. From a justice perspective it matters because personal belief, although perceived by some as antediluvian or simply bizarre, may be fundamental to an individual's selfhood and participation in a specific community. In a pluralist society we should accordingly be wary of assumptions that everyone recognises and embraces norms regarding physical integrity pre- and post-mortem, or that "traditional" beliefs are always and appropriately superseded by bureaucratic convenience or science.

Australian law recognises exceptions to legal norms regarding bodies, ie formally or tacitly provides dispensations for members of particular groups on the basis of faith or ethnicity. We characterise that dispensation as cultural exceptionalism. It is not comprehensive and does not, for example, involve parallel legal systems, systematic imposition of disabilities or freedom from civil responsibilities on the basis of religious affinity or ethnic identity.

An examination of cultural exceptions is useful because they potentially tell us something about the nature of Australian law, in much the same way that the civil disability experienced by people through prohibition of same-sex marriage offers insights about legal values and

---

[15] Adelaide Company of Jehovah's Witnesses Incorporated v Commonwealth [1943] HCA 12; (1943) 67 CLR 116.

[16] Australian Law Reform Commission, *The Recognition of Aboriginal Customary Laws*, ALRC Report No 31 (1986); Ann Black and Kerrie Sadiq, 'Good and Bad Sharia: Australia's Mixed Response to Islamic Law' (2011) 34(1) *University of New South Wales Law Journal* 383.

[17] See also: Racial and Religious Toleration Act 2001 (Vic).

[18] Markus Davidsen, 'Jediism: A Convergence of Star Wars Fan Culture and Salad Bar Spirituality' (2011) 51 *Die Filosoof* 24.

[19] See, for example: Marion Maddox, God Under John Howard: The Rise of the Religious Right in Australia (Allen & Unwin, 2008).

power relationships. As indicated above, our snapshots come from the boundaries of law, where values may be quite visceral and contestation a marker of belonging in a pluralist society. The snapshots reflect the chapter's origins as a paper in a symposium on justice, where the authors aspired to encourage discussion rather than simply articulate settled law and undisputed principles.

How have we made sense of the exceptions?

In considering Australian and overseas law we have eschewed grand theory[20] and instead relied on legal pragmatism, in practice an inquiring state of mind rather than a coherent but innately reductive heuristic.[21] Reductiveness is to be avoided because grand simplifications are inconsistent with the reality of legal practice, elide diversity in lived experience and disregard human dignity by conceptualising the subjects of law as manifestations of stereotypes rather than individuals.

The enquiring state of mind — what Posner characterises as "practical, instrumental, forward-looking, activist, empirical, skeptical, antidogmatic, experimental"[22] — is marked by an interest in what actually happens in law. It emphasises outcomes rather than what are claimed to be foundational principles.

It is also marked by willingness to ask questions that do not result in clear, definitive answers. That openness to different qualities and values is captured in the early comment by phenomenologist William James that pragmatism

---

[20] Quentin Skinner, 'The Return of Grand Theory', in Quentin Skinner (ed), *The Return of Grand Theory in the Human Sciences* (Cambridge University Press, 1985) 1.

[21] Among discussions of legal pragmatism see: Margaret Radin, 'The Pragmatist and the Feminist' (1990) 63 *Southern California Law Review* 1699; Richard Posner, 'What Has Pragmatism To Offer Law?' (1990) 63 *Southern California Law Review* 1661; Michael Sullivan, 'Pragmatism and Precedent: A Response to Dworkin' (1990) 26(2) *Transactions of the Charles S. Peirce Society* 225; Thomas Grey 'Holmes and Legal Pragmatism' (1989) 41 *Stanford Law Review* 787. For recent critiques, see: David Luban, *Legal Modernism* (University of Michigan Press, 1997) 126; Susan Haack, 'On Legal Pragmatism: Where Does "The Path of the Law" Lead Us?' (2012) 3(1) *Pragmatism Today* 8.

[22] Richard Posner, *Overcoming Law* (Harvard University Press, 1995) 11. For a response see: Ronald Dworkin, 'In Praise of Theory' (1997) 29 *Arizona State Law Journal* 364; 'Pragmatism, Right Answers and True Banality', in Michael Brint and William Weaver (eds) *Pragmatism in Law and Society* (Westview Press, 1990) 359; and, more broadly: Michael Sullivan and Daniel Solove, 'Can Pragmatism Be Radical: Richard Posner and Legal Pragmatism' (2003) 113 *Yale Law Journal* 687.

> has, in fact, no prejudices whatever, no obstructive dogmas, no rigid canons of what shall count as proof. She is completely genial. She will entertain any hypothesis, she will consider any evidence.[23]

Legal pragmatist Oliver Wendell Holmes Jr is described by Brian Tamanaha as having irreverently pierced the

> prevailing mode of analysing common law concepts as if they were essentialist notions of timeless provenance with a necessary internal structure and set of external relations. His favorite debunking technique was to employ historical analysis to demonstrate that these abstract concepts have a terrestrial origin in a specific context, derived from particular and contingent needs, and not infrequently based upon mistake. Holmes argued that legal rules should serve human purposes and must therefore be shaped to meet these purposes.[24]

Martha Minow and Elizabeth Spelman echo Posner in noting the importance of looking at realities rather than reductively at abstractions. They comment that

> the demand to look at the context often means a demand to look at the structures of power, gender, race, or class relationships, or the effects of age and physical vulnerability on people's abilities to protect themselves.[25]

The following examination of exceptionalism is grounded in a recognition that people are not the means to an end[26] and that at the borders of law there are tensions regarding autonomy and social goods that in a liberal democratic State are not easily resolved.

---

[23] William James, 'What Pragmatism Means', in Doris Olin (ed), *William James: Pragmatism in Focus* (Routledge, 1992) 53.

[24] Brian Tamanaha, 'Pragmatism in U.S. Legal Theory: Its Application to Normative Jurisprudence, Sociolegal Studies, and the Fact-Value Distinction' (1996) 41 *American Journal of Jurisprudence* 315.

[25] Martha Minow and Elizabeth Spelman, 'In Context' (1990) 63 *Southern California Law Review* 1651. See also: Ibid.

[26] Immanuel Kant, *The Metaphysics of Morals* (Mary Gregor trans, Cambridge University Press, 1996) [trans of *Die Metaphysik der Sitten* (first published 1797)] 186.

Autopsies and the Indigenous Body

We can see some of those tensions in action when we look at the law's treatment of coronial autopsies, ie urgent decision-making by coroners and courts about autopsies for forensic rather than research purposes.[27]

There is a public interest in knowing how people died, with rationales such as serving justice through fact-based criminal investigation and protecting public health through research into disease or injury. That knowledge in some instances can only be authoritatively gained through an examination of the body, something that might involve delays in burial and the removal of organs. Such examination valorises State authority over the interests of individuals or community groups. It has also been claimed to privilege medical knowledge over law.[28]

Statute law in Australian and overseas jurisdictions mandates that a coroner can order an autopsy, irrespective of the religious or other beliefs of the dead person (who has no standing) and the person's survivors.[29] Some statutes provide for interested parties to challenge authorisation of an autopsy.[30] That challenge is usually urgent and when successful typically embodies cultural exceptionalism, ie law recognising that in some circumstances the values of particular groups will be taken into account and indeed override a practice norm.[31]

We can see cultural exceptionalism in action by looking at decisions in Australia regarding challenges to autopsies on Indigenous people. Those challenges reflect differences in faith and the experience of Indigenous

---

[27] Ian Freckelton and David Ranson, *Death Investigation and the Coroner's Inquest* (Oxford University Press, 2006).

[28] Belinda Carpenter and Gordon Tait, 'The Autopsy Imperative: Medicine, Law, and the Coronial Investigation' (2010) 31(3) *Journal of Medical Humanities* 205–221.

[29] Coroners Act 2003 (SA) s 22; Coroners Act 1996 (WA) s 34; Coroners Act 2003 (Qld) s 13; Coroners Act 2008 (Vic) s 25; Coroners Act 2009 (NSW) s 89; Coroners Act 1995 (Tas) s 36; Coroners Act (NT) s 20; Coroners Act 1997 (ACT) s 21. See also: Coroners Act 2006 (NZ) s 31; Coroner's Act 1959 (North Ireland) s 27; Coroner's Act (Ontario) s 15.

[30] Prue Vines, 'The Sacred and the Profane: Property Concepts in Post-mortem Examinations' (2007) 29(2) *Sydney Law Review* 235, 252

[31] Coroners Act 1996 (WA) s 37; Coroners Act 2003 (Qld) s 19; Coroners Act 2008 (Vic) ss 8, 79; Coroners Act 2009 (NSW) ss 89, 96; Coroners Act 1995 (Tas) s 38; Coroners Act (NT) s 23; Coroners Act 1997 (ACT) ss 20, 28.

people since white settlement regarding the collection of human remains for anthropological or other collections.[32]

In *Evans v Northern Territory Coroner*[33] the Northern Territory Supreme Court agreed to prevent an autopsy on an Indigenous minor who may have died from SIDS. The "sudden and tragic death of a young child at Borroloola" had been followed by a preliminary investigation and a subsequent determination, reflecting "expert advice", by the Coroner that it was "necessary for a direction to be given to a medical practitioner to perform an autopsy on the body of the deceased child". The father of the deceased infant sought an order under section 23(3) of the *Coroners Act* (NT) that an autopsy not be performed.

The judgment notes that the father of the child was notified of the death, then

> spoke with the doctor and enquired whether there would be an autopsy. The doctor alerted him to the possibility that he may be able to stop any autopsy from taking place. The father subsequently obtained legal advice and brought these proceedings as a consequence.
>
> In his affidavit filed in support of the application the father advised that he lives a traditional life with his wife and children. He said that he did not want the autopsy to take place as "it is against our way and culture". He explained the processes that would usually follow upon a death and went on to say:
>
> I do not want my son to undergo an autopsy because the *Jungayi* [elders] can refuse to look after him and prepare him for burial. This would be devastating to me and my family.
>
> If the autopsy takes place my son will not be able to enter the spiritual country and be with his ancestral family because his body would not be whole. He will be alone with nowhere to go and no one to look after him. This would be very distressing to me and my family if my son's spirit had to go on without his ancestors to look after him.[34]

The father expressed concern that if the autopsy took place "bad things will happen to family members" and that his son would be "lost with nowhere to go because our law has been broken".

---

[32] See, for example: Tiffany Jenkins, Contesting Human Remains in Museum Collections: The Crisis of Cultural Authority (Routledge, 2011); Helen MacDonald, Human Remains: Episodes in Human Dissection (Melbourne University Press, 2005).

[33] Evans v Northern Territory Coroner [2011] NTSC 100.

[34] Ibid, [5].

In *Unchango*[35] Walsh J was receptive to that argument in overriding the Coroner's decision regarding autopsy of another Indigenous infant whose death was suspected to have resulted from SIDS. He commented that

> Whilst there is undoubtedly potential for a post mortem report to reveal that death could well not have been caused by sudden infant death syndrome but by a natural cause such as infection, nonetheless that would not really advance the matter a great deal in circumstances such as this. One should take into account the very strong cultural beliefs held by the relatives and by the community at Kalumburu and the effect that the post mortem would have on them by way of emotional trauma, particularly in view of the fact that it would prohibit, in their view, the spirit of the deceased remaining in the body and returning to the body and would leave the spirit roaming at large.

In *Evans* Riley CJ commented that —

> There was no dispute that proceeding with the autopsy would cause the father, the mother, the family of the deceased child and others "great heartache and distress". The views expressed by the father on behalf of himself and his family were clearly, deeply and genuinely held.[36]

The Coroner had sought expert advice, hearing that "unless an autopsy is performed there will usually be no way that these conditions can be identified" and that "the results of autopsies may help the community, both lay and professional, to gain an understanding of issues around such deaths that may be useful in formulating future preventative strategies".[37]

In refusing the autopsy the Court noted that

> it is incumbent upon the Court to resolve a conflict between the decision of the Coroner that an autopsy is necessary and the competing wishes of family, relatives or friends of the deceased person generally based upon cultural or religious beliefs that are genuinely and strongly held. In some cases it has been held that ascertaining the precise cause of death is less important than the spiritual and cultural beliefs of the family in the particular circumstances.[38]

---

[35] Re Death of Simon Unchango (Jnr); ex parte Simon Unchango (Snr) (1997) 95 A Crim R 65.

[36] Evans v Northern Territory Coroner [2011] NTSC 100, [8].

[37] Ibid, [11].

[38] Ibid, [21].

The Court took a pragmatic view, referring to its decision in *Wuridjal v The Northern Territory Coroner*[39] and stating that

> there were grounds upon which the Coroner was justified in requiring a post-mortem examination including an autopsy. The Coroner reasonably believed that it was necessary for an autopsy to be performed. Without an autopsy the cause of death could not, finally, be determined. There is a public interest in knowing the exact cause of death.
>
> On the other hand the public interest in knowing the cause of this death must be weighed against thepublic interest in giving deeply held spiritual and cultural beliefs proper recognition and respect. In this case I was satisfied that the spiritual beliefs of the family of the child were genuinely held. To perform an autopsy would compound the great grief and distress already being suffered by the family ... In all the circumstances the likelihood was that the performance of an autopsy would not provide any additional information as to what actually caused the death of the child, although it may have done so. If there was any additional information to be obtained from the autopsy it was likely to be quite limited. The findings resulting from an autopsy were unlikely to contribute in any meaningful way to a better understanding of the death of this child or to contribute in any meaningful way to efforts being made to improve health outcomes for other infants.
>
> In all the circumstances I considered that, in this case, the interests of the family outweighed the public interest in determining the precise cause of death and I ordered that no autopsy be performed.[40]

In *Raymond-Hewitt*[41] the Court similarly granted a family's application under section 23(3) of the NT *Coroners Act* to prevent an autopsy of a person killed in a road crash.

It noted that its exercise of discretion under section 23(3) involved balancing the interests of the deceased person's family "in following and maintaining their Aboriginal culture and law" against "the interests of the community on the other that the cause of an otherwise unexplained death be ascertained if possible". That balance reflects a recognition that "if there are any suspicious circumstances surrounding the death, or there are other compelling reasons why it is in the public interest that an autopsy be performed, those cultural and spiritual considerations must take second place to the public interest".[42]

---

[39] Wuridjal v Northern Territory Coroner [2001] NTSC 99.
[40] Evans v Northern Territory Coroner [2011] NTSC 100, [26].
[41] Raymond-Hewitt v Northern Territory Coroner [2011] NTSC 94.
[42] Ibid.

In this instance the Court endorsed the comment in *Green v Johnstone*[43] that —

> In a multicultural society such as we have in this country, it is my opinion that great weight should be given to the cultural and spiritual laws and practices of the various cultural groups forming our society, and that great care should be taken to ensure that their laws and practices, assuming they are otherwise lawful, are not disregarded or abused.

Was the autopsy essential? The Court adopted a pragmatic approach, emphasising outcomes rather than principles. It noted that —

> It was further submitted that knowing that the cause of this death was the deceased's heart condition, rather than the presence of alcohol or drugs in his system, may ensure that the deceased's dependents obtain the full benefits available to them under the *Motor Accidents (Compensation) Act*. I was informed that toxicology results were pending, meaning that information about whether the deceased had alcohol or other drugs in his system at the time of death will become available as a result of blood samples and that it is not necessary to perform an autopsy to achieve this result …
>
> It was further submitted on behalf of the coroner that understanding the cause of this death may give rise to consideration and discussion of the entitlement to drive of persons with serious heart conditions, the capacity and obligation of treating medical personnel to report such conditions to the licensing authorities, and the power and duty of those authorities to consider and determine a driver's entitlement. There is a real possibility that this man's death was caused or contributed to by heart disease, and an autopsy will do nothing to establish the cause of the collision. In those circumstances, it seems to me that the coroner has all the information he is ever going to get, autopsy or no autopsy, on which to base any such comments or recommendations.

Disquiet about autopsies (or more broadly about delays in burial/cremation of a body) is not restricted to Indigenous people. As noted above most Australian jurisdictions make some allowance for personal and cultural concerns, and practice documents such as the Queensland *State Coroners Guidelines* highlight the need for sensitivity. Familial distress, however, is insufficient grounds for overriding a coronial decision to conduct an autopsy.

---

[43] *Alan James Green v Graeme Douglas Johnstone* [1995] VSC 34; [1995] VICSC 34; [1995] 2 VR 176.

In *Krantz*[44] Wood CJ accepted a Jewish family's appeal regarding a planned autopsy of an 86 year old woman. Wood noted that

> [Rabbi Apple commented that] "Among the foremost of the precepts concerning reverence for the dead is one which is of particular importance in the context of the present Application. Put simply, according to Jewish religion, an autopsy is an action of desecration, and as such is inimical to our deepest principles and feelings".
>
> The plaintiff has said that it would be a matter of anguish, both by reason of his mother's beliefs and his own beliefs, if her remains were to be dissected for a post mortem examination. He has invited the Coroner to conduct an alternative non-intrusive examination and for that purpose has offered to bear any additional costs associated therewith.[45]

Wood concluded

> I observe that I am quite unpersuaded by the argument that the wrong message would be sent to the public in a case such as this, if the matter was allowed to proceed without a post mortem examination. For the reasons identified by Walsh J, in *Unchango*, this case and similar cases can never be taken as a general precedent. In every case a discretion has to be exercised having regard to the particular facts of the matter.
>
> I am satisfied in a case such as the present that the public would readily understand the lack of any need for a post mortem in respect of a frail 86 year old woman whose health was observed by independent observers to have been progressively declining, who had a supportive family, who died in her own home, where there was genuine evidence of strong religious beliefs shared both by her and by her family concerning the undesirable interference with a body at post mortem.[46]

That decision is consistent with jurisprudence overseas, such as *Callanan*[47] and *R v Westminster City Coroner, ex Parte, Rainer* QBD 112 SJ 882.

It is important to note that Australian courts, in deciding applications on cultural grounds to prevent autopsies or order immediate burial, have not given an automatic dispensation. Instead, although recognising sensitivities, they have decided on a case by case basis. Ethnicity is not a guarantee of exceptional outcomes. Riley J in *Wuridjal v Hand* [2001] NTSC 99 thus rejected an application by members of the Yolngu community.

---

[44] *Krantz v Hand* [1999] NSWSC 432.
[45] Ibid, [4]–[5].
[46] Ibid, [49]–[50]
[47] *Callanan v Geraghty* [2007] IEHC 419.

Coroners' decisions have been overturned, for example in *Green v Johnstone*, *Unchango*, and *Abernethy v Deitz* (1996) 39 NSWLR 701.

They have also been upheld, for example in *Magdziarz*, where McDonald J noted familial distress but endorsed the autopsy on the basis that the cause of death of an adult son was not discernable though external examination of the deceased. The Court noted the parents' claim that they were devout Catholics and believed "that an autopsy will simply serve to desecrate our son's body". Counsel for the parents had indicated that

> although it was not being advanced that there was a religious reason in particular against the autopsy in this case, nevertheless the Court should take into account the religious views of the parents of the deceased.[48]

In *Joe Traynor v Ors* in 2012, Digby J of the Victorian Supreme Court endorsed parental rejection of an autopsy of a seven year old girl who died after getting tangled in a skipping rope that was tied to a swing.[49] Her parents argued little could be gained from performing an autopsy and her family should be able to bury her intact. Ian Freckelton SC, co-author of the leading Australian text on coronial investigation, argued on the family's behalf that the child's identity was already known, as was the cause of her death. There was no indication of foul play: nothing would be gained by the "intrusive dissection of her body" aside from causing unnecessary distress to her family. "The child died in unusual circumstances in a tragic and distressing way and there is minimal to be gained and no necessity to perform actions of this intrusive kind". He argued that there was no reason why a finding could not be made that she had died of constriction of the neck "quite adequately without the gratuitous causing of distress to her parents" and that it was "utter speculation that [an autopsy] is going to provide any information that will be useful".

Digby J appears to have agreed, reportedly commenting that the girl's father was not able to bear the thought of an autopsy being performed on his deceased daughter and his partner just wanted her daughter back for burial. He had weighed up the public interest in learning the cause of the death, against the anguish and grief experienced by the parents, rejecting the State's argument that an autopsy was necessary for the coroner to fulfil its statutory obligation in determining the cause of the death of a "young child who died in extremely … unusual circumstances" and provide

---

48 *Magdziarz v Heffey* [1995] VSC 201 [18]. See also: *Pope & Pope v State Coroner* [1998] SASC 6526.

49 *Joe Traynor v Ors* (Unreported, Supreme Court of Victoria, 2012).

recommendations, wherever possible, that could prevent any further deaths the same way.

In 2009 prominent Indigenous artist Banduk Marika[50] unsuccessfully sought an injunction against the Northern Territory Coroner's authorisation of an autopsy on her son after his death in a road accident.[51] Marika reportedly argued that an autopsy is inconsistent with traditional law. She had told police after her son's death that she did not want an autopsy. She was told by the coroner during the next day that an autopsy would be carried out in 48 hours, timing that potentially disadvantages people without immediate access to legal support. During the injunction hearing Marika reportedly told the Court that her family felt "disfigurement" of her son's body was unnecessary, that the family had not seen any evidence from police to justify it and that when a body is interfered with by a foreign hand the dead person's spirit is prevented from moving forward into the next world.

Some people, however, are concerned about what is happening to living bodies in this rather than the next world.

Rejecting the Fluid of Life

On 21 September 2006, Abbott J of the Irish High Court made an ex parte order that an African woman from the Democratic Republic of the Congo, who spoke limited English, and professed to be a Jehovah's Witness, receive a blood transfusion against her wishes.[52] The order authorised the use of restraint in the event that she resisted.

Although the case is over six years old, and occurred in another common law jurisdiction with a separate strain of jurispolitics[53] underpinning maternal-child relations, this particular case is of interest because on the facts, it forced the court to consider nearly all the complex issues facing courts in the common law world hearing matters involving refusal to consent to blood transfusion on religious ground: autonomy,

---

[50] George Milpurrurru, Banduk Marika, Tim Payunka and the Public Trustee of the Northern Territory v Indofurn Pty Ltd, Brian Alexander Bethune, George Raymond King and Robert James Rylands [1994] FCA 1544.

[51] The Northern Territory Supreme Court decision is unreported. See: 'Clash of Laws Over Indigenous Autopsy', *Australian Broadcasting Corporation* (online), 30 December 2009, <http://www.abc.net.au/news/2009-12-30/clash-of-laws-over-indigenous-autopsy/1193818>.

[52] Fitzpatrick & Anor v K & Anor [2008] IEHC 104.

[53] For jurispolitics see Ronald Howell, 'The Search for Jurispolitical Philosophy' (1958) 44 *Virginia Law Review* 409.

capacity, consent, "best interests of the child", paramount interest in preserving life, respect for religious beliefs, and discrimination on the basis of ethno-religious beliefs.

There is much about *Fitzpatrick & Anor v K & Anor* (*K's case*) which can be of use to Australian courts in interpreting similar situations.

Blood transfusion is a relatively common therapy, used to treat a range of conditions including blood loss caused by trauma, such as childbirth and postoperative trauma, certain types of cancers and complications from other infections. The Australian Red Cross estimates that one in three of Australia's 23 million citizens will require a blood transfusion at some point, and yet only one in 30 are donors, and that more than 27 000 donations are required per week, or 1.4 million donations per year.[54] For some patients, transfusion is used to treat an acute condition, requiring one or more units of blood to rectify a deficiency that, once addressed, is unlikely to recur — for example surgery requirements or trauma. Other patients require blood transfusions and blood products on an ongoing basis, to treat chronic conditions such as cancer or immunological disorders.[55]

In spite of the well-established history of transfusions as a therapy, there are some patients who refuse to consent to blood transfusions. Two of the more common reasons for refusal are: 1) concern about the safety of transfused blood products, particularly based on concerns around diseases such as AIDS, hepatitis, and other blood-borne infections; and 2) religious beliefs, most notably when the proposed recipient is a member of the Jehovah's Witnesses.[56] This chapter, with its focus on ethno-religious exceptionalism, examines the latter reason for refusal, and the law's response to it.

For many people, the refusal of Jehovah's Witnesses to accept blood transfusions or perform military service is the limit of their knowledge of the religious beliefs of this group.[57] The "exception" is the "identity". It is

---

[54] Blood Service Statistics January 2012 (2012) Australian Red Cross <http://www.donateblood.com.au/files/pdfs/Blood%20Service%20Statistics%20Jan%202012R.pdf>.

[55] Jacqueline Shortt et al, 'Assessment of the Urgency and Deferability of Transfusion to Inform Emergency Blood Planning and Triage: The Bloodhound Prospective Audit of Red Blood Cell Use' (2009) 11 *Transfusion* 2296.

[56] See, for example: M S Gohel et al, 'How to Approach Major Surgery Where Patients Refuse Blood Transfusion' (2005) 87 *Annals of the Royal College of Surgeons England* 3.

[57] Questions of service were highlighted in: *Adelaide Company of Jehovah's Witnesses Incorporated v Commonwealth* [1943] HCA 12; (1943) 67 CLR 116.

estimated that there are approximately seven million Jehovah's Witnesses worldwide,[58] including 1.5 million in Europe, 1.2 million in Africa, three million in the Americas, and half a million in Asia and the Middle East.

Since 1945, Jehovah's Witnesses have been instructed to abstain from blood transfusion, as it is interpreted as contrary to their religious teachings.[59] This view is largely based on interpretation of *Acts* 15:22 (eat no food that has been offered to idols; eat no blood; eat no animal that has been strangled); *Genesis* 9:4 (The one thing you must not eat is meat with blood still in it; I forbid this because the life is in the blood); and *Leviticus* 17:13–14 ("If any Israelite or any foreigner living in the community catches an animal or bird which is ritually clean, he must pour its blood out on the ground and cover it with dirt. The life of every living thing is in the blood, and that is why the LORD has told the people of Israel that they shall not eat any meat with blood still in it and that anyone who does so will no longer be considered one of his people").[60] Since 1961, accepting a blood transfusion, even under circumstances of life or death, has attracted the sanction of "disfellowship" — punitive exclusion from the congregation.[61]

There has been a perceived softening of this approach in recent years: while transfusion of whole blood, red cells, white cells, or plasma remains prohibited by mainstream Jehovah's Witnesses, acceptance of other products derived from donated blood is an issue which is left more to the personal choice of the patient.[62]

Clinical studies to date have demonstrated that Jehovah's Witnesses experience greater incidence of morbidity and mortality than the general population in some, but not all, of the contexts examined.[63,64]

---

[58] Watchtower Bible and Tract Society of Jehovah's Witnesses, *2011 Yearbook of Jehovah's Witnesses* (2011).

[59] *The Watchtower*, 1 July 1945, 198.

[60] *Good News Bible* (Australian Edition) (1988).

[61] *The Watchtower*, 15 January 1961, 63.

[62] Osamu Muramoto, 'Bioethical Aspects of Recent Changes in the Policy of Refusal of Blood by Jehovah's Witnesses' (2001) 322 *British Medical Journal* 37; Lee Elder, 'Why Some Jehovah's Witnesses Accept Blood and Conscientiously Reject Official Watchtower Society Blood Policy' (2000) 26 *Journal of Medical Ethics* 375. Muramoto and Elder argue that this perceived "softening" actually forces the patient to exclude themselves if they consent to treatment with these products, as opposed to being formally excluded by the Congregation.

[63] M E Van Wolfswinkel et al, 'Maternal Mortality and Serious Maternal Morbidity in Jehovah's Witnesses in The Netherlands' (2009) 116(8) *British Journal of Obstetrics & Gynaecology* 1103; N Massiah et al, 'Obstetric Care of Jehovah's Witnesses: A 14-year Observational Study' (2007) 276(4) *Archives of Gynaecological Obstetrics* 339.

Critical to this chapter is consideration of three particular scenarios: the emergency patient who requires an urgent blood transfusion to replace lost blood; the child who requires blood transfusion as part of treatment regime for cancer, or an immune disorder; and, as in *K's Case,*[65] the delivering mother who has a post-partum haemorrhage.

Prima facie, providing any medical treatment to a patient without lawful justification constitutes a battery in tort law.[66] Lawful justification includes treatment provided under emergency circumstances, where the threat to the life or health of the patient necessitates immediate intervention,[67] or provision of consent by the patient, or a person authorised to make decisions on their behalf.[68]

In the case of emergency, therefore, the law should appear to be fairly straightforward. Lawful justification of emergency or necessity in this context has been reflected in legislation in some jurisdictions.[69] It may, however, become complicated if the practitioner becomes aware that the treatment they are, or are planning, to administer, is in conflict with the express wishes of the patient.[70]

Many Jehovah's Witnesses carry cards on their person expressing their opposition to blood transfusion, while others have executed other types of Advanced Directive appropriate to the legislation in their home jurisdiction. In the event that a practitioner becomes aware of the existence of such a directive, the lawful justification or necessity will cease to operate in their defence.

Cases that attract media attention in this context have more traditionally involved children, where the lawful justification of emergency has not been appropriate, or other questions about the capacity of the person to provide consent.

---

64 J Kepros, 'Refusal of Transfusions for Cardiac Surgery Was Not Associated with Shorter Long-term Survival' (2012) 157 (10) *Annals of Internal Medicine* JC5; A S Jassar et al, 'Cardiac Surgery in Jehovah's Witness Patients: Ten-year Experience' (2012) 93(1) *Annals of Thoracic Surgery* 19.

65 Fitzpatrick & Anor v K & Anor [2008] IEHC 104.

66 *Schloendorff v The Society of the New York Hospital* 211 N.Y. 125, 105 N.E. 92 (1914), cited with approval by Mason CJ, Dawson Toohey and Gaudron JJ in: *Department of Health & Community Services v JWB & SMB* ("*Marion's Case*") (1992) 175 CLR 218.

67 *Rogers v Whitaker* (1992) 175 CLR 479, [14] (Mason CJ Brennan, Dawson, Toohey and McHugh JJ).

68 For example, under the *Guardianship* or *Powers of Attorney* legislation.

69 For example: Emergency Medical Operations Act (NT) s3; Consent to Medical Treatment and Palliative Care Act 1998 (SA) s 13.

70 Hunter and New England Area Health Service v A [2009] 74 NSWLR 88, [40].

tribunal appointing the guardian can impose limits on the authority of the guardian as the circumstances require.[83]

In the case of a Jehovah's Witness patient lacking capacity, without a valid advance directive, but requiring a blood transfusion, decision-making capacity may be vested in either the Attorney or Guardian, or the Tribunal, depending on the legislation for the relevant jurisdiction.[84]

The situation with respect to children is more complex by far. Generally, it is accepted that parents have the right to make decisions about medical treatment on behalf of their children.[85] This right is, however, not without boundaries. The Supreme Court of each State exercises an inherent *parens patriae* jurisdiction, which enables them to overrule the decisions of the parent in the event that it is in the best interests of the child that they do so.[86] A similar power exists in the Federal jurisdiction, under Part VII of the *Family Law Act*;[87] until 1999 the cross-vesting laws allowed it to be exercised in State Supreme Courts.[88]

In the event that a Jehovah's Witness parent withholds consent for a blood transfusion for his or her child, the care provider can seek an order of the court authorising the transfusion to proceed. Even in the case of a child who is mature enough to be deemed "Gillick" competent[89] — capable of making valid decisions about their treatment based on understanding of the consequences — the courts have demonstrated their willingness to disregard the express wishes of the child when they feel they are inconsistent with the best interests[90] of the child. Such was the case in *Royal Alexandra Hospital for Children v J & Ors,*[91] where the patient in question was a 16 year old male Jehovah's Witness with acute lymphoblastic leukaemia, with a 50 per cent chance of dying within 24 hours in the absence of a transfusion.[92]

---

83 Guardianship and Management of Property Act 1991 (ACT) s 7.

84 Qumsieh v Guardianship and Administration Board & Anor [1998] VSCA 45.

85 Family Law Act 1975 (Cth) s 61.

86 See, for example: Supreme Court Act 1935 (SA) s 17(2), discussed in: Children, Youth & Women's Health Services Inc v YJL, MHL and TL (By his next friend) [2010] SASC 175.

87 *Family Law Act 1975* (Cth) Part VII.

88 Jurisdiction of Courts (Cross-Vesting) Act 1987 (Cth) s41(1).

89 Gillick v West Norfolk and Wisbech Area Health Authority [1985] 3 All ER 402.

90 *Family Law Act 1975* (Cth) ss 60CA, 60CC

91 Royal Alexandra Hospital for Children t/a Children's Hospital at Westmead v J & Ors [2005] NSWSC 465.

92 Royal Alexandra Hospital v Joseph & Ors [2005] NSWSC 422.

The courts will temper this with consideration of the best interests in a holistic sense, including the impact any transfusion would have on the parents' acceptance of the child. It is notable that some parents, although unwilling to consent to transfusions themselves, indicate that they will not excommunicate the child after the child receives the transfusion (as is, nominally at least, required by the teachings of the main Jehovah's Witness faith).[93] The courts will also, where appropriate, include a requirement that all other options be tried before the transfusion is performed; the transfusion is thus authorised, but only as a last resort.[94]

This provides a clear indication of the courts attempts to recognise the importance of religious and social practice within the Jehovah's Witness community, while balancing it against the paramount interest of preserving the life of the child, who may in fact not have been permitted any choice in the matter of religion.

Another class of case attracting significant publicity, but limited attention from the courts, is that of Jehovah's Witness mothers who experience complications, such as post-partum haemorrhage, associated with childbirth. Ironically, this is the class of patients for whom the most clinical data exists: studies demonstrate that Jehovah's Witness women who refuse transfusions for treatment of childbirth-related complications experience increased risk to life and health than their non-Jehovah's Witness counterparts.[95]

All of which brings us back to the somewhat anomalous *K's case*. The patient was conscious and, apparently, alert after the birth of her baby, and her refusal seemed, on the face of it, based on religious beliefs. Prima facie, her wishes should have been respected, and the transfusion not performed. However the hospital apparently felt that there were issues surrounding her capacity: she did not speak English, and relied on a friend, who later was identified as a relative, to translate, and there was great confusion about both her religious status, and the whereabouts of the baby's father. Questions about her understanding, and the validity of her consent, may have been reasonable; however use of a professional translator to overcome any comprehension issues affecting the validity of her decision may have been more appropriate than seeking a court order disregarding it. Ultimately, the court found that she lacked capacity, although this was determined at a later hearing held after the initial ex

---

93 Women's and Children's Health Network Inc v JC, JC, and KC (By her litigation guardian) [2012] SASC 104; Children, Youth &Women's Health Services Inc v YJL, MHL and TL (By his next friend) [2010] SASC 175.

94 *Re Bernard* [2009] NSWSC 11.

95 Fitzpatrick & Anor v K & Anor [2008] IEHC 104.

parte order was made. The critical issue in making the ex parte order, it appears, was the best interests, not of the mother, but of her newborn son.[96] In making the ex parte order, the court privileged the needs of the baby, whom it believed, mistakenly as was later established, would have been left parentless in a foreign country had the order not been made, and the patient died of blood loss.

This decision triggered significant public criticism, and, although the issuing of the order was upheld in a later review, the judgment avoided considering the question of whether it was appropriate to privilege the rights of the baby over those of the mother, but made it clear that the Court wanted to avoid similar cases in future.[97] It raises significant questions about application in future cases. Did the perceived "single parent" status of the mother at the time the ex parte order was made make her religious beliefs less significant, on the basis of her marital status? What role do the mother's wishes have? Would it have been different if her refusal was based on fear of contracting an infection from the transfusion, for example?

It is also at odds with a similar story reported just 12 months later where the refusal to consent to transfusion of a recently-delivered Jehovah's Witness mother of twins was respected, and the mother subsequently died[98] — unarguably also a less than satisfactory outcome.

Conclusion

Moliere's M Jourdain discovered, to his astonishment, that he'd been speaking prose all his life. In considering cultural exceptionalism regarding bodies we might ask whether many of Australia's judges and legislators are unacknowledged speakers of legal pragmatism, unacknowledged because they do not refer to theorists such as Minow,

---

[96] Ibid.

[97] Ibid.

[98] Liz Hull, Andy Dolan and Dan Newling, 'Jehovah's Witness Mother Dies after Refusing Blood Transfusion after Giving Birth to Twins', *Daily Mail* (online), 5 November 2007, <http://www.dailymail.co.uk/news/article-491791/Jehovahs-Witness-mother-dies-refusing-blood-transfusion-giving-birth-twins.html#ixzz2D16juHMX>; Fred Attewill, 'Jehovah's Witness Mother Dies after Refusing Blood Transfusion', *The Guardian* (online), 5 November 2007, <http://www.guardian.co.uk/uk/2007/nov/05/health.religion>; 'Mother Dies after Refusing Blood', *BBC News* (online), 5 November 2007, <www.news.bbc.co.uk/2/hi/uk_news/England/Shropshire/7078455.stm>.

Posner and Holmes and indeed rarely characterise legal decision-making in terms of legal theory as such.

That lack of acknowledgment is unsurprising, given that proficiency in legal theory or possession of a law degree is not a prerequisite for election to a legislature and that the judiciary looks for practical solutions rather than aiming to develop philosophical constructions that are engaging in academic seminars but are of uncertain value in dealing with the realities of disputes before the bench.

What is practical? The introduction to this chapter suggested the conceptual validity of legal pragmatism is indicated by the extent to which it provides a useable understanding of the law, ie an understanding that is conceptually coherent and consistent with the operation of the justice system. In dealing with disputes about blood and bodies Australian courts are guided by precedent in interpreting statute law and making sense of discretion. That precedent has the predictive character highlighted by Holmes' encapsulation of law as "The prophecies of what the courts will do in fact" and "prediction, the prediction of the incidence of public force through the instrumentality of the courts".[99] Practicality, in lower courts, means decision-making that is consistent with precedent and unlikely to be overturned on appeal.

What we can see in looking at the snapshots in the preceding paragraphs is that Australian law is accommodating difference on a practical basis, with scope for decision-making by authorities that recognises conflicting cultural values and beliefs but does not necessarily privilege a particular faith, ethnicity or other identity. Minow and Spelman comment that legal insight comes

> not from turning away from human relationships in search of some essential form of reason, but instead from encountering the differences among people, the critical perspectives afforded by the facts of our differences, and the struggle to move between contexts in the search for temporary solutions to our problems.[100]

In practice Australian law-making and implementation has that concern for context and Kantian respect for diversity and dignity rather than enshrining absolutes.

---

[99] Oliver Wendell Holmes Jr, 'The Path Of The Law', in Sheldon Novick (ed), *The Collected Works of Justice Holmes* (University of Chicago Press, 1995) vol 3, 393.

[100] Martha Minow and Elizabeth Spelman, 'In Context' (1990) 63 *Southern California Law Review* 1649.

CHAPTER NINE

THE MOUNT RENNIE RAPE CASE OF 1886: POLITICS, MERCY AND JUSTICE IN LATE NINETEENTH CENTURY AUSTRALIA

WENDY KUKULIES-SMITH AND SUSAN PRIEST

> Six men's lives trembling in the balance, and the Chief Justice in New Zealand, the Attorney-General in Tasmania, and the judge who tried the case having sailed for England.[1]

Introduction

These poignant words were written by the then Governor of New South Wales, Lord Charles Robert Carrington, on 4 January 1887.[2] They serve as an introduction to the sense of isolation as well as the burden of responsibility he felt at the time of writing. The circumstances of the Mount Rennie case, which his words refer to, had taken its toll. The Mount Rennie case involved the violent rape of a young 16 year old girl called Mary Jane Hicks by a local gang of young men. The case was described at the time as being a crime of the most "revolting brutality and ferocity"[3] and the Mount Rennie case remains one of the most well-known cases in Colonial Australian criminal history. The crime occurred in Moore Park, an area then of low-lying scrub and swampland on the outskirts of the City

---

[1] Lord Carrington, 'The Mount Rennie Case December 1886–January 1887', The Colonial Secretary Special Bundle, NSW State Records 2/8095B.2, 4.

[2] In 1887, Carrington had been the Governor of NSW for approximately three years. See: A W Martin, *Carrington, Charles Robert (Marquess of Lincolnshire) (1843-1928)* (2012) Australian Dictionary of Biography — National Centre of Biography <http://www.adb.online.anu.edu.au/biogs/A030334b.htm>.

[3] Lord Carrington, 'Minute from The Governor for The Executive Council', The Colonial Secretary Special Bundle, NSW State Records 2/8095B.2, 1.

of Sydney, adjoining the industrial suburb of Waterloo.[4] The place was known locally as Mount Rennie. The circumstances surrounding this notorious case were subsequently branded in the colonial press as “The Waterloo Outrage”[5] or the “Mount Rennie Outrage”[6]. The first term is clearly a reference to the location of the crime. The second term, “outrage”, was employed widely throughout the daily press in the reporting of the case and appears from its use to be a term synonymous with “rape”.[7]

An examination of this high profile crime enables us to gain insight into the workings of the colonial justice system between November 1886 and January 1887. It also tells us something about the nature of the changing values of the society. Previous scholarship on the Mount Rennie case has analysed the “colonial mythology”[8] of rape operating in the Colony, the colonial perceptions of women, and the views of youth

---

[4] ‘Terrible Outrage on a Girl’, Sydney Morning Herald (Sydney), Saturday 11 September 1886, 10; The Historical Atlas of Sydney, Atlas of Suburbs of Sydney ca 1885-1890 Sydney, City of Sydney map and Waterloo map, Higinbotham & Robinson Publishers, http://www.photosau.com.au/CoSMaps/scripts/display.asp

[5] ‘The Waterloo Outrage, Trial of the Prisoners’, *Sydney Morning Herald* (Sydney), Tuesday 23 November 1886, 4.

[6] ‘The Hanging of Coleman and the Mt Rennie Outrage’, *Barrier Miner* (Broken Hill), Friday 3 July 1908, 2; ‘Mt Rennie Outrage’, *Sunday Times* (Perth), Sunday 29 January 1905, 8; ‘Mt Rennie Outrage’, *Kalgoorlie Miner* (WA), Friday 26 June 1896, 3; ‘Horrible Outrage’, *Queanbeyan Age* (NSW), Saturday 9 November 1895, 2.

[7] See, for example, the use of outrage in this manner in the *Barrier Miner* “… two of the lads were innocent of any complicity in that alleged outrage”: ‘The Hanging of Coleman and the Mt Rennie Outrage’, *Barrier Miner* (Broken Hill), Friday 3 July 1908, 2. See also, the term’s use in the sense of an “outrage upon a girl”. For example, the *Queanbeyan Age* reported ‘A Terrible Story is to Hand of an Outrage Upon a Girl … Horrible Outrage’, *Queanbeyan Age* (NSW), Saturday 9 November 1895, 2; ‘Terrible Outrage on a Girl’, *Sydney Morning Herald* (Sydney), Saturday 11 September 1886, 10.

[8] N Philadelphoff-Puren, ‘Reading Rape in Colonial Australia: Barbara Baynton’s ‘The Tramp’, *The Bulletin* and Cultural Criticism’ (2010) (Special Issue: Common Reader and Cultural Critics) *Journal of the Association for the Study of Australian Literature* 1, 2.

including the culture of larrikins or larrikinism.[9] The aims of this chapter are to consider the ramifications of the sentence imposed upon the nine youths found guilty of the outrage, particularly in terms of the politics of justice operating at the time the crime occurred. Further, unlike previous scholarship, this chapter is less concerned with the details of the crime itself and focuses more exclusively on the implications of the death sentence imposed on the young offenders and the enormity of the decision faced by the then Governor of New South Wales as to whether to exercise Executive clemency.

This perspective has been developed through a close analysis of available primary resources. The New South Wales State Records have a collection of materials known as the Colonial Secretary's Special Bundle, which contain Lord Carrington's notes on the Mount Rennie case.[10] There are further Carrington papers available at the State Library of New South Wales but these are accessible on a read-only basis and are subject to stringent publication restrictions. Official court documents for the Mount Rennie case are scarce.[11] However, there was extensive reporting of the trial throughout the Colony in the daily newspapers and in regional broadsheets. These proved to be a rich source of material. The newspapers were also valuable with regards to understanding the public responses to the trial and the intimate workings of the colonial legal system; as those in the limelight, the Judge, the Governor and the Premier were all called upon to respond to the controversy created by this case.

Public attention surrounding the case at the time was extremely high not only because of the shocking nature of the crime, but because it accentuated the problems of social morality and the unruly gangs of youths within Sydney. Such sentiments were reflected in the letters to the Editors of the daily press including those of Francis Myers who complained about the "[u]ndisciplined licentious boys wandering uncontrolled through

[9] See, for example, A Kaladelfos, 'The Politics of Punishment Rape and the Death Penalty in Colonial Australia 1841-1901' (2012) 9(1) *History Australia* 155; A Kaladelfos, *Crime and Outrage: Sexual Villains and Sexual Violence in New South Wales 1870-1930* (PhD, Department of History, University of Sydney 2010); N Philadelphoff-Puren, above n 8, 1; D Walker, 'Youth on Trial: The Mt Rennie Case' (1986) 48–51 (50) *Labour History* 28.

[10] Lord Carrington, above n 1, 2.

[11] David Walker writing on the case in 1986 noted that "Archival holdings on the trial have proved elusive": Walker, above n 9, 28 (footnote 3). The NSW State Records currently holds a number of depositions from the Mount Rennie Trial.

the scrub through long hours of leisure …"[12] and of Frank Ward who considered that "the parents of the unfortunate boys are in the first instance answerable for the crime they have committed, having reared them in crowded and unwholesome localities …"[13] The age of the offenders in this case was also a matter of significance and moreover was pivotal to the debates about whether the death sentence should be carried out.

In 1886, when the crime occurred, rape was a capital charge in New South Wales.[14] It was no longer, however, a capital offence in England. Since 1841, murder and treason remained the only capital offences in England.[15] The exercise of the death penalty against British subjects had subsided with the move to transportation and later to a system of penal servitude.[16] The Mount Rennie case can then also be seen to shed light on changing public views that were occurring around the turn of the century on the death sentence in Australia. The case highlights that there were serious concerns about what the nature of this crime said overseas of the character of the Colony when Australia was in the throes of celebrations for the upcoming Queen's Jubilee year in 1887[17] As portrayed in the words of Lord Carrington in the quote at the outset of this chapter, "the Judge who tried the case having sailed for England" to take part in these centenary commemorations.

Windeyer's Justice: An "Unyielding Heel of Iron"[18]

The Mount Rennie trial commenced on Monday 22 November 1886. On the first day of proceedings, 11 young men aged between 17 and 22

---

[12] Francis Myers, 'The Mount Rennie Outrage To the Editor of the Herald', *Sydney Morning Herald* (Sydney), Wednesday 29 December 1886, 8.
[13] Frank Ward, 'The Mount Rennie Outrage', *Sydney Morning Herald* (Sydney), Friday 31 December 1886, 5.
[14] Persons found guilty of rape were liable to be sentenced to death. See: *Criminal Law Amendment Act 1883* (NSW) s 39.
[15] J Chan and D Oxley, 'The Deterrent Effect of Capital Punishment: A Review of the Research Evidence' (2004) 84 *Contemporary Issues in Crime and Justice* 3.
[16] *Penal Servitude Act 1857*, c. 3 (Regnal. 20 and 21 Vict), s 2.
[17] Lord Carrington, above n 1, 3.
[18] In an article looking back on the Mount Rennie Outrage the *Sunday Times* reported that despite coming under harsh comment in the press at the time of the Mount Rennie Outrage for his severe sentence upon the youths, Justice Windeyer had broken the youth gangs and impacted rates of carnal crime in NSW as a result of his "method of stamping it out — with an unyielding heel of iron". See 'Worse Than Mt Rennie', *Sunday Times* (Perth), Sunday 9 December 1917, 5.

years of age[19] stood in the dock of the Central Criminal Court having all been charged with "ravishing and carnally knowing Mary Jane Hicks against her consent".[20] The matter was heard before his Honour Justice William Charles Windeyer and ran for six full days.

The matter, as recounted in the Central Criminal Court of New South Wales by the *Sydney Morning Herald*, tells us that Mary Jane Hicks was a domestic servant.[21] On the morning of 9 September 1886, she had set out from her lodging to go to a registry office in Sydney seeking work.[22] She travelled on foot along Sussex Street when she alleged that a cabman approached her and offered her a ride into town.[23] Hicks accepted the ride. She entered the cab but instead of being taken to the agreed location, the cabman took her a couple of miles away to scrubland in Moore Park. It was claimed at the trial that the cabman, Charles Sweetman,[24] then exited the cab and gave her some flowers.[25] He had attempted to have liberties with her when a group of young men appeared on the scene and pulled Hicks from the cab. Charles Sweetman immediately drove away.[26] This group of young men, alleged to have been a gang known as "the push", then brutally raped Mary Jane Hicks. William Stanley, a shipwright, was walking from Randwick racecourse when he heard Hicks's screams.[27] He ran in the direction of the screams and attempted to rescue her but was surrounded by three men and was attacked by them.[28] He escaped and ran to the Redfern police station to seek help.[29] Stanley became a key witness in the Prosecution's case and told the Court that "He need not detail the girl's story beyond saying that all the prisoners except three violated her in a most brutal manner some even when she was in a semi-conscious state"[30] Thomas Smith, a jockey, was also a key witness. Smith gave

---

[19] William Hill, George Duffy, William Newman, Michael Donnellan, Thomas Oscroft, Joseph Martin, William Boyce, Hugh Miller, Robert George Read, George Keegan, Michael Mangan.

[20] 'The Waterloo Outrage' above n 5, 4.

[21] Ibid.

[22] Ibid.

[23] Ibid.

[24] 'The Mount Rennie Outrage Case', *The South Australian Advertiser* (Adelaide), 30 November 1886, 5.

[25] 'The Waterloo Outrage' above n 5, 4.

[26] Ibid.

[27] 'The Waterloo Outrage, Trial of the Prisoners', *Sydney Morning Herald* (Sydney), Thursday 25 November 1886, 4.

[28] Ibid.

[29] Ibid.

[30] Ibid.

evidence identifying six of the prisoners,[31] whom he claimed to have seen assaulting the victim.[32] The identification of the youths was a key aspect of this case with many of the prisoners claiming that either they had not been present on Mount Rennie at the time or that they had only arrived at the scene after the offence had taken place.

Justice Windeyer, appointed to preside over the trial, was regarded as a stern judge who was renowned as possessing "a rigorous and unrelenting sense of retribution that he believed criminal justice demanded".[33] J F Archibald, the editor of *The Bulletin*, portrayed Windeyer as a brutal member of the bench and part of a dying system of rough colonial justice.[34] Archibald had sat through the entire proceedings of the Mount Rennie case and had taken extensive notes.[35] He later drafted a treatise of the Mount Rennie case drawing on his observations in court during the trial and also on his recollections of the broader circumstances surrounding the case.[36]

J F Archibald clearly disliked Justice Windeyer and the system of brutal colonial justice that this judge represented. During the Mount Rennie trial Archibald was very critical of Justice Windeyer for running the case in a way to suit his own agenda rather than ensuring that justice be done. In particular, Archibald drew attention to the length of the daily sittings adopted by court when hearing this matter.[37] Archibald observed

---

[31] William Hill, George Duffy, William Newman, Michael Donnellan, Thomas Oscroft, Joseph Martin.

[32] 'The Waterloo Outrage', above n 27, 4.

[33] *Windeyer, Sir William Charles (1834–1897)* (2012) Australian Dictionary of Biography, National Centre of Biography <http://adb.anu.edu.au/biography/windeyer-sir-william-charles-1062/text8145>.

[34] J F Archibald, 'An Appeal to Caesar. The Story of Mount Rennie. A Suppressed Chapter of NSW History Sydney Version', State Library of Australia MLA2254/Vol 5, John Feltham Archibald Papers, 3–9.

[35] Katherine Thomson, 'Australia On Trial, Episode One The Mount Rennie Outrage' (2012) Screen Hub <http://www.screenhub.com.au/industry/production_detail.php?productionID=2443>.

[36] The State Library of New South Wales holds a collection of Archibald papers within this collection are a number of drafts of the unpublished treatise on the Mt Rennie case written by Archibald. See, for example: J F Archibald, 'An Appeal to Caesar. The Story of Mount Rennie. A Suppressed Chapter of NSW History Sydney Version', State Library of Australia MLA2254/Vol 5, John Feltham Archibald Papers.

[37] Ibid, 13–14; Thomson, above n 35.

that under the usual hours of court, the court would commence at 10 am.[38] Of the six days it took to hear this case, Archibald recorded that the court sat for the first time on Monday 22 November 1886 between the hours of 10 am until 9:50 pm, Tuesday from 9 am until 11:30 pm, Wednesday 9 am until 7 pm, Thursday 9 am until 7 pm and Friday 9 am until 3:30 am on Saturday morning. The court reconvened five and a half hours later for its final day of sitting on Saturday 27 November 1886 at 9 am until 11:40 pm.[39] These times were also readily confirmed by other newspaper reports on the trial.[40]

Archibald believed that the 7 pm adjournments on the Wednesday and Thursday evenings of proceedings were to accommodate Justice Windeyer's dinner appointments. He recalled that "On Friday … [t]he Court, to make up for time expended over the dinner-table … opened at nine, [rather than 10 am] and sat right on night and day until half past three on Saturday morning".[41] Justice Windeyer was apparently keen to finish the case as quickly as possible as he was shortly to set sail for England.[42] Archibald graphically described the mood of the court in the early hours of Saturday morning:

> … Counsel, who had vainly implored the judge to adjourn, addressed a comatose jury, up and down whose ranks a bottle of powerful salts was being passed to keep the arbiters of life or death awake … The exhausted and bewildered jury, drawn mainly from a class of men quite unused to protracted mental exertion …[43]

---

[38] Archibald, above n 34, 13.
[39] Ibid, 13–14.
[40] 'The Waterloo Outrage', above n 5, 4; 'The Waterloo Outrage, Trial of the Prisoners', *Sydney Morning Herald* (Sydney), Wednesday 24 November 1886, 6; 'The Waterloo Outrage, Trial of the Prisoners', above n 27, 4; 'The Waterloo Outrage, Trial of the Prisoners', *Sydney Morning Herald* (Sydney), Friday 26 November 1886, 4; 'The Waterloo Outrage, Trial of the Prisoners', *Sydney Morning Herald* (Sydney), Saturday 27 November 1886, 8; 'The Waterloo Outrage, Trial of the Prisoners', *Sydney Morning Herald* (Sydney), Monday 29 November 1886, 5.
[41] Archibald, above n 34, 14.
[42] Thomson, above n 35; The *Sydney Morning Herald* reported Justice Windeyer to be departing for England on Friday 31 December 1886. See: 'Testimonial to Mr Justice Windeyer and Mrs Windeyer', *Sydney Morning Herald* (Sydney), Wednesday 22 December 1886, 5.
[43] Archibald, above n 34, 14.

So incensed was Archibald by the Court's sitting schedule that he later commenced the Sydney version of his piece on the case with the following statement: "And wretches swung that Windeyer might dine".[44]

The trial ended on Saturday 27 November in spectacular circumstances. Justice Windeyer is documented as taking almost 10 hours to sum up the case before the jury retired at approximately 20 minutes past eight on Saturday evening and returned at approximately 11 pm with its verdict. The jury delivered a guilty verdict upon nine of the 11 youths,[45] but with a recommendation of mercy.[46] Justice Windeyer then took approximately 40 minutes to deliver his sentence upon the nine youths. He sentenced all nine youths to death.[47] The nine condemned youths comprised: William Boyce (19 years), Michael Donnellan (17 years), George Duffy (17 years), William Hill (22 years), George Keegan (19 years), Joseph Martin (17 years), Hugh Miller (18 years), William Newman (18 years) and Robert George Read (19 years).[48] Therefore at the conclusion of the trial at 11:40 pm on Saturday evening, of the 11 youths arraigned, nine had been found guilty. The cabman had also been found guilty for his part in the crime and was sentenced to 14 years hard labour with two floggings.[49]

If these death sentences were carried out, it would be a significant display of might. Executing such a number would see New South Wales going against the declining practice of exercising the death penalty

---

[44] Ibid, 1. See also: above n 36.

[45] Michael Mangan and Thomas Oscroft were both discharged by the jury. See: 'The Summing Up', *Sydney Morning Herald* (Sydney), Monday 29 November 1886, 5.

[46] Second hand evidence exists that the jury recommended mercy in this case. W B Dalley comments on this aspect of the trial in his deputation to Lord Carrington on 5 January 1887. See: Lord Carrington, above n 1, 5. Comments are also recorded about the Jury's recommendation for mercy in this case in quotes reported in the daily press of the public meetings. See: 'The Mount Rennie Outrage', *Sydney Morning Herald* (Sydney) Wednesday 5 January 1887, 6.

[47] 'The Summing Up', above n 45, 5.

[48] Lord Carrington, above n 1, 1.

[49] The number of floggings was reported as lenient due to ill health. See: 'The Mount Rennie Outrage Case' *South Australian Advertiser* (Adelaide) Tuesday 30 November 1886, 5.

elsewhere in the Colony.[50] Nonetheless, Justice Windeyer was clearly pleased with the jury's verdict and reportedly stated:

> Prisoners, you have been convicted of a most atrocious crime, a crime so horrible that every lover of his country must feel that it is a disgrace to our civilisation. I am glad to find that this case has been tried by a jury that has the intelligence to see through the perjury upon perjury that has been committed on your behalf, and the courage to declare the truth as they see it.[51]

His Honour then imposed a sentence of death by hanging upon each of the prisoners. He is reported to have said, "I warn you to prepare for death. No hope of mercy can I extend to you. Be sure no weakness of the Executive. No maudlin feeling of pity, will save you from the death you so richly deserve".[52] Archibald later depicted the case in his treatise as a "story … which years ago imprinted upon the legal administration of New South Wales a burning brand of shame that hisses still".[53]

Lord Carrington's Bind

When news of the sentence was published in the press, extensive debate arose about the fate of the youths and whether nine young men should face the gallows. The newspapers reported on all sides of this debate. The virtue of Mary Jane Hicks was subject to close scrutiny, but the newspapers appeared to accept the horrendous nature of the crime itself and that *perhaps* all women in the eyes of the law were sacred.[54] Historian David Walker describes the time as "intense conflict about how best to act in the face of a youth problem enigmatically embedded in the shifting cultural formation of colonial society".[55] This period was also a

---

[50] For example, Mark Finnane notes that in 1870 Victoria executed 10 males, which is only one more than those sentenced to death in the Mount Rennie Case. See: M Finnane, *Punishment in Australian Society* (Oxford University Press, 1997) 32. See also the decline in the rates of executions carried out across the colonies in Table 1 in: Ivan Potas and John Walker, 'Capital Punishment' (Trends and Issues in Crime and Criminal Justice No 3, Australian Institute of Criminology, 1987)

[51] 'The Summing Up', above n 45, 5.

[52] 'The Waterloo Outrage Conclusion of the Trial Nine Men Sentenced to Death Sydney Version', *The Echo* (NSW) Monday 26 November 1886, 5.

[53] Archibald, above n 34, 21.

[54] See, further: Archibald, above n 34, 12; Philadelphoff-Puren, above n 8, 1, 3–5; Walker, above n 9, 28, 38.

[55] Walker, above n 9, 28, 29.

time when public opinion about the death penalty was changing, not just in England but also in its colonies including Australia.

Public opinion appeared to be divided in respect as to whether the death sentences should be carried out in the circumstances surrounding the Mount Rennie case. Throughout the months of December 1886 and January 1887, a series of public meetings were convened around New South Wales including Sydney City, Lithgow, Newcastle and Balmain.[56] Those who attended these meetings discussed, in detail, whether mercy ought to be exercised by the Governor in favour of the Mount Rennie youths. The voices calling for the youths to be executed were particularly strong. As David Walker describes: "there was a widely endorsed theory that one more act of leniency towards criminal youths would generate a wave of similar crimes".[57]

On Wednesday 1 December 1886, the *Sydney Morning Herald* added a further dimension to the discourse. It announced that "the trial of the prisoners for the Waterloo outrage at Sydney has attracted considerable attention in England".[58] This attention led to spiralling concerns within the Executive over the importance of saving face within the British Empire. The Premier, Sir Henry Parkes brought this issue directly to Lord Carrington, with Carrington recording in his notes on the case dated 25 December 1886 that:

> I had a long interview with Sir Henry, in which he dwelt on the great harm which would accrue to the Colony if these youths were hanged in the year before the Centennial ...[59]

Therefore the pressure upon the Governor to exercise Executive clemency to the nine youths was mounting. The question of commuting the sentences was becoming not just one of mercy, but also one of politics.

---

[56] For example: 'The Mount Rennie Case (Public Meeting Sydney)', *Sydney Morning Herald* (Sydney), Monday 13 December 1886, 4; 'The Mount Rennie Outrage (Public Meeting Sydney Town Hall)', *Sydney Morning Herald* (Sydney), Wednesday 22 December 1886, 5; 'The Mount Rennie Outrage (Public Meeting Lithgow)', *Sydney Morning Herald* (Sydney), Friday 24 December 1886, 8; 'The Mount Rennie Outrage (Public Meeting Newcastle)', *Sydney Morning Herald* (Sydney), Saturday 25 December 1886, 7; 'The Mount Rennie Outrage (Public Meeting Balmain)', *Sydney Morning Herald* (Sydney), Wednesday 5 January 1887, 6.

[57] Walker, above n 9, 28, 29.

[58] 'Latest Intelligence', *Sydney Morning Herald* (Sydney) Wednesday 1 December 1886, 9.

[59] Lord Carrington, above n 1, 2.

As will be seen below, this was a position that Sir Henry Parkes was to repeatedly advance in several upcoming forums before the Governor.

Meeting of the Executive Council

As set out in section 12 of the Royal Instruction above, the Executive Council was convened to give advice to the Governor. The first meeting of the Executive Council was held on Thursday 16 December 1886.[70] Lord Carrington's notes document that, also in accordance with the Royal Instructions he had already received a written report from Justice Windeyer.[71] It is not documented in Carrington's notes whether this document was taken into consideration at the first meeting of the Executive Council in accordance with the procedure set out in the Royal Instructions.[72] Certainly the views of Justice Windeyer on the Mount Rennie Case would have been made clear to the Executive because, as sanctioned by the Royal Instructions, Justice Windeyer had been summoned and did attend the first Executive Council meeting.[73]

At this meeting, a decision was reached that the lives should be spared of three of the nine prisoners; Michael Donnellan, Hugh Miller and George Keegan.[74] The decision reached by the Executive Council was that the death sentence for these three offenders be commuted to one of "penal servitude for life with the first three years in irons".[75] Justice Windeyer had recommended mercy be exercised on behalf of William Hill.[76] However, the Executive Council advised that the remaining six prisoners, William Boyce, George Duffy, William Hill, Joseph Martin, William

---

[70] Ibid, 2.

[71] Ibid, 6.

[72] The Minister of Justice would later rely on this document in his review of the case. See: 'News of the Day', *Sydney Morning Herald* (Sydney), Monday 30 July 1888, 7. However, whether he raised these concerns at time of the first Executive Council meeting with Justice Windeyer and whether he did have access to this document at the time of the first meeting is unknown.

[73] Ibid, 2.

[74] Ibid.

[75] Ibid.

[76] Following the trial Justice Windeyer had changed his mind in respect to William Hill. By the time of the meeting of the Executive Council, the Judge was recommending mercy for Hill. Lord Carrington's notes state that Justice Windeyer recommended mercy for Hill in his written report to the Governor, see: Lord Carrington, above n 1, 6.

Newman and Robert George Read should suffer the death penalty.[77] Lord Carrington acted on this advice.[78]

Throughout December the Mount Rennie case remained a political burden upon the Executive. Public opinion gave weight to a view that two of the six condemned men were innocent.[79] On 4 January 1887, the Executive Council decided to meet again to discuss the case.[80] Justice Windeyer had now left for England so was not present at this meeting. The Chief Justice Sir Alfred Stephen, was also outside the jurisdiction and unable to attend. Moreover, the Attorney-General was absent, having travelled to Tasmania. The Attorney-General's absence had particular significance because it meant that there was now an even number of members present.

At the second meeting of the Executive Council "the whole of the evidence, the statements from the prisoners and of the witness on their behalf, petitions presented and resolutions passes in favour of their reprieve were carefully gone into …"[81] The Council was split with four members for carrying out the death sentences and four against. Lord Carrington records in his notes on the meeting, that two ministers who had previously voted for the death sentence being carried out had changed their position since the first meeting of the Executive Council.[82] He complained in his notes of the Attorney-General's absence and stated:

> [t]hey were both sides absolutely determined, and the matter then rested absolutely on me — a serious condition of things. Six men's lives trembling in the balance, and the Chief Justice in New Zealand, the Attorney-General in Tasmania, and the Judge who tried the case having sailed for England.[83]

---

[77] Ibid, 2.

[78] The outcome of the Executive Council meeting was reported in the newspapers, see: 'The Mount Rennie Outrage', *Sydney Herald* (Sydney), Thursday 23 December 1886, 3. Letters to the editor detail that the Governor had exercised mercy for three of the youths. See, for example: Robert Horniman, 'The Mount Rennie Outrage, To the Editor of the Herald', *Sydney Herald* (Sydney), Thursday 23 December 1886, 5.

[79] Latest Telegrams, *Northern Territory Times and Gazette* (Darwin), Saturday 1 January 1887, 3.

[80] Lord Carrington, above n 1, 4.

[81] 'The Mt Rennie Outrage, The Law To Take Its Course', *The South Australian Register* (Adelaide), Wednesday 5 January 1887, 5.

[82] Lord Carrington, above n 1, 4.

[83] Ibid.

Because the Council were not unanimous at this second meeting, it left Lord Carrington with no clear direction from his "constitutional advisors"[84] other than the advice from the first meeting of the Executive Council that the death sentence for the remaining six youths should stand.[85] The six youths were facing execution on Friday 7 January 1887, unless the Governor decided to exercise the prerogative of mercy.[86]

The deputations

The following day, 5 January 1887, with approximately 48 hours remaining before the executions were scheduled to take place, Lord Carrington received correspondence from Cardinal Moran pleading for mercy on behalf of the six condemned prisoners.[87] Later on the same day, a deputation of influential men comprising of Sir Henry Parkes, the Right Honourable W B Dalley, Cardinal Moran and Bishop Barry called on the Governor to make a final appeal for the exercise of the royal prerogative of mercy for all remaining six lives.[88]

Sir Henry Parkes spoke first and made a lengthy plea on behalf of the prisoners. Parkes once again focused on the reputation of the Colony abroad and of the damage that he believed would be done if the sentences were carried out.[89] The *South Australian Advertiser* reported Parkes' appeal to Lord Carrington on this occasion in the following manner:

> He did not ask for the prerogative to be exercised in favour of the men on behalf of mercy, but he thought that the hanging of these men would not do anything in vindication of the law while it would hurt our reputation at home.[90]

W B Dalley is reported to have concurred with Parkes' concerns about the reputation of the Colony overseas.[91] Dalley also addressed matters in respect to the conduct of the trial including the questionable nature of the

---

[84] This is the term given to the Executive Council. See: 'The Condemned Youth Strong Feeling in Sydney' above n 61, 5.

[85] Lord Carrington, above n 1, 4. This was also the position as reported in the press. See, for example: 'The Mt Rennie Outrage, The Law to Take Its Course', *The South Australian Register* (Adelaide), Wednesday 5 January 1887, 5.

[86] 'The Mt Rennie Outrage, The Law to Take Its Course', above n 85, 5.

[87] Lord Carrington, above n 1, 4.

[88] Ibid, 5.

[89] Ibid.

[90] 'The Condemned Youth Strong Feeling in Sydney', above n 61, 5.

[91] Ibid; Lord Carrington, above n 1, 5.

identification evidence that was relied upon. He spoke of public policy concerns about the reluctance of juries to convict in criminal matters if their recommendations of mercy "were held of no account".[92] He further observed that "[h]e knew of no English judge who ever insisted on the counsel and jury being forced to go on with such a trial when their physical energies were exhausted and their intellects were not equal to the occasion".[93] This was expressing concerns of the same tenor as those expressed by Archibald (see above in *Windeyer's Justice: An "Unyielding Heel of Iron"*).[94]

The next to address the Governor was Cardinal Moran. He admitted "he had little to add to his letter".[95] However, he is recorded as having criticised the blood lust that was present in the daily press and also emphasised the ignorance and youth of the prisoners.[96] The final submission was by Bishop Barry who was reported to have said little on the matter other than to remind the Governor that the prerogative of mercy could still be exercised up until the last moment. He sympathised with the Governor's plight and reportedly said that "the position that you have taken up is unassailable".[97] Despite this obvious show of power, Lord Carrington's recollection of this meeting, as recorded in his notes, was that "[i]t seemed to be a very strong deputation, but in reality it was not".[98]

On 6 January 1887, the eve of the execution, Lord Carrington received yet another group of prominent gentlemen presenting a deputation. Mr Thomas Ewing, John Davies and A H M'Culloch, members of the Legislative Assembly of New South Wales, presented a petition that had been signed by thirteen members of the Legislative Assembly and also by Sir Henry Parkes.[99] The signed petition requested that Carrington commute the sentence of death imposed upon all prisoners and once again

---

[92] The Condemned Youth Strong Feeling in Sydney', above n 61, 5.

[93] Ibid.

[94] This is perhaps not surprising if you accept Archibald's recollections of the events. He attributes Francis Myers and himself as the parties responsible for organising this high profile deputation. See: Archibald, above n 34, 19.

[95] Lord Carrington, above n 1, 5.

[96] Ibid.

[97] Ibid. In Archibald's recollections of this time he reports that Bishop Barry had been pressured into attending this meeting, having earlier written to Archibald stating that "as the criminals had been duly tried according to law he could not see his way to interfere". See: Archibald, above n 34, 19.

[98] Lord Carrington, above n 1, 5.

[99] 'Deputation to the Governor', *Sydney Morning Herald* (Sydney), Friday 7 January 1887, 3.

attention was drawn to the reputation of the Colony overseas.[100] It was reported in the *Sydney Morning Herald* that the petition had been hastily prepared the night before and that if there had been more time to prepare the document then more members of the Assembly could have been reached and a greater number of signatures provided.[101]

Mercy for Hill and Newman and the fate of the remaining four

While Lord Carrington does not document that he was motivated by either of these deputations in his notes, on the same day 6 January 1887, he reports that "after long and careful consideration"[102] he decided to grant mercy to two of the six condemned men: William Hill and William Newman. They were both granted a conditional pardon of "penal servitude for life with the first three years in irons".[103] These were the same conditions as those imposed on Donnellan, Miller and Keegan in December following the first Executive Council meeting. On hearing the news of clemency, the *Sydney Morning Herald* documented that Hill supposedly stated: "That's worse than death. I would rather die. I would rather go to the gallows. I don't want to live,"[104] while it was observed that Newman "appeared to be dazed and said nothing".[105]

As stated above, Justice Windeyer's written report to the Governor of 9 December 1886 had recommended mercy for Hill.[106] The decision of the Governor in respect to granting clemency to Hill is therefore interesting. Carrington had chosen to accept the recommendations of the judge for this prisoner over those of that the Executive Council. We have indicated earlier that the Executive Council on 16 December 1886, in a meeting at which Justice Windeyer was present, advised the Governor that the death sentence should proceed for Hill. Of course, we have also seen that Lord Carrington was under considerable external pressure to exercise clemency since this meeting and perhaps this was a concession he was prepared to make given he had judicial support for mercy for this prisoner.

The recommendation for mercy for Newman had also originated from Justice Windeyer. Unlike Hill, however, Justice Windeyer appeared to

---

[100] Ibid.
[101] Ibid.
[102] Lord Carrington, above n 1, 6.
[103] Lord Carrington, above n 3, 2.
[104] 'The Mount Rennie Outrage', *Sydney Morning Herald* (Sydney), Friday 7 January 1887, 3.
[105] Ibid.
[106] Lord Carrington, above n 1, 5; Lord Carrington, above n 3, 2.

have a change of heart in respect to Newman's position immediately prior to his departure for England. He is reported to have sent a memo to Lord Carrington at this time.[107] Newman was depicted as an 18 year old man of low intelligence[108] whose quiet demeanour had impressed gaol officials and attracted sympathy for his position. Lord Carrington recorded in his notes that he also received information from two Sisters of Mercy who visited the prisoners that all of the prisoners had claimed that Newman was not present at the scene of the crime and was innocent.[109]

In respect of the remaining four condemned youths, Lord Carrington felt that "he had no alternative but to enforce the law as he found it"[110] and uphold the opinion of the Executive Council. On the morning of Friday 7 January 1887, George Duffy, Joseph Martin, William Boyce and George Read were executed on the gallows at Darlinghurst Gaol.[111] The news of their execution and the public spectacle that took place spread throughout the Colony.[112] A record number of people had turned out for the execution.[113] Prisoner Read produced a document which was to be read after his death. In this document he professed his innocence.[114]

In December 1886, Miller, Keegan and Donnellan, three of the youths who were now under sentence of penal servitude, each sent a letter to the Minister of Justice setting out their recollections of the day of outrage and asking for the Minister's further consideration of the case.[115] The Minister of Justice did follow up on these letters. The newspapers documented that as late as July 1888, the Minister of Justice had raised with Justice Windeyer discrepancies that he had identified in the evidence in the

---

[107] Lord Carrington, above n 1, 6.
[108] Ibid.
[109] Ibid.
[110] 'The Mount Rennie Outrage Execution of the Criminals, Firmness on the Scaffold, Statement by Read, Death Not Instantaneous', *The Echo* (NSW), Saturday 8 January 1887, 5.
[111] 'The Mount Rennie Outrage, Execution of Four of the Criminals', *Sydney Morning Herald* (Sydney), Saturday 8 January 1887, 8.
[112] See, for example: 'The Mt Rennie Outrage', *The Brisbane Courier* (Brisbane), Saturday 8 January 1887, 5; 'The Mount Rennie Outrage, Execution of Four of the Criminals', above n 111, 8; 'The Mount Rennie Outrage Execution of the Criminals, Firmness on the Scaffold, Statement by Read, Death Not Instantaneous', *The Echo* (NSW), Friday 7 January 1887, 5.
[113] 'The Mount Rennie Outrage, Execution of Four of the Criminals', above n 111, 8.
[114] 'The Mount Rennie Outrage Execution of the Criminals, Firmness on the Scaffold, Statement by Read, Death Not Instantaneous', above n 111, 8.
[115] Lord Carrington, above n 3, 2.

case.[116] A series of correspondence took place between the Judge and the Minister where it was ultimately determined that the men had, in fact, been properly convicted.[117] This demonstrated the extraordinary nature of the issues surrounding this matter and that 18 months after four youths were executed for the crime, concern still existed about the circumstances and about the involvement of those convicted.

The primary sources referred to in this chapter have revealed that a series of remarkable events took place to shape the outcome of the fate of the youths found guilty of the Mount Rennie outrage. Nonetheless, a postscript remains. As we have seen, five of the nine youths sentenced to death were granted a conditional pardon. It is reported that Donnellan and Newman served their sentence in Darlinghurst Gaol, Miller and Keegan in Parramatta Gaol and Hill in Trial Bay Gaol.[118] These five youths were all released after having served 10 years.[119] With regards to the fate of Mary Jane Hicks, it is thought that she left Sydney for New Zealand and took up employment in that country shortly after the trial.[120]

Conclusion

The evidence presented in this chapter demonstrates that there were procedural practices in use in the Colony in this period with respect to the exercise of Executive clemency. In determining the fate of the nine condemned youths for the Mount Rennie Outrage, the Executive closely followed the practice set out in section 12 of the Royal Instructions. The actions of the Executive in calling a second meeting to debate the circumstances of the case is significant. It shows, not only the controversial nature of the case, but also that the Executive was prepared to revisit earlier decisions in order to ensure that justice be seen to be done. Lord Carrington's notes on the Mount Rennie Case reveal the inner workings of the system at this time. These documents highlight the mounting pressure that Lord Carrington was under and reveal that he operated within a conservative practice. He would later complain that if he had known the burden of the decisions that he would be called upon to

[116] Particularly with respect to Newman, Miller and Keegan. See: 'News of the Day', *Sydney Morning Herald* (Sydney), Monday 30 July 1888, 7.
[117] Ibid.
[118] 'Mount Rennie Prisoners Released', *Zeehan and Dundas Herald* (Tasmania), Friday 4 December 1896, 2.
[119] Ibid.
[120] Thomson, above n 35.

make as the Governor of New South Wales, he would never have come to the Colony.[121]

The circumstances of the case as it transpired also highlight that the Colony was ready to rethink current practices surrounding the use of capital punishment, particularly for the offence of rape. In his notes Lord Carrington intimates this and he recorded that the whole matter was:

> a very trying time, but of the guilt of the four condemned prisoners there can be no question. Whether the law will be altered or not after this terrible tragedy is another matter, and one for the people of New South Wales to determine.[122]

Capital punishment continued to be a significant political issue within the Colony. The following year the debate over the use of the death penalty would reach new heights in Sydney with the Louisa Collins Case.[123] This case concerned a female charged with murder by poisoning and Justice Windeyer, Premier Sir Henry Parkes and the Governor Lord Carrington, operating pursuant to the Royal Instructions were called upon once more to determine the fate of the accused.[124] The Mount Rennie case had a significant impact in colonial Australia and the debates that it ignited continued to shape the direction of the colonial justice system.

---

[121] 'THE YAWNING GUV'NAH and the YAWNING GRAVE', *The Bulletin* (Sydney), 12 January 1889, 1. See further: Wendy Kukulies-Smith and Susan Priest, '"No Hope of Mercy" for the Borgia of Botany Bay: Louisa May Collins, the Last Woman Executed in NSW, 1889' (2011) 10(2) *Canberra Law Review* 144, 156.

[122] Lord Carrington, above n 1, 9.

[123] See: Kukulies-Smith and Priest, above n 121, 144.

[124] Ibid.

PART IV

JUSTICE IN A COMPARATIVE CONTEXT

INTRODUCTION

MARGARET THORNTON

Justice as Performance

The search for justice is comparable to the search for the Holy Grail because justice is an ideal, the quest for which is never realised. The fact that a dispute necessarily involves conflict hints at the impossibility of a definitive meaning, for there is always going to be disagreement when we move away from philosophical abstractions to the particular. To capture a sense of the permeability of justice, I draw on the insights of postmodernism to suggest that justice is a performative idea that is played out differently in different sites by different actors.

Conventional theorists of justice, whether from Antiquity, such as Aristotle,[1] or from modern times, such as Rawls,[2] invariably approach justice as an abstraction, the principles of which can be applied universally. More recently, there has been a reaction against universality. Amartya Sen, for example, insists that cognisance be taken of the lives that individuals actually live.[3] Derrida's idea of the performative takes the subjectivity of justice a step further in showing how its permeability produces or transforms a situation.[4] Judith Butler elaborates on Derrida's idea of the performative. Although focusing on gender, her insight illuminates the understanding of justice. The performative *act* involves repetition, ritual and legitimation in a public setting.[5] Variations in the sites of justice produce multiple meanings despite the endless repetition of

---

[1] Aristotle (edited and translated by J Warrington), *Politics* (Everyman's Library, J M Dent & Sons,1961), esp §1282b.
[2] John Rawls, *A Theory of Justice* (Oxford University Press, 1971).
[3] Amartya Sen, *The Idea of Justice* (Belknap Press of Harvard University Press, 2009). Cf Martha C Nussbaum and Jonathan Glover (eds), *Women, Culture, and Development: A Study of Human Capabilities* (Clarendon Press, 1995).
[4] Jacques Derrida, 'The Supplement of Origin', in Barry Stocker (ed), *Jacques Derrida: Basic Writings* (Routledge, 2007) 124.
[5] Judith Butler, Gender Trouble: Feminism and the Subversion of Identity (Routledge, 1990) 140.

rituals in settings, such as courtrooms. The idea of each enactment of dispute resolution as performance imaginatively encompasses the complex web of meanings within the rubric of justice.

In this way it can be seen that justice is not the sole prerogative of judges adjudicating in formal courts, although justice is closely imbricated with the ritual of law, and law and justice are often assumed to be synonymous. The inequality of bargaining power between the parties to a dispute may produce an unjust outcome but faith in liberal legalism and the rule of law encourages or plays down that inequality. Indeed, actors other than judges within the legal system may pursue justice more assiduously. Such actors include arbitrators, legislators, bureaucrats, lawyers and litigants themselves. The sites in which justice emerge are also many and varied and by no means confined to a courtroom presided over by a judge.

The vastly different contexts of the three chapters in this section, viz, corruption and the rule of law in developing nations of the Pacific, the role of religion in international commercial arbitration and environmental justice in Europe, highlight the futility of fastening on a single definition of justice, a single agent of justice or a single site for the production of justice. I therefore commend to the reader the idea of justice as performance.

Chapter Ten: Tony Krone, Corruption and the Rule of Law: A Case Study of Solomon Islands

This chapter highlights the limitations of the formal justice system when there is a gross inequality of bargaining power. The colonial dispossession of land and resources pose particular problems for indigenous peoples, including those in the developing nations of the Pacific where corruption may be endemic. Tony Krone analyses a number of cases of official corruption dealt with through the formal justice system, only one of which resulted in a successful prosecution. Cases brought against ministers for changing their allegiance also failed. While critics might argue that there should have been more prosecutions, a corrupt process frustrates the realisation of substantive justice.

The struggle for justice by indigenous peoples in the Pacific could go on for years and, even then, there is no guarantee of a just outcome within a formal court system. The struggle is also being conducted concurrently within traditional law and legal structures with no greater prospect of success. Nevertheless, the fact that academics such as Tony Krone are writing about the corruption and exposing it to the scrutiny of the international community might itself be understood as a performative step towards the realisation of justice for the indigenous peoples of the Pacific.

Chapter Eleven: Dalma Demeter and Thilini Perera, Religious Influences over Arbitral Proceedings: Personalising or Jeopardising Justice?

Dalma Demeter and Thilini Perera consider arbitration as a way of achieving justice outside the courtroom. Despite the private nature of arbitration under Shari'a and Judaic law, the terms of settlement on which the parties agree are enforceable. That would seem to be unexceptional as a form of justice has been arrived at by means of a negotiated settlement between the parties. However, that is not the end of the matter because the identity of the arbitrator is prescribed. That person must be male which causes us to confront the conflictual nature of justice head-on. This chapter shows that the attainment of justice is not restricted to the parties to a dispute alone as third parties, including the community as a whole, also have an interest.

While Demeter and Perera do not support gender discrimination per se, they do support party autonomy as a valued principle of arbitration. However, it is precisely this autonomy that enables gender discrimination to thrive. While the autonomy of the parties is a significant principle in the performance of justice in commercial arbitration, that autonomy may be disturbed by deference to religion. Even if the legal actors within an arbitral situation may themselves feel that both the process and the outcome are just, the ramifications of justice widen when third parties, that is, members of the public or the community as a whole, object that the process is unjust by virtue of the religious strictures. The collision of autonomy, religion and the non-discrimination principle in an unusual factual situation highlights the inadequacy of a closed definition of justice in favour of a performative understanding.

Chapter Twelve: Mirjana Drenovak-Ivanovic, Environmental Justice in a Comparative Context

Environmental justice underscores a broad idealised understanding of justice. It embraces both procedural and substantive elements, although the term "environmental justice" is no less elusive than justice itself. Like the preceding chapter, albeit expressly rather than impliedly, this chapter recognises the importance of members of the public being included as legal actors in the pursuit of justice.

Ivanovic infers that environmental justice based on theories of both distributive justice and social recognition can be achieved through a process of public participation in decision-making — but only if the public is adequately informed. Adequate public participation includes the familiar rituals of procedural fairness, including timely notice and reasonableness in the allocated time for public participation and a right of review. Ivanovic equates environmental justice with environmental democracy in the right to participate in decision-making, but that right is subject to the principles associated with procedural fairness, including a right of access to information.

Conclusion

These three chapters with their discrete scenarios illustrate well the impossibility of a universal definition of justice and the aptness of the idea of justice as performance. The chapters also underscore the variety of legal actors who have an interest in justice other than the paradigmatic aggrieved person or individual judge, for the relevant constituency may include a range of actors extending to the community as a whole.

CHAPTER TEN

NATURAL RESOURCES, CORRUPTION AND THE RULE OF LAW:

A CASE STUDY OF SOLOMON ISLANDS

TONY KRONE

Introduction

Solomon Islands is one of a number of Pacific nations that have fallen in and out of serious conflicts and crises since gaining independence.[1] Following serious conflict or civil disorder in Fiji, Papua New Guinea, Solomon Islands, Vanuatu and Tonga, the Pacific Islands Forum Secretariat responded in 2006 by commissioning a land management and conflict minimisation project. In a 2008 report for the Pacific Islands Forum Secretariat, Wilson summarised the cost of conflict in the Pacific as follows:[2]

> these conflicts have exerted substantial social, economic and political costs on the states and communities involved. Several thousand civilians and security personnel have died, and tens of thousands have been displaced. Violence and instability has deterred tourism and foreign investment and caused already fragile economies to contract.

Wilson examines in detail the role of disputes concerning traditional land tenure in the escalation of civil conflict in the Pacific. Three case studies used are Bougainville, Solomon Islands and Fiji. As Wilson reports, these struggles have occurred in Melanesia and have often been

---

[1] Fiji gained independence in 1970, followed by Papua New Guinea in 1975, Solomon Islands in 1978 and Vanuatu in 1980.

[2] Chris Wilson, *Land and Conflict in the Pacific Region* (2008) Report prepared for the Pacific Islands Forum Secretariat, 7.

associated with contests over the use of traditionally owned land with a particular focus on extractive resource industries or landscape changing industries.[3] Wilson concludes that the disruption of traditional Indigenous land ownership brought about by particular forms of economic development is a major contributor to conflict in the region.

This chapter uses a case study of forestry law in Solomon Islands to explore the complex way in which law mediates the relationship between customary ownership and exploitation of land or of land based resources. What has not worked well is the relationship between traditional law and legal structures and the formal legal system.

I argue that the forestry law in Solomon Islands is currently framed in a way that undermines traditional ownership and fosters corruption in three ways:

1. By disrupting traditional land ownership. Traditional owners are cut off from their traditional land or the products of that land resulting in a loss of resources, while also disabling traditional methods for conflict resolution related to land and resources.
2. Weak laws facilitating exploitation but not environmental control.
3. Weak laws facilitating exploitation but not the regulation of logs taken or payment of taxes on the number of logs taken. These laws are difficult to police or are open to corruption that cannot be prosecuted.

To investigate the significance of anti-corruption laws in relation to forestry in Solomon Islands a review of reported corruption prosecutions in Solomon Islands is presented. This was done using the Pacific Legal Information Institute (PacLII) collection of Solomon Islands High Court and Court of Appeal cases.[4] There are various problems with the accuracy

---

[3] Ibid, 41. Examples are the Ok Tedi mine in the Highlands of Papua New Guinea and the Panguna mine in Bougainville. In Solomon Islands the Gold Ridge mine on Guadalcanal has caused localised tensions.

[4] Cases have been selected for this chapter by using the search functions available in the PacLII database for Solomon Islands.

of text entered into PacLII and a full survey of PacLII reported cases would require going through the text of each case individually.[5]

Background Context

Sources of development based on natural resource exploitation

National economic development for Pacific island nations is a pressing concern. The first permanent forms of landscape-changing development involved plantation agriculture.[6] Many Pacific nations share a history of colonial development based on the establishment of commercial plantations. Important plantation crops have changed over the twentieth century from coconuts for copra, to palm oil, cocoa and coffee.

In Melanesia, forestry has also been an important resource for the economies of Papua New Guinea, Bougainville, Solomon Islands, New Caledonia and Fiji.

In Melanesia, the land mass of these nations is comprised mainly of islands of volcanic origin or of land mass that is highly prospective for the exploitation of economically valuable minerals, and in the case of Papua New Guinea, natural gas deposits. In Polynesia, mining of phosphate was established in Nauru in the early 1900s and has had a devastating ecological impact.

Impacts on traditional Indigenous land ownership patterns

In Melanesia, social organisation remains rooted in traditional relationships to land and among kinship or language groups. Arguments for development often cite the need to free-up traditional forms of land

---

[5] Using reported cases provides an insight only into those cases that have firstly been prosecuted and then reported. The circumstances surrounding a case and the whole of the arguments put in a case are not always reflected in the reported judgment. This is not unusual in legal research but it does present special difficulties in researching cases from jurisdictions where the full context in which a case is brought may be difficult to discern. See, for example: Ken Averre, 'Correction to an Article by Miranda Forsyth in the Journal of South Pacific Law' (2008) 12(1) *Journal of South Pacific Law* 39.

[6] Judith A Bennett, *Pacific Forests* (The White Horse Press, Cambridge, 2000) 36–61.

ownership to facilitate investment and growth. However, dismantling traditional patterns of resource ownership disrupts resources and traditional systems that enable communities to be self-reliant and on which traditional patterns of interdependence and social stability are based.

The "Resource Curse"

In 1993, Auty used the term "the resource curse" to describe the apparent paradox whereby nations rich in natural resources often do not enjoy economic growth, experience conflict and instability and have poor standards of governance.[7] According to Stiglitz,[8] poor economic and social outcomes result from the distorted distribution of resource wealth. This requires action to address governance issues and the distribution of wealth within a natural resource dependent economy.

Conflict over natural resource development

Wilson notes that a consequence of some land-based mining is the spoiling of the land being mined and the environmental degradation of downstream lands.[9] This affects traditional land owners for whom the land is their primary resource. It is from the land that they extract all that they require for a traditionally based lifestyle. There is very little that traditional owners may receive or expect from the State in return.

With poor levels of service delivery in these nations the traditional owners of mined land are hit doubly. They lose their land and they get very little back in the form of State provided services.[10]

A Case Study: Solomon Islands Forestry

Commercial forestry is another form of land use with the potential to dramatically change the ecosystem and landscape. However, conflicts concerning the exploitation of forest resources generally lack a permanent site for disputation and disruption as timber cutters move from one forested area to another.

---

[7] Richard Auty, Sustaining Development in Mineral Economies: The Resource Curse Thesis (Routledge London, 1993)

[8] Joseph Stiglitz, *Making Globalization Work* (WW Norton & Company New York, 2006)

[9] Wilson, above n 2, 41.

[10] Ibid, 39.

Traditional ownership is disrupted

The history of timber exploitation in Solomon Islands is documented by Judith Bennett in *Pacific Forests*.[11] In Solomon Islands the exploitation of forest resources is regulated under the *Forest Resources and Timber Utilisation Act [Cap 40]*. An important aspect of this law is the disconnection of control of the timber resource from the traditional ownership of the land it grows on.

The law favours unsustainable logging

In 1994, following considerable pressure from environmental groups, Australia's Prime Minister, Paul Keating, led a push for South Pacific Forum Governments to take action to conserve the remaining forest resources in their countries. As Bennett records, the South Pacific Forum released its Brisbane communique, which expressed concern "at the way in which forests throughout the region and the world are being harvested in a highly destructive manner".[12] At the same forum meeting, Prime Minister Billy Hilly of Solomon Islands announced that the logging licence of a Malaysian logging company was suspended for breaching legal requirements. According to Bennett, a "debt for nature swap" involving payment of AUD$2 million to Solomon Islands Government was to secure forest preservation in the Morovo Lagoon area.[13]

As Bennett argues, these two events played out badly in Solomon Islands politics, with the opposition leader, Solomon Mamolomi, portraying Hilly as a "puppet" of Australia, and Australia as dictating policy to a sovereign Pacific nation. Mamolomi subsequently became Prime Minister. In the struggle for power, logging interests sought and received favour. The result was an expansion of unsustainable logging.[14]

There were repeated attempts to place Solomon Islands forestry onto a sustainable basis in the late 1990s. Eventually the *Forestry Act 1999* was passed, heralding sweeping reform.[15] The new Forestry Act would have set out measures to ensure that forest resource extraction is carried out on

---

[11] Bennett, above n 6.

[12] South Pacific Forum Secretariat, *Forum Communiqué* (Twenty-Fifth South Pacific Forum Brisbane, Australia, 1 August 1994) 11.

[13] Bennett, above n 6, 344.

[14] Ibid, 345.

[15] *Forests Act 1999* (Solomon Islands). The text of this Act is not available on PacLII but can be found at: *The Forests Act 1999* (Solomon Islands) (2012) Legal Office: FAOLEX <http://faolex.fao.org/docs/pdf/sol18884.pdf>.

a sustainable basis and that where possible despoliation of the environment be minimised. However, the forestry sector has not been affected, as this new Act was passed but was not gazetted, and as a result has no legal effect.[16]

The law fosters or is inadequate to deal with corruption

In Solomon Islands, there are two parts of the *Penal Code 1963 [Cap 26]* that deal with corruption. The first is "Part X Corruption and the abuse of office", which regulates the behaviour of those in public office. The second is "Part XXXVIII Secret commissions and corrupt practices."

The principal provision in Part X is section 91(a), which states:

> Any person who,
> (a) being employed in the Public Service, and being charged with the performance of any duty by virtue of such employment, corruptly asks for, solicits, receives or obtains, or agrees or attempts to receive or obtain, any property or benefit of any kind for himself or any other person on account of anything already done or omitted to be done, or to be afterwards done or omitted to be done, by him in the discharge of the duties of his office … is guilty of a felony and shall be liable to imprisonment for seven years.

In addition, there are provisions in the *Leadership Code (Further Provisions) Act [Cap 86]* that allow for findings of guilt for improper behaviour with minor penalties. There are 31 reported cases dealing with corruption and these are shown in Table 10-1, although this is not presented as an exhaustive list of all corruption cases in Solomon Islands.

---

[16] Richard L Pauku, *Asia-Pacific Forestry Sector Outlook Study II* (Food And Agriculture Organization Of The United Nations Regional Office For Asia And The Pacific, Bangkok, 2009) 16.

Table 10-1 Corruption cases in Solomon Islands High Court and Court of Appeal judgments

Conversion by police officer	*Sahu v Regina* [2012] SBHC 122	2012
Electoral fraud allegation	*Inoke v Tran* [2012] SBHC 49	2012
Electoral fraud allegation	*Fono v Fiulaua* [2011] SBHC 6	2011
Corruptly granting citizenship Two co-accused, four judgments	*Regina v Kaliuae* [2010] SBHC 25 *Regina v Kaliuae* [2010] SBHC 30 Rojumana v Reginam [2009] SBCA 9 Rojumana v Regina [2008] SBHC 23	2010 2009 2008
Corruption — delay in prosecuting — stay refused	Base v Director of Public Prosecutions [2010] SBHC 98	2010
Inland revenue case dropped — costs application	*Regina v Pohe* [2010] SBHC 29	2010
Larceny by a police officer — stay refused	Pitabelama v Attorney General [2010] SBHC 77	2010
Sentence for receiving gifts	*Regina v Tebolo* [2010] SBHC 27	2010
Conversion of Ministerial fund	Dausabea v Regina [2008] SBHC 30	2008
Electoral fraud allegation	Fuilorentino v Regina [2008] SBHC 47	2008
Bribe offered to tax officer — sentence appeal	*Yee v Reginam* [2007] SBHC 28	2007
Compensation payment — acquitted	*Regina v Kii* [2007] SBHC 137	2007
Minister giving stamp duty exemption	*Zama v Regina* [2007] SBHC 113	2007
Police accused of assault	*Regina v Anita* [2005] SBHC 154	2005
Bail following conviction and sentence	Regina v Bartlett [2004] SBHC 130	2004
Bail following conviction and sentence	*Wong v Regina* [2004] SBHC 135	2004
Electoral fraud allegation	Rukale v Kemakeza [2004] SBHC 116	2004
NPF scandal — validity of dismissal of public servants	Zaku v Public Service Commission [2003] SBHC 58	2003
Judicial comment that bureaucratic process invites corruption	Pacific Architects Ltd v Commissioner of Lands [1997] SBHC 10	1997
Inducement to change allegiance to PM	Regina v Musuota [1997] SBHC 9	1997

Inducement to change allegiance to PM	*Regina v Zapo* [1997] SBHC 25	1997
Inducement to change allegiance to PM	Regina v Orodani [1996] SBHC 69	1996
Corruption conviction overturned	*Regina v Yam* [1994] SBHC 70	1994
Immigration officer — acquitted	*Ansah v Attorney-General* [1994] SBHC 14	1994
Electoral fraud allegation	*Maetia v Dausabea* [1993] SBHC 29	1993
Electoral fraud allegation	*Hite v Paul* [1993] SBHC 76	1993
Electoral fraud allegation	*Lekelalu v Zapo* [1993] SBHC 79	1993
Electoral fraud allegation	*Thugea v Paeni* [1985] SBHC 585)	1985

Eight cases involved allegations of corruption by way of electoral fraud. Three cases concerned allegations of illegal police behaviour that was labelled by the court as corrupt because of the status of the defendants as police officers.

Two Ministers were prosecuted separately for corruption. In the first case the issue was the fraudulent granting of citizenship and in the second case it was the waiving of stamp duty charges. These two cases were each prosecuted under section 91(a) of the *Penal Code*.

One Minister was prosecuted for the abuse of Ministerial funds, which was referred to by the court as a corrupt practice.

The list of cases highlights the absence of reported corruption cases concerning either mining or forestry operations. There are, however, very many cases in the PacLII database concerning civil disputes under the relevant mining[17] and forestry laws.[18]

There are three separate cases from 1996–7 that indirectly involve the corrupting influence of the logging industry on politics in Solomon Islands. In these cases, three Ministers were prosecuted for alleged corruption involving the receipt of benefits to switch allegiance from the government of Francis Hilly Billy to support the formation of a new government under Solomon Mamalomi. As Nelson argues, "A basic understanding of some of the ways that Melanesian governments operate is essential to those contemplating intervention in the region. The very

[17] Mines and Minerals Act [Cap 42] (Solomon Islands).

[18] To better understand how resource disputes have contributed to national conflict in Solomon Islands future research could examine all of the civil cases reported on PacLii involving the many disputes brought to court under the *Mines and Minerals Act [Cap 42]* (Solomon Islands) or the *Forest Resource and Timber Utilisation Act [Cap 40]* (Solomon Islands).

way that governments are created and supported establishes corruption — of the distribution of State assets and often the members themselves".[19]

The *Penal Code* provision sought to be applied in these cases was section 374 in Part XXXVIII, which relevantly states:

> If— (a) any agent corruptly accepts or obtains, or agrees to accept or attempts to obtain, from any person, for himself or for any other person, any gift or consideration as an inducement or reward for doing or forbearing to do or for having done or forborne to do, any act in relation to his principal's affairs or business or for showing or forbearing to show favour or disfavour to any person in relation to his principal's affairs or business ... he is guilty of a misdemeanour, and shall be liable to imprisonment for two years or to a fine of six hundred dollars.

Only Musuota was successfully prosecuted and then for the lesser charge of allowing his integrity to be called into question under the *Leadership Code (Further Provisions) Act [Cap 86]*. All corruption charges against the three accused were dismissed by the Court.

In each of these cases, the allegations involved the Ministers receiving a benefit from a representative of Chinese Malaysian logging interests to shift their support from Hilly Billy to Mamolomi. The loggers were facing increasing regulation and control from the Government of Hilly Billy and a proposed lack of regulation under Mamolomi.

Basically, the court in each case found that shifting support from one Prime Minister to another candidate could not be characterised as corruption for the purposes of the *Penal Code*, as the act of quitting removed the member of Parliament from a position in which he could perform an act or refrain from performing an act for the Crown. In Musuota's case, the judge summed up the situation in these terms:

> What Goh (representing Malaysian logging interests) did is reprehensible and in common parlance, political corruption. Is it corruption in terms of the law in section (374) of the *Penal Code* which requires that the benefit, in this case, the use of hired car, be a gift or consideration, for Musuota to forbear — omit to do any act in relation to the business of his principal, the Crown?
>
> It was inducement for them to resign but certainly not to refuse to do a job which was waiting to be done or to do that office work in favour of

[19] Hank Nelson, Collier in Melanesia: A discussion of Paul Collier's "The Bottom Billion": Why the Poorest Countries are Failing and What Can be Done about It (State Society and Governance in Melanesia Working Paper No 2008/1, State Society and Governance in Melanesia Program, ANU College of Asia and the Pacific Canberra, 2008) 8.

> Goh or any other person. The act that Musuota was to omit to do cannot be said to be an act in relation to the principal's business. Musuota quit completely the business of the Crown, his principal. He was not simply forbearing or omitting to do the principal's business. He terminated the whole relationship between him and his principal; he terminated the whole mandate. He removed himself from the post of a cabinet minister and so from the authority of the Crown, the principal, which relate to duties of a cabinet minister. Section (374) is not meant to cover that situation; it is meant to punish people who are, to use the common expression, "bought" in the performance of their duty so that they show favour in actioning the interest of the person who has offered the benefit, or so that those "bought" avoid taking action correctly, if that action affects adversely the interest of the person who has offered benefit.[20]

These three cases from 1996–7 are the only ones that are found in the reports of Solomon Islands available on PacLII dealing with corruption associated with the forestry industry. Despite the lack of reported prosecutions, the Auditor-General for Solomon Islands makes clear in a report from 2007 that corruption is both a widespread and a long-standing problem.[21] In particular, the Auditor-General notes that "poor management and administration" and a "lack of accountability and transparency in granting timber exemptions" led to a significant loss to national revenue consistently over many years.[22]

The Auditor-General is referring to the impact on the national accounts from sloppy or corrupt practices that allowed round logs to be exported from Solomon Islands without paying the correct duty or any duty at all.

Conclusion

On Thursday 24 July 2003, the Regional Assistance Mission to Solomon Islands (RAMSI) commenced operation following serious but contained conflict in Solomon Islands between 1999 and 2003. In 2010 Braithwaite et al produced a comprehensive review of RAMSI as part of the Peacekeeping Compared Project.[23] As they argue, the tensions in Solomon Islands have been repeatedly characterised as the manifestation

---

[20] *Regina v Musuota* [1997] SBHC 9.

[21] Floyd A Fatai, An Auditor-General's Insights into Corruption in Solomon Islands Government (Office of the Auditor-General, Honiara, 2007)

[22] Ibid, 10.

[23] John Braithwaite et al, *Pillars and Shadows: Statebuilding as Peacebuilding in Solomon Islands* (November 2010) Australian National University <http://epress.anu.edu.au?p=76041>.

of ethnic conflict. Ultimately however, the conflict was about traditional land, access to resources and the failure of the State to provide the expected benefits of development to the people, leading to a trashing of the State and its treasury. The authors cite Allen and Dinnen, who revealed how the State was substantially weakened by:

> the disruption to political patronage networks engendered by the combined impact, in the late 1990s, of declining demand for Solomons log exports due to the Asian financial crisis and the reform agenda of the Ulufa'alu government.[24]

As Braithwaite et al note, this fostered the conditions in which the treasury was drained by spurious compensation claims and "ethnic divisions" came to be exploited for political purposes by members of an elite struggling to control fewer and fewer resources. The authors identify a number of shortcomings of RAMSI that relate to a failure to deal with the problems associated with natural resource extractive industry in Solomon Islands. They assert that the following actions should have been implemented:[25]

- Prosecution of foreign loggers for breaches of the law;
- Prosecution of international commercial interests for:
    - corrupting the Solomons Islands' tax system and its customs administration;
    - funding the buying of votes of no confidence in the Parliament;
    - destroying the sustainability of the export industries of logging and fishing;
- Prosecution of Solomon Islands elites involved in corrupt conduct concerning logging and fishing.

It is regrettable that the effort in 1994 to enact a new forestry management regime in Solomon Islands failed. In reality, the law for the regulation of forestry in Solomon Islands is probably inadequate to the tasks suggested. There are likely to be only limited opportunities for prosecution for past excesses under existing law.

It may seem surprising that the 2003 RAMSI intervention did not lead to the implementation of a new forestry regulatory regime for sustainable exploitation of the resources then remaining. However, this could be explained in terms of the self-interests of the political elites in Solomon

---

[24] Mathew Allen and Sinclair Dinnen, 'The North Down Under: Antinomies of Conflict and Intervention in Solomon Islands' (2010) *Conflict, Security & Development* 10(3) 299.

[25] Braithwaite, above n 23, 152.

Islands with whom RAMSI had to negotiate. However, it would be lamentable if after 10 years there is still no progress on this issue. It may be that a failure to address this, and the system for managing land use conflicts more generally, may compromise the long term legacy of RAMSI.

There are some areas for optimism, provided we learn from the past and focus on finding new ways to promote sustainable resource use with equitable distribution of the proceeds of resource exploitation. While much of the forests of Solomon Islands have been lost in their natural state, there is some potential for forest resources to be rehabilitated in the long term, for example, through re-afforestation.

For the future, a new forestry law is required. In devising any new law, careful attention must be paid to the protection of indigenous landowning interests in a holistic way.

CHAPTER ELEVEN

RELIGIOUS INFLUENCES OVER ARBITRAL PROCEEDINGS: PERSONALISING OR JEOPARDISING JUSTICE?

DALMA DEMETER AND THILINI PERERA

Introduction

Arbitration, while apparently a topic not easily fitting in the theme of "Justice Connections"[1] is in fact just another way to achieve justice, albeit outside of the court system; a method that has become the mainstream dispute resolution mechanism in the international business arena.[2] Its purpose of being a fast and personalised quasi-judicial process achieving the same legal outcome as the one provided through State courts, but through a more efficient procedure, is ensured by legal recognition and flexibility.

Legal recognition of arbitration is provided through national legislation[3] and international conventions[4] which create legal harmonisation and

[1] The themes of the *Justice Connections Symposium* are: "Justice Behind the Scenes"; "Justice in the Workplace"; "Justice, the Individual and the Courtroom"; and "Justice in a Comparative Context".
[2] See: ICC, *Arbitration: Introduction to Arbitration* (2012) International Chamber of Commerce
<http://www.iccwbo.org/products-and-services/arbitration-and-adr/arbitration/>.
[3] Most often in the form of arbitration acts (for example: *Australian International Arbitration Act 2011* (Cth)), occasionally in the form of chapters in civil procedure codes (for example: *Code of Civil Procedure* (France) Title II of Book IV), or private international law acts (for example: *Federal Statute on Private International Law 1987* (Swiss) Ch.12), all recognising arbitral decisions as having the same legal force as court judgments.

uniform treatment of arbitration within different legal systems.[5] The certainty generated by similar legislation across borders — so essential in international disputes between parties having different backgrounds — is then, almost paradoxically, complemented with flexibility. This allows the parties to shape arbitration to their individual preferences and the particular needs of each dispute. The flexible character that allows arbitration to function as a personalised justice mechanism represents a unique advantage over State court litigation — while also presenting some risks.

In order to achieve flexibility, international arbitration is regulated by a complex combination of sources of norms that can be classified into State laws (also including international conventions, as adopted by their member States), institutional rules,[6] party autonomy,[7] and the arbitral tribunal's discretion. While these sources of norms are independent from each other and apparently self-standing, they are affected by influences originating from socio-political, cultural, or religious norms. We analyse the influences that religion — manifested through State law or party autonomy — can have over arbitral procedures. The aim of this analysis is to see whether such religious influences affect the efficiency and effectiveness of arbitration, and consequently transform arbitration into a more personalised or a more ponderous dispute resolution mechanism.

Limitations of this chapter — while not absolute — include the international and commercial character of arbitration. International arbitration is the area most likely to face conflicts between different sources of norms and different legal systems and international arbitration is used to solve mainly commercial disputes. Consequently, while not intentionally excluded, the chapter will not focus on domestic or non-

---

4 For example: *Convention on the Recognition and Enforcement of Foreign Arbitral Awards 1958*, 21 U.S.T. 2517, 330 U.N.T.S. 38 (hereafter *NY Convention*). For more see: *Related Arbitration Links* (2012) International Council for Commercial Arbitration <http://www.arbitration-icca.org/related-links.html#01>.

5 The *NY Convention* has the widest coverage, its 147 signatories (as at 23 October 2012) recognising and enforcing foreign arbitral awards under almost identical conditions.

6 Procedural rules adopted by arbitral institutions that disputing parties can freely chose to administer their case.

7 In arbitration, the term "party autonomy" is used to reflect both the parties' freedom to choose the law governing the merits in a dispute, as well as the freedom to choose the law and the rules governing the arbitral procedure. For the purpose of the present chapter, only the latter will become relevant, as no substantive issues are part of the analysis proposed.

commercial arbitration. A second limitation could be that our analysis is targeting only procedural aspects, in order to see whether the arbitration process itself is influenced for better or worse by accommodating religious influences. Consequently, no data on the merits of any dispute subject to arbitration will be considered, as procedure and substance can easily be separated and religious influences over the merits in arbitration have already been extensively researched.[8]

We first consider the role of religion in international commercial arbitration, with special emphasis on Islam and Judaism having a strong presence in the sphere of international business, and reflecting similarities in their influence over arbitral procedures. We then analyse how these two religions affect the constitution of an arbitral tribunal, the arbitral proceedings proper and the recognition and enforcement of arbitral awards, as well as the broader implications of such religious influences over arbitration generally. The analysis will be based on consideration of sources of religious norms (such as the Qur'an and the *halacha*), of relevant State laws, of arbitral rules of various arbitral institutions (such as the American Beth Din), and of international conventions on arbitration. We also consider case law identifying issues created by religious influence over arbitral procedure, as well as a range of secondary sources, with no resort to empirical research.

Analysing the effect of religion on international commercial arbitration does not have the sole purpose of satisfying theoretical curiosity, but serves an essential and practical benefit. Members of the business community and legal practitioners facing or handling international disputes should consider these often less visible aspects when deciding whether a dispute could be better solved through religious arbitration or by other means. On one hand, if disregarded, religious norms may have an unexpected and often undesired impact over arbitration. On the other hand, however, arbitration can be the only forum where religious preferences can influence the procedure. Therefore, whether parties aim to personalise arbitration through religious influences or try to avoid possible pitfalls created by such influences, this chapter can provide the understanding of the possible consequences that free choice may trigger in international commercial arbitration. This chapter can provide the understanding of the possible consequences that free choice may trigger in international

---

[8] See El-Ahdab and Jalal El-Ahdab, *Arbitration with the Arab Countries* (Kluwer Law International, 2011); Samir Saleh, *Commercial Arbitration in the Arab Middle East: A Study in Shari'a and Statute Law* (Graham & Trotman, 1984); Anthony Shoult (ed), *Doing Business with Saudi Arabia* (GMB Publishing Ltd, 2006).

commercial arbitration, whether aiming to personalise through religious influences or trying to avoid possible pitfalls created by such influences.

The Role of Religion in International Commercial Arbitration

Arbitration is capable of accommodating religious norms due to its "guiding principle in determining the procedure to be followed" being party autonomy,[9] but also as a result of religion-based State laws affecting international arbitration. Religious expectations or regulations can affect any phase of the arbitral procedure, from the composition of the arbitral tribunal appointed to render a decision in the dispute, through to the arbitral procedure proper including the procedural steps taken during the running of the case, and to the post-award phase in which the arbitral award rendered in the case obtains legal recognition and is finally enforced. Religious norms taking the form of mandatory State law, while not common, can affect all three steps, while religious preferences manifested through party autonomy can only affect the first two, as recognition and enforcement are subject exclusively to legislation, not leaving room for party autonomy to shape this phase.

Whilst trade and commerce in western countries may not commonly involve religious influences, the same is not true of religious legal systems, where arbitration can be directly or indirectly regulated by religious scripture, even though that is not part of their main objective. Not surprisingly, the impact of religious norms over arbitration is most evident in cultures having strong religious traditions, notwithstanding the existence of modern statutes adopted with the aim of legislative harmonisation.[10]

Religion as law is based on the principle that the word of God is law,[11] and as such cannot be amended or legislated against by judges or governments. Nevertheless, scripture never provides a thorough and detailed legal system, but often serves as the basis for further legislation.

---

[9] Nigel Blackbaby, Constatine Partasides, Alan Redfern and Martin Hunter, *Redfern and Hunter on International Arbitration* (Oxford University Press, 5th ed, 2009), 365.

[10] Ahmed S El Kosheri, 'Islamic Law', in Albert Jan van den Berg (ed), *Planning Efficient Arbitration Proceedings: The Law Applicable in International Arbitration, ICCA Congress Series* (Kluwer Law International, 1996) vol 7, 506–512.

[11] For example: the Jewish *halacha* and the Islamic Shari'a both mean the "path to follow".

The Qur'an[12] for example, although containing some law, acts primarily as a source of further law through interpretation[13] and precedent, forming the body of law known as Shari'a.[14] The only country basing its entire legal system on Shari'a is Saudi Arabia; most other Muslim countries have a mixed system, combining Shari'a with codified, non-religious legislation.[15] In contrast, the use of the Jewish Halakha (which includes biblical[16] and rabbinic law[17]), while still used by some Israeli communities, is not mandatory under Israeli law.[18] Judaic religious principles, however, are commonly used within Jewish communities even in western, non-religious legal systems, where the legal consequences of such rules are often recognised.[19]

The traditional presence of Jewish investment and the desire to attract Islamic finance in western economies play a significant role in shaping international commercial arbitration, since theoretically any financial relationship may end up in a dispute. As no other religion has such a strong presence in the international business world as Islam and Judaism, this chapter will only focus on the influence of these two religions on international commercial arbitration.

---

[12] The Qur'an is the Holy Book of Muslims and the main source of Islamic law and jurisprudence, also directly regulating arbitration.

[13] Qiyas refers to "reasoning by analogy" and Ijma refers to "consensus".

[14] Omar M H Aljazy, 'Jurisdiction of Arbitral Tribunals in Islamic Law (Shari'a)', in M Á Fernández-Ballesteros and David Arias (eds), *Liber Amicorum Bernardo Cremade* (La Ley, 2010) 65–99.

[15] Ibid.

[16] Including the Torah which is the Old Testament in the Pentateuch, the Five Books of Moses. See: Marylin Johnson Raisch, *Religious Legal Systems: A Guide to Research and Its Role in Comparative Law* (2006) Hauser Global Law School Program at NYU School of Law <http://www.nyulawglobal.org/globalex/religious_legal_systems.htm>.

[17] The Talmud, which is a collection of Jewish teachings, and the Mishnah, which is a commentary on the Torah: Ibid.

[18] The current Israel legal system is a hybrid of common law and civil law: Ruth Levush, *Israeli Law Guide, Law and Technology Resources for Legal Professionals* (November 2007) <http://www.llrx.com/features/israel3.htm#hebrewofficialsources>.

[19] Where the Maryland courts in the U.S.A. recognise the validity of arbitration proceedings before a Beth Din despite the Beth Din failing to strictly comply with *Maryland Uniform Arbitration Act*. See: *Blitz v Beth Isaac Adas Israel Congregation* 352 Md. 31, 720 A.2d 912 (Md. 1998), No 72, September Term, 1997. Dated September 14 1998. Opinion clarified December 14 1998. Opinion by J Bell.

Religious Norms Affecting the Constitution of an Arbitral Tribunal

The primary feature that makes arbitration so appealing to the business community is the ability to choose the arbitrators to decide a dispute; a right that arbitrating parties prefer to hold on to.[20] The ability to choose one's arbitrator and the chance for a fast and effective dispute resolution, however, can be affected by religious influences. In some jurisdictions State law may impose religious restrictions on the composition of an arbitral tribunal, posing a severe limitation to the universal principle of party autonomy governing arbitration. Conversely, where arbitration laws provide for maximum freedom in choosing one's arbitrator, personal preferences originating in religious norms or perceptions can also affect the composition of a tribunal to an extent that undermines the efficiency of the entire process. In addition, the effects of religion on arbitration can range from the core definition of what arbitration is, to the role and qualifications of the arbitrators, creating a potentially problematic interaction between religion and arbitration.

The definition of an arbitrator under Islamic and modern arbitration

Under Shari'a law, all private arrangements mutually agreed between the parties are enforceable, as long as they are not contrary to Islamic norms.[21] The Qur'an acknowledges and encourages the settlement of disputes through arbitration, but the rules created during the 7th–8th centuries were limited to existing disputes, to be submitted to "a given person or persons already known and appreciated by the parties as being in possession of a high degree of integrity".[22] This leaves no room for the choice of arbitrators through a third person or appointing authority, as often practiced in modern arbitration.[23] In addition, the followers of the *Maliki* school of thought, for example, perceive arbitrators to be agents

[20] White & Case and the Queen Mary University of London, The 2012 International Arbitration Survey: Current and Preferred Practices in the Arbitral Process (2012) <http://www.whitecase.com/files/Uploads/Documents/Arbitration/Queen-Mary-University-London-International-Arbitration-Survey-2012.pdf>.

[21] Nudrat B Majeed, Good Faith and Due Process: Lessons from the Shari'ah, Arbitration International (Kluwer Law International, 2004) vol 20, 97–112.

[22] El Kosheri, above n 10, 494.

[23] Blackbaby et al, above n 9, 251.

appointed by and working for the parties to the dispute, while followers of the *Hanafi* school consider arbitrators in some aspects as similar to agents; a perception still present in the arbitral jurisprudence,[24] even though in direct contradiction with the "fundamental principle in international arbitration that every arbitrator must be and remain independent and impartial of the parties and the dispute".[25] Even schools that do not follow fundamentalist Islamic rules, dictate that the arbitrator's appointment — based on personal knowledge and trust — can be unilaterally revoked at any time, simply for a loss in confidence.[26] The procedure practiced under Islamic law appears in this sense a hybrid combination of arbitration and conciliation, in which the arbitrator(s) consult both parties in private, in order to reach a mutually satisfactory solution.

Although these practices did make sense in the times they were created, their rigid application today by fundamentalist Islamic lawyers conflicts with universal arbitration principles and practices. The consequences of disregarding arbitration principles may easily jeopardise the recognition of the dispute resolution process itself as arbitration, potentially depriving it of the legal recognition a proper arbitration would have ensured.

Arbitrators' qualifications in Islamic tribunals and their presence in a modern arbitration environment

The four major schools of Islamic Jurisprudence[27] agree that there are no limitations applicable to the number of arbitrators to be appointed in order to constitute the arbitral tribunal.[28] According to the *Medjella*,[29] however, an arbitrator has to be a male Muslim of age who is wise, free

[24] Essam Al Tamimi shared his own experience of serving on an arbitral tribunals where one of the arbitrators from an Islamic country tried to act as an agent for the party that had appointed him.: Essam Al Tamimi, 'Islamic Influences on International Arbitration' (Speech delivered at the 2011 The Clayton Utz Sydney University International Arbitration Lecture, The Federal Court (Sydney), 08 November 2011) <http://www.claytonutz.com/ialecture/2011/transcript_2011.html>.

[25] Blackbaby et al, above n 9, 266.

[26] El Kosheri, above n 10, 495.

[27] The *Hanafi* school, the *Shafi'e* school, the *Maliki* school and the *Hanbali* school.

[28] Ahmad Alkhamees, 'International Arbitration and Shari'a Law: Context, Scope, and Intersections' (2011) 28(3) *Journal of International Arbitration*, 255–264.

[29] The *Medjella* is deemed the first codification of Shari'a under the Ottoman Empire.

and fair.[30] Some schools of Islamic jurisprudence[31] believe that the religious affiliation requirement must be applied strictly, as it is based on a Qur'anic rule.[32] The reluctance to accept non-Muslim arbitrators even in cases involving a non-Muslim party, rather "imposing a mandatory condition, that the arbitrator should be of Islamic faith, since a non-Muslim could not exercise authority (Walaya) over a Muslim",[33] was previously a strict requirement when arbitrating in Saudi Arabia, where the condition relating to faith and knowledge of Islamic law and local customs and traditions was even incorporated in the Arbitration Regulation.[34] However, parties sought to avoid use of this law. Being perceived as difficult and inefficient in resolving commercial disputes,[35] this law was used infrequently. As a result, Saudi Arabia amended its Arbitration Law recently through the *New Arbitration Law 1433H (2012G)*, joining the global trend of legal harmonisation based on the *UNCITRAL Model Law on International Commercial Arbitration* (the *Model Law*).[36]

Although the enactment of the *New Arbitration Law* makes significant improvements to reduce the difficulties and inefficiencies experienced under the *Old Arbitration Law*, it is important to note that the benefits of the *Model Law* will not be experienced in its entirety, as Saudi Arabia has not incorporated the *Model Law* verbatim, but only used it as a starting point to make some improvements.[37] The *New Arbitration Law* is meant to be accompanied by Implementing Regulations to explain in detail how the new law is to be implemented, but these are yet to be released.[38]

---

[30] Ahdab, above n 8, 36.

[31] Namely the *Maliki* and *Shafi'i* schools.

[32] Namely that unbelievers should not be given advantage over believers. See: Saleh, above n 8, 36.

[33] El Kosheri, above n 10, 498.

[34] Section 3 of the *Saudi Arabian Arbitration Regulation* 27.05.1985G (08.09.1405H) 27 May 1985: "The arbitrator shall be a Saudi national or Muslim expatriate from the free profession section or others … In the case of more than one arbitrator, the umpire shall have a knowledge of sharia rules, commercial regulations, customs and traditions applicable in Saudi Arabia".

[35] Saud Al-Ammari and Tim Martin, *Saudi Arabia Modernizes Arbitration Laws* (2012) Lexology <http://www.lexology.com/library/detail.aspx?g=7b26fd08-7cad-4b88-82fa-1a52fbfdb4f1>.

[36] The Council of Ministers approved the *New Arbitration Law* on 9 April 2012 and a Royal Decree on the law was issued on 16 April 2012. The law came into force on 9 July 2012 being the 30th day after the date of its publication.

[37] Al-Ammari and Martin, above n 35.

[38] Ibid.

Although the strict application of Shari'a law only allows males to be Muslim judges, the question of whether a non-Muslim or a female can be appointed in modern arbitration is not settled in contemporary jurisprudence[39] and is yet to be resolved by Caliphs. There are Islamic scholars who are of the view that a non-Muslim male can act an arbitrator, as long as the award rendered is compatible with Shari'a law and the parties to the dispute are also non-Muslims.[40] Others see the debate to be a purely academic one[41] since all these issues are now regulated through codified laws and the procedural rules of arbitral institutions, in accordance with the global trend. Modern laws are, indeed, codified in most Gulf countries where the Qur'an is not directly applied,[42] but even there legal principles are often rooted in Shari'a principles.[43] A welcome modernisation of Islamic legal systems is evidenced by the Egyptian and Jordanian arbitration laws no longer imposing religious or gender criteria to the appointment of arbitrators.[44] This may also be the case under the *New Arbitration Law* in Saudi Arabia, apparently seeking to replace the former requirement that arbitrators had to be either citizens of Saudi Arabia or a Muslim with a professional background,[45] but in any case be male and Muslim.[46] Relaxing the conditions to some degree, the *New Arbitration Law* requires that arbitrators be *inter alia* of good conduct and reputation, and have a university degree in either Shari'a science or law. Where the tribunal has more than one arbitrator, only the chair of the panel has to meet this last condition. Considering the very recent change in regulation, it is too early to know whether this liberal approach will be accepted without strong negative reactions.

---

[39] Al Tamimi, above n 24.

[40] A view is upheld by the International Islamic Centre of Reconciliation and Arbitration (IICRA). See: The Chart of the IICRA (2005), article 10 available at: <www.iicra.net/English/m4_1.htm>.

[41] Al Tamimi, above n 24.

[42] Except Saudi Arabia, where the Qur'an is strictly applied. article 1 of the *Saudi Arabia Constitution* states that "God's Book and the Sunnah of His Prophet are the country's constitution": *Saudi Arabia Constitution* (1992) Ch 1.

[43] Al Tamimi, above n 24.

[44] Ibid.

[45] See: article 3 of the Implementing Regulations of the Old Arbitration Law.

[46] Al-Ammari and Martin, above n 35.

Non-religious arbitral tribunals affected by Islamic norms

In jurisdictions that do not impose any religion-based limitations to the composition of an arbitral tribunal, appointments can be based on preferences that range from professional qualifications to nationality.[47] Despite commercial disputes being decided on law, equity and/or business considerations, arbitral decision-making also has a strong component of personal trust vested in the members of the tribunal appointed to adjudicate the dispute. This trust, similar to the trust referred to in Islamic principles above, together with the procedure's flexibility and the outcome's global recognition, make arbitration achieve true justice. The same trust, however, requires the parties to be entitled to choose the arbitrators based on whatever criteria they find relevant, including religious affiliation.

Accordingly, arbitration involving Islamic issues is not exclusive to religious systems, but is a heavily debated subject in European countries as well, its effects being also recognised in non-religious legal systems.[48] Due to concerns raised by English courts not accepting Shari'a law,[49] a Commission, established by the French financial organisation Paris Europlace to research the potential difficulties that Islamic finance may incur in France, published a Proposal.[50] While dealing mostly with substance-related issues, it also touches upon the procedural aspects of Islamic finance, particularly addressing the doubts of jurisdiction of a Muslim over a non-Muslim and of a woman over a man.[51] The Commission, recognising the principle of party autonomy in arbitration, stated that both the gender and the religious requirements are based on other teachings than the Qur'an itself, and as such, are not to be rigidly followed. While this clarification serves as a much needed bridge over the differences between western arbitration legislation and religious dogma,

---

[47] Alan Redfern, Law and Practice of International Commercial Arbitration (Sweet & Maxwell, 2004) 194–204.

[48] Hervé de Charette, No to the Rejection of Islam, Yes to Islamic Finance, in Our Country's Interest! (February 2010) Institute Francaise de Finance Islamique <http://www.institutfrancaisdefinanceislamique.fr/en/index.php>.

[49] Shamil Bank of Bahrein EC v Beximco Pharmaceuticals Ltd [2004] EWCA Civ. 19; [2004] 4 All ER 1072.

[50] G Affaki , Fadlallah, D Hascher, A Pézard, F-X Train (eds), *Proposal: Group on Governing Law and Dispute Resolution in Islamic Finance* (September 2009) (to be published).

[51] Ibid, 25–26.

reality shows that even appointments in modern arbitration can and often do reflect the same old principles, manifested as personal preferences.

Current practices tend to depart from the old beliefs[52] and adopt the "view according to which the relevance of the Islamic legal traditions is limited to these few basic aspects not subject to any possible controversy or difference of opinion"[53] — a perception that allows the application of modern arbitration practices and rules without finding them contradictory with mandatory rules of the Qur'an. However, religious preconceptions still have an impact over the composition of otherwise non-religious arbitral tribunals. Such preconceptions take the form of party choice and may occasionally conflict with other rules and laws governing arbitration. However, balancing freedom of religion against other legal principles may prove difficult enough to undermine all advantages arbitration has against court litigation in achieving justice.

A perfect example of such an outcome is the landmark case of *Hashwani v Jivraj*,[54] where the English Court of Appeal found an arbitration agreement void for breach of anti-discrimination principles. The agreement required arbitrators to be "respected members of the Ismaili community and holders of high office within the community" and for the chairman to be "the President of the HH Aga Khan National Council for the United Kingdom for the time being".[55] This requirement was found by the Court to go beyond the accepted practice of "arbitrators' special characteristics", since the arbitrators were asked to apply English law, for which no special religious qualification is required.[56] Thus, the only exception permitted by the Regulation, namely that of a proportionate and genuine requirement of a job for a particular ethos or belief,[57] was not applicable. Although this decision of the Court of Appeal has been overturned by the Supreme Court, the recognition of the importance of the parties' right to determine the composition of an arbitral tribunal followed

---

[52] Or 'ijtihad', which means opinion.

[53] El Kosheri, above n 10, 496.

[54] Sadruddin Hashwani v Nurdin Jivraj [2010] EWCA Civ 712.

[55] Excerpts from the arbitration agreement reproduced in the judgment of the court.

[56] In order to reach this conclusion, the Court qualified arbitrators as employees for the purpose of *The Employment Equality (Religion and Belief) Regulations 2003* (UK) and held that the agreement breached Regulation 3. Discrimination on grounds of religion or belief
<http://www.legislation.gov.uk/uksi/2003/1660/regulation/3/made>

[57] *Employment Equality (Religion and Belief) Regulations 2003* (UK) Regulation 7 — "Exception for genuine occupational requirement"
< http://www.legislation.gov.uk/uksi/2003/1660/regulation/7/made>

by the entire arbitral agreement being declared void precisely for the exercise of such choice[58] raised serious pro-arbitration concerns. And while the apparent clash between the party autonomy arbitration principle and anti-discrimination principles were eventually solved by the Supreme Court,[59] the concern still remains.

Despite the Supreme Court restoring — at least for a while — certainty by finding that "the requirement of an Ismaili arbitrator can be regarded as a genuine occupational requirement",[60] the *Jivraj* saga is far from reaching its end. As the Supreme Court refused to refer any of the issues to the European Court of Justice,[61] Mr Hashwani has recently filed a complaint with the European Commission against this decision,[62] bringing back the uncertainty regarding the freedom to appoint arbitrators possessing not only professional, but also religious characteristics. The business and arbitration community can now only sit and wait to see whether the acknowledgement made by the Supreme Court that "One of the distinguishing features of arbitration that sets it apart from proceedings in national courts is the breadth of discretion left to the parties and the arbitrator to structure the process for resolution of the dispute"[63] survives the case, or whether "The stipulation that an arbitrator be of a particular religion or belief can be relevant to this aspect of arbitration"[64] will become unacceptable all over again. In any case, the fear of religious appointments potentially being labelled as discriminatory again will inevitably influence the effectiveness and the positive perception of arbitration.

---

[58] Sadruddin Hashwani v Nurdin Jivraj [2010] EWCA Civ 712, [34].

[59] *Jivraj v Hashwani* [2011] UKSC 40 (27 July 2011).

[60] Ibid, [68].

[61] "If a national court is in doubt about the interpretation or validity of a European Union law, it may — and sometimes must — ask the Court of Justice of the European Union for advice. This advice is called a 'preliminary ruling'". See: *Court of Justice of the European Union* (2012) European Union <http://europa.eu/about-eu/institutions-bodies/court-justice/index_en.htm>.

[62] The complaint, based on article 267(a) of the *Treaty on the Functioning of the European Union*, claims that the UK Supreme Court adopted an erroneous interpretation of the *Council Framework Directive 2000/78/EC* for equal treatment in employment and occupation.

[63] *Jivraj v Hashwani* [2011] UKSC 40 (27 July 2011), [61].

[64] Ibid.

Judaic arbitral tribunals

Jewish arbitration also faces difficulties in finding its place in a modern arbitration environment. In Orthodox Judaism, a Beth Din[65] consists of religious Jewish men, at least one of whom is widely knowledgeable in Jewish law and is capable of instructing the other members in any such matters applicable to the case being heard.[66] Strict Jewish Law specifically prohibits women from serving as arbitrators,[67] although in progressive communities women may serve on the Beth Din.[68] A Beth Din usually consists of three judges[69] with no formal requirement as to their qualifications,[70] but the procedures of each Beth Din panel differ[71] and the appointment of arbitrators depends on the rules of the Beth Din in a particular area. For example, the rules of the Beth Din of America require at least one arbitrator to be a rabbi, and up to two others to be religiously observant individuals with expertise relevant to the dispute.[72]

Thus, similarly to strict Islamic rules, certain aspects of Jewish norms may appear discriminatory or in conflict with general arbitration principles. These concerns can undermine not only equality and fairness in arbitration, but also the reliability and uniform legal recognition of arbitration at a global level.[73]

---

[65] A Beth Din or beit din is a Jewish rabbinical court invested with legal powers in a number of religious matters in Jewish communities, where its judgments hold varying degrees of authority (depending upon the jurisdiction and subject matter).
[66] Amanda M Baker, A Higher Authority: Judicial Review of Religious Arbitration (2012) 37 *Vermont Law Rev*iew (forthcoming), 19 <http://ssrn.com/abstract=2145094>.
[67] Michael C Grossman, 'Is This Arbitration?: Religious Tribunals, Judicial Review, and Due Process' (2007) 170 *Columbia Law Review* 169, 181.
[68] Ibid.
[69] Ginnie Fried, 'The Collision of Church and State: A Primer to Beth Din Arbitration and the New York Secular Courts' (2003) 31(2) *Fordham Urban Law Journal* 633, 641.
[70] Grossman, above n 67, 180.
[71] Ibid.
[72] Beth Din of America, *Rules and Procedures of the Beth Din of America,* <www.bethdin.org/docs/PDF2-Rules_and_Procedures.pdf>, s 1(e).
[73] See below, under the heading: Religious Norms Affecting the Recognition and Enforcement of Arbitral Awards.

The wider implications of religious influences over arbitral tribunals

Even though "discriminatory" preferences may be within the acceptable norm when it comes to the freedom of appointing arbitrators, the *Jivraj* experience, reflecting a general conflict between religious norms and legal principles, brings up concerns that go beyond religious expectations of arbitrating parties. While it is unlikely that religious qualification requirements in appointing arbitrators will become prohibited, the chain of events in the *Jivraj* saga leaves the arbitration community with two secondary, but nevertheless important concerns that affect arbitration as a personalised justice mechanism. On one hand, as the lower Court observed, the "decision has a far wider significance than the present case".[74] In the unlikely event that religious qualification becomes unacceptable following the complaint at the EC, such decision would put all arbitration agreements that provide for arbitrators having specific religious characteristics at great risk, due to the Regulation's retroactive effect.

In addition, the *Jivraj* case opens the door to other arbitrator characteristics (like nationality) also possibly being qualified as discriminatory. Nationality restrictions are regularly used in international arbitration to ensure neutrality and language skills of arbitrators. However, nationality in itself might not easily satisfy the "genuine occupational requirement" test, and a case similar to *Jivraj v Hashwani* on the nationality of arbitrators could reopen Pandora's box, leading to a lengthy analysis of yet another arbitrator preference being permissible or not. Legislation regulating gender-based discrimination may also come into focus, whenever gender is an appointment criterion for parties whose religion provides for differential treatment between men and women. A Muslim party may wish to exclude female arbitrators from the composition of the tribunal, as they may feel uncomfortable (or even find it highly inappropriate) to let a woman decide and impose her decision over men. Such preferences, based on religious norms not having any legal manifestation, would most probably contradict either religion-based or gender-based discrimination regulations. This is a conflict that is now becoming imminent, with the English draft Mediation and Arbitration

[74] Sadruddin Hashwani v Nurdin Jivraj [2010] EWCA Civ 712, [9].

Services (Equality) Bill[75] directly targeting gender discrimination in arbitration.[76]

While the authors of this chapter do not argue in favour of gender-based discrimination in any area of life, further limitations imposed upon the appointment of arbitrators would severely restrict party autonomy. Although values protected by anti-discriminatory regulations are undoubtedly important for any democratic society, this protection should not be enforced at the cost of another much valued principle of party autonomy in arbitration. If done so, preference to arbitrate in any country that has strong anti-discrimination legislation may decrease significantly among religious communities — not because any of these communities would favour discriminative agreements, but because the distinctive line between "acceptable" and "unacceptable" discrimination is very fine, and a strict interpretation of anti-discrimination regulations restricts certain manifestations of the freedom of religion.

Secondly, the *Jivraj* saga has severely impacted on the actual and perceived benefits of arbitration overall. As mentioned above,[77] arbitration is the preferred method to achieve justice in the international business community due to its time and cost efficiency paired with maximum legal recognition. The *Jivraj* saga, however, impacts on the perception of arbitration being at least potentially fast by virtue of the duration of this case which is years away from being concluded. If a preliminary issue about the composition of the arbitral tribunal could not be finally solved in years[78] with the underlying dispute itself yet to be resolved, then arbitration is not the time and cost efficient method one would prefer over litigation.

---

[75] The Arbitration and Mediation Services (Equality) Bill [HL] (2012–13), had its second reading in the House of Lords on 19 October 2012.

[76] The Bill is aimed to amend the *Equality Act 2010* (UK) by prohibiting any term of an arbitration agreement or process which discriminates on the grounds of sex.

[77] See the Introduction section to this chapter.

[78] The appointment in dispute was first indicated in a letter dated 31 July 2008, and the expected procedure following the EC complaint could take years to resolve. See: *The Treaty on the Functioning of the European Union*, art 258, 260 <http://eur-lex.europa.eu/LexUriServ/LexUriServ.do?uri=OJ:C:2010:083:0047:0200:en:PDF>.

Religion in the Arbitral Proceedings

In addition to preliminary issues like the composition of arbitral tribunals, conflicts between religious traditions and other sources of norms regulating arbitration may also occur at later stages of arbitral proceedings. In contrast to court proceedings, arbitration is flexible enough to accommodate religious practices, but their observance is still left to the discretion of arbitrators in most cases, as there are hardly any rules or laws that expressly provide for compliance with such traditions.

Shari'a arbitration

The only recognition of Shari'a law in arbitral procedure appears to be in the very recent Arbitration Rules of the Kuala Lumpur Regional Centre for Arbitration,[79] created for disputes that "arise from commercial transactions that may contain Shariah elements or premised on Shariah principles",[80] reflecting some of the procedural issues such disputes face in international arbitration. Although the rules do not require arbitrators to be Muslims, they do impose that all Shari'a related issues be referred to the Shariah Advisory Council,[81] whose decision is binding upon the tribunal and the parties.[82] International arbitration is apparently "beyond the purview of the relevant council",[83] but in such cases, all Shari'a issues are to be referred to a Shari'a expert, whose ruling "the arbitrator shall apply … when deciding the dispute and giving the award".[84] Even though this rule seems to ameliorate an imposed external decision by transforming it into evidence, this evidence has the same mandatory application as the

---

[79] The i-Arbitration Rules, where i stands for Shari'a compliance, were launched at the 2012 Global Islamic Finance Forum.

[80] Introduction to the i-Arbitration rules, as explained on the Kuala Lumpur Regional Centre for Arbitration (KLRCA) website at: *KLRCA i-Arbitration Rules* (2012) Kuala Lumpur Regional Centre for Arbitration <http://www.rcakl.org.my/scripts/view-anchor.asp?cat=30#289>.

[81] Note to Rule 8 of the i-Arbitration Rules of KLRCA: "Shariah Advisory Council so established by the Central Bank under the Central Bank of Malaysia Act 2009 or the Shariah Advisory Council established by the Securities Commission under the Securities Commission Act 1993".

[82] Rule 8.5 of the i-Arbitration Rules of KLRCA. Also see: *Learn about the Bank* (2012) Bank Negara Malaysia (Central Bank of Malaysia) <http://www.bnm.gov.my/index.php?ch=7&pg=715&ac=802>.

[83] Introduction to the i-Arbitration rules, as explained at: *KLRCA i-Arbitration Rules*, above n 80.

[84] Rule 8.5 of the i-Arbitration Rules of KLRCA.

Council's decision — the only difference being in the identity of the person(s) providing that ruling. Such mandatory delegation of decision-making raises serious concerns as to the arbitrators' authority and the arbitral jurisdiction in general. One inevitably wonders whether this unique arbitral procedure is accommodating Islamic needs in modern arbitration, or in fact deprives arbitration of its decision-making character.

International arbitration affected by the parties' religion

The religious affiliation of arbitrating parties may affect disputes that are otherwise not qualified as religious arbitration, especially when the tribunal does not share the same religious beliefs. In the absence of any rules incorporating religious norms in the arbitral procedure, however, there is no legal consequence — either at national or at international level — for disregarding such preferences.[85] For this reason, it becomes essential to have arbitrators who understand and respect religious practices, and are open to give primacy to religion over a rigid efficiency-driven procedure. Alternatively, a conflict with religious customs would in most cases end with religion being "the losing party", since the price for protecting one's religious beliefs may be losing the case. In a Jakarta case,[86] for example, the chairman scheduled hearings during *Idul Fitr*,[87] despite the objections of the involved Indonesian counsel and witnesses. In light of the threat of a default award, should the parties fail to appear at the hearing, the leading counsel and the witnesses could not obey the traditional ceremonies of their religion. They could have made a different choice, of course, by prioritising their religious norms and refusing to comply with the rules imposed by the tribunal. The consequences of such a choice, however, would have been far worse than mere disappointment: a default award against the party represented by the Islamic counsel and supported by Islamic witnesses leaving more behind than just a bad impression on arbitration.

This unfortunate example shows that, while theoretically arbitration is the forum where religion could easily find its place due to party autonomy

---

[85] An arbitrator's conduct biased in this sense does not represent violation of due process to be considered as basis for annulment or refusing recognition and enforcement of an award under the *NY Convention*.

[86] Karen Mills, 'The Importance of Recognising Cultural Differences in International Dispute Resolution', in Michael Pryles and Michael Moser (eds), *The Asian Leading Arbitrators' Guide to International Arbitration* (Juris Publishing, Inc, 2007), 66.

[87] The biggest Islamic holiday.

and an overall malleable procedure, it is difficult to balance the flexibility of arbitration, including religious preferences, and the pursued efficiency of the process. One may find that arbitration can work at its best only by satisfying one, but not both expectations (ie making justice achievable either fast, or in a personalised form).

Religious impacts on taking evidence in arbitration

Religious influences can also become obvious with regard to taking evidence in arbitration, mainly affecting the witness testimony of women — an issue present under both Islamic and Jewish tradition. Proceedings conducted under Shari'a law require the oral testimony of two adult Muslim male witnesses.[88] However, some Islamic schools of thought provide that, should two adult Muslim males be unavailable as witnesses, the oral testimony of one male and two female witnesses will suffice, "thus indicating that the word of two women is equal to the word of one man".[89] Strict Jewish law — although not reflected by current jurisprudence — also excludes women, invalids and non-Jewish individuals from testifying as witnesses.[90]

These limitations on the acceptance of witness testimonies may be deemed discriminatory in the secular system and may also be seen as undermining due process. Should arbitration — more possible in religious, less likely in modern arbitration — prove to be flexible enough to allow such religious rules to find their way in arbitral proceedings, although would probably please any fundamentalist participants to that arbitration, their conflict with rules of natural justice would undermine the recognition of arbitration in the international arena.

Religious Norms Affecting the Recognition and Enforcement of Arbitral Awards

The Europlace Commission found that the application of traditional Islamic rules in arbitration processes "risks annulling the award by contradicting the public policy … Arbitrators should therefore refrain from applying these discriminatory rules since it is their duty to ensure the effectiveness of their awards".[91] By recognising that a potential conflict

[88] Baker, above n 66, 51.
[89] Ibid.
[90] Ibid, 50.
[91] Kosheri, above n 10, 26.

between religious and legislative norms can be avoided by observing public laws instead of following religious dogma in order to ensure a valid and enforceable award, the Commission also recognised that the influence of religion over arbitration does not end with the closing of the arbitral procedures.

Islamic rules on recognition and enforcement

Normally, arbitral awards are easily enforceable in any jurisdiction, the *Model Law* and the *NY Convention*,[92] ensuring that the vast majority of jurisdictions will give legal force to arbitral awards whether rendered within or outside of that jurisdiction.[93] According to these uniform rules, the possible grounds to refuse recognition and enforcement of arbitral awards are very limited, mainly focusing on procedural fairness and public policy.[94] The limits of these grounds, however, can be stretched by aspects not considered when drafting these legal harmonisation tools, like the influence of religion over arbitral proceedings.

In addition to the very limited grounds listed in the *NY Convention*,[95] recognition and enforcement of an arbitral award may be denied in Islamic countries on the ground that it does not meet the compliance requirements of Shari'a law.[96] In this sense, awards made in Saudi Arabia under foreign law by an arbitrator who does not fulfil Shari'a qualifications were deemed non-compliant with Shari'a law under the *Old Arbitration Law*, irrespective of the content of the award.[97] Although the *New Arbitration Law* does not contain the same requirement anymore, the requirement for the award not to contravene Shari'a and the public order of Saudi Arabia, still exists.[98]

---

[92] See above n 4.

[93] See: *UNCITRAL Model Law on International Commercial Arbitration*, UN Doc (A/CN.9/309) (Note by the Secretariat) 122–123 <http://www.uncitral.org/pdf/english/yearbooks/yb-1988-e/vol19-p117-123-e.pdf>.

[94] See: NY Convention, art V; UNCITRAL Model Law, art 34–36.

[95] Mainly restricted to a last check of arbitral jurisdiction, to due process and party autonomy principles being observed during arbitration, and to the award not conflicting with the enforcing country's international public policy — see: *NY Convention*, art V.

[96] Latham and Watkin LLP, *Doing Business in Saudi Arabia* (2010) 10 <www.lw.com/upload/pubcontent/_pdf/pub3507_1.pdf>.

[97] Saleh, above n 8, 322.

[98] Al-Ammari et al, above n 35.

Under the *Old Arbitration Law*, in addition to checking the arbitrators' qualification, the Saudi Board of Grievance[99] also conducted a full review of the case, to ensure that the award did not conflict with any principles of Shari'a law.[100] Reviewing an arbitration case on its merits stretches beyond acceptable limits the *ex officio* verification of public policy compliance introduced by the *NY Convention*. Applying public policy in a manner that allowed the Board of Grievance to, in effect, re-litigate the case,[101] implicitly denied the final and binding character of arbitral awards. As a result, apparently there was little or no precedent for the recognition and enforcement of foreign arbitral awards by the Board of Grievance[102] — a hurdle that was not reasonably foreseen by foreign arbitrating parties when undertaking arbitration in the first instance.

Under the *New Arbitration Law*, however, Saudi Arabia appears to be in alignment with the common international practice that an arbitral award is recognised as being valid and is enforced to the extent that it does not contravene public policy or is not set aside due to other contingencies that are provided for under the *Model Law*.[103] Accordingly, the *New Arbitration Law* provides that "… the arbitration award issued in accordance with this Law shall be valid and in force" (article 52), and "are not to be challenged in any way except through the filing of a lawsuit to nullify an arbitration award according to the provisions of this Law" (article 49). Whether these new provisions generally reflecting the same grounds for challenge provided for under the *Model Law* will be in line with contemporary cultural thinking of the Saudi population and institutions, or whether the traditional, dogmatic perceptions will somehow infiltrate in the application of new law, is yet to be seen.

---

[99] Latham and Watkins LLP, above n 96.

[100] James R Silkenat, Jeffrey M Aresty & Jacqueline Klosek, *The ABA Guide to International Business Negotiations: A Comparison of Cross-Cultural Issues and Successful Approaches* (American Bar Association, 2009), 884; Shoult, above n 8, 108.

[101] Silkenat et al, above n 100, 884; Shoult, above n 8, 108.

[102] Thomas Childs King and Spalding International LLP, 'Enforcement of Foreign Arbitral Awards in Egypt, Syria and Saudi Arabia' (2010) *International Bar Association*: *Arbitration Newsletter*, 72; Sikenat et al, above n 100; Adhab et al, above n 8, 667.

[103] Al-Ammari et al, above n 35.

Post-award consequences of prior Islamic influence over the arbitration

Religious influences that take place in an arbitration's earlier phase may also reveal their undesired consequences when the resulting award is tested for recognition and enforcement in a secular legal system. The perception of a spiritual leader as an arbitrator may, for example, prove to be erroneous only after the entire dispute resolution process has been completed. This may occur if the nature and role of the spiritual leader's involvement in the resolution of the dispute and whether this spiritual leader was to be involved with a view to producing a legally enforceable result, is not decided or precisely formulated by the parties.[104] Non-recognition of an "award" rendered under these circumstances erodes the benefits of religious arbitration, and indeed arbitration itself.

Whilst awards in the context of religious arbitration may be subject to stringent conditions and may not be enforceable due to non-compliance with religious norms, the same may be true of awards rendered by religious arbitral tribunals that do not comply with secular legal requirements. Indeed, arbitral awards rendered under religious influences may also fail legal recognition, if the arbitration process is subjected to religious norms that are deemed to be discriminatory under the legislation of the country where the resulting award is sought to be enforced. In this sense, arbitral awards rendered under the *Old Arbitration Law* in Saudi Arabia, which imposed religious and gender-based restrictions on arbitrators against the parties' will, were perceived to be in breach of public policy in any jurisdiction where anti-discriminatory principles are highly valued. Similarly, traditional Islamic (or Judaic) rules limiting the freedom or the value of a woman's witness testimony, would be found to seriously affect due process principles, and as such, lead to non-recognition and enforcement of that arbitral award in a secular system — creating undesired uncertainty in the international business environment.

Recognition and enforcement of Judaic arbitral awards

Difficulties in the post-award phase are also encountered by members of Jewish communities, who are often compelled to resolve their disputes before their respective religious institutions. The qualification of such institutions and the enforcement of their decisions by State courts can be

[104] See: Ghalib Hussain Abdul Sattar v Wycombe Islamic Mission and Mosque Trust Limited, High Court of Justice 290 of 2010, 20 April 2011.

problematic and this difficulty may even be seen to undermine religious autonomy. A decision by a dayanim[105] that any future disputes between the parties in regard to their disputed contract must be decided by the Beth Din was, for example, qualified by the State court as retention of future jurisdiction exceeding the authority of the Beth Din.[106] The judgment generated wide-spread concerns in the Jewish community. Organisations like the Agudath Israel of America, the Orthodox Union, and the American Jewish Congress filed amicus briefs in support of the Beth Din's decision, pointing to the relationship between religious and State courts.

The fear of the Beth Din system being devastated by State courts was eventually dissipated by the commitment expressed through the decision of the Supreme Court's Appellate Division[107] to respect an award rendered by a Beth Din without re-litigating the merits of the case. The recognition that the Beth Din is a private dispute resolution body just as any arbitral institution, even though its decisions are based exclusively on religious rules other than the "profane" legislative provisions, does not fit easily within the framework of what arbitration or an arbitral award is assumed to be in modern arbitration. Hence, the Supreme Court's decision serves as a much appreciated bridge between secular and religious arbitration, reconciling the conflicts between the two systems.

Characteristics of Judaic arbitration may, however, also exceed the acceptable limits of classical arbitration, leading to the non-recognition of the award resulted. In another fairly recent US case,[108] the Court denied enforcement of a Beth Din award for one of the parties having been compelled to use only counsel acceptable to the Beth Din. In traditional Jewish law, litigants were discouraged from retaining counsel, because lawyers were viewed as canvassing the cause of their client as opposed to pursing justice as mandated in the *halacha*.[109] The issue of whether representation is permitted in modern arbitration is yet to be settled,[110] but

---

[105] Judge of the Beth Din.

[106] New York Supreme Court Kings County order of December 18 2008, denying to confirm the award rendered by the Beth Din of America on July 10 2007.

[107] *Brisman v Hebrew Academy of Five Towns & Rockaway*, Supreme Court of the State of New York, Appellate Division: Second Judicial Department, 22 January 2010.

[108] *Joseph Kahan aka Yosef Kahan v Sarah Rosner aka Sara Rosner et al* No 2008-08484 (N.Y. App. Div. 2d Dep't Nov. 19, 2009), N.Y.L.J., 23 November 2009, 17, col 3.

[109] "Justice, justice thou shalt pursue": *Deuteronomy* 48:20; Fried, above n 63, 645–646.

[110] *Deuteronomy*, above n 109, 48:20; Fried, above n 63, 645–646; Grossman, above, n 67, 180.

in the case mentioned, whilst the petitioning party was not denied his right to appoint a representative, he was denied the right to a counsel of his choice, eventually proceeding without representation. This restriction proved to be in conflict with the laws of the State of New York which grant individuals the right to select counsel they believe is best able to provide them with competent representation,[111] Thus, although the Beth Din was only enforcing traditional Jewish principles, the modern legal environment did not prove to be flexible enough to accommodate such religion-induced processes. As a result, since arbitration is dependent on legal recognition, instead of achieving the binding outcome reasonably expected from arbitration through a personalised process accommodating religious tradition, the religious arbitration proved to be a futile exercise leading to no final solution to the dispute.

Conclusion

The trade mark of arbitration is flexibility and party autonomy, whereby parties are able to choose their own arbitrators and the rules and laws to which they agree to be subject. In this context, parties essentially have the freedom to make choices that will best service their dispute resolution requirements, thus benefitting from one of the most important features and advantages of arbitration: that is, its "user-friendly" nature, which makes it adaptable to suit even the most unconventional expectations of the parties, and thereby satisfying the sometimes unique needs of human nature which do not ordinarily fit well within court systems.

Religion, although not often recognised as a source of norms directly regulating international commercial arbitration, may play a significant role in shaping arbitration. Its influences, whether in the form of mandatory rules rooted in religious dogma applicable to a given arbitration, or in the form of personal preferences, may equally personalise arbitration or transform it into a dead end, standing in the way of timely and efficient justice, instead of individualising it. The turning point between these two possible outcomes is a fine line of a fragile balance between general legal principles from the different areas of law involved and arbitration based on party autonomy, freedom of religion, and non-discrimination principles. Legal harmonisation and judicial recognition of individual rights shaping

---

[111] *Joseph Kahan aka Yosef Kahan v Sarah Rosner aka Sara Rosner et al* No 2008-08484 (N.Y. App. Div. 2d Dep't Nov. 19, 2009), published in N.Y.L.J., 23 November 2009, 17, col 3.

arbitration are constantly refining the international arena of arbitration practice. But whenever the rules of the rest of a legal system are enforced under the flag of equality or religious rights, yet in a manner that annihilates party autonomy, the advantage of arbitration is slowly but certainly diminished and its legal recognition becomes questionable.

Given that the price of these laborious debates being inevitably borne by arbitrating parties in the form of excessive time and costs spent on a final outcome, it is particularly important to have a mutual understanding and respect of the laws and cultural norms relevant to their dispute. Especially in the context of international commercial arbitration conducted in today's globalised world, the key to the successful resolution of disputes through international arbitration lies in this understanding and mutual respect, making the difference between religion transforming arbitration into a more personalised or a more ponderous dispute resolution mechanism.

CHAPTER TWELVE

ENVIRONMENTAL JUSTICE IN A COMPARATIVE CONTEXT

MIRJANA DRENOVAK-IVANOVIC

Introduction

There are environmental risks which affect only individuals or specific groups, such as uranium mine workers, people who live near nuclear power plants or hazardous waste landfills, fishermen who fish in bays with high-frequency oil tanker traffic. Are these cases of discrimination or the calculated decisions of those who will bear a certain environmental risk? The industrial development of modern society inevitably leads to the occurence of these examples, and there will always be individuals or groups exposed to a higher degree of environmental risk. Environmental justice does not refer to the question of how to achieve a risk-free environment. The focus of environmental justice is the matter of ensuring equal distribution of environmental values and risks and eliminating the possibility that certain individuals or groups are disproportionately exposed to environmental risks.[1]

The first part of the chapter analyses how the definition of the term "environment" influences the definition of the term "environmental justice". In this sense, I will introduce anthropocentric, ecocentric and economic understandings of the environment and the influence that theories about justice have on the definition of environmental justice. By means of comparative analysis of the constitutional and legal regulation of environmental protection, in the second part of the chapter, I will try to reach a conclusion as to which approach is used in contemporary law.

---

[1] Joseph L Sax, 'The Searching for Environmental Rights' (1993) 6 *Journal of Land Use and Environmental Law* 99.

Understanding the Term "Environmental Justice"

Understanding the term "environment"

The term "environmental justice" belongs to a group of terms that comparative environmental law considers closely, but which are so complex that there is no consensus on what they mean in theory. There are two main reasons for this. The first reason is the absence of a unique term "environment" (see below) and consensus on the term "environmental rights". Another reason why defining environmental justice causes controversy and a lack of theoretical unity is that the concept of environmental justice largely depends on how we determine the concept of justice itself. The following sections will explain the theoretical basis of defining the term environment and the influence that theories about justice have on the environmental justice definition.

The term "environment" in theory

Defining the term environmental justice depends on how we define the term environment, ie whether it is determined from the aspect of anthropocentric, ecocentric or economic understandings of the environment. This further reflects on the question of how we define the meaning of environmental rights. The anthropocentric understanding of the environment aims to establish mechanisms of care for natural environmental relations which provide human well-being and care for the future generations. Anthropocentic environmental law aims to prevent and remedy environmental problems insofar as they affect humans.[2]

---

[2] "Pollution-prevention laws are the best example of anthropocentric environmental laws. Although a pollution-free environment obviously benefits all aspects of the environment, the main aim of these laws is to prevent pollution that is detrimental to humans": Joshua J Bruckerhoff, 'Giving Nature Constitutional Protection: A Less Anthropocentric Interpretation of Environmental Rights' (2007–2008) 86 *Texas Law Review* 618.

Ecological theories arise as a response to the dominant role of science in formulating the environmental law. Ecological theories are developed through "deep ecology",[3] social ecology[4] and ecofeminism.[5] There are radical ideas in modern environmental law which emphasise the necessity of establishing a new branch of law — "the wild law". According to Cullinan,

> The wild law expresses Earth jurisprudence ... As an approach it seeks both to foster passionate and intimate connections between people and nature and to deepen our connection with the wild aspect of our own natures ... Wild laws are laws that regulate humans in a manner that creates the freedom for all members of the Earth Community to play a role in the continuing co-evolution of the planet.[6]

Ecological theories assume that all aspects of the world have a value in the whole of nature. This theory claims that nature is of value for itself, and therefore it is necessary to establish the form that will protect environmental rights.[7]

An economic understanding of the environment sees environmental protection as protection of natural resources from the aspect of economic benefits. A key point is to analyse whether there is a cost of production not recognised in the final cost of the product. This can be achieved by means of cost–benefit analysis. This theoretical approach is prone to criticism. There are some harmful activities to the environment and human health that do not occur at the same time as the environmental polution activities. Those

---

[3] See: Aldo Leopold, *A Sand Country Almanac* (Ballantine Books, 1968); Arne Naess, 'The Shallow and the Deep, Long Range Ecology Movement: A Summary' (1973) 16 *Inquiry: An Interdisciplinary Journal of Philosophy*; Daniel B Botkin, *Discordant Harmonies: A New Ecology for the Twenty-First Century* (Replica Book, 2001).

[4] See: Ben Boer, 'Social Ecology and Environmental Law', in Ram Babu Singh and Suresh Misra (eds) *Environmental Law in India: Issues and Responses* (Concept Publishing Company, 1996) 35–81.

[5] Dorceta E Taylor, 'Women of Color, Environmental Justice and Ecofeminism', in Karen J Warren (ed), *Women, Culture, Nature* (Indiana University Press, 1977) 38–81. On critical feminist descriptions of social inequality and concerns for environmental mistreatment see: Carol Merchant, *The Death of Nature: Women, Ecology and the Scientific Revolution* (San Francisco, 1980).

[6] Cormac Cullinan, *Wild Law: A Manifesto to Earth Justice* (Green Books, 2003) 32.

[7] On "legal-operational aspects" and "physic and socio-physic aspects" of natural object and "its own legal rights" see: Christopher D Stone, *Should Trees Have Standing?* (Oxford University Press, 2010).

harmful activities are caused by the polution activities, so should be taken into account.[8] Also, the degree of violation of environment and human health must be determined.

> [t]he basic problem of narrow economic analysis of health and environmental protection is that human life, health and nature cannot be described meaningfully in monetary terms; they are priceless … To say that life, health and nature are priceless is not to say that we should spend an infinite amount of money to protect them. Rather, it is to say that translating life, health and nature into dollars is not a fruitful way of deciding how much protection they should be provided with. A different way of thinking and deciding about them is required.[9]

The term "environmental rights" and constitutional protection

In order to determine the meaning of the term "environmental rights" in contemporary law, I will compare how the right to live in a healthy environment is normalised at the constitutional level. After that, I will point out the extent to which certain theoretical approaches to the term environment are present in positive legal definitions of environmental rights. The right to live in a healthy environment is recognised and stipulated by the constitution as a basic human right in a number of countries. The *Constitution of the Republic of Serbia* stipulates every person's right to a healthy environment and full information on its condition.[10] Becoming a rule stipulated by the Constitution and not only by the law under the Constitution, the right to a healthy environment is provided with a greater degree of protection than the rights stipulated by other laws, not only because it requires a more complex procedure of amendment than the law, but also because it provides the possibility of additional legal protection. The role of the law in further elaboration of the right to a healthy environment, especially in regulating the right to public participation in environmental decision-making, is indispensable, primarily due to the inability of the Constitution to stipulate the legal framework for the application of environmental standards aiming to achieve environmental protection.

---

[8] Richard L Revesz, Environmental Regulation, Cost-Benefit Analysis and the Discounting of Human Lives (Berkeley Program in Law and Economics, US Berkeley, 1999).

[9] Frank Ackerman and Lisa Heinzerling, Priceless: On Knowing the Price of Everything and the Value of Nothing (New Press, 2004) 8–9.

[10] Constitution of the Republic of Serbia, 30 September 2006, art 74(1).

The *Constitution of the Kingdom of Norway* distinguishes between environment and natural environment. In this sense, "every person has a right to an environment that is conductive to health and to a natural environment whose productivity and diversity are maintained."[11] According to this Constitution, apart from the right to a healthy environment, environmental rights also consist of the right of every person to a life in the environment where special attention is given to the preservation of natural diversity.

According to the *Constitution of Greece*, the term environmental rights refers to the "natural and cultural environment".[12] It includes "preservation in the context of [the] sustainability principle", "rehabilitation of existing residental areas" and "the protection of monuments and historic areas". Special attention is given to the protection of the forest ecosystem. The Greek Constitution stipulates that the matters related to protection of forests and forest expanses are regulated by law. However, stressing the importance of forest resources, the Constitution prescribes that "alteration of the use of forests and forest expanses is prohibited, except where agricultural development or other uses, which are imposed as the public interest, prevail for the benefit of the national economy".[13]

Since 2004, the *Constitution of France* contains the *Charter for the Environment*. The Charter states that "Everyone has the right to live in a balanced environment which shows due respect for the health" [of people].[14] Unlike the other examples already mentioned, the French Constitution does not define the environment as "healthy", but introduces additional criteria implying "balance", which is of such quality that it provides "due respect for the health".

Environmental protection in the *Constitution of Germany* is defined in such a manner that it does not grant an actionable right to the citizens.[15] The Constitution stipulates the obligation of the State, ie the legislative, executive and judicial authorities, in considering its responsibility for future generations, to "protect the natural foundations of life and animals". The *Constitution of Germany* does not mention the term "environment". Article 20a, which deals with this issue, is titled "Protection of the natural foundations of life and animals", which indicates the application of the

[11] Constitution of the Kingdom of Norway, art 110b.
[12] Constitution of Greece, art 24.
[13] Ibid, art 24(1).
[14] *La Constitution du 4 octobre 1958, Charte de l'environnement de 2004* [French Consitution of 4 October 1958, Environmental Charter of 2004] art 1.
[15] *Grundgesetz für die Bundesrepublik Deutschland* [Basic Law of the Federal Republic of Germany] art 20a.

ecocentric understanding of the environment. However, an "environmental duty" for individuals does not exist in the German constitutional system, although the obligation of individuals in environmental protection matters, in specific cases, may be established by law.[16]

Statements about advancing environmental rights are found in the *Constitution of the Republic of the Philippines* and the *Constitution of the Federative Republic of Brazil*. The first one stipulates: "The States shall protect and advance the right of the people to a balanced and healthful ecology in accord with the rhythm and harmony of nature".[17] More broadly, environmental rights are protected in the *Constitution of the Federative Republic of Brazil*. It stipulates: "All have the right to an ecologically balanced environment, which is an asset of common use and essential to a healthy quality of life, and both the Government and the community shall have the duty to defend and preserve it for present and future generations".[18]

The influence of theories of justice on theories of environmental justice

From the earliest times, a number of lawyers and philosophers, from Aristotle, Plato, Socrates, St Thomas Aquinas, Hugo Grotius, John Stuart Mill and Hans Kelsen, to John Rawls, Robert Nozick and Ronald Dworkin, aimed to build a concept of justice. The term environmental justice became current with the development of environmental movements in the 1960s and 1970s. One group of authors sought to determine the term environmental justice within existing theories of justice. Another group of authors, finding elements indicative of a contemporary need to protect the environment, using the requirements of environmental movements as a basis and emphasising the need for active public participation, aimed to find a unique term for environmental justice. The following section outlines the development of the environmental justice theory.

[16] Michael Rodi, 'Public Environmental Law in Germany', in René J G H Seerden et al (eds), *Public Environmental Law in the European Union and the United States* (Kluwer Law International, 2002) 207.

[17] *1987 Saligang Batas ng Pilipinas* [1987 Constitution of the Republic of the Philippines] art II, s 16.

[18] Constitution of the Federative Republic of Brazil, art 225.

The theory of distributive justice and environmental justice

Distributive justice suggests “the right to equal treatment, ie the equitable distribution of resources and opportunities so that every individual has rights, opportunities and obligations that are equal to rights, opportunities and obligations of any other individual”.[19] The concept of justice as distribution was first found in the works of Aristotle, who perceived the concept of justice as the distribution of honours, wealth, and other common values that are divisible and which can be assigned to members of the community.[20] Thus defined, the term justice focused on the question of fair distribution of values, not the procedure leading to it.

John Rawls defined justice as “the standard by which the distributive aspects of the basic structure of society are established”.[21] Further, this means that justice determines “the exemplary division of social values”.[22] The basic problem of distributive justice theory is finding a model for establishing the principle of fair distribution. To develop distributive justice theory, according to Rawls, it is necessary to start from the “original position”, which Rawls defined as the position in which we do not know our strengths and weaknesses, nor our social position.[23] The generally accepted term fair justice can be formulated only if isolated from the knowledge of one’s own social status and value. Rawls further argued that, by acting impartially from the perspective of “original position”, we can formulate a system in which everyone has equal political rights and an equal position in the distribution of economic and social inequality. Since everyone in the above model is positioned in the same way and there is no possibility that the specific position of an individual is favoured, the principle of justice is the result of fair agreement and understanding. It is a principle that will always lead to justice in terms of fair distribution of social, political and economic “goods” and “bads”.[24] Justice would constitute fair distribution, independent from materialisation of the individual idea of the notion of good.[25]

---

[19] Ronald Dworkin, *Taking Rights Seriously* (Harvard University Press, 1977) 273.
[20] Michael Pakaluk, *Aristotle’s Nicomachean Ethics: An Introduction* (Cambridge University Press, 2005) 181.
[21] John Rawls, *A Theory of Justice* (Harvard University Press, 1999) 8.
[22] Ibid, 9.
[23] Freeman, Samuel (ed), *John Rawls: Lectures on the History of Political Philosophy* (Harvard University Press, 2007) 19.
[24] Rawls, above n 21, 11.
[25] Ibid, 12.

The concept of distributive justice as a basic form of justice was accepted by a number of legal theorists. Thus, in comparative literature, since the first edition of Rawls' work *A Theory of Justice* in 1972, justice has been defined as justice in the distribution of social goods. In this sense, Brian Barry, a follower of Rawls' idea of distributive justice, also considers the concept of justice as a fair distribution, free of any materialisation of what the person believes is good.[26] Unlike other distributive justice theories that are based on analysis of the distribution subject (goods, rights, options) or which principles of distribution should be applied, Barry believes that the process of formulating rules for distribution has the key role in achieving distributive justice. He points out that achieving free and equal participation of all is possible only in the process of establishing policies.[27] This process must be impartial and independent of the subjective ideas of individuals who participate in it.[28] The distributive justice theories understand environmental justice as a fair and equitable distribution of environmental impacts and risks. They refer to morally accountable distribution of environmental "goods and bads" among the members of a particular community.[29]

Social recognition and environmental justice

Confronted with the actual social framework and research which indicates that certain minority groups face a higher degree of environmental risk, do not have equal access to environmental values and have less ability to control environmental injustice they are confronted with, the opinion that social recognition is an essential element for achieving environmental justice finds its way into the theory of environmental justice.[30] The lack of recognition in the social and political environment prevents the application of Rawls' model that would lead to distributive justice.[31]

---

[26] Brian Barry, *Justice as Impartiality* (Oxford University Press, 1995) IX.
[27] Ibid, 52.
[28] Ibid, 200–201.
[29] David E Newton, *Environmental Justice* (ABC-CLIO, 1996) 1–3.
[30] Kristin Shrader-Frechette, *Environmental Justice — Creating Equality* (Oxford University Press, 2002) 3.
[31] Nancy Frazer, Axel Honneth, Redistribution or Recognition? A Political–Philosophical Exchange (London 2003) 33.

The influence of social recognition ideas on environmental justice theory is first found in the work of Iris Young — *Justice and the Politics of Difference*.[32] She asserts that, in distributive justice theory, a model is formulated and a procedure for achieving proper distribution described, but that the social, cultural and institutional conditions that put certain groups at a disadvantage before applying this model are not described.[33] In the case of differences which place social groups in a disadvantageous position when compared each other, it is necessary to identify the elements that cause the disadvantage, in order to marginalise their influence.[34] Therefore, the key question should not be 'which distribution model is the best?', but 'under which circumstances does maldistribution occur?'[35]

Iris Young is particularly attentive to the elements that distributive justice theory does not take into account, in particular, structure and decision-making. The decision-making process does not apply only to the question of who has the right, according to their position, to make certain decisions, and what kind of decisions can be made, but also to the question of *how* decisions are made.[36] The decision-making process must be based on public participation, but it is important to establish mechanisms that ensure the participation of individuals and various groups in decision-making. For groups to have an opportunity for effective participation in decision-making, it is necessary to encourage: 1) self-organisation of group members, which results not only in connecting the ideas of the group members, but also an understanding of common interests; and 2) creation of an institutional framework in which the decision-maker is required to take the opinion of the group into account, resulting in a more intensive role of groups in formulating specific policies (eg environmental policy) and/or the analysis of already proposed policy.[37]

Another author who considers the issue of social recognition as a key element in achieving justice is Charles Taylor. By developing the principle of universal equality, Taylor starts from the issue of recognition of

---

[32] Iris Young, *Justice and the Politics of Difference* (Princeton University Press, 1990). The theoretical sequence of ideas can be found in her later work: Iris Young, 'Communication and the Other', in Seyla Benhabib (ed), *Democracy and Difference: Contesting the Boundaries of the Political* (Princeton University Press, 1996); Iris Young, *Inclusion and Demosracy* (Oxford University Press, 2000).

[33] Iris Young, *Justice and the Politics of Difference* (Princeton University Press, 1990) 15.

[34] Ibid, 21–22.

[35] Ibid, 3–4.

[36] Ibid, 24.

[37] Ibid, 184–185.

individuals and groups, and the possibility of their influence and participation in public.[38] In this sense, he states that any person or group should be granted a unique identity, thus avoiding the possibility of being ignored. Taylor further identifies two types of recognition: recognition of a person as an individual worthy of respect (universal dignity); and recognition of a person as an individual of particular distinctiveness.[39]

He finds the basis of recognition in the concept that all people are entitled to equal respect. What makes every individual worthy of respect is "a universal human potential", which belongs to everyone and which ensures that every individual is equally respected.[40] Universal human potential also forms the basis for creating and defining one's identity as an individual. However, Taylor criticises the standpoint that an individual should be evaluated with regard to the cultural development of his or her community, because it would lead to the negation of the principle of "universal human potential". [41] By applying Taylor's principle of equality, each individual or group would have the same set of rights, regardless of their differences. If the differences, as an important characteristic of an individual or a group, are not recognised, this results in discrimination. Taylor argues that the lack of social and political recognition results in injustice, in both direct and indirect ways: directly, because individuals and groups are limited in exercising their rights, and indirectly, since the lack of recognition creates a basis for distributive injustice.[42]

The basic elements of environmental justice

There are different standpoints about basic elements of environmental justice. Nancy Fraser advocates the concept of distributive justice and social recognition as basic elements of (environmental) justice. Like Iris Young, Fraser considers the issue of the social context of unjust distribution to be the essential element in achieving justice and eliminating existing injustice. She particularly criticises the distributive justice theorists who consider the adequate distribution of rights to be sufficient for elimination of misrecognition. Misrecognition or malrecognition is a

[38] Charles Taylor, 'The Politics of Recognition', in Gutman Amy (ed), *Multiculturalism* (Princeton University Press, 1994) 37–39.
[39] Ibid, 38.
[40] Ibid, 41.
[41] Ibid, 41–42.
[42] Ibid, 43–44.

form of institutional injustice and as such is "rooted in social patterns of representation, interpretation and communication".[43]

The central part of Fraser's work is focused on developing models for achieving the integration of justice as distribution and justice as recognition in a single normative framework. As a result, we have a two-dimensional conception of justice.[44] The concept of "two-dimensional justice" accepts distribution and recognition as independent elements of justice, whose merging provides a wider and more substantial foundation. Fraser finds the normative basis of the concept of two-dimensional justice in participatory parity. In order to achieve equal participation, it is necessary to meet the previous conditions. Those are the objective condition and "intersubjective condition".[45] The objective condition is met only if the material resource distribution provides stakeholder independence. In this case, the elements that have a negative impact on equal participation are excluded. The intersubjective condition of equal participation is met only if the institutional framework of a society has an established system of respect for the cultural values which enables equal evaluation of every individual. The application of the intersubjective condition excludes the normative framework which systematically and *a priori* depreciates certain social categories. In addition, the use of the intersubjective condition excludes the institutionalisation of the value system that would deny some stakeholders the status of equal participation.[46]

Based on these theoretical approaches, several conclusions can be drawn about the basic elements of environmental justice. Environmental justice can only be achieved by public participation in environmental decision-making, without any form of discrimination. The question then arises whether any public participation leads to achieving environmental justice. I believe that the public can, qualitatively, contribute to achieving environmental justice only if certain conditions are met. Firstly, it is necessary to keep the public informed about the state of the environment and all the elements that influence decision-making in a particular case. Secondly, it is necessary to provide adequate protection of the right to public participation in environmental decision-making.

---

[43] Nancy Frazer, 'Social Justice in the Age of Identity Politics: Redistribution, Recognition, and Participation', in Grethe B Peterson (ed), *The Tanner Lectures on Human Values* (Salt Lake City, 1998) no 19, 7–8.

[44] Nancy Frazer and Axel Honneth, Redistribution or Recognition? A Political–Philosophical Exchange (London, 2003) 35.

[45] Ibid, 36.

[46] Ibid.

Uneven distribution of environmental "goods" and "bads" is not the cause of the non-existence of environmental justice, but the result of a broader institutional and social context.[47] The absence of environmental justice is an expression of the inability of those who are exposed to disproportionate environmental risks to change that institutional and social context, and thus establish a system of environmental justice.[48] The institutional context includes any structure or activity, rule or standard that affects the functioning of the structure or enforcement of activities, as well as language and symbols that mediate social interaction.[49] The institutional context can tell us about the fairness of the conditions that provide people with the opportunity to participate in decision-making which influences their practices and the conditions that give them the opportunity to develop and apply their potential.

I will now analyse the positive law of Germany and Serbia and decisions of the European Court of Justice (ECJ) and draw some conclusions on the degree of application of environmental justice theories in comparative law.

The Theories of Environmental Justice and Comparative Environmental Law

Environmental justice and EU law

Before proceeding to the analysis of the relationship between participatory parity and positive law, I should point out some basic views on environmental justice in the EU countries. The legal rules of the EU relating to environmental protection, as well as the judgments of the ECJ, do not contain the term environmental justice.[50] Ludwig Krämer provides an interesting notion on the (non) existence of the use of the term environmental justice in the legislation and case law of the EU. In this sense, he notes that if we were to ask someone who practises European

---

[47] Young, above n 33, 25.

[48] Stevan Lilic, 'Ekološka Pravda' (2006) 1–3 *Strani Pravni Život* 197–198; Richard J Lazarus, 'Pursuing "Environmental Justice": the Distributional Effects of Environmental Protection' (1993) *Northwestern University Law Review* 787–788.

[49] Sheila Foster, 'Justice from the Ground Up: Distributive Inequities, Grassroots Resistance, and the Transformative Politics of the Environmental Justice Movement' (1998) *California Law Review* 790.

[50] Ludwig Krämer, Jonas Ebbesson and Phoebe Okowa (eds), *Environmental Law and Justice in Context* (Cambridge University Press, 2009) 195.

law, but is not familiar with the discussions in the US that have been going on for the past 30 years about what environmental justice is, we would probably get the answer that it is an attempt at fair treatment of the environment inasmuch as, in the process of balancing interests in environmental decision-making, the environment is not always the loser.[51] Discussions on the concept of environmental justice in EU are related to the 1998 *Aarhus Convention on Access to Information, Public Participation in Decision-making and Access to Legal Protection*, which has become an integral part of the EU in accordance with article 300(7) of the *Treaty on the European Union*. The Convention provides that everyone has the right to freely access information held by the authorities, the right to participate in decision-making about activities that may have an environmental impact from an early stage, and the right to challenge a decision that has not been made in accordance with the rules of the Convention or regulations on the environmental protection before the court or other independent public authority. Administrative authorities are obliged to make environmental information available and to create conditions for the active participation of citizens and environmental organisations in making environmental programs, plans and environmental projects. The *Aarhus Convention* generated the possibility of creating an open society in which decisions are made publicly, with the full participation of interested parties. In order for all members of the public to be as equally informed as the administrative authorities, the *Aarhus Convention* provides the right of all citizens and their organisations to freely access environmental information.

The ECJ does not have any reported cases of discrimination in decision-making or implementation of environmental policy and environmental legislation on the basis of a minority background.[52] However, there are numerous cases where the public was not allowed to participate in environmental decision-making, did not have access to environmental information or protection of rights in environmental matters. The question then arises as to how the EU members interpret the concept of participatory parity and in which cases we can say that stakeholders have an equal right to participate in environmental decision-making.

---

[51] Ibid, 197.

[52] Ludwig Krämer, 'Statistics on Environmental Judgments by the EC Court of Justice' (2006) 3 *Journal of Environmental Law* 407–421.

Public participation in environmental decision-making in comparative law and jurisprudence

In order to determine how the specific legislation regulates the public's right to participate in environmental decision-making, we should determine the definition of "public" and the procedure for allowing public participation. We must determine who constitutes the public in a particular case, whether a particular law distinguishes between the general public and the public concerned, and whether non-governmental organisations (NGOs) are allowed to participate.[53] Some national laws distinguish between the terms "public" and "public concerned". Others do not. For that reason, it is important to analyse if specific national laws distinguish between the public and the public concerned. In the analysis of the public participation procedure, the assumption is that the procedure that allows public participation is a special administrative procedure that is carried out in accordance with pre-established rules and has been designed in accordance with the environmental decision-making specificities.

Public participation in German law

The analysis of public participation in environmental law should start with the conventional distinction between public participation in specific decision-making, public participation in policy-making and public participation in legislative drafting and rule-making. If we begin with the anthropocentric understanding of the environment, the public has a more important role in cases when there are direct negative effects of certain activities to health and the environment. A general impact of the activity on the public does not give the public a significant role in decision-making. I conclude that the generally accepted structure "ladder of public participation"[54] in environmental law has the anthropocentric understanding of the term environment as a basis. However, introducing the possibility that NGOs, as bearers of collective interest, the interest of future generations and protection of the interests of environmental protection,

---

[53] The public means one or more natural or legal persons and, in accordance with national legislation or practice, their associations or groups. The public concerned means the public affected or likely to be affected by, or having an interest in, the environmental decision-making. See: *Aarhus Convention*, art 2(4) and art 2(5).

[54] Jerzy Jendroska, 'Public Information and Participation in EC Environmental Law; Origins, Milestones and Trends', in Richard Macrory (ed), *Reflection on 30 Years of EU Environmental Law — A High Level of Protection?* (Europa Law Publishing, 2005) 75.

participate in decision-making as a part of the public, represents penetration of the ecocentric approach into the concept of the environment in a set of procedural rules to be followed by environmental authorities.[55]

Public participation in environmental decision-making in German law is recognised as an expression of implementing the co-operation principle.[56] This is a principle that involves participation of institutions, groups and citizens who may be affected by the decision. The German *Federal Immissions Control Act* defines harmful effects on the environment as emissions which, according to their nature, extent or duration, are liable to cause hazards, considerable disandvantage or considerable nuisance to the general public or the neighbourhood.[57] Persons who may be affected by the effect of, for example, an installation, are a part of the general public. Neighbours are persons who could be affected by the harmful effect of the installation situated in the surroundings.[58] Neighbours includes owners and tenants of residential property as well as those who work in the sphere of harmful effect influence.[59] In some cases, a special ad hoc group may represent the public.

---

[55] Eleanor Sharpston, Advocate General of the Court of Justice of the European Union, gave an interesting opinion about the importance of NGOs participation: "The provisions on access to justice in environmental matters here at issue start from the premise that the natural environment belongs to us all. Preventing environmental damage is society's responsibility, not just the responsibility of individuals or isolated interests. Viewed in that light, the provisions of the *Aarhus Convention* and *Directive 85/337*, as amended, give legal form to the logic of collective action. The individual is protected by acting in a group and the group is collectively strengthened by its individual members. Both the individual and the general interest are thus better protected; and the benefits for all concerned outweigh the disadvantages. This is why both measures accord an important role to non-governmental organizations promoting environmental protection": Opinion of Advocate General Sharpston delivered on 2 July 2009: *Djurgården-Lilla Värtans Miljöskyddsförening v Stockholms kommun genom dess marknämnd* (C-263/08, 15 October 2009) [59].

[56] Horst Schlemminger and Claus-Peter Martens (eds), *German Environmental Law for Practioners* (Kluwer Law International, 2004) 36.

[57] Gesetz zum Schutz vor schädlichen Umwelteinwirkungen, Geräusche, Erschütterungen und ähnliche Vorgänge (Bundes Immisions schutzgesetz) [Law to Protect Against Harmful Environmental Effects, Noise, Vibration and Related Events (Federal Immisions Protection Act)] (Germany) 26 September 2002, BimSchG, art 3(1).

[58] Ibid, art 3(1), art 4, art 5(1), art 5(3).

[59] Schlemminger and Martens, above n 56, 54.

> To the extent that provision is made in any authorisation for the issue of ordinances and general administrative regulations that the parties concerned shall be heard, an ad hoc group will be constituted from time to time from among representatives of the scientific community, those directly affected, trade and industry and the traffic sector, in so far as involved, and the supreme land authorities responsible for emission control shall be heard.[60]

When the protection of nature is in question, the legal system in Germany provides an opportunity for involvement of associations. The *Federal Nature Protection Act* of 2002 stipulates that if an environmental association is recognised by the Ministry of the Environment and its sphere of tasks defined in its charter is affected by the project, the association has the right to state its opinion and to inspect the relevant expert opinions.[61] The *Federal Nature Protection Act* of 2002 provides a right for recognised associations to bring an action even where they are not affected by the measures to which they object.[62]

In the particular licensing procedure, the competent authority must give public notice of the project. The application and the supporting documents must be available for public inspection for one month, from the day of notification.[63] The public and neighbours are able to lodge

---

[60] Gesetz zum Schutz vor schädlichen Umwelteinwirkungen, Geräusche, Erschütterungen und ähnliche Vorgänge (Bundes Immisions schutzgesetz) [Law to Protect Against Harmful Environmental Effects, Noise, Vibration and Related Events (Federal Immisions Protection Act)] (Germany) 26 September 2002, BimSchG, art 51. Hearings of Parties Concerned is stipulated in article 60 of the Gesetz zur Förderung der Kreislaufwirtschaft und Sicherung der umweltverträglichen Beseitigung von Abfällen (Kreislaufwirtschafts und Abfallgesetz) [Law to Promote Circular Economy and Esure Environmentally Friendly Disposal of Waste (Recycling Waste Management Act)] (Germany), KrW/AbfG: "As far as the authorisations for issuing statutory ordinances and general administrative provisions prescribe hearing of the parties concerned, representatives should be selected, and heard, from scientists, those involved, involved commercial and industrial sectors, the supreme authorities responsible for waste management, the communities and community associations".

[61] *Gesetz über Naturschutz und Landschaftspflege (Bundesnaturschutzgesetz)* [Law on Nature Conservation and Landscape Management (Nature Conservation Act)] 25 March 2002, BnatSchG, art 58(1).

[62] Ibid, art 61.

[63] Gesetz zum Schutz vor schädlichen Umwelteinwirkungen, Geräusche, Erschütterungen und ähnliche Vorgänge (Bundes Immisions schutzgesetz) [Law to Protect Against Harmful Environmental Effects, Noise, Vibration and Related Events (Federal Immisions Protection Act)] (Germany) 26 September 2002, BimSchG, art 10(3).

objections against the project within two weeks from the expiry of the inspection period.[64] The public authority responsible for issuing the license must discuss the objections not only with those who raised them, but also with the applicant for the project.[65] The final decision includes a written statement of the grounds for the decision. It should be delivered to the applicant and any person who lodges an objection.[66] The public must be notified of the final decision. The public notice contains instructions about the place and time where the public may inspect the final decision.[67] The term for inspection is two weeks. The German *Environmental Impact Assessment Act* stipulates that the competent public authority must grant a hearing to the general public about the environmental impact assessment of the project. The public should be heard for a second time if the public authority asks a project developer to alter the project's documents and there are fears of additional or other significant effects on the environment.[68]

In 2006, by adopting the *Act Concerning Supplemental Provisions on Appeals in Environmental Matters Pursuant to EC Directive 2003/35/EC* (the *Environmental Appeals Act*), Germany transformed European law into national legislation.[69] *The Federal Nature Conservation Act* was amended, and, in 2009, the Act to amend nature conservation and landscape preservation law came into effect.[70] The procedures of associations' recognition are stipulated by the *Environmental Appeals Act*. Recognised environmental associations may contest decisions from purely environmental perspectives. It is not necessary for environmental associations to show that their own rights have been infringed.[71] An association's appeal is justified if the decision, made by the public authority, or failure to take such decision, "violates statutory provisions that protect environment, establish environmental rights, and are of importance for the decision, and the violation involves issues of environmental protection that are among

---

[64] Ibid.

[65] Ibid, art 10(6).

[66] Ibid, art 10(7).

[67] Ibid, art 10(8).

[68] *Gesetz über die Umweltverträglichkeitsprüfung* [Law on Environmental Impact Assessment] (Germany) 5 September 2001, BGBI, art 9(1).

[69] *Umwelt-Rechtsbehelfsgesetz* [Environmental Appeals Act] (Germany) 1 March 2012, UmwRG.

[70] *Gesetz zur Neuregelung des Rechts des Naturschutzes und der Landschaftspflege* [Law Amending the Law of Nature Conservation and Landscape Management] (Germany) 29 July 2009, new BNatSchG.

[71] *Umwelt-Rechtsbehelfsgesetz* [Environmental Appeals Act] (Germany) 1 March 2012, UmwRG, art 2.

the objectives to be promoted by the association according to its bylaws".[72]

Public participation in Serbian law

The Serbian *Law on Environmental Impact Assessment*[73] regulates the integral system of environmental protection, which provides the right to live in a healthy environment, as well as a balanced relationship between economic development and environmental protection. In addition, the environmental protection system is comprised of measures, conditions and instruments for the sustainable management of natural resources and for the prevention, control, reduction and recovery of all forms of environmental pollution. Basic definitions of the issue of public participation can be found in the standards of the *Law on Environmental Protection* and related regulations.[74] In this sense, everyone has the right to be informed about the state of the environment and to participate in the decision-making process whose implementation could affect the environment.[75] In accordance with the *Law on Environmental Protection*, the public has the right to participate in decision-making on: a) environmental impact assessment projects whose implementation can lead to environmental pollution or pose a risk to the environment and human

---

[72] Ibid, art 2(5)1.

[73] *Law on Environmental Impact Assessment*, 'Official Gazette of the Republic of Serbia', no 135/04; *Law on Amendments to Law on Environmental Impact Assessment*, 'Official Gazette of the Republic of Serbia', no 36/09.

[74] *Law on Environmental Protection*, 'Official Gazette of the Republic of Serbia', no 135/04 and *Law on Amendments to Law on Environmental Protection*, 'Official Gazette of the Republic of Serbia', no 36/09, art 1. Those are the following by-laws, which fill out this law: *Decree on Establishing the List of Projects for which Impact Assessment is Mandatory and the List of Projects for which the Environmental Impact Assessment may be Required*, 'Official Gazette of Republic of Serbia', no 114/08; *Regulation on the Content of the Inquiry for Deciding on the Need of Impact Studies and Content of Inquiry for Determining the Scope and Content of the Environmental Impact Assessment*, 'Official Gazette of Republic of Serbia', no 69/05; *Regulation on the Content of the Environmental Impact Assessment Study*, 'Official Gazette of Republic of Serbia', no 69/05; *Regulation on Public Display, Presentation and Public Discussion of the Environmental Impact Assessment Study*, 'Official Gazette of Republic of Serbia', no 58/05.

[75] *Law on Environmental Protection*, 'Official Gazette of the Republic of Serbia', no 135/04, art 9.

health;[76] b) strategic impact assessment of plans and programs to the environment; and c) the approval of new or existing facilities.[77] Public participation in decision-making on environmental impact assessment is carried out at public project presentations and public hearings, and public participation in terms of strategic impact assessment is provided in the presentation of spatial and urban planning in public. Public participation in decisions on the release of new or existing facilities is conducted in the process of issuing permits for integrated pollution prevention and control. The important restriction of public participation refers to the possibility that the Government of the Republic of Serbia may restrict public participation in making these decisions for the purpose of protecting the interests of the defence and security of the country.[78]

Laws governing the right of public participation in decision-making on specific activities use the terms the "public" and the "public concerned". The public consists of one or more individuals or legal persons, their associations, organisations or groups.[79] The public concerned consists of the public affected or likely to be affected by the project, including NGOs that deal with environmental protection and are registered with the competent authority.[80] There are two conditions relating to the legal capacity of NGOs in the cases in which they participate in the environmental impact assessment as the public concerned. The first condition refers to the obligation of the NGOs to engage in environmental protection. The second condition is registering NGOs with the competent authority. The public concerned is entrusted with significant influence on the process of decision-making, especially by the delegation of powers to directly participate in the decision-making process, and the right to file an appeal or a lawsuit. The *Law on Environmental Impact Assessment*, in article 2, paragraph 1, item 8, identifies, as authorities and organisations concerned, those bodies and organisations of the republic, autonomous provinces and local governments and enterprises, which are authorised to determine the conditions for granting licenses, permits and approvals for the construction of facilities,

---

[76] See: Mirjana Drenovak Ivanovic, 'The Application of Information Technology and Environmental Protection' (2012) *International Review of Administrative Science* 4, 9–11.

[77] *Law on Environmental Protection*, 'Official Gazette of the Republic of Serbia', no 135/04, art 81 (1).

[78] Ibid, art 82.

[79] Ibid, art 3, item 26; *Law on Environmental Impact Assessment*, 'Official Gazette of the Republic of Serbia', no 135/04, art 2, paragraph 1, item 1.

[80] *Law on Environmental Impact Assessment*, 'Official Gazette of the Republic of Serbia', no 135/04, art 2, paragraph 1, item 7.

planning and development, environmental monitoring, performance of activities and protection and use of natural and man-made resources. It may be noted that the terminology in Serbian legislation defines the concept of the public and the public concerned in accordance with provisions of the *Aarhus Convention.*[81]

The public participation procedure in practice of the ECJ and the Aarhus Convention Compliance Committee

As mentioned earlier, a procedure that allows public participation is a special administrative procedure. Only a procedure that is carried out in accordance with pre-determined rules and conditions may result in the application of participatory parity. A prerequisite for the equal public participation in environmental decision-making is an equal opportunity of access to all information that may be relevant for environmental decision-making. Even though everyone should have free access to environmental information, there are a lot of exemptions.[82] The judgment *of IFAW International Tierschutz-Fonds gGmbH v European Commision* provides an example.[83] IFAW International Tierschutz-Fonds gGmbH is a non-governmental organisation, active in the field of the preservation of animal welfare and nature conservation. When the Commission gave a positive opinion on the Airbus company project on building a private airport in a Natura 2000 area, the NGO requested access to various documents received by the Commission from the German authorities related to the examination of the industrial project. The NGO was particularly interested in a letter which the then German Chancellor Gerhard Schröder had written to the President of the Commission in 2001. Although the Commission granted access to some documents, it refused access to this letter. This decision was upheld by judgment of the General Court,[84] but it was annulled on appeal by the Court of Justice.[85] In 2008, the NGO repeated its request for access to the documents. The German authorities

[81] Mirjana Drenovak Ivanovic, 'Implementation of the *Aarhus Convention* in Serbia' (2011) 2 *European Energy and Environmental Law Review*, 58–71.

[82] Convention on Access to Information, Public Participation in Decision-Making and Access to Justice in Environmental Matters (Aarhus Convention) (1998), art 1(3), art 1(4).

[83] IFAW International Tierschutz-Fonds gGmbH v European Commision (General Court) (T-362/08, 13 January 2011).

[84] See: IFAW Internationaler Tierschutz-Fonds v Commission (T-168/02) [2004] ECR II-4135.

[85] See: *Sweden v Commission* (C-64/05) [2007] ECR I-11389.

stated that "disclosure of the German Chancellor's letter would undermine the protection of the public interest as regards the international relations and the economic policy of the Federal Republic of Germany within the meaning of the third and fourth indents of article 4(1)(a) of *Regulation No 1049/2001*".[86] The Court of Justice found that the General Court should have consulted the Schröder letter. Without such consultation, the General Court was not in a position to assess if access to the document could have been validly refused by the German authorities.[87] It thus set aside the judgment of the General Court and sent the case back for a new decision.

Adequate public participation in environmental decision-making exists only when the public is allowed to participate in decision-making from an early stage, when it can affect the content of the decision. An example of ineffective public participation can be found in the case of granting a permit to a waste disposal incinerator located in Fos-sur-Mer, in the south of France. In this case, a French municipal authority made two decisions about the installation without the involvement of the public. In 2003, it decided about the incineration as a method of waste disposal, decided on the location of the incinerator, and held a public tender. In 2005, the public authority decided on the award of the contract, which included further modalities of processing the waste, after which public participation took place. The question that arises is: was the public participation too late, since not all opinions had been informed on time and there was no public debate, but only a public inquiry? In 2009, the Aarhus Convention Compliance Committe found that "all options were still open when the Prefect authorised the project in 2006. One of the main arguments was that in fact 50 decisions per year were handed down by the Prefect and this shows that the Prefect is in the position to decide on the subject matters of the case".[88] Public participation makes sense particularly when the public influences the decision-making about activities that affect the environment, in coordination with the government. In this sense, the public should have been involved in decision-making about the incineration as a method of waste disposal, as well as determining the location.

---

[86] IFAW International Tierschutz-Fonds gGmbH v European Commision (T-362/08) [2004] ECR II-4135, [24].

[87] IFAW International Tierschutz-Fonds gGmbH v European Commision (T-362/08) [2004] ECR II-4135, [93], [122].

[88] Aarhus Convention Compliance Committee (ACCC/C/2007/22), A Andrusevych, T Alge, C Konrad (eds), *Case Law of the Aarhus Convention Compliance Committee (2004-2011)* (RACSE, Lviv, 2011) 155.

The right to public partcipation must be equaly recognized in earlier and in later stages of the environmental decision-making. Some national legislations give extensive opportunity for public participation at an early stage of decision-making, but give an opportunity to the public to dispute the final court decision under very restrictive conditions . This approach is criticised by the ECJ in the case of Djurgarden-Lilla Vartans Miljoskyddsforening v Stockholm kommun municipality genome dess marknämnd.[89]

The opportunity of equal participation in environmental decision-making means the possibility of timely access to environmental information and timely notice of the proceedings in which the public can participate. Participatory parity cannot be achieved if the public is not adequately informed about the process of environmental decision-making. Participatory parity cannot be achieved if the process does not determine a reasonable deadline for public participation, sufficient for stakeholders to access environmental information, review the experts' opinions on the effects of certain actions and to consider alternatives to making decisions. A decision of the Aarhus Convention Compliance Committee provides an example. In 2009, a Spanish NGO, *Platforma Contra la Contaminación de Almendralejo*, submitted a communication claiming that public authorities failed to provide environmental information in a prompt manner in a reasonable time. Because of that, the public did not have enough time to access the information and project documentation. The Committee found that Spain failed to comply with articles 4(1)(b) and 6(6) of the *Aarhus Convention*, as public authorities did not allow access to information in the requested form. The Committee found that requiring members of the public who were interested in participation to travel 30–120 km to read project information on two computers was an "inhibitive condition".[90]

The importance of establishing a reasonable period of time for public participation is emphasised in the European Parliament resolution of 14 June 2012 on public consultations and their availability in all EU languages.[91] The resolution, among other things, states that:

> the public involvement is a fundamental component of democratic governance, whereas well designed and communicated public consultations are one of the main tools giving substance to the EU's policy

---

[89] *Djurgarden-Lilla Vartans Miljoskyddsforening v Stockholms kommun genom dess marknämnd* (C-263/08, 15 October 2009) <http://ec.europa.eu/dgs/legal_service/arrets/08c263_en.pdf>.

[90] Aarhus Convention Compliance Committee, above n 88, 175.

[91] European Parliament Resolution of 14 June 2012 on Public Consultations and Their Availability in all EU Languages [2012] OJ 11/06/2012, 121.

> of transparency, and whereas to date their potential for bridging the communication and information gap between citizens and the EU has not been fully exploited … The Commission should ensure that all consultations are understandable to ordinary citizens and are carried out over a sufficiently long period of time to allow for increased participation.[92]

In the participation procedure, the public, for example, in the environmental impact assessment procedure, has a right to comment, to state opinions, to view analyses of the impact that the particular project has on the environment and to object to the implementation of the proposed activities.[93] A competent administrative authority is obliged to take into account the views presented to the public, which means that the competent authority must explain a decision that rejects an opinion, comment or complaint.[94] The European Ombudsman has an important role in controlling the regulation of administrative authorities' work, particularly in terms of the regulation of the procedure of public participation and taking into account the opinions expressed. For example, in the case of the proposed enlargement of Vienna Airport, the European Ombudsman conducted an investigation on the environmental impact assessment in late 2011. On this occasion, special attention was given to the question of whether the public was allowed to participate in the environmental impact assessment. In 2006, 27 citizens submitted an initiative to the Commission fighting against the negative consequences of the expansion of the airport. The Commission concluded that an environmental impact assessment was not obligatory, but agreed with the Austrian authorities that an ex-post environmental impact assessment should be carried out. In 2008, complainants turned to the European Ombudsman, claiming that the public authority in charge of the ex post environmental impact assessment was the same authority that had granted permits and that the public did not have access to the ex post environmental impact assessment. With respect to these allegations, the Commission informed the Ombudsman that it would close the infringement case against Austria only upon establishing that the Austrian authorities had taken the necessary steps. As the review procedure was ongoing, the Ombudsman closed the case. But, in 2010, the complainants turned to the Ombudsman for the third time. After this inquiry, the Ombudsman found that there had been nothing to suggest that the

---

[92] Ibid, art C, art 3.
[93] *Aarhus Convention*, above n 82, art 7.
[94] Ibid, art 8, art 9.

complainants' arguments had been discussed in writing with the Austrian authorities. The Ombudsman concluded that the Commission did not take his finding from the previous inquiry into account. Instead, the Commission waited for the final report to be submitted by the Austrian authorities. The Ombudsman made the following recommendation:

> The Commission should reconsider its approach in regard to the handling of the complainants' infringement complaint concerning Vienna Airport and address the deficiencies highlighted by the Ombudsman. This means that the Commission's further actions in the infringement proceedings should take into account the obligation of the national authorities to ensure that (i) the complainants have access to a review procedure.[95]

It is important to stress that the ex-post environmental impact assessment was discussed in *Commission v Ireland* by the ECJ. "Paragraph 57 of the judgment indicates that 'regularisation' after the event, of otherwise operations or measures, may be permissible in certain exceptional cases. The ECJ did not elaborate on these aspects of its ruling and it is not clear what exceptional circumstances might be acceptable in this context."[96]

Conclusion

The idea of environmental justice is based on the principles of environmental democracy. The realisation of environmental protection and sustainable development can be achieved only if the administrative authorities, public and industry representatives participate in making decisions about activities that may have a significant impact on the environment.

The question that arises is: What is the meaning of the term "environment" in comparative law? This chapter has shown that there is a large influence of the anthropocentric understanding of the environment in comparative law, exemplified in the positive legal definition of environmental rights. In some constitutions, like that of Serbia, the

---

[95] Special Report of the European Ombudsman Concerning His Inquiry into Complaint 2591/2010/CG against the European Commission (2012) European Ombudsman <http://www.ombudsman.europa.eu/cases/specialreport.faces/en/11558/html.bookmark?>.

[96] Aine Ryall, 'Case C-215&06, *Commission v Ireland*, Judgment of the European Court of Justice (Second Chamber) 3 July 2008' (2009) 2 *Review of European Community and International Environmental Law*, 213.

anthropocentric understanding of the environment is directly applied in the definition of environmental rights. By giving every person the right to a healthy environment, the *Constitution of the Republic of Serbia* associates the term environment only to the health of people. The *Constitution of France* introduces the term "balanced environment", which could indicate a broader definition. However, further elaboration ("balanced environment which shows due respect for the health") reveals a narrow definition of environmental rights. The *Constitution of the Kingdom of Norway* clearly advocates the broader definition of environmental rights, defining this right cumulatively, as "a right to an environment that is conductive to health" and as "a right to a natural environment whose productivity and diversity are maintained". The *Constitution of Greece* stipulates that "the protection of the natural and cultural environment constitutes the right of every person", which leads me to the conclusion that it is a broader definition of environmental rights. In the *Constitution of the Federative Republic of Brazil*, there is a considerable influence of ecological theories. In this sense, the constitution uses the term "ecologically balanced environment" and indicates that the environment is "an asset of common use". However, the formulation that the environment, with listed qualities, is "essential to a healthy quality of life" brings the term environmental rights closer to the anthropocentric understanding of the environment. On the other hand, ecological theories did predominantly influence the *Constitution of the Republic of the Philippines*. That Constitution uses the term "balanced and healthful ecology" and indicates the need to coordinate the state of the environment with "the rhythm and harmony of nature".

The question that arises is the meaning of environmental justice. If we define environmental justice as the equitable distribution of environmental values and environmental risks, we have to determine the conditions for establishing the equal protection of participants in that distribution. Another matter is how to identify who has the right to participate in decision-making. If an individual or group is not recognised as a holder of rights, they will not be in a legal position to participate in decision-making. The fact that the public is recognised as a participant in decision-making in environmental matters does not mean that the public will have a significant impact on decision-making. When it comes to making environmental decisions, it is necessary to provide the public with access to environmental information relevant to decision-making, so that members of the public are able to understand the motives of administrative bodies when making certain decisions in environmental matters. In other words, environmental justice can be achieved only if the public has a right of access to environmental information.

The overview of ECJ practice shows that the process of public participation in environmental decision-making is a special administrative procedure. The ECJ jurisprudence shows that complete application of participatory parity is possible only when: a) the public is promptly informed of the participatory decision-making process; b) the public has a right to equal access to the environmental information that is important for decision-making; c) the public has a right to participate in environmental decision-making from an early stage, with a possibility of influencing the content of the decision, which does not rule out the possibility of participating in the later stages of the decision-making; d) the public participation process is arranged in such manner that, at each stage, the public is provided with sufficient time to adequately prepare and take part in the procedure; and e) the public has a right to present comments, opinions, new analyses of the environmental impact of the concrete project and to file an objection to the implementation of the proposed activities (with the authorities' obligation to explain a decision that rejects an opinion, comment or complaint).

CONCLUSION

LORRAINE WALKER

As a magistrate and coroner, delving in to the world of research and academia in relation to legal philosophy during the working week is a rare privilege. Yet many of these chapters proved to have a real relevance to my daily work.

There are four strands to the chapters in this book which are hugely disparate in detail and context. Yet there are significant themes discernible within them.

From microcosmic discussions of particular provisions regarding the giving of evidence in sexual assault cases and the question of the right to self-determination of arbitration proceedings in an international setting to the broader discussions of the rights to privacy and control over one's genetic information, the notion of respect for the individual and their personal characteristics underpins the analyses.

The theme of the evolution of what constitutes justice is explored from the review of the Mount Rennie rape case in 1886 to an exploration of the development of the rule of law in the Pacific. Both chapters are a reminder that whilst the principle of the rule of law is a constant in civilised society, its form is very much an evolving beast.

The significance of recognising and protecting the potentially vulnerable is explored in the chapters on the giving evidence in sexual assault cases, the relevance of Aboriginality in sentencing, sexual harassment in the bush and formal recognition of the debilitating effect of family violence in the workplace. They are a reminder that what is implemented or considered as a protection may not be perceived as such by the purported beneficiary. The risk of misguided paternalism is also to be guarded against.

Recognition of the significance of the public interest, recognising and reflecting it, are highlighted by the chapters dealing with the need for public awareness of sentencing practices along with public participation in decision-making in the environmental justice context.

His Honour, former Justice Kirby, addressed the Symposium that evolved into this book. He stressed the need for vigilance in the pursuit and protection of justice. This book is evidence of such vigilance.